Wiley CPAexcel®

Auditing and Attestation

Donald E. Tidrick, Ph.D., CPA, CMA, CIA
Robert A. Prentice, J.D.

Wiley Efficient Learning™

Published by John Wiley & Sons, Inc., Hoboken, New Jersey.

For general information on our other products and services or for technical support, please contact our Customer Care Department within the United States at (800) 762-2974, outside the United States at (317) 572-3993 or fax (317) 572-4002.

Wiley publishes in a variety of print and electronic formats and by print-on-demand. Some material included with standard print versions of this book may not be included in e-books or in print-on-demand. If this book refers to media such as a CD or DVD that is not included in the version you purchased, you may download this material at http://booksupport.wiley.com. For more information about Wiley products, visit www.wiley.com.

Library of Congress Cataloging-in-Publication Data:
ISBN 978-1-11908320-7
Version 7.11

Printed in the United States of America

10 9 8 7 6 5 4 3 2 1

OUR AUTHORS

CPAexcel™ content is authored by a team of accounting professors and CPA exam experts from top accounting colleges such as the University of Texas at Austin (frequently ranked the #1 accounting school in the country), California State University at Sacramento, Northern Illinois University, and University of North Alabama.

Professor Allen H. Bizzell
CPAexcel Author, Mentor and Video Lecturer
Ph.D., CPA
Former Associate Dean and Accounting Faculty, University of Texas (Retired)
Associate Professor, Department of Accounting, Texas State University (Retired)

Professor Ervin L. Black
CPAexcel Author and Video Lecturer
Ph.D.
Brigham Young University - Lecturer in international accounting and financial accounting.

Professor Gregory Carnes
CPAexcel Author and Video Lecturer
Ph.D., CPA
Raburn Eminent Scholar of Accounting, University of North Alabama
Former Dean, College of Business, Lipscomb University
Former Chair, Department of Accountancy, Northern Illinois University

Professor B. Douglas Clinton
CPAexcel Author and Video Lecturer
Ph.D., CPA, CMA
Alta Via Consulting Professor of Management Accountancy, Department of Accountancy, Northern Illinois University

Professor Charles J. Davis
CPAexcel Author, Mentor and Video Lecturer
Ph.D., CPA
Professor of Accounting, Department of Accounting, College of Business Administration, California State University - Sacramento

Professor Donald R. Deis Jr.
CPAexcel Author and Video Lecturer
Ph.D., CPA, MBA
Ennis & Virginia Joslin Endowed Chair in Accounting, College of Business, Texas A&M University - Corpus Christi
Former Director of the School of Accountancy, University of Missouri - Columbia
Former Professor and Director of the Accounting Ph.D. Program, Louisiana State University - Baton Rouge

Robert A. Prentice
CPAexcel Business Law Co-Author
Ed and Molly Smith Centennial Professor In Business Law and Distinguished Teaching Professor, J.D.
McCombs School of Business, University of Texas - Austin

Professor Pam Smith
CPAexcel Author and Video Lecturer
Ph.D., MBA, CPA
KPMG Professor of Accountancy, Department of Accountancy, Northern Illinois University

Professor Dan Stone
CPAexcel Author and Video Lecturer
Ph.D., MPA
Gatton Endowed Chair, Von Allmen School of Accountancy and the Department of Management, University of Kentucky

Professor Donald Tidrick
CPAexcel Author and Video Lecturer
Ph.D., CPA, CMA, CIA
Deloitte Professor of Accountancy, Northern Illinois University, Former Associate Chairman of the Department of Accounting, Director of the Professional Program in Accounting and Director of the CPA Review Course, University of Texas at Austin, 1991 - 2000

Table of Contents

Auditing and Attestation

Welcome

Passing the Auditing/Attestation Part of the CPA Exam
Candidates sometimes have a misperception about the Auditing and Attestation part of the CPA examination, believing that auditing is primarily a practice-oriented part of the exam. They may believe that having had first-hand experience doing audit work is sufficient for success on this part, or that not having had such experience is insurmountable. Sometimes candidates have a false sense of security, expressing the view that "Auditing is just common sense!" However, their view often changes when they see the specificity of the CPA exam questions that focus on the relevant concepts and the applicable professional standards. Passing the auditing part of the CPA examination is fundamentally an academic endeavor. I believe that everything you need to pass is contained in CPAexcel -- all that is required is your commitment to carefully study it.

AICPA Professional Standards
The Auditing and Attestation part of the CPA examination focuses heavily on candidates' familiarity with the applicable AICPA Professional Standards. Since the AICPA prepares the exam, it should not be surprising that they emphasize their professional literature. Indeed, a substantial majority of the points in auditing focuses on candidates' knowledge of the AICPA's Statements on Auditing Standards, the Statements on Standards for Attestation Engagements, the Statements on Standards for Accounting and Review Services, and, to a lesser extent, the Statements on Quality Control Standards. The entire set of AICPA Professional Standards tested in the Auditing and Attestation area have been outlined and are addressed. Of course, the PCAOB auditing standards and IFAC's International Standards on Auditing are "fair game" for testing and are also appropriately covered in CPAexcel. Fortunately, the AICPA's "clarified" auditing standards have now substantially reduced the significance of differences between the AICPA's Statements on Auditing Standards and the International Standards on Auditing.

CPAexcel materials
These CPAexcel materials strive to achieve an optimal balance between **technical depth**, covering the topics on the AICPA Content Specification Outlines, and **efficiency**, focusing on the task at hand without excess verbiage and unnecessary detail. The materials emphasize the professional standards and important concepts that are the primary object of testing in the Auditing and Attestation area.

I encourage you to review the study text basically in sequence, since auditing has something of a chronological order -- including planning, evidence gathering, and reporting. Read the study text carefully, and review the available supplemental outlines of the important AICPA Professional Standards, particularly for unfamiliar topics. And, very importantly, take the time to work on the proficiency questions and the multiple-choice questions that are integral to CPAexcel's successful approach.

Multiple-choice questions
Even though the number of professional standards has increased over the years, these standards often deal with only incremental changes to similar prior standards. In many cases, the underlying concepts have not changed very much. This part of the exam is not quantitative by nature, so questions cannot be updated by simply changing the "numbers." If you make a diligent effort studying these past exams' multiple-choice questions, you will very likely see some "old friends" on your examination, or, at the very least, some questions that are very similar to what you have practiced.

Final review
In addition to diligently studying the study text and the supplemental outlines of important professional standards and practicing proficiency questions and exam questions, candidates invariably benefit from an intensive final review. The study text is designed to facilitate an efficient review and I encourage you to spend a few days reviewing the study text to refresh your memory of important concepts immediately prior to testing.

Work hard and enjoy the accomplishment of becoming a CPA for the rest of your life!

~ Professor Donald Tidrick

In AUD, I am responsible for the 16%-20% of the CPA Exam that is devoted to Professional Responsibilities, including primarily the AICPA's Code of Professional Conduct, PCAOB and SEC ethics rules, GAO and DOL ethics guidelines, and the IFAC Code of Ethics for Professional Accountants.

Most of the attention in this part has always been upon the AICPA Code of Professional Conduct and I expect that to continue to be the case with the promulgation in summer 2014 of a new, electronic version of the Code. Most of the new Code goes into effect as of December 15, 2014. The "conceptual framework" portions go into effect December 15, 2015. The Code is now easily accessed at the AICPA website: http://pub.aicpa.org/codeofconduct/Ethics.aspx. It will be easily updated and is now organized along functional lines. Most of the Code addresses the attest work done by "Members in Public Practice." Some of the Code addresses the work done by "Members in Business," such as management accountants, internal auditors, accountants working for government agencies and NGOs, etc. A small portion of the Code addresses "Other Members," such as CPAs who are unemployed or retired.

The new version of the Code, which makes many substantive changes and huge organizational changes, more closely resembles the IFAC Code than before. Mastering the AICPA's Code of Professional Conduct will be very helpful to understanding the IFAC Code and the ethics code provisions of the Government Accountability Office (GAO) and the Department of Labor (DOL).

Remember that AICPA's tax-related ethics rules are located in the Regulation section. Many provisions of the Code covered here—such as those related to integrity, objectivity, advertising, and the like—apply to CPAs in all lines of endeavor—audit, tax, advisory services, etc.

The SEC and PCAOB material contained in this part deals primarily, though not exclusively, with additional Sarbanes-Oxley provisions aimed generally at improving the quality of financial information flowing to investors. Some of these are discussed inside our material on the AICPA Code of Professional Conduct because they override the Code's provisions where there is a conflict.

~ Prof. Robert Prentice

Auditing and Attestation Professors

Professor Donald E. Tidrick is currently Deloitte Professor of Accountancy in the Department of Accounting at Northern Illinois University. From 1991 - 2000, Dr. Tidrick was on faculty at the University of Texas at Austin, where he was Associate Chairman of the Department of Accounting, Director of the Professional Program in Accounting and Director of UT's CPA Review Course. Among other professional distinctions, Dr. Tidrick serves on the Educators' Advisory Panel for the Comptroller General of the United States and he is a member of the Ethics Committee of the Illinois CPA Society.

Professor Robert A. Prentice is the Ed and Molly Smith Centennial Professor of Business Law at the University of Texas at Austin and has taught both UT's and other CPA courses for fifteen years. He created a new course in accounting ethics and regulation that he has taught for the last decade. Professor Prentice has written several textbooks, many major law review articles on securities regulation and accountants' liability, and has won more than thirty teaching awards.

Financial Statement Audits

Accounting vs. Auditing

After studying this lesson, you should be able to:

1. *Explain the respective responsibilities of management and the auditor in financial reporting.*
2. *Outline the role of and distinction between GAAP and GAAS.*

I. **Financial Accounting --** The accounting focuses primarily on the preparation and distribution of the general-purpose, historical financial statements (balance sheet, income statement, statement of cash flows, and statement of retained earnings), which are representations of management.

  A. These financial statements are distributed to interested parties outside of the reporting entity itself, such as actual or potential shareholders and creditors, major customers and suppliers, employees, regulators, and others for their decision-making (resource allocation) needs.

  B. Users' specific decision-making circumstances will involve different issues and they may have different information priorities and concerns, but most will want to evaluate whether management has performed well.

  C. Since management's performance will be evaluated, at least in part, by financial statements prepared by management itself, users need to know whether the financial statements are reliable when evaluating the performance of management.

II. **Auditing --** The auditor's primary role is to provide an impartial (independent) report on the reliability of management's financial statements.

> Purpose of an audit -- "The purpose of an audit is to provide financial statement users with an opinion by the auditor on whether the financial statements are presented fairly, in all material respects, in accordance with the applicable financial reporting framework. An auditor's opinion enhances the degree of confidence that the intended users can place in the financial statements."
>
> From the AICPA's Preface to *Codifications of Statements on Auditing Standards, Principles Underlying an Audit Conducted in Accordance with Generally Accepted Auditing Standards.*

III. **The Role of Standards --** Think of "standards" as the criteria by which quality will be evaluated. The preparation of the financial statements and the performance of the audit are subject to very different standards.

  A. Standards applicable to evaluating the presentation of the financial statements

> **Applicable financial reporting framework** "The financial reporting framework adopted by management and, where appropriate, those charged with governance in the preparation of the financial statements that is acceptable in view of the nature of the entity and the objective of the financial statements, or that is required by law or regulation."
>
> **Financial reporting framework** "A set of criteria used to determine measurement, recognition, presentation, and disclosure of all material items appearing in the financial statements; for example: U.S. generally accepted accounting principles (GAAP), International Financial Reporting Standards (IFRSs), issued by the International Accounting Standards Board (IASB), or a special purpose framework."

    1. The financial reporting framework adopted by an entity for its financial statement presentation in the U.S.A. may be based on IFRSs (issued by the IASB) or U.S. GAAP.

2. Accounting standards setters associated with U.S. GAAP -- The nature of the reporting entity determines which particular accounting standards must be followed under the label of U.S. GAAP.
   a. Federal governmental entities follow pronouncements of the Federal Accounting Standards Advisory Board (FASAB).
   b. State and local governmental entities follow pronouncements of the Governmental Accounting Standards Board (GASB).
   c. Other entities (such as corporations) follow pronouncements of the Financial Accounting Standards Board (FASB).

B. Standards applicable to evaluating the auditor's performance
1. **Outside of the U.S.A. --** "International Standards on Auditing" (ISAs) are issued by the International Auditing and Assurance Standards Board, an audit-related standard-setting body within the International Federation of Accountants, known as IFAC.
2. **Within the U.S.A. --** The nature of the reporting entity determines which auditing standards are applicable to an audit of the entity's financial statements.
   a. Governmental entities -- When required by law, regulation, or agreement, Generally Accepted Government Auditing Standards (GAGAS), issued by the U.S. Government Accountability Office (GAO) are applicable.
   b. Public companies (companies registered with the Securities and Exchange Commission, also referred to as "issuers," that is, issuers of securities to the public) -- the auditing standards of the Public Company Accounting Oversight Board (PCAOB) are applicable.
   c. Private companies (referred to as "nonissuers") and other entities -- the auditing standards of the AICPA's Auditing Standards Board are applicable; these pronouncements collectively are referred to by the AICPA as generally accepted auditing standards (GAAS).

> **AICPA's "clarity and convergence" project** The AICPA reissued substantially all of their existing Statements on Auditing Standards (SASs) in a clarified format intended to make the SASs easier to understand. In addition, the AICPA substantially converged their auditing standards to be consistent with the requirements of IFAC's International Standards on Auditing. Although some differences in those respective requirements remain (and will be covered elsewhere in CPAexcel), those standards are now very, very similar. The recent AICPA pronouncements are referred to as "Clarified Standards."
>
> The PCAOB adopted the then-existing AICPA auditing standards in April 2003 as "interim standards, on an initial, transitional basis." Since that time, the PCAOB has been issuing its own Auditing Standards. Much of the existing PCAOB auditing standards remain those of the AICPA existing as of April 16, 2003.

GAAS and Principles

After studying this lesson, you should be able to:

1. *Identify the 7 principles underlying an audit conducted in accordance with GAAS under the AICPA's "Clarified" auditing standards.*
2. *Identify the 10 Generally Accepted Auditing Standards (GAAS) associated with the AICPA's past auditing standards, which still remain as part of the PCAOB auditing standards.*

> **Study Tip:** Remember the acronym **"TID-PIE-GCDO"** -- Training; Independence; Due care (general standards); Planning; Internal control; Evidence (field work standards); GAAP; Consistency; Disclosure; Opinion (reporting standards) -- A mnemonic for remembering the 10 standards of GAAS. The "key" words are part of the memory aid. The "standard" is the whole phrase that follows each of the key words.

I. **Generally Accepted Auditing Standards (GAAS)** -- Historically, the AICPA identified 10 standards comprising GAAS that used to serve as a framework for U.S. auditing standards. The AICPA replaced these 10 standards with 7 principles in connection with its Clarified Auditing Standards. (The AICPA no longer uses the term "GAAS" to refer to these 10 standards. Rather, the AICPA uses the term GAAS to refer to the body of professional standards issued in the form of Statements on Auditing Standards.) However, the PCAOB still incorporates the 10 traditional GAAS standards as a framework relevant to the PCAOB auditing standards. From a PCAOB perspective, there are 10 standards that comprise the traditional GAAS and that used to serve as the criteria to evaluate the quality of the auditor's performance.

   A. **General Standards** -- There are 3 of these (**"TID"**). They are "personal" in nature as they relate to qualities that the auditor brings to the assignment:

      1. **Training** -- "The auditor must have adequate technical training and proficiency to perform the audit."
      2. **Independence** -- "The auditor must maintain independence in mental attitude in all matters relating to the audit."
      3. **Due care** -- "The auditor must exercise due professional care in the performance of the audit and the preparation of the report."

   B. **Field Work Standards** -- There are 3 of these (**"PIE"**). They are related to the evidence-gathering activities that form the foundation for the auditor's conclusions.

      1. **Planning and supervision** -- "The auditor must adequately plan the work and must properly supervise any assistants."
      2. **Internal control** -- "The auditor must obtain a sufficient understanding of the entity and its environment, including its internal control, to assess the risk of material misstatement of the financial statements whether due to fraud or error, and to design the nature, timing, and extent of further audit procedures."
      3. **Evidence** -- "The auditor must obtain sufficient appropriate audit evidence by performing audit procedures to afford a reasonable basis for an opinion regarding the financial statements under audit."

   C. **Reporting Standards** -- There are 4 of these (**"GCDO"**). Each of them says something about the language that is required in the auditor's report.

      1. **GAAP** -- "The auditor must state in the auditor's report whether the financial statements are presented in accordance with generally accepted accounting principles (GAAP)."
      2. **Consistency** -- "The auditor must identify in the auditor's report those circumstances in which such principles have not been consistently observed in the current period in relation to the preceding period."

3. **Disclosure --** "When the auditor determines that informative disclosures are not reasonably adequate, the auditor must so state in the auditor's report."

4. **Opinion --** "The auditor must either express an opinion regarding the financial statements, taken as a whole, or state that an opinion cannot be expressed, in the auditor's report. When the auditor cannot express an overall opinion, the auditor should state the reasons therefore in the auditor's report. In all cases where an auditor's name is associated with financial statements, the auditor should clearly indicate the character of the auditor's work, if any, and the degree of responsibility the auditor is taking, in the auditor's report."

II. **Clarity and Convergence Project --** In connection with its "clarity and convergence project" the AICPA has replaced its Statements on Auditing Standards to be similar to the International Standards on Auditing (ISAs) issued by the International Federation of Accountants (specifically IFAC's International Auditing & Assurance Standards Board, IAASB). As part of that effort, the AICPA has also replaced its use of 10 "Generally Accepted Auditing Standards" with 7 "principles" to provide a framework for understanding and explaining an audit.

A. The 7 principles are not requirements and have no authoritative status. However, they are intended to be helpful as a framework for audit standard setting.

B. The 7 principles reflect most of the considerations that had been addressed in the previous 10 generally accepted auditing standards (the former reporting standards seem to have changed the most relative to these principles).

C. The 7 principles are organized around 4 primary themes -- (1) purpose/premise; (2) responsibilities; (3) performance; and (4) reporting (as a memory aid, remember: "PR-PR").

III. **Purpose of an Audit and Premise Upon Which an Audit is Conducted**

A. The purpose of an audit is to provide financial statement users with an opinion by the auditor on whether the financial statements are presented fairly, in all material respects, in accordance with the applicable financial reporting framework. An auditor's opinion enhances the degree of confidence that intended users can place in the financial statements.

B. An audit in accordance with generally accepted auditing standards is conducted on the premise that management and, where appropriate, those charged with governance, have responsibility for

1. The preparation and fair presentation of the financial statements in accordance with the applicable financial reporting framework; this includes the design, implementation, and maintenance of internal control relevant to the preparation and fair presentation of financial statements that are free from material misstatement, whether due to fraud or error; and

2. Providing the auditor with all information, such as records, documentation, and other matters that are relevant to the preparation and fair presentation of the financial statements; any additional information that the auditor may request from management and, where appropriate, those charged with governance; and unrestricted access to those within the entity from whom the auditor determines it necessary to obtain audit evidence.

C. **Responsibilities --** Note that the term *responsibilities principle* takes the place of what previously had been called General Standards describing characteristics the auditor brings to the engagement.

1. Auditors are responsible for having appropriate competence and capabilities to perform the audit; complying with relevant ethical requirements; and maintaining professional skepticism and exercising professional judgment, throughout the planning and performance of the audit.

D. **Performance --** Note that the term *performance principle* takes the place of what previously had been called Fieldwork Standards governing the auditor's evidence-gathering activities.

1. To express an opinion, the auditor obtains reasonable assurance about whether the financial statements as a whole are free from material misstatement, whether due to fraud or error.

2. To obtain reasonable assurance, which is a high, but not absolute, level of assurance, the auditor

    a. Plans the work and properly supervises any assistants;

    b. Determines and applies appropriate materiality level or levels throughout the audit;

    c. Identifies and assesses risks of material misstatement, whether due to fraud or error, based on an understanding of the entity and its environment, including the entity's internal control; and

    d. Obtains sufficient appropriate audit evidence about whether material misstatements exist, through designing and implementing appropriate responses to the assessed risks.

3. The auditor is unable to obtain absolute assurance that the financial statements are free from material misstatement because of inherent limitations, which arise from

    a. The nature of financial reporting;

    b. The nature of audit procedures; and

    c. The need for the audit to be conducted within a reasonable period of time and so as to achieve a balance between benefit and cost.

E. **Reporting**

1. Based on an evaluation of the audit evidence obtained, the auditor expresses, in the form of a written report, an opinion in accordance with the auditor's findings, or states that an opinion cannot be expressed. The opinion states whether the financial statements are presented fairly, in all material respects, in accordance with the applicable financial reporting framework.

Professional Standards

After studying this lesson you should be able to:

1. *Understand the role of guidance associated with Statements on Auditing Standards including interpretive publications and other auditing publications.*
2. *Identify the 2 types of professional requirements (unconditional requirements and presumptively mandatory requirements) and the wording associated with each.*

I. The AICPA's Use of the Term *GAAS* and Guidance Associated with It

A. **Statements on Auditing Standards (SASs) --** The SASs constitute GAAS and must be followed by auditors when AICPA auditing standards are applicable. (Specifically, Rule 202, "Compliance With Standards," of the AICPA Code of Professional Conduct requires that auditors adhere to the standards promulgated by the Auditing Standards Board.) Under the clarified auditing standards, any reference to GAAS specifically means this body of professional standards (SASs) issued by the Auditing Standards Board.

1. The auditor is expected to have sufficient knowledge of the SASs to identify those applicable to the audit.
2. The auditor should be prepared to justify any departures from the SASs.
3. Materiality and audit risk also underlie the application of the SASs, particularly those related to performing the audit (evidence gathering) and reporting.

B. **"Interpretive publications" --** Consist of the appendices to the SASs, auditing interpretations of the SASs, auditing guidance included in AICPA Audit and Accounting Guides, and AICPA auditing Statements of Position.

1. Interpretive publications are **not** considered to be auditing standards, however.
2. These are issued under the authority of the Auditing Standards Board after all ASB members have had an opportunity to comment on the interpretive publication.
3. Auditors should be aware of (and consider) interpretive publications applicable to their audits. When auditors do not apply such auditing guidance, they should be prepared to explain how they complied with the SAS provisions related to such interpretive publications.

C. **"Other auditing publications" --** Include articles in the *Journal of Accountancy* and the AICPA's *CPA Letter* (and other professional publications), continuing professional education programs, textbooks, etc.

1. Other auditing publications have no authoritative status - they may be useful to the auditor in understanding and applying the SASs, however.
2. To assess the appropriateness of the other auditing publications - consider the degree to degree to which the publication is recognized as helpful in applying the SASs and the degree to which the author is recognized as an authority on auditing matters. (Other auditing publications reviewed by the AICPA Audit and Attest Standards staff are presumed to be appropriate.)

II. Categories of Professional Requirements --

The various AICPA standards (i.e., Statements on Auditing Standards, Statements on Standards for Attestation Engagements, Statements on Standards for Accounting and Review Services, and Statements on Quality Control Standards) distinguish between **two types of professional requirements:**

A. **"Unconditional requirements" --** Must comply with the requirement without exception (indicated by "must" in applicable standards);

1. **"Presumptively mandatory requirements" --** In rare circumstances, the practitioner may depart from such a "requirement," but must document the justification for the departure and how the alternate procedures performed were adequate to meet the objective of the "requirement" (indicated by "should" in applicable standards).

> **Note:**
> **Explanatory material** -- descriptive guidance within the body of the standards that does not impose a "requirement" (indicated by "may," "might," or "could" in applicable standards).

Quality Control Standards (SQCS)

After studying this lesson, you should be able to:

1. *Describe the relationship of GAAS to the AICPA's Statements on Quality Control Standards (SQCS).*
2. *List the 6 elements that comprise a firm's quality control system.*

I. **Relationship of GAAS to the SQCS --** An individual audit engagement is governed by GAAS, whereas a CPA firm's collective portfolio of accounting and auditing services (sometimes called the "A&A" practice, which involves entities' financial statements and, thereby, involves the "public interest") is governed by the AICPA's SQCS. SQCS are issued by the AICPA's Auditing Standards Board (in particular, the section of the SQCS dealing with "A Firm's System of Quality Control" is QC10). The relevant AICPA guidance applicable to an individual audit engagement is provided by AU 220: "Quality Control for an Engagement Conducted in Accordance with [GAAS]."

Note:
The purpose of AU 220 on "Quality Control for an Engagement Conducted in Accordance with [GAAS]" is to assist the auditor in implementing the firm's quality control procedures specifically at the engagement level. This pronouncement states that the auditor's objective is to implement quality control procedures at the engagement level that provide reasonable assurance that (a) the audit complies with professional standards and applicable legal and regulatory requirements and (b) the auditor issues an appropriate report.

II. **Focus of the System of Quality Control --** A CPA firm is required to have a "system of quality control" for its accounting and auditing services (covering audit, attestation, compilation, and review services; note that the SQCS are not applicable to tax or consulting services) to provide reasonable assurance that engagements are performed in accordance with professional standards and applicable regulatory and legal requirements, and that the issuance of reports are appropriate in the circumstances.

   A. **Nature and scope --** The policies and procedures will vary with the circumstances (e.g., firm size and number of offices, complexity of services offered, and the level of experience of the professional staff).

   B. **Inherent limitations --** Similar to any internal control system, a quality control system provides "reasonable" (a high, but not absolute) assurance, reflecting implicit cost-benefit trade-offs.

III. **Six Elements of a Quality Control System --** These are interrelated (e.g., monitoring and the quality of personnel involved affect the other elements).

   A. **Leadership responsibilities for quality --** Policies and procedures should promote an internal culture that emphasizes a commitment to quality (sometimes called the "tone at the top"). For an individual audit engagement, the engagement partner should take responsibility for overall audit quality, although performance of certain procedures may, of course, be delegated to other members of the engagement team.

   B. **Relevant ethical requirements --** Policies and procedures should address the independence of personnel as necessary (should obtain written confirmation of compliance with independence requirements from all appropriate personnel at least annually).

   C. **Acceptance and continuance of client-relationships and engagements --** Policies and procedures should carefully assess the risks associated with each engagement (including issues related to management integrity) and the firm should only undertake engagements that can be completed with professional competence.

Note:
If the engagement team identifies a threat to independence that safeguards may not eliminate or reduce to an acceptable level, the engagement partner is required to report the matter to the relevant person(s) in the firm to determine the appropriate action (to either eliminate the threat or withdraw from the engagement when withdrawal is allowed under applicable law or regulation).

D. **Human resources --** Policies and procedures should address important personnel issues (including initial hiring, assignments to engagements, professional development and continuing professional education, and promotion decisions).

E. **Engagement performance --** Policies and procedures should focus on compliance with all applicable firm and professional standards and applicable regulatory requirements, and encourage personnel to consult as necessary with professional (or other) literature or other human resources within or outside of the firm for appropriate guidance.

F. **Monitoring --** Policies and procedures should provide an ongoing assessment of the adequacy of the design and the operating effectiveness of the system of quality control. Controls that are effective at one point in time, may deteriorate over time owing to neglect or changed circumstances. It is important that the controls are properly monitored so that timely adjustments can be made as necessary to keep the quality control policies and procedures working effectively over time.

IV. **Differences of Opinion --** The firm should establish policies and procedures for dealing with and resolving differences of opinion within the engagement team, with those consulted, and between the engagement partner and the engagement quality control reviewer (including that the conclusions reached are documented and implemented and that the report is not released until the matter is resolved).

V. **Documentation of the Operation of Quality Control Policies and Procedures --** The firm should establish policies and procedures requiring appropriate documentation of the operation of each element of the system of quality control.

VI. **Definitions**

A. **Engagement partner --** The person in the firm who is responsible for the audit engagement and its performance and for the auditor's report.

B. **Engagement quality control review --** A process designed to provide an objective evaluation, before the report is released, of the significant judgments the engagement team made and the conclusions it reached in formulating the auditor's report. (The engagement quality control review process is only for those audit engagements, if any, for which the firm has determined that an engagement quality control review is required, in accordance with its policies and procedures.)

C. **Engagement quality control reviewer --** This is the person in the firm, a suitably qualified external person, or a team made up of such individuals, none of whom is part of the engagement team, with sufficient and appropriate experience and authority to objectively evaluate the significant judgments that the engagement team made and the conclusions it reached in formulating the auditor's report.

VII. **The Main Difference Between the Clarified SAS and the Corresponding International Standard on Auditing --** The SAS requires that the quality control review must be completed before the engagement partner **releases** the auditor's report, whereas the ISA requires that the quality control review be completed before the engagement partner **dates** the auditor's report

Overview of Audit Process

After studying this lesson, you should be able to:

1. *Identify the primary dimensions that comprise the audit process: a) engagement planning; b) internal control considerations; c) reporting.*

I. Engagement Planning

A. Decide whether to accept (or continue) the engagement - Recall the quality control standards regarding client acceptance/continuation issues.

B. Perform risk assessment procedures to address the risks of material misstatement, whether duc to crror or fraud.

C. Evaluate requirements for staffing and supervision.

D. Prepare the required written audit plan (sometimes called the *audit program*) that specifies the nature, timing, and extent of auditing procedures for every audit area (which is usually prepared after control risk has been assessed, so that detection risk can be appropriately set in each audit area).

II. Internal Control Considerations

A. Obtain an understanding of internal control for planning purposes as required, emphasizing the assessment of the risk of material misstatement in individual audit areas and document the understanding of internal control.

B. If contemplating "reliance" on certain identified internal control strengths as a basis for reducing substantive testing, the auditor must then perform appropriate "tests of control" to determine that those specific controls are operating effectively, that is, working as intended.

III. Substantive Audit Procedures (evidence gathering procedures whose purpose is to detect material misstatements, if there are any)

-- Note that the word *substantive* is derived from *substantiate*, which means "to verify." These are evidence-gathering procedures designed to verify the financial statement elements and to detect any material misstatements.

A. Analytical procedures -- Those evidence-gathering procedures that suggest "reasonableness" (or "unreasonableness") based upon a comparison to appropriate expectations or benchmarks, such as prior year's financial statements, comparability to industry data (including ratios) or other interrelationships involving financial and/or nonfinancial data.

B. Tests of details -- Those evidence-gathering procedures consisting of either of two types:

1. **Tests of ending balances --** Where the final balance is assessed by testing the composition of the year-end balance (e.g., testing a sample of individual customers' account balances that make up the general ledger accounts receivable control account balance).
2. **Tests of transactions --** Where the final balance is assessed by examining those debits and credits that caused the balance to change from last year's audited balance to the current year's balance.

IV. Reporting

-- Conclusions are expressed in writing using standardized language to avoid miscommunication.

Overview of Auditor's Report

After studying this lesson, you should be able to:

1. *Describe the structure and content of the so-called standard unqualified audit report under the AICPA's Clarified Standards .*

I. Prior to the issuance of the Clarified Standards, the so-called standard unqualified audit report under AICPA Professional Standards consisted of 3 paragraphs (comprised of a total of 9 sentences). The change in the audit reporting language is one of the major differences caused by the Clarified Standards.

A. **Introductory Paragraph --** 3 sentences:

1. Identify the entity's financial statements;
2. Identify management's responsibilities; and
3. Identify the auditor's responsibilities.

B. **Scope Paragraph --** 5 sentences:

1. Audit conducted in accordance with GAAS;
2. Audit provides reasonable assurance;
3. Audit examines evidence on a test basis;
4. Audit includes assessing accounting principles used and significant estimates made;
5. Audit provides a reasonable basis for the opinion.

C. **Opinion Paragraph --** 1 long sentence:

1. Express an opinion that the financial statements are fairly stated in conformity with GAAP (or other applicable accounting framework).

> A sample unqualified audit report under the "old" (now superseded) standards is provided below, so that the differences relative to the sample unqualified audit report under the "new" Clarified Standards will be more clearly recognized.

See the following report.

Standard Unqualified Auditor's Report -- Under the "old" AICPA Professional Standards

Independent Auditor's Report

We have audited the balance sheets of ABC Company at December 31, 20X2 and 20X1, and the related statements of income, retained earnings, and cash flows for the years then ended. These financial statements are the responsibility of the Company's management. Our responsibility is to express an opinion on these financial statements based on our audits.

We conducted our audits in accordance with auditing standards generally accepted in the United States of America. Those standards require that we plan and perform the audit to obtain reasonable assurance about whether the financial statements are free of material misstatement. An audit includes examining, on a test basis, evidence supporting the amounts and disclosures in the financial statements. An audit also includes assessing the accounting principles used and significant estimates made by management, as well as evaluating the overall financial statement presentation. We believe that our audits provide a reasonable basis for our opinion.

In our opinion, the financial statements referred to above present fairly, in all material respects, the financial position of ABC Company at December 31, 20X2 and 20X1, and the results of their operations and their cash flows for the years then ended, in conformity with accounting principles generally accepted in the United States of America.

/s/ CPA firm (signed by audit engagement partner)

Date (The auditor's report should not be dated earlier than the date on which the auditor has obtained sufficient appropriate audit evidence to support the opinion.)

II. **Auditor's Report --** Under the AICPA's Clarified Standards, the auditor's report has been reformatted and expanded to reflect 4 main sections:

A. The first section has no label, but it identifies the nature of the engagement and the entity's financial statements involved (consists of 1 sentence).

B. The second section is labeled **"Management's Responsibility for the Financial Statements"** -- (1 sentence) it states that management is responsible for the fair presentation of the financial statements and the implementation of internal control.

C. The third section is labeled **"Auditor's Responsibility,"** which consists of 3 separate paragraphs.

1. The first consists of 3 sentences
    a. Responsibility to express an opinion;
    b. Conducted the audit in accordance with (GAAS); and
    c. Plan and perform the audit to provide reasonable assurance.
2. The second consists of 5 sentences
    a. Perform procedures to obtain audit evidence about the amounts and disclosures;
    b. The procedures depend on the auditor's judgment, including assessment of risks of material misstatement, whether due to fraud or error;
    c. In making those risk assessments, the auditor considers internal control;
    d. The auditor expresses no such opinion (*on internal control, when not engaged to report on internal control in an "integrated audit"*); and
    e. An audit includes evaluating the appropriateness of accounting policies used and the reasonableness of significant accounting estimates.
3. The third consists of 1 sentence -- expressing the auditor's belief that the audit evidence is sufficient and appropriate to provide a basis for the opinion.

D. The fourth section is labeled **"Opinion"** -- (1 sentence) it expresses the auditor's opinion (in the same wording as that used in the previous AICPA standards).

In the Clarified Standards, the AICPA has replaced the term *unqualified* with *unmodified*. Two versions of the sample unmodified auditor's report are provided below. The first presents the typical unmodified audit report in paragraph form; and the second presents it on a sentence-by-sentence basis for ease of review.

Sample Unmodified Auditor's Report Under AICPA Clarified Standards

<u>Independent Auditor's Report</u>

[Appropriate Addressee]

We have audited the accompanying consolidated financial statements of ABC Company and its subsidiaries, which comprise the consolidated balance sheets as of December 31, 20X1 and 20X0, and the related consolidated statements of income, changes in stockholders' equity and cash flows for the years then ended, and the related notes to the financial statements.

Management's Responsibility for the Financial Statements

Management is responsible for the preparation and fair presentation of these consolidated financial statements in accordance with accounting principles generally accepted in the United States of America; this includes the design, implementation, and maintenance of internal control relevant to the preparation and fair presentation of consolidated financial statements that are free from material misstatement, whether due to fraud or error.

Auditor's Responsibility

Our responsibility is to express an opinion on these consolidated financial statements based on our audits. We conducted our audits in accordance with auditing standards generally accepted in the United States of America. Those standards require that we plan and perform the audit to obtain reasonable assurance about whether the consolidated financial statements are free from material misstatement.

An audit involves performing procedures to obtain audit evidence about the amounts and disclosures in the consolidated financial statements. The procedures selected depend on the auditor's judgment, including the assessment of the risks of material misstatement of the consolidated financial statements, whether owing to fraud or error. In making those risk assessments, the auditor considers internal control relevant to the entity's preparation and fair presentation of the consolidated financial statements in order to design audit procedures that are appropriate in the circumstances, but not for the purpose of expressing an opinion on the effectiveness of the entity's internal control. Accordingly, we express no such opinion. An audit also includes evaluating the appropriateness of accounting policies used and the reasonableness of significant accounting estimates made by management, as well as evaluating the overall presentation of the consolidated financial statements.

We believe that the audit evidence we have obtained is sufficient and appropriate to provide a basis for our audit opinion.

Opinion

In our opinion, the consolidated financial statements referred to above present fairly, in all material respects, the financial position of ABC Company and its subsidiaries as of December 31, 20X1 and 20X0, and the results of their operations and their cash flows for the years then ended in accordance with accounting principles generally accepted in the United States of America.

[Auditor's signature -- firm name, signed by audit engagement partner]

[**Auditor's city and state** -- this is a new requirement under the Clarified Standards]

[Date of the auditor's report -- when the auditor has obtained sufficient appropriate audit evidence as a reasonable basis for the opinion]

Sample Unmodified Auditor's Report Under AICPA Clarified Standards (Sentence-By-Sentence):

Independent Auditor's Report

[Introductory Paragraph]

1. We have audited the accompanying consolidated financial statements of ABC Company and its subsidiaries, which comprise the consolidated balance sheets as of December 31, 20X1 and 20X0, and the related consolidated statements of income, changes in stockholders' equity and cash flows for the years then ended, and the related notes to the financial statements.

Management's Responsibility for the Financial Statements

1. Management is responsible for the preparation and fair presentation of these consolidated financial statements in accordance with accounting principles generally accepted in the United States of America; this includes the design, implementation, and maintenance of internal control relevant to the preparation and fair presentation of consolidated financial statements that are free from material misstatement, whether owing to fraud or error.

Auditor's Responsibility

[First of 3 paragraphs]

1. Our responsibility is to express an opinion on these consolidated financial statements based on our audits.

2. We conducted our audits in accordance with auditing standards generally accepted in the United States of America.

3. Those standards require that we plan and perform the audit to obtain reasonable assurance about whether the consolidated financial statements are free from material misstatement.

[Second of 3 paragraphs]

4. An audit involves performing procedures to obtain audit evidence about the amounts and disclosures in the consolidated financial statements.

5. The procedures selected depend on the auditor's judgment, including the assessment of the risks of material misstatement of the consolidated financial statements, whether owing to fraud or error.

6. In making those risk assessments, the auditor considers internal control relevant to the entity's preparation and fair presentation of the consolidated financial statements in order to design audit procedures that are appropriate in the circumstances, but not for the purpose of expressing an opinion on the effectiveness of the entity's internal control.

7. Accordingly, we express no such opinion.

8. An audit also includes evaluating the appropriateness of accounting policies used and the reasonableness of significant accounting estimates made by management, as well as evaluating the overall presentation of the consolidated financial statements.

[Third of 3 paragraphs]

9. We believe that the audit evidence we have obtained is sufficient and appropriate to provide a basis for our audit opinion.

Opinion

1. In our opinion, the consolidated financial statements referred to above present fairly, in all material respects, the financial position of ABC Company and its subsidiaries as of December 31, 20X1 and 20X0, and the results of their operations and their cash flows for the years then ended in accordance with accounting principles generally accepted in the United States of America.

Different Types of Engagements

After studying this lesson, you should be able to:

1. *Recognize which AICPA Professional Standards are applicable to engagements to review and/or compile financial statements of a private company and which are applicable to other attestation engagements.*
2. *Be aware that "engagement letters" are required for any engagement to audit, review, or compile an entity's financial statements under AICPA Professional Standards.*

I. **AICPA's Statements on Standards for Accounting and Review Services (SSARSs) --** These are applicable when the CPA is associated with the financial statements of a private company, but that association is something less than a full-scope "audit" engagement.

   A. **Compilation --** This occurs when the CPA is engaged simply to assemble into financial statement format the financial records of a private company, without expressing any degree of assurance on the reliability of those financial statements.

   B. **Review --** This occurs when the CPA is engaged to provide a lower level of assurance (relative to that of an audit) on financial statements of a private company by performing limited procedures, including reading the financial statements, performing analytical procedures, and making appropriate inquiries of client personnel.

II. **AICPA's Statements on Standards for Attestation Engagements (SSAEs) --** These are applicable when the CPA provides assurance about written representations or subject matter other than historical financial statements (e.g., management may make representations about its superior product performance that may be made more reliable by the CPA's independent verification and report).

III. **Responsibilities Vary for Different Types of Engagements**

   A. **Understanding with the client --** When associated with financial statement subject matter, AICPA Professional Standards require the CPA to establish an understanding with the entity involved as to the services to be rendered and the parties' respective responsibilities. The CPA must document that understanding in a written engagement letter between the CPA and the client entity. This should not be surprising, since the "public interest" is associated with such financial statement subject matter.

   > **Note:**
   > A written engagement letter must be obtained for engagements to audit, review, or compile an entity's financial statements under AICPA Professional Standards.

   B. **Levels of assurance --** The level of assurance varies with the type of service involved and should be clearly addressed in the engagement letter between the CPA and the client entity.

      1. **Audit --** An audit conveys a high level of assurance about the reliability of the financial statements, and is expressed as positive assurance in the form of an opinion (recall that the SASs apply to audits of "nonissuers").
      2. **Review --** A review conveys a lower (i.e., "moderate") level of assurance about financial statements (for a private company under the AICPA's SSARSs).
      3. **Compilation --** A compilation conveys no assurance about the reliability of the financial statements (for a private company under the AICPA's SSARSs).

IV. **Other attest engagements --** The CPA may convey either a high or moderate level of assurance about nonfinancial statement representations under the SSAEs. (The subject matter of the engagement involves something other than historical financial statements, and, hence, more flexibility exists to negotiate with the entity about the level of assurance to be conveyed and/or the procedures to be used as a basis for conclusions.)

NOTE: The SSARSs and SSAEs will be explored in detail at an appropriate point later in the course materials. They are merely introduced here so that candidates will be reminded early on that the AICPA Professional Standards encompass a variety of types of standards governing different services associated with the CPA profession.

Planning Activities

Pre-Engagement Planning Issues

After studying this lesson, you should be able to:

1. *Understand the auditor's requirement under the applicable Statements on Quality Control Standards as they are used to specifically consider the "acceptance and continuance of clients and engagements."*
2. *Understand the auditor's responsibilities in agreeing upon the terms of the audit engagement with management.*
3. *Understand the auditor's responsibilities to communicate with the predecessor auditor when an entity changes auditors.*

I. **Statements on Quality Control Standards --** Recall the AICPA's "Statements on Quality Control Standards (SQCS)" that are applicable to a CPA's financial statement related services.

A. One of the six elements of a quality control system is "acceptance and continuance of clients and engagements." Auditors should avoid clients whose management lacks integrity or clients who are viewed as too risky owing to industry considerations or entity-specific issues.

B. The auditor should also evaluate the compliance with applicable ethics requirements, especially regarding independence issues and competencies to properly perform the engagement, before proceeding with other significant audit-related activities.

> ? **Question:** What if the successor believes that the financial statements covered by the predecessor's report require revision?
>
> **Answer:**
> Try to arrange a meeting with the three parties (i.e., the successor, predecessor, and client management) -- if the client refuses to meet to discuss issues reflecting on the appropriateness of the previously issued financial statements, the successor should consider the risks of being the entity's auditor.

> ? **Question:** What if the auditor is unable to observe the beginning inventory?
>
> **Answer:**
> If unable to verify the beginning inventory, the auditor may be unable to reach a conclusion about the cost of goods sold and, hence, the net income. As a result, the auditor may not be able to express an opinion on the fairness of the income statement, statement of cash flows, or statement of retained earnings. However, the auditor could still express an opinion on the balance sheet itself.

II. **"Terms of Engagement" --** The relevant AICPA guidance is provided by AU 210: "Terms of Engagement." This pronouncement addresses the auditor's responsibilities in agreeing upon the terms of the audit engagement with management (and those charged with governance, when appropriate).

A. Auditor's objective under AU 210 -- The auditor's objective is to accept an audit engagement involving a new or existing audit client only when the basis for the audit has been agreed upon by (1) establishing when the "preconditions for an audit" are present; and (2) confirming that a common understanding of the terms of the engagement exists between the auditor and management (and those charged with governance, as applicable).

> **Definition:**
> *Preconditions for an audit*: The use by management of an acceptable financial reporting framework in the preparation of the financial statements and the agreement of management to the premise on which an audit is conducted.

1. Management should acknowledge its responsibility for (a) the fair presentation of the financial statements; (b) the design and implementation of effective internal control over financial reporting; and (c) providing the auditor with all information relevant to the financial statements and any additional information requested by the auditor, and providing access to all entity personnel relevant to the audit of the financial statements. (The auditor should determine whether the financial reporting framework is appropriate and obtain an agreement that management acknowledges and understands its responsibilities.)
2. If the preconditions are not present -- the auditor should not accept the engagement; instead, the auditor should discuss the matter with management.
3. If management imposes a limitation on the scope of the audit that the auditor believes would result in a disclaimer of opinion (called a "limited engagement") -- the auditor normally should not accept the engagement. If such an entity is required by law or regulation to have an audit, the auditor is then allowed to accept the "limited engagement," so as long as a disclaimer of opinion is acceptable under the applicable law or regulation.
4. Agreement on audit engagement terms -- The agreement of the terms of the engagement should be documented in an audit "engagement letter" and address the following:
    a. The objective and scope of the audit;
    b. The auditor's responsibilities;
    c. Management's responsibilities;
    d. A statement about the inherent limitations of an audit;
    e. A statement identifying the applicable financial reporting framework;
    f. Reference to the expected content of any reports to be issued; and
    g. Other matters as warranted in the auditor's judgment.

B. **Initial audits --** *Initial audit* refers to when the prior year's financial statements have been audited by a different auditor (referred to as the "predecessor auditor").

1. Before accepting the engagement -- The auditor should request that management authorize the predecessor auditor to respond to the auditor's inquiries relevant to the decision whether to accept the engagement.
2. The predecessor is expected to respond fully and to indicate when the response is limited. The auditor should evaluate the predecessor's response in deciding whether to accept the engagement. If management does not authorize the predecessor to respond (or otherwise limits the predecessor's response), the auditor should consider that fact in deciding whether to accept the engagement.
3. The auditor's communication with the predecessor auditor may be written or verbal -- typical matters expected to be addressed include the following:
    a. Information that might bear on the integrity of management;
    b. Any disagreements with management about accounting or auditing issues;
    c. Communications involving those charged with governance with respect to fraud and/or noncompliance with applicable laws or regulations;

d. Communications involving management and those charged with governance regarding significant deficiencies in internal control; and

e. The predecessor's understanding about the reasons for the entity's change in auditors.

> **Question:**
> What if the auditor believes that the financial statements covered by the predecessor's report require revision?
>
> **Answer:**
> Try to arrange a 3-way meeting involving the auditor, predecessor, and entity management. If management refuses to meet to discuss issues related to the appropriateness of previously issued financial statements, the auditor should consider those matters in deciding whether to accept the engagement.

C. **Recurring audit engagements --** If the auditor concludes that the terms of the preceding engagement are still applicable to the current engagement, the auditor should remind management of the terms of the engagement (and document that reminder).

1. The auditor may remind management of the terms of the engagement in writing or verbally. When the communication is oral, it is desirable to document the significant matters discussed (including with whom and when).

2. It may be appropriate to revise the terms of the previous engagement --This is the case, for example, when there is a change in senior management or a significant change in ownership; when there is a change in the financial reporting framework adopted; when there is a change in legal or regulatory requirements; when there is any indication that management misunderstands the nature of the audit; or when there are special terms to the engagement.

D. Acceptance of a change in the terms of the audit engagement

1. If the auditor is asked to change the audit engagement to an engagement resulting in a lower level of assurance (prior to completing the audit engagement) -- The auditor should determine whether reasonable justification for doing so exists; if not, the auditor should decline the request.

2. Suppose that the auditor concludes no reasonable justification for such a change exists, but management will not permit the auditor to continue the original audit engagement. The auditor should: (a) withdraw from the audit engagement when possible; (b) communicate the circumstances to those charged with governance; and (c) determine whether there is any legal or other obligation to report the matter to any other parties.

3. Reasonable basis for a change -- Reasonable justification would exist when there is a change in circumstances affecting management's requirements, or if there was a misunderstanding about the nature of the service originally requested. The resulting report should not refer to any audit procedures performed prior to changing the engagement to a review or other service.

III. Sample Engagement Letter

> **CPA Firm's Letterhead**
>
> (Date)
>
> Ms. Nancy Pritchett*
>
> ABC Company**
>
> 1803 King Avenue
>
> Columbus, OH 43212

Dear Ms. Pritchett:

This letter confirms our understanding of the services we will provide to ABC Company for the fiscal year ended December 31, 20XX. Moreover, this letter constitutes the entire agreement between us regarding the services covered by this letter, and it supersedes any prior proposals, correspondence, and understandings, whether written or oral.

Services and Related Report

We will audit the balance sheet of ABC Company as of December 21, 20XX, and the related statements of income, retained earnings, and cash flows for the year then ended, for the purpose of expressing an opinion on them. Upon completion of our audit, we will provide you with our audit report on those financial statements.

Our Responsibilities and Limitations

Our responsibility is to express an opinion on the financial statements based on our audit, and is limited to the period covered by our audit. If circumstances preclude us from issuing an unqualified opinion, we will discuss the reasons with you in advance. If, for any reason, we are unable to complete the audit or are unable to form an opinion, we may decline to express an opinion or decline to issue a report for the engagement.

We are responsible for conducting the audit in accordance with generally accepted auditing standards. Those standards require that we obtain reasonable, but not absolute, assurance about whether the financial statements are free of errors or fraud that would have a material effect on the financial statements, as well as other illegal acts having a direct and material effect on the financial statements. Accordingly, a material misstatement may remain undetected. An audit is not designed to detect errors, fraud, or the effects of illegal acts that might be immaterial to the financial statements. We will inform you of all matters of fraud that come to our attention. We will also inform you of any illegal acts that come to our attention, unless they are clearly inconsequential.

We will obtain an understanding of internal control over financial reporting sufficient to properly plan the audit and to determine the nature, timing, and extent of audit procedures to be performed. The audit will not be designed to provide assurance on internal control over financial reporting or to detect significant deficiencies in internal control. However, we will report to you any significant deficiencies in internal control that we identify.

An audit includes examining, on a test basis, evidence supporting the amounts and disclosures in the financial statements. Judgment is required in determining the areas and number of transactions selected for our testing. An audit also includes assessing the accounting principles used and significant estimates made by management, as well as evaluating the overall financial statement presentation. Our procedures will include appropriate tests of documentary evidence supporting the transactions recorded in the accounts, tests of the physical existence of inventory, and direct confirmation of accounts receivable and certain other assets and liabilities by correspondence with selected customers, banks, legal counsel, and creditors. At the conclusion of our audit, we will request certain written representations from senior management about the financial statements and related matters.

Management's Responsibilities

The financial statements are the responsibility of the Company's management. That responsibility includes properly recording transactions in the accounting records and establishing and maintaining internal control sufficient to permit the preparation of financial statements in conformity with generally accepted accounting principles.

The Company's management is responsible for adjusting the financial statements to correct any material misstatements and for affirming to us in the representation letter that the effects of any uncorrected misstatements aggregated by us during the engagement and pertaining to the latest period presented are immaterial, both individually and in the aggregate, to the financial statements taken as a whole. Management is also responsible for ensuring that the Company complies with all applicable laws and regulations.

The Company's management is also responsible for making available to us, on a timely basis, all of the Company's original accounting records and related information, documentation, and company personnel to whom we may direct our inquiries. That includes providing access to us to the minutes of all meetings of stockholders, the board of directors, and committees of the board of directors for which such minutes are taken.

Timing, Fees, and Other Matters

Assistance to be supplied by the Company's personnel, including the preparation of certain specific schedules and analyses of accounts, is described in a separate attachment. Timely completion of this work is necessary for us to complete our audit on a timely basis.

The results of our audit tests, the responses to our inquiries, and the written representation furnished by management, comprise the evidence that we will reply upon in forming our opinion on the financial statements. The resulting audit documentation for this engagement is the property of (*name of the CPA firm*) and access will be limited to authorized persons to protect the confidentiality of company-specific information.

As part of our engagement for the year ending December 31, 20XX, we will review the federal and state income tax returns for ABC Company. We will be available during the year to consult with you on the tax effects of any proposed transactions or anticipated changes in your business activities.

Our fees will be billed as work progresses and are based on the amount of time required plus out-of-pocket expenses incurred by our audit team. Individual hourly rates vary according to the degree of responsibility involved and the experience and skill required. We will notify you on a timely basis of any circumstances we encounter that might affect our initial estimate of total fees, which we anticipate will range from $xx,xxx to $xx,xxx, excluding the aforementioned out-of-pocket expenses. Invoices are payable upon presentation.

If this letter accurately reflects your understanding, please sign where indicated in the space provided below and return it to us. We appreciate the opportunity to serve you and look forward to a mutually enjoyable association.

Sincerely yours,

(Name of the CPA Firm)

____

Engagement Partner's Signature

Accepted and agreed to:

____

(ABC Company Representative's Signature)

(Title)

(Date)

*The engagement letter should be addressed to whoever engaged the CPA firm (which might be the entity's CEO, board of directors, or someone else). The client representative responsible for the engagement who signs the engagement letter should be given a copy of the signed engagement letter and the CPA firm should retain the original letter for engagement documentation purposes.

**Assume that ABC Company is a "nonissuer" (i.e., a private company) such that PCAOB auditing standards do not apply. Hence, there is no mention here of PCAOB auditing standards or the audit of internal control that is applicable to SEC registrants under the Sarbanes-Oxley Act of 2002.

Planning an Audit

After studying this lesson, you should be able to:

1. *Understand the auditor's responsibility to adequately plan an audit engagement based on applicable AICPA Professional Standards.*

> Recall the AICPA's specific "Performance Principle" dealing with "planning, materiality, risk assessment, and evidence," which states: "To obtain reasonable assurance, which is a high, but not absolute, level of assurance, the auditor: plans the work and properly supervises any assistants."
> For PCAOB auditing standards, recall the First Field-work Standard of GAAS "The auditor must adequately plan the work and must properly supervise any assistants."

I. **AICPA Guidance --** The relevant AICPA guidance is provided by AU 300: "Planning An Audit." This pronouncement states that the auditor's objective is to plan the audit so that it will be performed in an effective manner.

   A. Involvement of key engagement team members -- The engagement partner and other key members of the audit team should be involved in planning activities.

      1. The nature and extent of planning varies with the size and complexity of the entity, the audit team's experience with the entity, and changes in circumstances occurring during the engagement. Likewise, the extent of supervision and review can vary depending upon the size and complexity of the entity, the nature of the audit area involved, the assessed risks of material misstatement, and the competence of the audit personnel involved.

      2. Planning is an ongoing iterative process, not a one-time activity. Planning encompasses risk assessment procedures, understanding the applicable legal and regulatory framework, the determination of materiality, the involvement of specialists, and so forth.

      3. The engagement partner may delegate portions of planning and supervision to other personnel, but a discussion about the risk of material misstatement (including fraud risks) among key members of the audit team, including the engagement partner, is required.

   B. Preliminary engagement activities -- The auditor should address the following matters at the beginning of the engagement:

      1. Perform appropriate procedures to address quality control issues related to the continuance of the client relationship and the specific audit engagement (including consideration of issues regarding management integrity);

      2. Evaluate compliance with relevant ethical requirements related to quality control considerations (particularly regarding independence issues);

      3. Establish an understanding of the terms of the engagement.

   C. **Planning activities**

      1. The auditor should establish an "overall audit strategy" dealing with the scope and timing of the audit work, which affects the development of the required "audit plan." (An audit plan is more detailed than the overall strategy and deals with the nature, timing, and extent of audit procedures to be performed.) In establishing the overall audit strategy, the auditor should:

         a. Identify relevant characteristics of the engagement affecting its scope;

         b. Identify the reporting objectives of the engagement and required communications;

c. Consider the factors that are significant in utilizing the audit team;

d. Consider the results of preliminary engagement activities, and

e. Determine the nature, timing, and extent of necessary resources for the engagement.

f. The overall strategy affects the auditor's decisions regarding the allocation of audit resources to specific audit areas and how those resources are managed and supervised.

g. Communication with those charged with governance -- The auditor is required to communicate with those charged with governance about an overview of the planned scope and timing of the engagement. The auditor may discuss planning issues with management, but should be careful to avoid divulging details that might reduce the effectiveness of the audit by making the auditor's procedures and scope too predictable.

2. The auditor should also develop an "audit plan." (In practice, the term "audit program" is often used in place of what the AICPA calls the "audit plan.") The audit plan encompasses (a) the nature and extent of planned risk assessment procedures; (b) the nature, timing, and extent of planned "further audit procedures" at the relevant assertion level; and (c) other planned audit procedures necessary to comply with GAAS. Note: Because planning is an iterative process, the auditor should make appropriate changes to the overall strategy and to the audit plan as necessary during the course of the audit if unexpected circumstances are encountered.

D. Specialized skills -- The auditor should determine whether there is a need for specialized skills on the engagement. In the past, the AICPA used the term *specialist* to describe what they now call "a professional possessing specialized skills."

1. A professional having specialized skills may be someone within or outside of the audit firm. Examples include valuation experts, appraisers, actuaries, tax specialists, IT professionals, etcetera.

2. The auditor should be sufficiently knowledgeable about the matters involved to communicate the objectives of the work, to evaluate whether the planned procedures will meet the auditor's needs, and to evaluate the results of the procedures performed.

E. Documentation -- The auditor should address the following matters in the audit documentation: (1) the overall audit strategy; (2) the audit plan; and (3) any significant changes made to the audit strategy or the audit plan during the audit engagement, along with the reasons for any such changes.

II. **PCAOB Standards --** The relevant PCAOB guidance is provided by Auditing Standard No. 9, "Audit Planning." The auditor's planning-related responsibilities are virtually the same under the PCAOB standards as they are under the AICPA standards.

Materiality

After studying this lesson, you should be able to:

1. *Recognize the meaning of the term "performance materiality."*
2. *Understand the concept of materiality, which is essential in evaluating the "fairness" of the financial statements within some range of acceptability.*
3. *Understand the role of both quantitative and qualitative considerations that might influence the auditor's judgments about materiality.*

I. **AICPA Guidance --** The relevant AICPA guidance is provided by AU 320: "Materiality in Planning and Performing An Audit." This pronouncement states that the auditor's objective is to apply the concept of materiality appropriately in planning and performing the audit.

II. **"Materiality" --** The concept of materiality can be described as "an understanding of what is important" in financial reporting based on the auditor's perception of the users' needs.

A. A definition of "materiality:" from the FASB's Conceptual Framework project (specifically, Statement on Financial Accounting Concepts No. 2) follows:

> "The magnitude of an omission or misstatement of accounting information that, in the light of surrounding circumstances, makes it probable that the judgment of a reasonable person relying on the information would have been changed or influenced by the omission or misstatement." (Note that this definition emphasizes that materiality judgments involve both quantitative and qualitative considerations.)

B. The determination of materiality is a matter of professional judgment, and involves both **quantitative** (the relative magnitude of the items in question) and **qualitative** (the surrounding circumstances) considerations.

C. The auditor considers the concept of materiality throughout the audit process, including (a) in planning and performing the audit; (b) in evaluating the effect of uncorrected misstatements on the entity's financial statements; and (c) in forming the auditor's opinion.

1. In planning the audit -- The auditor should determine the materiality for the financial statements as a whole in connection with establishing the overall audit strategy. The auditor should determine **"performance materiality"** in connection with assessing the risks of material misstatement and determining the nature, timing, and extent of further audit procedures at the relevant assertion level.

> **Note:**
> Previous AICPA auditing standards distinguished between "planning-stage materiality" and "evaluation-stage materiality." Current standards no longer make that distinction, but, instead, introduce the term *performance materiality*, which seems similar to what was meant by the term *planning-stage materiality* in the past.

> **"Performance materiality"** -- The amount(s) set by the auditor at less than materiality for the financial statements as a whole to reduce to an appropriately low level the probability that the aggregate of uncorrected and undetected misstatements exceeds materiality for the financial statements as a whole; if applicable, it is also the amount(s) set by the auditor at less than the materiality level(s) for particular classes of transactions, account balances, or disclosures.
>
> **"Tolerable misstatement"** -- The application of performance materiality to a particular sampling procedure.

2. Revision during the audit -- The auditor should revise materiality for the financial statements as a whole and, if applicable, the materiality level(s) for specific classes of transactions or account balances when the auditor becomes aware of information affecting the auditor's initial judgments. The auditor should also determine whether "performance materiality" should be revised and whether the nature, timing, and extent of further audit procedures are appropriate.

D. **Documentation --** The auditor should document the following matters:

1. Materiality for the financial statements as a whole;
2. Materiality level(s) for particular classes of transactions, account balances, or disclosures, as applicable;
3. Performance materiality; and
4. Any revision of those considerations during the audit engagement.

E. Considerations that may affect the auditor's materiality judgment

1. **Quantitative guidelines --** In practice, auditors frequently apply a variety of "benchmarks" as a starting point in determining the appropriate materiality levels. A few examples of frequently used general guidelines follow (these are not specifically identified in the AICPA auditing standards, however):
   a. 5% - 10% of net income or earnings before taxes.
   b. 0.50% - 2% of the larger of net sales or total assets.
   c. 5% of owners' equity for private companies.
2. **Qualitative matters --** The surrounding circumstances and perceived risks might affect the auditor's judgment of what is material to the users. There are too many such factors to list here, but two examples follow:
   a. Public versus private companies -- A lower materiality threshold may apply to public companies owing to more exposure to litigation and because the owners of private companies may be closer to the day-to-day operations and, therefore, have different information needs.
   b. Unstable versus stable industry -- A lower materiality threshold may apply to a company in an unstable industry, which is by nature more susceptible to business failure.
3. **"Tolerable misstatement" --** (which, in practice, is sometimes referred to as "tolerable error") -- This term refers to the maximum error in a population that the auditor is willing to accept. This should be established in such a way that tolerable misstatement, combined for the entire audit plan, does not exceed materiality for the financial statements taken as a whole.

III. **PCAOB Standards --** The relevant PCAOB guidance is provided by Auditing Standard No. 11, "Consideration of Materiality in Planning and Performing an Audit." The auditor's responsibilities regarding materiality under the PCAOB standards are very similar to those under AICPA standards, although the PCAOB standard does not use the term "performance materiality."

Audit Risk

After studying this lesson, you should be able to:

1. *Understand the components of the "audit risk model" that are applicable to individual audit areas or major classes of transactions to be audited.*
2. *Understand the concept (and definition) of audit risk that underlies a risk-based audit approach relevant to planning, fieldwork, and audit reporting.*

I. "Audit Risk"

A. Definition of *Audit Risk* **--** "The risk that the auditor expresses an inappropriate audit opinion when the financial statements are materially misstated. Audit risk is a function of the risks of material misstatement and detection risk." (Source -- AU200: "Overall Objectives of the Independent Auditor and the Conduct of an Audit in Accordance with [GAAS].") Note that the concept of audit risk is really a probability and that audit risk and materiality are interrelated by the definition of audit risk.

B. The presence of audit risk is indicated in the auditor's report by reference to "reasonable assurance," meaning that audit risk cannot be reduced to a zero probability (which would imply "absolute assurance") owing to the inherent limitations of an audit. "Reasonable assurance" is defined as follows: "In the context of an audit of financial statements, a high, but not absolute, level of assurance." Note that *reasonable assurance* means a "high level of assurance" and a "low level of audit risk."

II. Basic Auditor Responsibility -- The auditor should properly plan and perform the audit to obtain reasonable assurance that material misstatements, whether caused by errors or fraud, are detected.

III. Considerations at the Financial Statement Level -- The one over riding audit planning objective is to limit audit risk to an appropriately low level (as determined by the auditor's judgment), which involves the following:

A. Determining the extent and nature of the auditor's risk assessment procedures.

B. Identifying and assessing the risk of material misstatement.

C. Determining the nature, timing, and extent of further audit procedures.

D. Evaluating whether the financial statements taken as a whole are presented fairly in conformity with GAAP.

IV. Risk of Material Misstatement -- The "risk of material misstatement" (RMM) is defined as: "The risk that the financial statements are materially misstated prior to the audit." RMM exists at two levels: (1) the overall financial statement level; and (2) the assertion level for classes of transactions, account balances, and disclosures.

A. RMM at the overall financial statement level -- This refers to risks that are "pervasive" to the financial statements and that potentially affect many assertions.

B. RMM at the assertion level -- The auditor assesses RMM at the assertion level for the purpose of determining the nature, timing, and extent of further audit procedures to obtain sufficient appropriate audit evidence. RMM at the assertion level consists of two components: (1) inherent risk; and (2) control risk (see below).

C. At the assertion level, "audit risk" consists of three component risk: (1) inherent risk (IR); (2) control risk (CR); and detection risk (DR). RMM consists of inherent risk and control risk.

$$AR = IR \times CR \times DR$$

Definitions:
Inherent risk (IR): The probability that a material misstatement would occur in the particular audit area in the absence of any internal control policies and procedures.

Control risk (CR): The probability that a material misstatement that occurred in the first place would not be detected and corrected by internal controls that are applicable.

Detection risk (DR): The probability that a material misstatement that was not prevented or detected and corrected by internal control was not detected by the auditor's substantive audit procedures (that is, an undetected material misstatement exists in a relevant assertion).

V. Variations on the above "Audit Risk Model"

A. AR = RMM × DR, where:

1. "Risk of material misstatement" (RMM) -- the auditor's combined assessment of inherent risk and control risk (if IR and CR are not separately assessed).

Note that RMM = IR × CR

B. AR = RMM × TD × AP, where:

1. DR can be broken into two components involving the likelihood that the auditor's two basic categories of substantive procedures fail to detect a material misstatement that exists (1) "tests of details risk" (TD) and (2) "substantive analytical procedures risk (AP)."

Note that DR = TD × AP

C. AR = IR × CR × TD × AP

VI. Quantification of the Risk Components

A. The component risks do not necessarily have to be quantified; for example, they could be assessed qualitatively as high, medium, or low.

B. Each component is considered from left to right in order: audit risk is set, then inherent risk is assessed, then control risk is assessed, and finally the implications for the appropriate level of detection risk are considered.

C. "Detection risk" is the only component risk that is specifically the auditor's responsibility -- "inherent risk" arises because of the particular audit area under investigation and "control risk" reflects management's responsibility to design and implement internal controls. Note that the auditor must "assess" inherent risk and control risk, but the auditor actually makes the decisions that, in effect, result in some level of detection risk, which should take into consideration the auditor's assessment of the risk of material misstatement.

1. If IR and CR are seen by the auditor as too high, the auditor must compensate by decreasing DR.

2. If IR and CR are perceived as low, the auditor may consider accepting a higher DR.

D. Increasing or decreasing DR is accomplished by adjusting the nature, timing, and/or extent of the auditor's substantive audit procedures. These might be viewed as the auditor's three strategic variables that, in effect, "set" DR based on the auditor's professional judgment about the following:

1. **Nature --** What specific audit procedures to perform (perhaps shifting the relative emphasis placed on the "soft evidence" analytical procedures versus the "hard evidence" tests of details)?
2. **Timing --** When will the procedures be performed, at an "interim" date (prior to year-end) or at "final" (after year-end when the books have been closed) and the auditor is actually auditing the numbers that the entity intends to report in its financial statements)?
3. **Extent --** Are large samples required for the auditor's test work or can somewhat smaller sample sizes be justified? How extensively should substantive procedures be performed?

Analytical Procedures

After studying this lesson, you should be able to:

1. *State the definition of analytical procedures.*
2. *Understand the 4 "key" considerations that determine the efficiency and effectiveness of the analytical procedures used for substantive purposes.*
3. *Identify the matters related to analytical procedures that should be included in the audit documentation.*

Definition:
Analytical procedures: Evaluations of financial information through analysis of plausible relationships among both **financial and nonfinancial** data. (This includes any necessary follow-up investigation of fluctuations, significant differences, or inconsistent relationships.)

I. **AICPA Guidance --** The relevant AICPA guidance is provided by AU 520: "Analytical Procedures." This pronouncement states that the auditor's objectives are to: (1) obtain relevant and reliable audit evidence when using substantive analytical procedures; and (2) design and perform analytical procedures near the end of the audit that assist the auditor when forming an overall conclusion about whether the financial statements are consistent with the auditor's understanding of the entity.

Note:
AU 520 replaces a previous AICPA auditing standard (then designated "AU 329"). The AICPA's nonauthoritative "Summary of Changes," addressing the Clarified Standards, pointed out, "The clarified SAS does not change or expand the requirements of extant AU section 329 in any significant respect."

A. **Substantive analytical procedures --** When performing analytical procedures for substantive purposes, the auditor should: (1) determine the suitability of the particular analytical procedures for given assertions; (2) evaluate the reliability of the data from which the auditor developed the expectation; (3) develop an expectation of recorded amounts (or ratios) and evaluate whether the expectation is sufficiently precise; and (4) compare the recorded amounts (or ratios) with the auditor's expectations and determine whether any difference is acceptable without further investigation.

1. Substantive procedures may consist of substantive analytical procedures, tests of details, or some combination of both. The auditor makes judgments about the effectiveness and efficiency of such procedures to limit the assessed risk of material misstatement to an acceptably low level.
2. **Nature of assertion --** The effectiveness and efficiency of analytical procedures used for substantive purposes depends on 4 important considerations: (1) the nature of the assertion involved; (2) the plausibility and predictability of the relationship; (3) the availability and reliability of the data used as a basis for developing the expectation; and (4) the precision of the expectation. Analytical procedures may be particularly effective in testing for omissions (regarding the "completeness" assertion) of transactions that would be hard to detect with procedures that focus on recorded amounts. In other words, tests of details may not be effective when underlying source documents do not exist for transactions that went totally unrecorded, so analytical procedures may represent the best chance of detecting such omissions.
3. **Plausibility and predictability of relationship --** Developing a meaningful "expectation" to compare to the entity's recorded amount is critically important to the skillful use of analytical procedures

a. Relationships in a stable environment are usually more predictable than those in a dynamic environment.

b. Relationships involving income statement accounts tend to be more predictable than those involving balance sheet accounts (since the income statement deals with a period of time rather than a single moment in time).

c. Relationships involving transactions subject to management discretion tend to be less predictable.

4. **Availability and Reliability of Data --** Reliability increases when the data used are reliable, which is enhanced when the data are (a) obtained from independent external sources; (b) are subject to audit testing (either currently or in the past); or (c) are developed under conditions of effective internal control.

5. **Precision of Expectation --** The likelihood of detecting a misstatement decreases as the level of aggregation of the data increases. In other words, relationships of interest to the auditor may be obscured by the noise in the data at high levels of aggregation. For example, analyzing sales by month broken down by product line is more likely to be helpful to the auditor than simply comparing the current year's sales in total to the prior year's sales.

B. **Analytical procedures when forming overall conclusions --** The auditor should perform analytical procedures near the end of the audit that assist the auditor in forming an overall conclusion as to whether the financial statements are consistent with the auditor's understanding of the entity. These procedures may be similar to those used as "risk assessment procedures," and include reading the financial statements and considering any unusual or unexpected relationships that were not previously identified. As a result, the auditor may revise the assessment of the risks of material misstatement and modify the planned further audit procedures.

C. **Investigating results of analytical procedures --** The auditor should investigate any identified significant differences by (1) inquiring of management (and corroborating management's responses with appropriate audit evidence, as necessary); and (2) performing other necessary audit procedures.

D. **Documentation --** The auditor should include the following matters in the audit documentation:

1. The auditor's expectation and the factors considered in developing it;

2. The results of the comparison of the recorded amounts (or ratios) with the expectations; and

3. Any additional auditing procedures performed to investigate significant differences identified by that comparison.

In summary, analytical procedures serve 3 audit purposes (two of which are required):

1. For risk assessment (required!);
2. For substantive purposes (widely used voluntarily, but not technically required); and
3. As a final review (required!).

Detecting Fraud

After studying this lesson, you should be able to:

1. *Identify and distinguish between the two types of "fraud" that might be relevant to a financial statement audit, as discussed in the AICPA Professional Standards.*
2. *Understand (and be able to state) the auditor's fundamental responsibility to detect and communicate matters related to fraud in a financial statement audit.*
3. *Identify the three categories of "risk factors" that the auditor is required to consider when assessing the risk of material misstatement due to fraud, based on AICPA Professional Standards.*

I. **AICPA Guidance --** The relevant AICPA guidance is provided by AU 240: "Consideration of Fraud in a Financial Statement Audit." This pronouncement states that the auditor's objectives are to: (1) identify and assess the risks of material misstatement due to fraud; (2) obtain sufficient appropriate audit evidence regarding the assessed risks of material misstatement due to fraud, through designing and implementing appropriate responses; and (3) respond appropriately to fraud or suspected fraud identified during the audit.

Definitions:
Fraud: An intentional act by one or more individuals among management, those charged with governance, employees, or third parties, involving the use of deception that results in a misstatement in the financial statements.

Fraud risk factors : Events or conditions that indicate (a) an incentive or pressure to perpetrate fraud; (b) provide an opportunity to commit fraud; or (c) indicate attitudes or rationalizations to justify a fraudulent action.

A. There are two different types of misstatements that are relevant to the auditor's consideration of fraud:

1. **Fraudulent financial reporting --** This type of fraud involves misstatements that are intended to deceive financial statement users (for example, the intent is to inflate the entity's stock price). Fraudulent financial reporting often involves management override of controls, recording fictitious journal entries, concealing facts, and altering underlying records to achieve the deception. This scenario is typically associated with a conspiracy involving multiple members of senior management to deceive the auditors, as well as financial statement users.
2. **Misappropriation of assets --** This type of fraud involves theft of assets causing the financial statements to be misstated owing to false entries intended to conceal the theft. Misappropriation of assets often involves embezzlement of receipts, stealing physical assets or intellectual property, and diverting the entity's assets for personal use. This scenario is typically associated with an individual bad actor operating individually to perpetrate and conceal the theft.

II. **The Auditor's Basic Responsibility Relates to Planning**

A. In general, the auditor is required to design (plan) the audit to provide "reasonable assurance" of detecting misstatements that are material to the financial statements. In particular, the auditor should specifically assess the risk of material misstatement due to fraud (in addition to error), and design the audit procedures to be responsive to that risk assessment. That risk assessment should be performed at both the financial statement level and the assertion level.

B. Specifically, key audit team members must have a "brainstorming" discussion to consider how and where the financial statements might be susceptible to material misstatement owing to fraud and to emphasize the importance of maintaining professional skepticism. That discussion involving key members of the engagement team should consider such matters as the following:

1. Known internal and external fraud risk factors relevant to the entity;
2. The risk of management override of controls;
3. Indications of "earnings management"
4. The importance of maintaining professional skepticism throughout the engagement; and
5. How the auditor might respond to the risk of material fraud.

> **Note:**
> AICPA Professional Standards focus on the auditor's responsibility for providing reasonable assurance of detecting material misstatements, whether due to error or fraud. The distinction depends upon whether the misstatement is intentional (which is the essence of fraud) or not. Intent may be difficult to determine, for example, when addressing accounting estimates, which are subjective by nature.

> **Question:**
> Does failure to detect a material misstatement imply a substandard audit?
>
> **Answer:**
> No! An auditor may be unable to detect a material misstatement owing to forgery, collusion, or upper management involvement, etc.

III. **Inquiry and Analytical Procedures** -- To obtain information needed to identify the risks of material fraud the auditor emphasizes "inquiry" and "analytical procedures." (The auditor's important inquiries should be documented in the "Management Representations Letter" at the end of fieldwork!)

A. **Inquiry** -- The auditor should question management personnel about their knowledge of fraud, suspected fraud, or allegations of fraud; inquire about specific controls that management has implemented to mitigate fraud risks; and inquire about management's communications with those charged with governance about fraud-related issues. The auditor may also choose to question others (e.g., audit committee, internal auditors, operating personnel, in-house legal counsel, etc.) about fraud-related issues.

B. **Analytical procedures** -- The auditor should perform analytical procedures involving revenue accounts, in particular. In general, the auditor should consider whether any unexpected results associated with analytical procedures might have been intentional.

C. There is a presumption that improper revenue recognition is a fraud risk. The auditor should ordinarily presume that there is a risk of material misstatement owing to fraud related to revenue recognition, and perform appropriate audit procedures (such as analytical procedures).

IV. **Fraud Risk Factors** -- The auditing standards identify three characteristics generally associated with fraud: (1) incentive/pressure; (2) opportunity; and (3) attitude/rationalization. These three categories of risk factors are sometimes referred to as the "fraud triangle."

A. **Fraudulent financial reporting** -- Example risk factors the auditor should consider:

1. **Incentive/pressure** -- Reasons that management might be motivated to commit fraudulent financial reporting.

a. Financial stability/profitability - When the entity is threatened by deteriorating economic conditions, for example: operating losses threaten bankruptcy; there are recurring negative cash flows from operations; there is vulnerability to rapid changes due to technology or other factors; there are increasing business failures in the industry; or the entity reports unusual profitability relative to others in the industry.

- **b.** Excessive pressure to meet the expectations of outsiders - Senior management may face significant pressure to meet external expectations, for example: there are overly optimistic press releases; the entity is only barely able to meet the stock exchange's listing requirements; the entity is having difficulty meeting debt covenants; or the entity must obtain additional outside financing to retool production to be competitive.

2. **Opportunities --** Circumstances that might give management a way to commit fraudulent financial reporting.
   - **a. Nature of the industry or the entity's operations --** For example: significant related-party transactions not in the ordinary course of business; ability to dominate suppliers or customers in a certain industry sector; unnecessarily complex transactions close to year-end raise "substance over form" issues; significant bank accounts or business operations in "tax-haven" jurisdictions with no clear business justification; major financial statement elements that involve significant estimates by management that are difficult to corroborate.
   - **b. Ineffective monitoring of management --** For example, domination of management by a single person or small group without compensating controls or; ineffective oversight by those charged with governance.
   - **c. Complex or unstable organizational structure --** For example, organization consists of unusual legal entities; high turnover of senior management, counsel, or board members.
   - **d. Internal controls are deficient --** For example, inadequate monitoring of controls; high turnover rates in accounting, internal auditing, and information technology staff; ineffective accounting and information systems (There are significant deficiencies that rise to the level of material weaknesses.
3. **Attitudes/rationalizations --** Attitudes, behaviors or justifications of management that might be associated with fraudulent financial reporting:
   - **a.** Lack of commitment to establishing and enforcing ethical standards.
   - **b.** Previous violations of securities laws (or other regulations).
   - **c.** Excessive focus by management on the entity's stock price.
   - **d.** Management's failure to correct reportable conditions.
   - **e.** Pattern of justifying inappropriate accounting as immaterial.
   - **f.** Management has a strained relationship with the predecessor or current auditor.

B. Misappropriation of assets -- Example risk factors the auditor should consider:

1. **Incentive/pressure --** An employee or member of management might be motivated to commit the misappropriation for a variety of reasons, such as the following: employees who have access to cash (or other assets susceptible to theft), may have personal financial problems, or they may have adverse relationships with the entity under audit, (perhaps in response to anticipated future layoffs or recent decreases to their benefits or compensation levels).
2. **Opportunities --** Circumstances that might give someone a way to commit the misappropriation include the following:
   - **a.** When assets are inherently vulnerable to theft -- For example, there are large amounts of liquid assets on hand, or inventory items are small, but valuable.
   - **b.** Inadequate internal control over assets -- For example, there is inadequate segregation separation of duties, inadequate documentation or reconciliation for assets, or inadequate management understanding related to information technology.

3. **Attitudes/rationalizations --** The individual perpetrating the misappropriation might possess attitudes or justifications that might be associated with that rationalize the improper behaviors and avoid any feelings of remorse for this misconduct. Generally, the auditor cannot normally observe these attitudes, but should consider the implications of such matters when they are discovered. The following might be of interest to the auditor:
   a. The employee's behavior indicates dissatisfaction with the entity under audit.
   b. There are changes in the employee's behavior or lifestyle that are suspicious.
   c. The employee exhibits a disregard for internal control related to assets by overriding existing controls or failing to correct known deficiencies.

C. **Consideration of the effects of the risk factors**

1. The auditor should use judgment in considering the individual or collective effects of the risk factors and recognize that the effects of these risk factors vary widely.
2. Specific controls may mitigate the associated risks, and specific control deficiencies may add to the risks.

D. Conditions may be discovered during fieldwork that cause the assessment of these risks in the planning stage to be modified. Factors that might cause the auditor's concerns to increase include the following examples:

1. There are discrepancies in the accounting records including inaccuracies or unsupported balances.
2. There is conflicting or missing evidence including missing documents or the absence of original documents that should be available (perhaps only photocopies are available).
3. There is a problematic relationship between the auditor and the entity including restricted access of the auditor to records or personnel and undue time pressures imposed by management.

E. **Responses to risk assessment --** In response to this risk assessment related to fraud, the auditor may conclude that the planned procedures should be modified or that control risk should be reconsidered. The auditor might make some "overall responses" (at the financial statement level, such as assigning more experienced staff to the engagement) and make other responses "at the assertion level" (by designing audit procedures for which the nature, timing, and extent of those procedures are responsive to the assessed risks of fraud).

1. **Overall responses --** The auditor may decide to assign more experienced personnel or information technology specialists to the engagement. The auditor should incorporate a degree of "unpredictability" in audit testing, whether at the financial statement level or the assertion level (for example, visiting some locations for inventory counts on an unannounced basis) or selecting some items for testing that are below materiality levels.
2. **Responses at the assertion level --** The auditor may decide to increase the emphasis on audit procedures that provide a stronger basis for conclusions or to confirm the terms of sales transactions, in addition to receivable balances; the auditor may move important audit testing to year-end, instead of performing those tests at an interim date; and/or the auditor may increase sample sizes for audit testing.
3. **Addressing management override of controls --** The auditor should obtain an understanding of the entity's controls over journal entries and inquire about unusual activity. Selected journal entries at the end of the period should be examined. The auditor should also review accounting estimates for bias, and might perform a "retrospective review" of significant accounting estimates in the prior year. The auditor should specifically evaluate any significant unusual transactions outside the entity's normal course of business.

F. **Management override --** Auditors should plan procedures specifically to address management override of internal control. Management override means that upper management may not be affected by controls that are imposed on subordinates throughout the organization. (Therefore, management may be able to sidestep those controls without leaving an audit trail for discovery.)

1. **Examine adjusting journal entries --** The auditor should be especially attentive to nonstandard journal entries (involving unusual accounts or amounts and those involving complex issues or significant uncertainty). Likewise, the auditor should also be especially attentive to journal entries near the end of the reporting period (both for the fiscal year and any applicable interim reporting periods, such as quarterly reports).
2. **Evaluate accounting estimates for bias --** The auditor should consider performing a "retrospective review," which means evaluating prior years' estimates for reasonableness in light of facts occurring after those estimates were made. In other words, did later events support or refute the appropriateness of management's estimates in prior periods? That may affect the auditor's perception of the reliability of management's estimates in the current period.
3. **Evaluate the business rationale for any unusual transactions --** The auditor should look for appropriate authorization of any unusual transactions by those charged with governance.

Fraud: Evaluation and Communication

After studying this lesson, you should be able to:

1. *Identify the specific fraud issues that the auditor should document.*
2. *Understand the auditor's responsibility to communicate the identified fraud issues to management, those charged with governance, or others.*
3. *Understand the auditor's responsibility to evaluate fraud issues in light of the overall results of the audit procedures performed.*

I. **Evaluation of Audit Test Results --** Near the end of the audit, the auditor should evaluate whether the results of the auditing procedures affect the auditor's initial assessment of material fraud risk. (The analytical procedures related to revenue should be performed through the end of the period.)

   A. When evaluating identified misstatements of the financial statements, the auditor should consider whether such misstatements might be indicative of fraud. For example, the auditor might consider the organizational level involved. If a misstatement may be the result of fraud involving management, the auditor should reevaluate the assessment of material fraud risk and the auditor's response to the assessed risks.

   B. If the misstatement is (or may be) the result of fraud and the effect could be material to the financial statements (or if the auditor has been unable to evaluate the materiality involved):

      1. Attempt to obtain additional evidence to determine the facts as to the cause and whether the financial statements are misstated. Discuss the issues and any further investigation required with an appropriate level of management (at least one level above those believed to be involved) and with those charged with governance (especially if senior management appears to be involved).

      2. If the auditor encounters circumstances related to fraud that call into question whether it is appropriate to continue the audit, the auditor should determine the applicable professional and legal responsibilities, and consider whether it is appropriate to withdraw from the engagement. If the auditor withdraws, then the matter should be discussed with management and those charged with governance. (Circumstances that may call into question the auditor's ability to continue the audit include the following: (a) the entity does not take appropriate action regarding fraud; (b) audit evidence suggests that there is a significant risk of pervasive fraud; and (c) the auditor has significant concerns about the competence or integrity of management or those charged with governance.)

II. **Required Documentation --** The auditor should document the following matters related to the consideration of fraud in the financial statement audit:

   A. The discussion among engagement personnel about fraud in planning the audit, including how and when the discussion occurred, the team members who participated, and the subject matter discussed;

   B. The procedures performed to obtain information necessary to assess the risks of material fraud.

   C. Specific risks of material fraud that were identified at the financial statement level and at the assertion level, including a description of how the auditor responded to those identified risks (including the linkage of audit procedures to the risk assessment);

   D. Reasons supporting the auditor's conclusion if revenue recognition was not identified as a fraud risk contrary to the presumption that revenue recognition is a fraud risk;

   E. The results of procedures performed to further address the risk of management override of controls;

- **F.** Other conditions and analytical relationships that caused the auditor to perform additional auditing procedures; and
- **G.** The nature of any communication about fraud made to management, those charged with governance, regulators, and others.

III. Required Communications when Fraud is Detected or Suspected -- The auditor's communication of fraud issues with management (or those charged with governance) may be written or oral, but should be timely. As indicated above, such communication should be documented in the audit documentation.

- **A.** If the fraud is not material to the financial statements and senior management is not involved in the fraud, the appropriate level of management (which is usually considered to be at least one level above where the fraud is believed to have occurred) should be notified. Determining the appropriate level of management for such communication is a matter of judgment, and includes consideration of the likelihood of collusion within management.
- **B.** If the fraud is material to the financial statements or if senior management is involved in the fraud, those charged with governance should be notified.
- **C. Other matters related to fraud --** The auditor may choose to discuss a variety of other matters with those charged with governance, including the following:
    1. Concerns about the adequacy of management's assessment of the entity's controls to prevent and detect fraud;
    2. Failure by management to respond appropriately to identified fraud or to address identified significant deficiencies in internal control;
    3. Concerns about the entity's control environment, including the competence or integrity of management;
    4. Concerns about management's efforts to "manage earnings"; and
    5. Concerns about the authorization of transactions that do not appear to be within the normal course of the entity's business.
- **D.** The auditor should consider whether any identified fraud risk factors may constitute a "significant deficiency" (or material weakness) regarding internal control that should be reported to senior management and those charged with governance.
- **E. "Whistle-blowing" --** Informing others (outside) the entity such as regulatory and enforcement authorities, is ordinarily prohibited by the auditor's confidentiality requirements, although the duty of confidentiality may be overridden by law or regulation (or the requirements of audits for governmental entities). Accordingly, it would be appropriate for the auditor to seek legal guidance when facing such circumstances. The auditing (and ethical) standards historically have identified 4 basic exceptions to the auditor's confidentiality requirements:
    1. The auditor must respond truthfully to a valid legal subpoena.
    2. The auditor must comply with applicable legal and regulatory requirements (including complying with the SEC's 8-K requirements about important matters, such as the entity's decision to change auditors).
    3. A predecessor auditor must respond appropriately to the successor auditor's inquiries when the former client has given permission for the predecessor auditor to respond to the auditor's questions.
    4. The auditor must report fraud to the applicable funding agency under the requirements of government auditing standards.

Detecting Illegal Acts

After studying this lesson, you should be able to:

1. *State the auditor's fundamental responsibility to detect and communicate illegal acts in a financial statement audit.*

I. **AICPA Guidance --** The relevant AICPA guidance is provided by AU 250: "Consideration of Laws and Regulations in an Audit of Financial Statements." This pronouncement states that the auditor's objectives are to: (1) obtain sufficient appropriate audit evidence regarding material amounts and disclosures about laws and regulations generally recognized to have a direct effect on the financial statements; (2) perform specified audit procedures that may identify instances of noncompliance with other laws and regulations that may have a material effect on the financial statements; and (3) respond appropriately to noncompliance (or suspected noncompliance) with laws and regulations identified during the audit.

> Legal and regulatory framework -- Those laws and regulations to which an entity is subject; noncompliance may result in fines, litigation, or other consequences that may have a material effect on the financial statements.

A. **Fundamental auditor responsibility --** The essence of the auditor's responsibility is to obtain reasonable assurance that the financial statements are free from material misstatement, whether caused by fraud or error, considering the applicable legal and regulatory framework.

1. **Inherent limitations --** The auditor cannot be expected to detect all noncompliance with all laws and regulations, since that is a legal determination and because many laws focus on an entity's operations instead of on the financial statements. (Note that the personal misconduct of management, those charged with governance, or others is outside the meaning of the term *noncompliance*.)

2. The SAS distinguishes between two categories of considerations:

a. Laws and regulations **having a direct effect** on the amounts and/or disclosures in the financial statements -- The auditor should obtain sufficient appropriate audit evidence regarding material amounts and disclosures.

b. Other laws and regulations **not having a direct effect** on the financial statements -- The auditor should perform specified audit procedures that may identify noncompliance that may have a material effect on the financial statements. The specified audit procedures include inquiry of management and those charged with governance about compliance issues, inspection of any correspondence with regulatory authorities, reading minutes, and so forth.

B. **Auditor's consideration of compliance with laws and regulations --** In obtaining an understanding of the entity and its environment, the auditor should obtain an understanding of

1. The entity's applicable legal and regulatory framework; and

2. How the entity is complying with that framework.

C. Audit procedures when noncompliance is identified or suspected

1. **If information suggests possible noncompliance --** The auditor should obtain an understanding of the circumstances of the act involved and gather further information to evaluate the financial statement effect. The auditor should also evaluate the implications of noncompliance to other aspects of the audit engagement, including risk assessment and the reliability of written representations.

2. **If the auditor suspects noncompliance --** The auditor should discuss the matter with management (at least one level above those suspected to be involved) and with those charged with governance, as appropriate.

3. **If unable to obtain sufficient information as to compliance --** The auditor should evaluate the effect of the lack of sufficient appropriate audit evidence on the auditor's report (and consider the need for obtaining legal advice).

D. **Reporting of identified or suspected noncompliance**

1. **Reporting noncompliance to those charged with governance --** The auditor should communicate with those charged with governance any noncompliance with laws and regulations (unless it is clearly inconsequential). When management or those charged with governance is involved, the auditor should communicate to the next higher level of authority. If no higher level of authority within the entity exists, the auditor should consider obtaining legal advice.

2. **Reporting noncompliance in the auditor's report --** If a material effect on the financial statements has not been appropriately reported, the auditor should modify the opinion (expressing either a qualified or adverse opinion). If the auditor has been prevented from obtaining sufficient appropriate audit evidence to evaluate the financial statement impact of the matter, the auditor should modify the opinion (expressing either a qualified opinion or disclaimer of opinion) for a scope limitation.

3. **Reporting noncompliance to regulatory/enforcement authorities --** The auditor should determine whether there is a responsibility to report the matter to parties outside the entity, which may take priority over confidentiality responsibilities. The auditor should consider obtaining legal advice about this issue.

4. **Withdrawal --** If the entity refuses to accept a modified opinion and if withdrawal is possible under applicable law or regulation, the auditor may withdraw from the engagement and inform those charged with governance of the reasons in writing. Likewise, if the entity does not take the appropriate corrective action regarding noncompliance issues, the auditor may withdraw if such action is permitted by applicable law or regulation.

E. **Documentation --** The auditor should document the identified or suspected noncompliance and the results of the discussion with management, those charged with governance, and others, as applicable. Such documentation might include

1. Copies of records or documents; and

2. Minutes of the discussion with management, those charged with governance, and others.

Using the Work of a 'Specialist'

After studying this lesson, you should be able to:

1. *Understand the distinction between the terms auditor's specialist and management's specialist as used by the AICPA.*
2. *Know when it would be appropriate for the auditor to reference the involvement of the auditor's specialist in the auditor's report.*
3. *Identify the considerations that would be relevant to an auditor's selection of a particular specialist*

I. **AICPA Guidance --** The relevant AICPA guidance is provided by AU 620: "Using the Work of an Auditor's Specialist." This pronouncement states that the auditor's objectives are to determine: (1) whether to use the work of an auditor's specialist; and (2) whether the work of the auditor's specialist is adequate for the auditor's purposes.

> **Definitions:**
> *Auditor's specialist*: An individual or organization possessing expertise in a field other than accounting or auditing, whose work in that field is used by the auditor to assist the auditor in obtaining sufficient appropriate audit evidence.
>
> *Management's specialist*: An individual or organization possessing expertise in a field other than accounting or auditing, whose work in that field is used by the entity to assist the entity in preparing the financial statements.

A. Note that the auditor is still responsible for the expressed opinion, so the auditor's responsibility is not reduced by using the work of an auditor's specialist.

B. Examples of a "field of expertise other than accounting or auditing" include the following: the valuation of complex financial instruments; actuarial calculations of liabilities for employee benefits; the valuation of environmental liabilities and cleanup costs; estimation of oil and other mineral reserves; and the interpretation of contracts, laws, and regulations; and so forth.

II. **Basic requirements of the auditor with respect to using an auditor's specialist --** Some considerations may differ for an "internal" auditor's specialist (who is affiliated with the auditor's firm or a firm that is part of an affiliated network) or an "external" auditor's specialist (who is not affiliated with the auditor's firm).

A. **Determining the need --** The auditor should determine whether an auditor's specialist is needed to obtain sufficient appropriate audit evidence, taking into consideration the following:

1. The nature of the matter involved;
2. The risks of material misstatement involved;
3. The significance of the matter to the audit;
4. The auditor's experience with any previous work of the auditor's specialist; and
5. Whether the auditor's specialist is subject to the audit firm's quality controls (which would apply to an "internal" specialist, but not to an "external" one).

B. **Competence, capabilities, and objectivity of the specialist --** The auditor should evaluate the competence, capabilities, and objectivity of the auditor's specialist for the auditor's purposes.

1. The auditor should consider information about the competence, capabilities, and objectivity of an auditor's specialist, which might be obtained from the following:

   a. Personal experience with the specialist's previous work;
   b. Discussions with the specialist or with other auditors familiar with the specialist;
   c. Knowledge of the specialist's credentials or professional/industry affiliations, including whether the work is subject to any particular technical performance standards or industry requirements; and
   d. Any journal articles or books written by the specialist.
2. For an "external" auditor's specialist, the auditor should inquire about any relationships that might threaten the specialist's objectivity. The auditor should consider any "threats" to the specialist's objectivity, along with any "safeguards" that might reduce such threats to an acceptable level.

C. **Obtaining an understanding of the field of expertise --** The auditor should obtain a sufficient understanding of the field of expertise of the auditor's specialist so that the auditor can
   1. Determine the nature, scope, and objectives of the work; and
   2. Evaluate the adequacy of that work for the auditor's purposes. This understanding may be obtained from having experience with other entities requiring that same field of expertise, through specific education in that field, or through discussion with the auditor's specialist.

D. **Agreement with the auditor's specialist --** The auditor and the auditor's specialist should agree (in writing when appropriate) about the following:
   1. The nature, scope, and objectives of the work involved;
   2. Their respective roles and responsibilities;
   3. The nature, timing, and extent of communications between the auditor and the auditor's specialist, including any reports to be delivered; and
   4. The requirements for the auditor's specialist to adhere to confidentiality considerations applicable to an audit engagement. The agreement between the auditor and the "external" specialist is usually in the form of an engagement letter.

E. **Evaluating the adequacy of the work**
   1. The auditor should evaluate the adequacy of the work performed by the auditor's specialist, including the following matters:
      a. The relevance and reasonableness of the conclusions;
      b. The relevance and reasonableness of any underlying assumptions and the methods used; and
      c. The relevance, completeness, and accuracy of any source data used by the auditor's specialist.
   2. The auditor may perform specific procedures to evaluate such work, including
      a. Making inquiries of the specialist;
      b. Reviewing the specialist's working papers; and
      c. Performing certain corroborative procedures, such as performing analytical procedures, examining published data, or confirming some matters with third parties, among other possibilities.

F. **If the work is not adequate --** The auditor and the auditor's specialist should agree on any further work to be performed, or the auditor should perform additional audit procedures that are appropriate to the circumstances (which could include engaging another auditor's specialist). If the auditor is unable to resolve the matter, it could constitute a scope limitation that would result in a modified opinion.

G. Reference to the auditor's specialist in the auditor's report

1. If the auditor's report contains an "unmodified" opinion, the auditor should not refer to the work of an auditor's specialist.
2. If the auditor's report contains a "modified" opinion and the auditor believes that it would help readers understand the reason for the modification, the auditor may reference the work of an "external" auditor's specialist. Normally, such a reference would first require the permission of the auditor's specialist. The auditor should also point out, in the auditor's report, that such a reference does not reduce the auditor's responsibility for the expressed opinion.

Required Communications with Those Charged with Governance

After studying this lesson, you should be able to:

1. *Understand the impact that ineffective two-way communication with those charged with governance may have on the audit engagement.*
2. *State the specific matters that the auditor is required to communicate "with those charged with governance" (and be able to define that term).*

I. **AICPA Guidance --** The relevant AICPA guidance is provided by AU 260: "The Auditor's Communication With Those Charged With Governance." This pronouncement states that the auditor's objectives are to: (1) communicate clearly the auditor's responsibilities related to the audit and an overview of the planned scope and timing of the audit and (2) obtain from those charged with governance information relevant to the audit.

> **Definitions:**
> *Those charged with governance*: The person(s) organization(s) with responsibility for overseeing the strategic direction of the entity and the obligations related to the accountability of the entity (encompasses the term "board of directors" or "audit committee" used elsewhere in the auditing standards).
>
> *Management*: The person(s) with executive responsibility for the conduct of the entity's operations.

A. **Basic auditor responsibility --** The auditor should communicate those matters that are significant and relevant to the responsibilities of those charged with governance in overseeing the financial reporting process.

> **Note:**
> The auditor is not required to perform any specific procedures to identify such matters to communicate with those charged with governance.

B. **Benefits --** Effective two-way communication with those charged with governance is important to having a constructive relationship, obtaining information relevant to the audit, and assisting those charged with governance in their role of overseeing financial reporting.

II. **Communication with Management --** The auditor may choose to discuss some matters with management before communicating them with those charged with governance, unless that is inappropriate. For example, the auditor would not normally discuss issues involving management's competence or integrity. Likewise, the auditor may choose to discuss some matters with the internal auditor(s) before communicating the matters with those charged with governance.

III. **Matters Required to be Communicated with Those Charged with Governance --** (Note that the auditor may choose to communicate additional matters.)

A. **The auditor's responsibilities under GAAS --** The auditor should communicate the auditor's responsibility for expressing an opinion on the fairness of the financial statements, and point out that management is responsible for presenting the financial statements in conformity with the applicable financial reporting framework. These responsibilities could be communicated by an engagement letter.

B. **The planned scope and timing of the audit --** The auditor should communicate an overview of the planned scope and timing of the audit engagement.

C. **Significant findings from the audit --** The auditor should communicate

1. The auditor's views about the qualitative aspects of the entity's significant accounting policies including the quality (not just the acceptability) of significant accounting practices, estimates, and disclosures;
2. Significant difficulties encountered during the audit including significant delays caused by management, unreasonable time pressure, unavailability of expected information, etc;
3. Disagreements with management over accounting and auditing matters whether or not those disagreements were satisfactorily resolved;
4. Any other matters that the auditor believes would be important to those charged with governance in their oversight of financial reporting;
5. **Uncorrected misstatements --** The auditor should request that uncorrected misstatements be corrected and communicate any uncorrected misstatements accumulated by the auditor, including the financial statement effect.
6. **Other matters --** The auditor should communicate the following matters:
    a. Material misstatements communicated to management that were corrected;
    b. Any significant findings or issues discussed with management;
    c. Any known instances where management consulted with other accountants about accounting or auditing matters; and
    d. The written representations that the auditor requested from management.

IV. **The Communication Process --** Clear communication by the auditor facilitates effective two-way communication with those charged with governance. Generally, the communication may be oral or in writing (effective communication may include formal presentations, written reports, or informal discussions, as determined by the auditor's judgment).

A. The auditor should communicate the significant findings from the audit in writing when oral communication is inadequate in the auditor's judgment.

B. When a significant matter is discussed with an individual member or subset of those charged with governance (such as the chair of the audit committee or others), the auditor should evaluate whether the matter should be summarized in a subsequent communication to all those charged with governance.

C. **Timing of communications --** The auditor should communicate on a timely basis so that those charged with governance can take appropriate action. However, that timing may vary depending upon the circumstances.

D. **Adequacy of the communication process --** The auditor should evaluate whether the two-way communication has been adequate for purposes of the audit.

1. An inadequate two-way communication may suggest an unsatisfactory control environment, which the auditor should consider.
2. If the two-way communication is inadequate, the auditor should consider whether a scope limitation may exist and consider the possible effect on the assessment of the risks of material misstatement. This might warrant modification of the opinion, or even withdrawal.

V. **Documentation of the Communication --** The auditor should document matters communicated orally, and (when communicated in writing, the auditor should keep a copy of that communication).

VI. **Other Statements on Auditing Standards --** Other statements require that certain specific matters should be communicated to those charged with governance regarding:

A. **Illegal acts --** The auditor should communicate any illegal acts that come to the auditor's attention.

B. **Going concern issues --** When substantial doubt about the entity's ability to continue as a going concern remains after considering management's strategy, the auditor should communicate (1) the nature of the conditions identified; (2) the possible effect on the financial statements and disclosures; and (3) the effects on the auditor's report.

C. **Fraud --** The auditor should

1. Inquire of the audit committee about the risks of fraud and the audit committee's knowledge of any fraud or suspected fraud;
2. Communicate any fraud discovered involving senior management and any fraud that causes a material misstatement (whether or not management is involved); and
3. Obtain an understanding with those charged with governance regarding communications about misappropriations committed by lower-level employees.

D. **Communicating internal control matters identified in an audit --** The auditor should communicate to management and those charged with governance any identified significant deficiencies in internal control (including material weaknesses).

Internal Control - Concepts and Standards

Internal Control Concepts 1

After studying this lesson, you should be able to:

1. *Understand the auditor's responsibility to obtain an understanding of an entity's internal control (in connection with the second Standard of Fieldwork under GAAS, which is now associated with one of the AICPA's "Performance" Principles underlying an audit under GAAS).*
2. *Explain three different ways that an auditor might document the understanding of internal control.*

I. **Review Phase --** The auditor should obtain an initial understanding of internal controls and document that understanding.

A. The auditor obtains an **understanding of internal control** and the flow of documents related to the entity's transactions primarily through:

1. Inquiry of appropriate personnel;
2. Observation of client activities;
3. Review of documentation -- The auditor reviews relevant documentation, including the client's accounting manuals, prior-year's audit documentation (working papers), etc.

B. The auditor's internal control analysis tends to focus on the entity's major transaction cycles.

C. **"Transaction cycle" --** Defined to be a group of essentially homogeneous transactions, that is, transactions of the same type.

D. **Implication --** A specific transaction cycle is the highest level of aggregation about which meaningful generalizations of control risk can be made, since control risk is constant within that transaction cycle. Each transaction within a specific transaction cycle is captured, processed, and recorded subject to the same set of internal control policies and procedures.

E. **Examples of typical transaction cycles --** Typical examples, include the following:

1. Revenue/receipts;
2. Expenditures/disbursements;
3. Payroll;
4. Financing/investing activities; and
5. Inventory, especially if inventory is manufactured, rather than purchased.

F. **Document the auditor's understanding --** The auditor should document that understanding of internal control. The extensiveness of the review and documentation varies with the circumstances (e.g., the emphasis on understanding internal controls increases if reliance on internal control is planned):

1. **Flow charts of transaction cycles --** A graphical depiction of the client's accounting systems for major categories of transactions with emphasis on the origination, processing, and distribution of important underlying accounting documents.

   a. **Advantages --** A fairly systematic approach that is unlikely to overlook important considerations; tailored to client-specific circumstances; fairly easy for others to review and understand; and fairly easy to update from year to year.

   b. **Disadvantages --** Can be rather tedious and time consuming to prepare initially although available commercial software today may eliminate much of that difficulty; the auditor might fail to recognize relevant internal control deficiencies by getting too absorbed in the details of documenting the client's system.

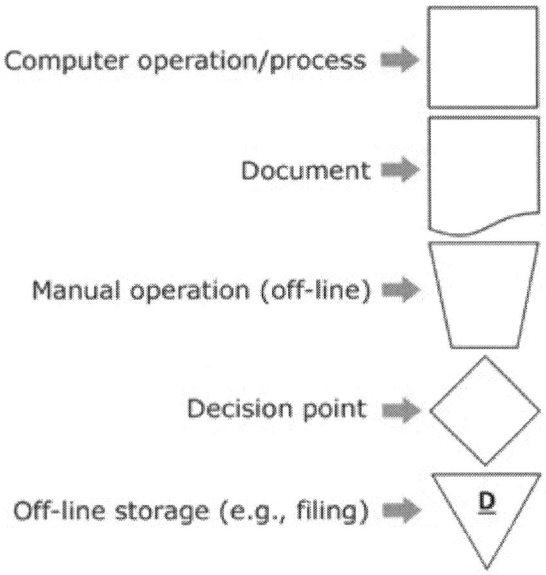

2. **Internal control questionnaires (ICQs) --** Questionnaires consisting of a listing of questions about client's control procedures and activities; a "no" answer is usually designed to indicate a control weakness.

   a. **Advantages --** Generic questionnaires can be prepared in advance for clients in various industry categories with every conceivable question, so that no important question related to controls is likely to be omitted; deficiencies are easily identified by a client's "no" response to any question.

   b. **Disadvantages --** Generic questionnaires are not tailored to client-specific circumstances and irrelevant questions are annoying to client personnel; the client personnel responding to the checklist of questions may conceal deficiencies by inaccurate answers without the auditor's knowledge.

3. **Narrative write-ups --** A written memo describing the important control-related activities in the transaction cycles under consideration.

   a. **Advantages --** Memos can be tailored to a client's unique circumstances, can be as detailed or general as desired, and are relatively easy to prepare (and easy for reviewers to read it).

   b. **Disadvantages --** It is relatively easy to overlook relevant internal control issues (strengths or weaknesses) because the analysis is fairly unstructured.

G. **Perform a "walkthrough" --** The auditor may select a few transactions to trace them through the client's accounting system. The purpose is merely to get some feedback as to whether the auditor has accurately understood (and documented) the way the client entity is processing transactions. The walkthrough is not considered "evidence" or a form of documentation and should not be confused with "tests of control"

Internal Control Concepts 2

After studying this lesson, you should be able to:

1. *Understand the implications of the assessment of control risk to the level of detection risk that may be appropriate (and, thereby, the effect on the "audit plan"—specifically on the nature, timing, and extent of the auditor's substantive procedures).*
2. *Understand the meaning of the term inherent limitations in connection with internal control.*
3. *Understand the purpose of performing "tests of control" and the circumstances that warrant performing such tests.*

I. **Preliminary Evaluation of Internal Control --** The auditor may initially consider whether "reliance" on certain specific internal control strengths is appropriate. The auditor may consider "assessing control risk at less than the maximum level."

   A. Consider the apparent **adequacy of controls (regarding "design" effectiveness)** -- If internal control is perceived to be "ineffective," the auditor would assess control risk at the maximum level.

      1. Consider the possible types of errors or problems that could occur.
      2. Consider the kinds of procedures that would prevent and/or detect such errors or problems.
      3. Determine whether such controls are in place.
      4. Evaluate the implications of any identified weaknesses.

   B. Consider **cost-benefit tradeoffs** -- Reliance on internal controls "buys" a reduction of substantive audit work to some degree, but it "costs" additional effort to perform tests of control (and this may or may not be cost beneficial, even if the design of internal control is perceived to be effective).

   C. The auditor should document the basis for conclusions about internal control -- either way, whether internal control is perceived to be effective or ineffective.

II. **Perform "Tests of Controls" --** If reliance is planned (regarding "operating effectiveness") -- "reliance" means the same thing as "to assess control risk at less than the maximum level" for purposes of accepting a somewhat higher level of detection risk.

   A. Perform "tests of controls" -- but only for those specific control policies and procedures (strengths that justify accepting a somewhat higher level of detection risk) on which reliance is planned.

   B. The purpose of performing tests of control is to verify that the controls that looked good "on paper" (design effectiveness) were actually working as intended throughout the period (**operating effectiveness**).

   C. Circumstances that warrant performing tests of control (associated with a "reliance" strategy): (1) when the auditor's risk assessment includes an expectation regarding the operating effectiveness of controls; or (2) when the performance of substantive procedures alone do not limit audit risk to an acceptably low level.

   D. **When performing "tests of controls" --** Select a sample of transactions and verify that the control procedures of interest were, in fact, performed on the transactions in the sample which usually requires that the control procedure be documented as it is performed. Undocumented controls may be tested by the auditor's "observation" of the entity's performance of such controls.

III. Reevaluate Planned Reliance Based on the Results of These Tests of Controls -- Determine whether the results of the tests of controls are consistent with the planned reliance on internal controls. (What looked good on paper may not be working satisfactorily in reality.)

IV. Develop a Detailed Audit Plan -- (Also referred to as an "audit program") The auditor should prepare a written audit plan that specifies the nature, timing, and extent of further audit procedures to be performed, and the auditor should document the conclusions about control risk in planning the audit:

A. A wholly substantive audit approach means "no reliance" on internal control (which means the same thing as "assessing control risk at the maximum level"). In other words, the auditor plans to meet the audit risk objectives by performing only substantive audit procedures without any expectation about the operating effectiveness of internal control. Tests of control would not be performed.

B. Auditors may base their audit conclusions on both tests of controls and substantive audit procedures, although the auditor must always perform substantive procedures to some extent (i.e., the auditor cannot rely entirely on the operating effectiveness of internal control as a sole basis for conclusions), related to "detection risk" in the audit risk model.

See the following example.

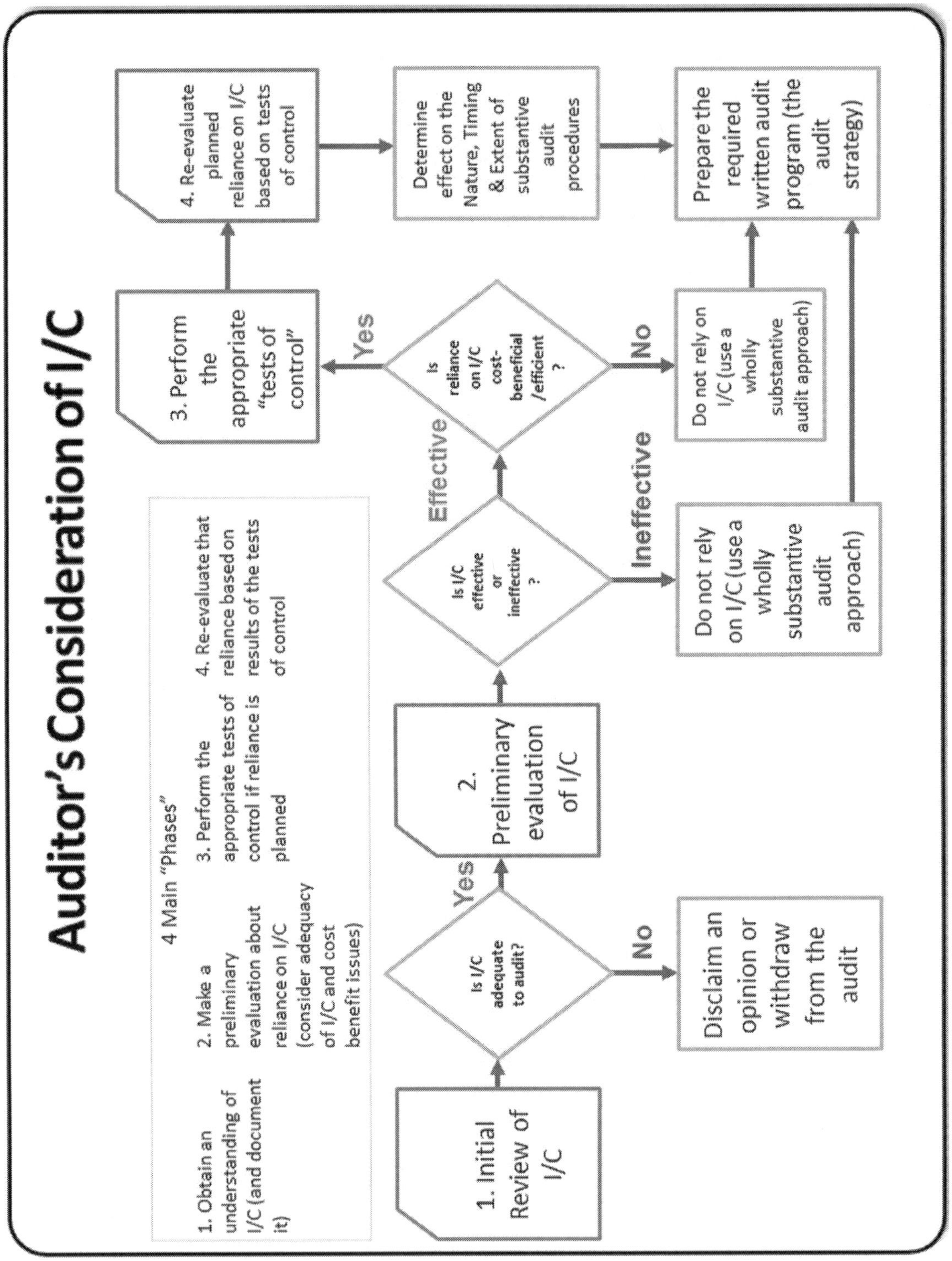
Auditor's Consideration of I/C
4 Main "Phases"
1. Obtain an understanding of I/C (and document it)
2. Make a preliminary evaluation about reliance on I/C (consider adequacy of I/C and cost benefit issues)
3. Perform the appropriate tests of control if reliance is planned
4. Re-evaluate that reliance based on results of the tests of control
1. Initial Review of I/C
Is I/C adequate to audit?
Yes
No
Disclaim an opinion or withdraw from the audit
2. Preliminary evaluation of I/C
Is I/C effective or ineffective ?
Effective
Ineffective
Do not rely on I/C (use a wholly substantive audit approach)
Is reliance on I/C cost-beneficial /efficient ?
Yes
No
Do not rely on I/C (use a wholly substantive audit approach)
3. Perform the appropriate "tests of control"
4. Re-evaluate planned reliance on I/C based on tests of control
Determine effect on the Nature, Timing & Extent of substantive audit procedures
Prepare the required written audit program (the audit strategy)

V. **Inherent Limitations --** The design and implementation of internal control is a management function (not the auditor's responsibility!) and management must evaluate the applicable costs and benefits in the design and implementation of their internal control policies and procedures.

A. The costs of internal controls should not outweigh the benefits attributable to those controls -- as a result, controls provide reasonable (not absolute) assurance.

B. Mistakes may occur as a result of employees' misunderstandings, misjudgments, carelessness, fatigue, etc.

C. Segregation of duties may break down due to collusion (a conspiracy among employees or management to circumvent internal controls) or management's "override" of controls -- override refers to management imposing controls downward on subordinates without intending to be affected by those controls themselves.

Question:
Why must auditors consider an entity's internal control in planning the audit engagement?

Answer:
In order to plan an effective and efficient audit, auditors must assess control risk as a basis for setting the appropriate level of "detection risk" related to their substantive auditing procedures (specifically, to determine the nature, timing, and extent of those substantive procedures).

Internal Control Standards 1

After studying this lesson, you should be able to:

1. *Understand the entity and its environment, including internal control (with emphasis on the 5 interrelated components of internal control), in accordance with AICPA Professional Standards.*
2. *Understand the auditor's responsibility to perform risk assessment procedures.*

I. Responsibilities under AICPA Professional Standards

A. "The relevant AICPA guidance is provided by AU 315: "Understanding the Entity and Its Environment and Assessing the Risks of Material Misstatement." This pronouncement states that the auditor's objective is to "identify and assess the risks of material misstatement, whether due to fraud or error, at the financial statement and relevant assertion levels through understanding the entity and its environment, including its internal control, thereby providing a basis for designing and implementing responses to the assessed risks of material misstatement."

> This SAS provides guidance regarding the second Standard of Fieldwork of GAAS: "The auditor must obtain a sufficient understanding of the entity and its environment, including its internal control, to assess the risk of material misstatement of the financial statements whether due to fraud or error, and to design the nature, timing, and extent of further audit procedures."
>
> That requirement is now embedded in one of the "Performance Principles." "To obtain reasonable assurance, which is a high, but not absolute, level of assurance, the auditor
>
> - identifies and assesses risks of material misstatement, whether due to fraud or error, based on an understanding of the entity and its environment, including the entity's internal control."

B. The AU section focuses on the auditor's requirements related to

1. Risk assessment procedures;
2. Understanding the entity and its environment, including its internal control;
3. Assessing the risks of material misstatement; and
4. Documentation.

II. Risk Assessment Procedures -- The auditor should perform "risk assessment procedures" to obtain an understanding of the entity and its environment, including its internal control (the nature, timing, and extent of the risk assessment procedures vary with the engagement's circumstances, such as the entity's size and complexity and the auditor's experience with it).

A. Inquiries of management and others -- The auditor should obtain information from inquiries made of management and others, including internal auditors, production and marketing personnel, those charged with governance, and outsiders (such as external legal counsel or valuation experts used by the entity).

B. Observation and inspection -- The auditor's risk assessment procedures should include observation of entity operations, inspection of documents (e.g., internal control manuals), reading reports prepared by management and those charged with governance (e.g., minutes of meetings), and visits to the entity's facilities

C. **Analytical procedures --** The auditor's analytical procedures performed in planning may assist the auditor in understanding the entity and its environment and identify specific risks relevant to the audit.

D. **Review information --** The auditor should review information about the entity and its environment obtained in prior periods. The auditor should consider whether changes may have affected the relevance of that information (perhaps by making inquiries or performing a walkthrough of transactions through the entity's systems).

E. **Discussion among audit team members --** The audit team should discuss the susceptibility of the entity's financial statements to material misstatements.

1. **Key members should be involved in the discussion --** But professional judgment is required to determine who should be included in that discussion. (For a multilocation audit, there may be multiple discussions for key members at each major location.)

2. **Objective of this discussion --** The purpose of the discussion is for members of the audit team to understand the potential for material misstatements of the financial statements (due to error or fraud) in specific areas assigned to them and how their work may affect other parts of the audit.

3. **The discussion should include "critical issues" --** Such matters include the areas of significant audit risk, the potential for management override of controls; important controls; materiality at the financial statement level and the relevant assertion level; etc.

III. **Understanding the Entity and Its Environment --** Including its internal control.

A. The auditor's understanding of the entity and its environment consists of understanding the following: (1) industry, regulatory, and other external factors; (2) nature of the entity; (3) objectives and strategies and related business risks that may cause material misstatement of the financial statements; (4) measurement and review of the entity's financial performance; and (5) internal control.

1. **Industry, regulatory, and other external factors --** There may be specific risks of material misstatement due to the nature of the business, the degree of regulation or other economic, technical, and competitive issues.

2. **Nature of the entity --** This refers to the entity's operations, ownership, governance, financing, etc. (Understanding these considerations may help the auditor understand the classes of transactions, account balances, and disclosures that are relevant to the financial statements.)

3. **Objectives and strategies --** The auditor should obtain an understanding of the entity's objectives and strategies, including any related business risks that may cause material misstatement of the financial statements. Strategies are operational approaches by which management intends to achieve its objectives. Business risks result from circumstances that could adversely affect the entity's ability to achieve its objectives. (Note that the auditor does not have a responsibility to identify all business risks.)

4. **Measurement and review of the entity's financial performance --** The auditor should obtain an understanding of the entity's performance measures (and their review) indicate aspects of the entity's performance that management considers important, which may help the auditor to understand whether such pressures increase the risks of material misstatement.

5. **Obtain a sufficient understanding of internal control --** The auditor should perform risk assessment procedures to evaluate the design of controls relevant to the audit to identify types of potential misstatements. Note that inquiry alone is not sufficient to evaluate the design and implementation of a control. Consider factors that affect the risks of material misstatement; and design the tests of controls, if applicable, and the substantive procedures that are appropriate in the circumstances.

> **Note:**
> The auditor must perform substantive tests to some degree for all significant audit areas - cannot assess control risk so low that substantive testing is omitted entirely!

B. The Auditor's Consideration of Internal Control -- Internal control may also be referred to as "internal control structure." The auditor should obtain a sufficient understanding of internal control to evaluate the design of controls relevant to the audit.

> **Definition:**
> *Internal control*: A process -- effected by those charged with governance, management, and other personnel -- that is designed to provide reasonable assurance about the achievement of the entity's objectives with regard to reliability of financial reporting, effectiveness and efficiency of operations, and compliance with applicable laws and regulations.

C. The auditor's primary consideration -- The auditor should consider whether (and how) a specific control prevents, or detects and corrects, material misstatements in relevant assertions related to classes of transactions, account balances, or disclosures.

D. Internal control consists of five interrelated components:

1. **Control environment --** The policies and procedures that determine the overall control consciousness of the entity, sometimes called "the tone at the top."

> The auditor should evaluate the following elements that comprise the entity's control environment:
>
> Communication and enforcement of integrity and ethical values;
>
> Commitment to competence;
>
> Participation of those charged with governance (including their interaction with internal and external auditors);
>
> Management's philosophy and operating style;
>
> The entity's organizational structure;
>
> The entity's assignment of authority and responsibility (including internal reporting relationships); and
>
> Human resource policies and practices.

2. **Risk assessment --** The policies and procedures involving the identification, prioritization, and analysis of relevant risks as a basis for managing those risks.

> The auditor's responsibilities include:
>
> Inquiring about business risks that management has identified relevant to financial reporting and considering their implications to the financial statements;
>
> Considering how management identified (and decided how to manage) business risks relevant to financial reporting; and
>
> Considering the implications to the risk assessment process when the auditor identifies business risks that management failed to identify.

3. **Information and communication systems --** The policies and procedures related to the identification, capture, and exchange of information in a form and time frame that enable people to carry out their responsibilities.

> The auditor's responsibilities include obtaining the following:
>
> Sufficient knowledge to understand the classes of transactions that are significant to the financial statements and the procedures and relevant documents related to financial reporting;
>
> An understanding of how incorrect processing of transactions is resolved;
>
> An understanding of the automated (IT) and manual procedures used to prepare the financial statements and how misstatements may occur;
>
> An understanding of how transactions originate with the entity's business processes; and
>
> Sufficient knowledge to understand how the entity communicates financial reporting roles and responsibilities.

4. **Control activities --** The policies and procedures that help ensure that management directives are carried out especially those related to
   a. Authorization,
   b. Segregation of duties,
   c. Performance reviews,
   d. Information processing, and
   e. Physical controls.

> The auditor's responsibilities include:
>
> Obtaining an understanding of how IT affects control activities relevant to planning the audit (especially with respect to "application controls" and "general controls"); and
>
> Considering whether the entity has established effective controls related to IT (especially with respect to maintaining the integrity of information and the security of data).

5. **Monitoring --** The policies and procedures involving the ongoing assessment of the quality of internal control effectiveness over time.

> The auditor should obtain an understanding of the sources of the information related to the entity's monitoring activities and the basis upon which management considers the information to be reliable.

E. **Inherent Limitations of Internal Control --** Internal control provides reasonable, not absolute, assurance about achieving the entity's objectives. Internal control may be ineffective owing to human failures (mistakes and misunderstandings) and controls may be circumvented by collusion or management override of controls. The cost of an internal control procedure should not exceed the benefit expected to be derived from it.

Internal Control Standards 2

After studying this lesson, you should be able to:

1. *Document various internal control matters.*
2. *Link audit responses to the risks of material misstatement at the financial-statement level and the relevant-assertion level, in accordance with AICPA Professional Standards.*
3. *Assess the risk of material misstatement.*

I. Responsibilities under AICPA Professional Standards

A. The primary relevant AICPA guidance is provided by AU 315: "Understanding the Entity and Its Environment and Assessing the Risks of Material Misstatement." This pronouncement states that the auditor's objective is to "identify and assess the risks of material misstatement, whether due to fraud or error, at the financial statement and relevant assertion levels through understanding the entity and its environment, including its internal control, thereby providing a basis for designing and implementing responses to the assessed risks of material misstatement."

B. Additional relevant guidance is provided by AU 330: "Performing Audit Procedures in Response to Assessed Risks and Evaluating the Audit Evidence Obtained." The auditor's objective is "to obtain sufficient appropriate audit evidence regarding the assessed risks of material misstatement through designing and implementing appropriate responses to those risks." (This standard will be introduced here, but discussed in more detail elsewhere in connection with "audit evidence.")

II. Assessing the Risk of Material Misstatement

A. Auditor's responsibility -- The auditor should identify and assess the risks of material misstatement

1. At the financial statement level; and
2. At the relevant assertion level related to classes of transactions, account balances, and disclosures.

B. Internal control considerations -- A weak control environment (such as management's lack of competence) may have pervasive financial statement effects and require an overall response by the auditor. The auditor's understanding of internal control may also raise questions about the auditability of the entity's financial statements (e.g., sufficient appropriate evidence may not be available).

C. "Significant risks" -- These are risks that the auditor believes require special audit consideration. The auditor should consider the nature of the risks identified (e.g., whether the risk may relate to fraud, significant economic developments, the complexity of transactions, related-party transactions, subjective measurement, or nonroutine transactions that are unusual for the entity).

D. Risks for which substantive procedures alone do not provide sufficient appropriate audit evidence -- The auditor should evaluate the design and implementation of controls over such risks, since it is not possible to reduce detection risk to an acceptably low level with substantive procedures by themselves: for example, when IT is a significant part of the entity's information system and transactions are initiated, authorized, recorded, processed, and reported electronically without an audit trail.

E. Revision of risk assessment -- Risk assessment is an iterative process and the assessment of risks may change as additional evidence is obtained. (For example, when performing tests of controls, evidence may be obtained that controls are ineffective, or when performing substantive procedures, misstatements may be detected that suggest that controls are ineffective.)

III. **Documentation --** The form of the documentation requires professional judgment and varies with the circumstances, including the complexity of the entity and the extent to which IT is used. The documentation may include narrative descriptions, questionnaires, flowcharts, and checklists.

A. The auditor should document the following matters:

1. The discussion with members of the audit team about the potential for misstatements due to error or fraud including how and when that discussion occurred, the subject matter discussed, the team members involved, and significant decisions reached about the planned responses to those risks;

2. Major elements of the understanding of each of the five components of internal control to assess the risk of material misstatement, the sources of information used for that understanding, and the risk assessment procedures performed; and

3. The assessment of the risks of material misstatement (both at the financial statement level and at the relevant assertion level) and the basis for that assessment.

4. The risks identified and the related controls the auditor evaluated.

B. Another standard (AU 330) focuses on the auditor's requirements related to:

1. Overall responses to the risks of material misstatement at the financial statement level;

2. Responses to the risks of material misstatement at the relevant assertion level (in determining the nature, timing, and extent of further audit procedures, including tests of the operating effectiveness of controls and substantive procedures);

3. Evaluating the sufficiency and appropriateness of the audit evidence obtained; and

4. Documentation.

IV. **Overall Responses to the Risks of Material Misstatement at the Financial Statement Level**

A. As the risk of material misstatement increases, the auditor may assign more experienced staff to the engagement; provide closer supervision; use specialists; use more unpredictable audit procedures; and/or make appropriate changes in the nature, timing, or extent of further audit procedures.

B. The assessment of the risk of material misstatement may influence the auditor's strategy in using a "substantive approach" or a "combined approach" that uses both tests of controls (regarding the operating effectiveness of controls) and substantive procedures.

V. **Responses to the Risks of Material Misstatement at the Relevant Assertion Level --** The assessment of the risk of material misstatement may affect the auditor's decisions regarding the nature, timing, and extent of further audit procedures, including the tests of the operating effectiveness of controls and the substantive procedures.

A. Substantive procedures must be performed to some degree for all relevant assertions related to each material class of transactions, account balance, or disclosure (that is, the auditor cannot rely totally on the effectiveness of the entity's internal controls).

B. **Nature --** This refers to the purpose of further audit procedures (tests of controls or substantive procedures) and their type (inspection, observation, inquiry, confirmation, recalculation, reperformance, or analytical procedures).

C. **Timing --** This refers to when the further audit procedures are performed (at year-end or before year-end, called "interim"); performing substantive procedures at year-end is usually more effective with a higher risk of material misstatement.

D. **Extent --** This refers to the quantity of an audit procedure to be performed (such as sample size) based on the auditor's judgment; computer-assisted audit techniques (CAATs) may be used to extensively test electronic transactions/files.

E. **Tests of Controls --** To determine the operating effectiveness of controls

1. The auditor should perform tests of controls when the auditor's risk assessment includes an expectation of the operating effectiveness of controls. (Note that this is frequently referred to as "relying" on internal control as a partial basis for the auditor's conclusions, or "assessing control risk at less than the maximum level.")

2. The auditor should also perform tests of control when substantive procedures alone do not provide sufficient appropriate evidence at the relevant assertion level. For example, when the entity uses IT extensively and no audit trail exists.

3. **Nature of tests of controls --** Tests of control might include making inquiries of entity personnel; inspection of documents, reports, or files, indicating performance of the control; observation of the application of the control; and auditor reperformance of the control. Note that inquiry alone is not sufficient to test controls. When controls are not documented, the auditor may be able to obtain evidence about their operating effectiveness by observation or the use of CAATs.

4. **Timing of tests of controls --** When obtaining evidence about the effectiveness of controls for an interim period, the auditor should determine what evidence is required for the remaining period. If planning to rely on controls that have changed since last tested, the auditor should test those controls currently. If planning to rely on controls that have not changed since last tested, the auditor should test the operating effectiveness of those controls at least every third year (that is, no more than two years should pass before retesting such controls).

> **Note:**
> When the auditor identifies a significant risk of material misstatement, but plans to rely on the effectiveness of controls that mitigate that risk, the auditor should test those controls in the current period.

5. **Extent of tests of controls --** When a control is applied on a "transaction basis" (for example, matching approved purchase orders to suppliers' invoices) and if the control operates frequently, the auditor should use audit sampling techniques to test operating effectiveness; when a control is applied on a "periodic basis" (for example, monthly reconciliation of the accounts receivable subsidiary ledger to the general ledger), the auditor should perform procedures appropriate for testing smaller populations.

F. **Substantive Procedures --** The issues related to the auditor's search for material misstatements will be discussed later in connection with "audit evidence" topics.

VI. Evaluating the Sufficiency and Appropriateness of the Audit Evidence Obtained

A. An audit is an iterative process, so the planned audit procedures may need to be modified; for example, identified misstatements from substantive procedures may alter the auditor's judgment about the effectiveness of controls.

B. Consider all relevant audit evidence -- The auditor should consider all relevant audit evidence, whether it appears to corroborate or contradict the relevant assertions.

VII. Documentation -- The auditor should document the following:

A. The overall responses to address the assessed risk of misstatement at the financial statement level;

B. The nature, timing, and extent of the further audit procedures;

C. The linkage of those procedures with the assessed risks at the relevant assertion level;

D. The results of the audit procedures; and

E. The conclusions reached in the current audit about the operating effectiveness of controls tested in a prior audit.

Internal Control—Required Communications

After studying this lesson, you should be able to:

1. *Understand the auditor's responsibility to communicate identified internal control deficiencies to management and those charged with governance, in accordance with AICPA Professional Standards.*
2. *Know the meaning of the terms significant deficiency and material weakness.*

I. Required Communications Related to Internal Control Deficiencies (weaknesses)

> **Definition:**
> *Control deficiency*: When the design or operation of a control does not allow management or employees, in the normal course of performing their assigned functions, to prevent or detect misstatements on a timely basis.
>
> *Deficiency in design:* When a control necessary to meet the control objective is missing, or when the control objective is not always met, even if the control operates as designed.
>
> *Deficiency in operation:* When a properly designed control does not operate as designed, or when the person performing the control does not have the authority or competence to effectively perform the control.
>
> *Significant deficiency:* A deficiency (or combination of deficiencies) in internal control that is less severe than a material weakness, yet important enough to merit attention by those charged with governance.
>
> *Material weakness:* A deficiency (or combination of deficiencies) in internal control such that there is a reasonable possibility that a material misstatement of the entity's financial statements will not be prevented or detected and corrected on a timely basis.

A. Evaluating Control Deficiencies -- The auditor must determine whether identified deficiencies are "significant deficiencies" or "material weaknesses."

1. The auditor should consider both the likelihood and potential magnitude of misstatement in making that evaluation - multiple control deficiencies affecting the same financial statement item increases the likelihood of misstatement.
2. The auditor may wish to consider the possible mitigating effects of compensating controls that can reduce the severity of the effects of a deficiency.
3. Risk factors that affect whether there is a reasonable possibility that a deficiency will result in a misstatement include the following:
   a. The nature of the accounts, classes of transactions, disclosures, and assertions involved;
   b. The susceptibility of the related asset or liability to loss or fraud;
   c. The subjectivity, complexity, or extent of judgment involved;
   d. The interaction or relationship of the control with other controls;
   e. The interaction among the deficiencies; and
   f. The possible future consequences of the deficiency.
4. Specific indicators of material weaknesses include the following:

a. Identification of any fraud involving senior management (whether or not material);

b. Restatement of previously issued financial statements to correct a material misstatement due to error or fraud;

c. Identification of a material misstatement in the financial statements by the auditor that would not have been identified by the entity's internal control; and

d. Ineffective oversight of the entity's financial reporting and internal control by those charged with governance.

II. **Communicating Identified Control Deficiencies --** The auditor must communicate the significant deficiencies and material weaknesses identified in the audit.

A. **Form of communication --** Identified significant deficiencies and material weaknesses must be communicated in writing to management and those charged with governance. Certain matters may not be communicated to management when communication would be inappropriate (for example, matters that raise questions about management integrity or competence). Lesser matters (not "significant deficiencies") may be communicated to the appropriate level of operational management with the authority to take remedial action. Such lesser matters may be communicated either orally or in writing.

B. **Timing --** The required communication is best made by the "report release date" and should be made no later than 60 days following the report release date. The "report release date" is the date that the auditor grants the entity permission to use the auditor's report in connection with the audited financial statements.

C. **Early communication is permitted --** The auditor may choose to verbally communicate certain significant deficiencies and material weaknesses during the audit (e.g., to permit timely correction). However, all identified significant deficiencies and material weaknesses must still be communicated in writing no later than 60 days following the report release date, including those matters communicated orally during the audit.

D. **Other matters --** The auditor may choose to communicate other matters believed to be beneficial to the entity (including deficiencies that are not "significant deficiencies") either in writing or verbally. If communicated verbally, the auditor must document such communication.

E. The written communication about significant deficiencies and material weaknesses should:

1. State that the purpose of the audit was to express an opinion on the financial statements, not to express an opinion on the effectiveness of internal control;
2. State that the auditor is not expressing an opinion on the effectiveness of internal control;
3. State that the auditor's consideration of internal control was not designed to identify all significant deficiencies or material weaknesses;
4. Include the definition of the terms *material weakness* and *significant deficiency*, as applicable.
5. Identify the matters that are considered to be material weaknesses and significant deficiencies, as applicable.
6. State that the communication is intended solely for the use of management, those charged with governance, and others within the organization (it should not be used by anyone other than those specified parties) - if such a communication is required to be given to a governmental authority, that specific reference may be added.

> **Note:**
> The auditor may include additional statements regarding the general inherent limitations of internal control, including the possibility of management override, but such comments are not required.

See the following sample.

Sample Written Communication about Internal Control Deficiencies:

In planning and performing our audit of the financial statements of ABC Company (the "Company") as of and for the year ended December 31, 20XX, in accordance with auditing standards generally accepted in the United States of America, we considered the Company's internal control over financial reporting (internal control) as a basis for designing our auditing procedures for the purpose of expressing our opinion on the financial statements, but not for the purpose of expressing an opinion on the effectiveness of the Company's internal control. Accordingly, we do not express an opinion on the effectiveness of the Company's internal control.

Our consideration of internal control was for the limited purpose described in the preceding paragraph and was not designed to identify all deficiencies in internal control that might be significant deficiencies or material weaknesses and therefore, there can be no assurance that all deficiencies, significant deficiencies, or material weaknesses have been identified. However, as discussed below, we identified certain deficiencies in internal control that we consider to be material weaknesses (and other deficiencies that we consider to be significant deficiencies - *add this phrase only if applicable*).

A deficiency in internal control exists when the design or operation of a control does not allow management or employees, in the normal course of performing their assigned functions, to prevent, or detect and correct misstatements on a timely basis. A material weakness is a deficiency, or a combination of deficiencies, in internal control, such that there is a reasonable possibility that a material misstatement of the entity's financial statements will not be prevented, or detected and corrected on a timely basis. (We consider the following deficiencies in the Company's internal control to be material weaknesses:)

(*Describe the material weaknesses that were identified.*)

(A significant deficiency is a deficiency, or a combination of deficiencies, in internal control that is less severe than a material weakness, yet important enough to merit attention by those charged with governance. We consider the following deficiencies to be significant deficiencies in internal control:)

(*Describe the significant deficiencies that were identified.*)

This communication is intended solely for the information and use of management, (*identify the body or individuals charged with governance*), others within the organization, and (*identify any specified governmental authorities*) and is not intended to be and should not be used by anyone other than these specified parties.

F. The auditor should not issue a written communication stating that no significant deficiencies were identified - however, the auditor is permitted to add a comment that no material weaknesses were identified, perhaps as requested to submit to a governmental authority.

G. Management may issue a written response to the auditor's communication to indicate corrective action taken or planned or stating management's belief that the costs of correction exceed the benefits - if such a written response is included with the auditor's communication, the auditor should add a paragraph to disclaim an opinion on management's written response.

Using the Work of an Internal Audit Function

After studying this lesson, you should be able to:

1. *Understand the independent auditor's responsibilities to evaluate the internal auditors' competence and objectivity when considering the role of an entity's internal audit function for purposes of assessing control risk and/or providing assistance with substantive procedures.*

I. **AICPA Guidance --** The relevant AICPA guidance is provided by AU 610 (SAS No. 128) "Using the Work of Internal Auditors," which has been clarified to be consistent with International Standards on Auditing.

> Note: The requirements of this standard do not apply if (1) the activities of the internal audit function are not relevant to the audit, or (2) the external auditor does not expect to use the work of the internal audit function in obtaining audit evidence. There is no requirement that external auditors use the work of an internal audit function.
>
> The AICPA defines an **"internal audit function"** as "a function of an entity that performs assurance and consulting activities designed to evaluate and improve the effectiveness of the entity's governance, risk management, and internal control processes."

II. **Two Ways to Use the Work of an Internal Audit Function --** The external auditor may use the internal audit function to (1) obtain audit evidence that modifies the nature, timing, or extent of audit procedures to be performed by the external auditor; and/or (2) provide direct assistance to the external auditor under the external auditor's direction, supervision, and review.

A. Using the internal audit function **"to obtain audit evidence"** means, in effect, substituting the internal auditors' work (related to tests of controls and/or substantive procedures) in place of work that would otherwise be performed by the external auditor.

1. There are three necessary conditions before the external auditor may use the internal audit function to obtain audit evidence

a. **Objectivity --** The internal audit function's organizational status (dealing with the level to whom the function reports, such as those charged with governance, rather than middle management) and relevant policies and procedures must support the objectivity of the internal auditors.

b. **Competence --** The internal auditors must be competent (related to their education, experience, certification, etc.) to perform reliable work.

c. **Systematic and disciplined approach --** The internal audit function must apply a "systematic and disciplined approach, including quality control." The external auditor should not rely on "internal audit-like" work that is conducted in an informal, unstructured, or ad hoc way. However, the degree of formality and structure may vary with the nature, size, and complexity of the entity involved.

2. Significant judgments—The external auditor should make all significant audit judgments.

3. The external auditor should perform more of the work directly when (a) the degree of judgment involved increases, (b) the assessed risk of material misstatement increases, (c) the organizational status and objectivity of the internal auditors decreases, or (d) the competence of the internal auditors decreases.

4. Procedures to be performed by the external auditor when using the work of the internal audit function to obtain audit evidence include the following:

a. The external auditor should read the internal audit function's reports related to the work the external auditor plans to use;

b. The external auditor should perform procedures to determine whether the internal audit function's work was adequately planned, performed, reviewed, and documented, and whether the conclusions reached were appropriate; and

c. The external auditor should reperform some of the internal audit function's work that the external auditor plans to use.

5. Communication with those charged with governance—The external auditor should communicate plans to use the work of the internal audit function to obtain audit evidence.

B. Using the internal audit function **"to provide direct assistance"** means using internal auditors to perform audit procedures subject to the external auditor's direction, supervision, and review.

1. There are two necessary conditions before the external auditor may use the internal audit function to obtain audit evidence.

a. **Objectivity --** The internal audit function's organizational status and relevant policies and procedures must support the objectivity of the internal auditors.

b. **Competence --** The internal auditors must be competent to perform reliable work.

2. Determining the nature and extent of the internal auditors' direct assistance—The external auditor should consider the internal audit function's objectivity and competence, the assessed risk of material misstatement, and the amount of judgment involved.

3. Procedures to be performed by the external auditor when using the internal audit function to provide direct assistance

> **Note:**
> A "systematic and disciplined approach" is not a requirement for using the internal audit function to provide direct assistance, since the internal auditors' work is subject to the direction, supervision, and review of the external auditor.

a. The external auditor should obtain written acknowledgment from management or those charged with governance (either as part of the engagement letter or as a separate document) that the internal auditors will be allowed to follow the external auditor's directives without interference.

b. The external auditor should appropriately direct, supervise, and review the work performed by the internal auditors.

c. The external auditor should test some of the work performed by the internal auditors.

4. Communication with those charged with governance—The external auditor should communicate how the auditor plans to use the internal auditors to provide direct assistance.

III. Documentation Requirements

A. When using the internal audit function to obtain audit evidence—the external auditor should document the following:

1. The evaluation of the internal audit function's organizational status and objectivity of the internal auditors, the function's competence, and the application of a systematic and disciplined approach;

2. The nature and extent of the work used and the basis for that decision; and

3. The external auditor's procedures performed to evaluate the work of the internal audit function.

B. When using the internal audit function to provide direct assistance— the external auditor should document the following:

1. The evaluation of the internal audit function's organizational status and objectivity of the internal auditors and the function's competence;
2. The basis for the external auditor's decision about the nature and extent of the work performed by the internal auditors; and
3. Identification of the working papers prepared by the internal auditors, and the nature and extent of the external auditor's review and testing of the internal auditors' work.

> **Note:**
> There is no "division of responsibility" regarding the work of the internal auditors. The external auditor's report should not refer to the internal auditors' work in the audit report! The external auditor remains fully responsible for all the conclusions expressed.

Internal Control - Transaction Cycles

Specific Transaction Cycles

After studying this lesson, you should be able to:

1. *Identify several examples of transaction cycles that an auditor might consider.*
2. *Understand what is meant by the term transaction cycle and why auditors tend to focus on transaction cycles when assessing control risk.*

I. **A "Transaction Cycle" --** A *transaction cycle* is a group of essentially homogeneous transactions, that is, transactions of a particular type. The bulk of a company's economic activities can be grouped into a relative few categories called transaction cycles.

II. **Implication --** Within a given category of transactions, control risk is essentially constant, since all transactions within that category are processed subject to the same configuration of internal control policies and procedures. A transaction cycle is, therefore, the highest level of aggregation for which control risk may be viewed as a constant.

III. **Transaction Cycles Covered in This Module**

A. Revenue/receipts.

B. Expenditures/disbursements.

C. Payroll.

D. Inventory, especially manufactured inventory (since purchased inventory would be similar to expenditures/disbursements as presented here).

E. Fixed assets.

F. Investing/financing.

> **Note:**
> The applicable SAS describes "control activities" in terms of five specific considerations: (1) authorization; (2) segregation of duties; (3) physical controls; (4) information processing; and (5) performance reviews.

> **Exam Hint:** As a tool to analyze the audit considerations of internal control policies and procedures in each transaction cycle, remember that internal controls should "SCARE"! Note that this is not a meaningful concept to the CPA examination graders (so do not write in your essay response that "Internal control activities should 'SCARE'" because the graders won't know what you mean!); but it is intended to be a helpful memory aid simply to recall some basic points of emphasis that are useful to auditors in looking at the relative strength or weakness of controls in a particular transaction cycle. In this context, "SCARE" represents:
>
> Segregation of duties,
>
> Controls (as in "Physical Controls"),
>
> Authorization,
>
> Reviews (as in "Performance Reviews"), and
>
> EDP/IT ("Information Processing").

IV. **The Framework "SCARE" --** This acronym is easy to remember and it is helpful in identifying relevant internal control considerations that are associated with "control activities" in the AICPA Professional Standards:

A. **Segregation of duties --** This is also referred to as "separation of duties" and involves separating "incompatible functions" to the extent possible. The same employee should not normally (1) authorize transactions (execution function), (2) have access to the related assets (custody function), and (3) perform accounting activities (record keeping function) in the ordinary course of duties. In essence, these three activities are like points on a triangle and each point of the triangle should ideally be vested in different employees, subject to cost-benefit considerations.

B. **Controls (physical controls) --** Access to assets (and to important accounting documents and computer systems) should be limited to authorized personnel. In addition, assets should be periodically counted, as appropriate, and compared to the corresponding accounting records for agreement. This is important in safeguarding assets and in establishing accountability for assets.

C. **Authorization --** Transactions should be executed in accordance with management's authorization.

D. **Reviews (performance reviews) --** Actual performance should be compared to appropriate budgets and forecasts. Internal data should be compared to external sources of information as appropriate. Analyses of relationships should be performed and investigative and corrective action should be taken as needed.

E. **EDP/IT (Information processing) --** Information technology (IT) controls consist of 2 basic categories:

1. "General controls," which are policies and procedures that have widespread effect on many specific applications; and
2. "Application controls," which refer specifically to the processing of particular computer applications.

> **Note:**
> "EDP" as used here is an outdated reference to "electronic data processing" that has been replaced by the more contemporary term *IT* for information technology.)

Revenue/Receipts - Sales

After studying this lesson, you should be able to:

1. *Identify the primary accounting documents and internal control objectives associated with an entity's revenue-receipts cycle (with emphasis on sales recognition).*
2. *Understand the primary control activities normally associated with an entity's revenue-receipts cycle (with emphasis on sales recognition).*

I. Flow Chart of Typical Internal Controls for Sales

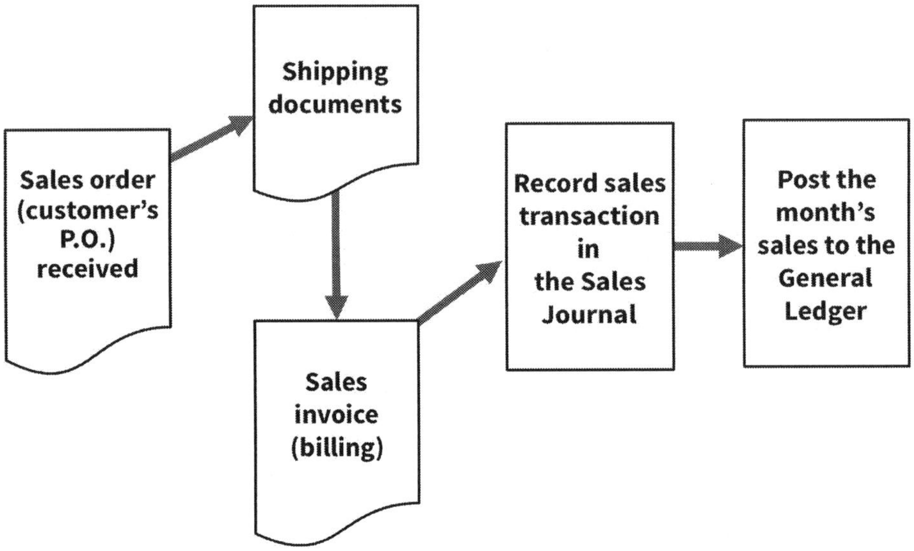

II. Internal Control Objectives

II. Internal Control Objectives -- The objectives of internal controls in this area are to provide reasonable assurance that:

- **A.** Goods and services are provided in accordance with management's authorization (and based on approved orders).
- **B.** Terms of sale (including prices and any discounts) are in accordance with management's authorization.
- **C.** Credit terms and limits are properly established (as authorized).
- **D.** Deliveries of goods and services result in accurate and timely billings.
- **E.** Any sales-related discounts and adjustments (including returns) are in accordance with management's authorization.

III. Audit Considerations (Framed by "SCARE") -- The entity's control activities should address the following matters:

A. **Segregation of duties --** Separate the execution (authorization), record-keeping (accounting), and custody (access) functions

1. Credit to customers should be granted by an independent department (separate from sales staff which may be paid on commission and which may have an incentive to view everyone as "creditworthy").
2. An independent employee should review the statements to customers.
3. Returns should be accounted for by an independent clerk in the shipping/receiving area.

B. **Controls (Physical Controls)**

1. Computer passwords should be used to limit unauthorized access to the accounting systems.
2. Any inventory involved should be secured with access limited to authorized personnel.

C. **Authorization --** The entity's transactions should be executed as authorized by management.

1. Management should review the terms of sales transactions and indicate that approval on the sales invoice (billing).
2. Management should usually establish "general" approvals of transactions within specified limits and specifically approve transactions outside of those prescribed limits.
3. Management should approve the entity's adjusting journal entries.

D. **Reviews(Performance Reviews)**

1. The entity's recorded sales should be compared to appropriate budgets and forecasts.
2. Related accounting documents should be compared on a timely basis - for example, sales invoices and shipping documents should be compared to verify that the sales transactions were recorded in the proper period, which is referred to as proper "cutoff."

E. **EDP/IT (Information Processing) --** The auditor should agree the financial statement amount(s) to the applicable general ledger account(s).

1. Important accounting documents (e.g., shipping documents and sales invoices) should be prenumbered and the numerical sequence should be accounted for.
2. An aged trial balance for accounts receivable should be agreed (or reconciled) to the general ledger control account; the aging provides important information about the quality of the receivables and the need for follow-up audit procedures.

Revenue/Receipts - Cash

After studying this lesson, you should be able to:

1. *Identify the primary accounting documents and internal control objectives associated with an entity's revenue-receipts cycle (with emphasis on cash collection).*
2. *Understand the primary control activities normally associated with an entity's revenue-receipts cycle (with emphasis on cash collection).*

I. Flow Chart of Typical Processing of Cash Receipts

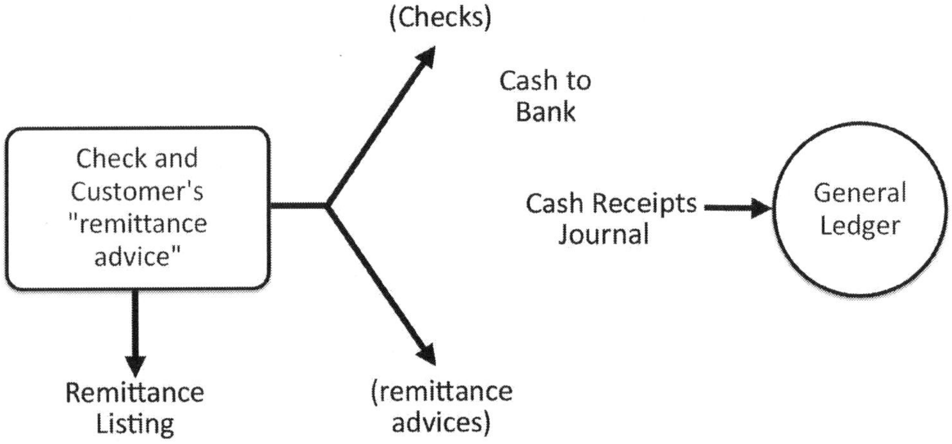

II. Internal Control Objectives -- The objectives of internal controls in this area are to provide reasonable assurance that:

A. Access to cash receipts records and accounts receivable records is limited to authorized personnel.

B. Detailed cash and account balance records are reconciled with control accounts and bank statements at least monthly.

C. All cash receipts are correctly recorded in the period received.

III. Audit Considerations (Framed by "SCARE") -- The entity's control activities should address the following matters:

A. Segregation of duties

1. A listing of cash receipts (sometimes referred to as a "remittance listing" or "log of cash receipts") is prepared upon opening the mail in the mail room; checks are restrictively endorsed immediately ("for deposit only...").
2. Cash-related activities, which are handled by separate personnel as appropriate are as follows:
   - **a.** Opening the mail: handling the checks received, and verifying the accuracy of the payment indicated on the enclosed "remittance advice" (the stub returned with the customer's payment on account).
   - **b.** Making the deposit -- deposits should be made daily.

c. Applying payments received to the appropriate customers' accounts receivable.

d. Preparing the bank reconciliation on a timely basis.

B. **Controls (Physical Controls)**

1. Employees with access to cash receipts should be "bonded," which is a type of insurance for which the employer pays an insurance premium and which involves background checks on the applicable employees.

2. Receipts should be deposited daily, not accumulated in someone's desk drawer for an occasional deposit.

3. Access to cash receipts (including access to documents) should be limited to those authorized -- that includes the appropriate use of passwords.

4. The company might use a "lockbox" whereby payments from customers are directly received by the bank, thereby avoiding the company's mail room.

C. **Authorization --** The entity's transactions should be executed as authorized by management.

1. Adjusting journal entries should be approved by management.

2. Bank reconciliations should be appropriately reviewed with the reviewer's approval indicated.

D. **Reviews (Performance Reviews)**

1. The initial cash receipts listing from the mail room should be compared to the total according to the cash receipts journal, and traced to that day's bank deposit to show that what was received was, in fact, deposited.

2. The cash accounts should be reconciled with the bank statements on a timely basis by someone not involved in handling cash receipts or updating the accounting records.

E. **EDP/IT (Information Processing)**

1. In general, there should be adequate documentation supporting transactions and account balances (important documents should be prenumbered and the numerical sequence properly accounted for).

2. For cash transactions received "on site," there should be adequate "point of sale" cash registers and use of prenumbered receipts.

Expenditures/Disbursements

After studying this lesson, you should be able to:

1. *Understand the primary control activities normally associated with an entity's expenditure/disbursements cycle.*
2. *Identify the primary accounting documents and internal control objectives associated with an entity's expenditure/disbursements cycle.*

I. Flow Chart of Typical Processing for Expenditures/Disbursements

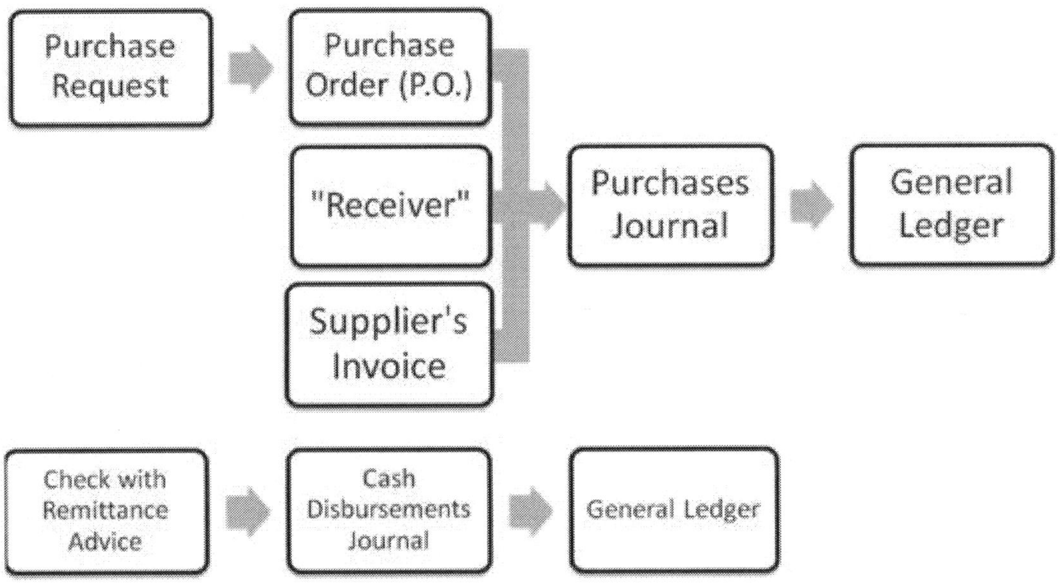

II. Objectives of Internal Controls over Purchases and Accounts Payable

Objectives of Internal Controls over Purchases and Accounts Payable -- The objectives are to provide reasonable assurance that:

- **A.** Goods and services are obtained in accordance with management's authorization and based on approved orders -- considering quantity, quality, vendors, etc. This is usually handled by a separate "Purchasing Department" to centralize these activities.
- **B.** The terms of acquisitions (including prices and quantities) are in accordance with management's authorization.
- **C.** All goods and services received are accurately accounted for on a timely basis.
- **D.** Adjustments to vendor accounts are made according to management's authorization.
- **E.** Only authorized goods and services are accepted and paid for (and payments are timely to take advantage of any cash discounts available for prompt payment).
- **F.** Amounts payable for goods and services received are accurately recorded and properly classified.
- **G.** Access to purchasing, receiving, and accounts payable records is limited to authorized personnel.

III. Objectives of Internal Controls over Cash Disbursements

Objectives of Internal Controls over Cash Disbursements -- The objectives are to provide reasonable assurance that:

- **A.** Disbursements are for authorized expenditures as approved by management.

B. Disbursements are recorded at the proper amounts and with the appropriate classifications.

C. Periodic comparisons are made between the supporting detailed accounting records (including bank reconciliations) and the general ledger control accounts.

D. Any adjusting journal entries for cash accounts are in accordance with management's authorization.

E. Access to cash and disbursement records is limited to authorized personnel.

IV. **Audit Considerations (Framed by "SCARE") --** The entity's control activities should address the following matters related to the expenditures/disbursement transactions cycle:

A. **Segregation of duties**

1. A separate purchasing department handles the purchasing activities (after a duly approved request for goods or services has been received from the department making the request).
2. The purchasing personnel (execution function) are independent of those in receiving (custody function) and in accounting (record-keeping function), including the accounts payable personnel. The accounts payable personnel should also be independent of those involved in processing the related cash disbursements.
3. Bank reconciliations are prepared by someone not having other involvement in handling cash receipts, cash disbursements, or record keeping.

B. **Controls (Physical Controls)**

1. There should be appropriate physical control over unused checks to limit access to authorized personnel.
2. Employees with the ability to initiate cash disbursements should be "bonded."
3. Access to cash disbursements or to related documents should be limited to authorized personnel.

C. **Authorization --** The entity's transactions should be executed as authorized by management.

1. All adjusting journal entries should be approved by management.
2. Only authorized personnel should be able to order goods and services on the company's behalf.
3. The department requesting the purchase of goods or services should indicate their acceptance of the goods or services received and approval, before payment is made.

D. **Reviews (Performance Reviews)**

1. An appropriate employee should compare the suppliers' monthly statements with recorded payables.
2. An appropriate employee should compare the purchase order, "receiver," and vendor's invoice for agreement to establish that the invoice is for goods and services received and as authorized. (The invoice should be approved before payment is made and available cash discounts for prompt payment should be taken.)

E. **EDP/IT (Information Processing)**

1. Detailed records should be maintained to support the general ledger payable account.
2. Prenumbered purchase orders should be used (and the numerical sequence accounted for).
3. Prenumbered checks should be used (and the numerical sequence accounted for).
4. The supporting documents (including vendors' invoices) should be canceled as "paid" immediately upon payment to prevent double payments.

5. Two signatures should be required on checks. (Any signature plates should be kept in a secure place to prevent unauthorized use.)

F. Note the difference between a "vouchers payable" system and an "accounts payable" system:

1. An **accounts payable** system keeps track of payables by the name of the vendor. (Hence, payables are identified by the total amount owed to the various individual suppliers.)

2. A **vouchers payable** system keeps track of individual transactions without summarizing amounts owed in total to individual vendors. (There can be numerous vouchers payable to an individual vendor, but the payables are identified by voucher number, not by vendor name. An entity that uses a vouchers payable system can confirm individual transactions, but cannot confirm the total amount owed to a given vendor, which has implications to the vendor's auditor and how confirmation requests should be designed.)

Payroll Cycle

After studying this lesson, you should be able to:

1. *Understand the primary control activities normally associated with an entity's payroll cycle.*
2. *Identify the primary accounting documents and internal control objectives associated with an entity's payroll cycle.*

I. Flow Chart of Typical Internal Controls for Payroll

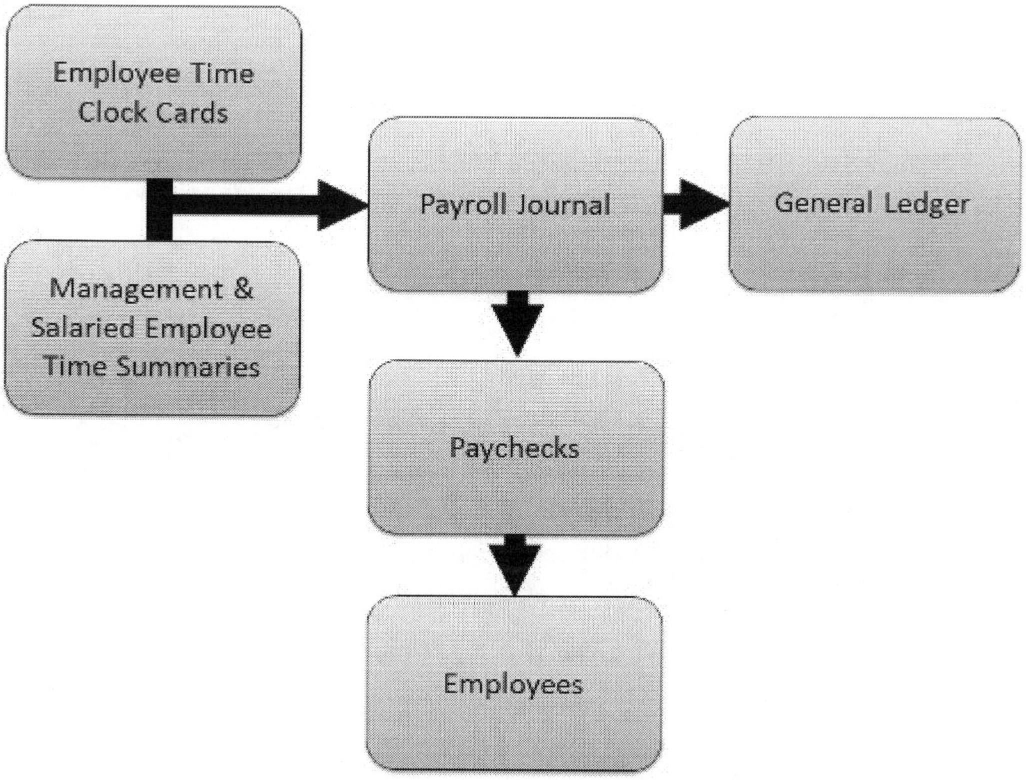

II. Objectives of Internal Controls over Payroll -- The objectives are to provide reasonable assurance that:

A. Payroll withholdings and deductions are based on appropriate supporting authorizations.

B. Compensation is made only to valid employees at authorized rates and for services actually rendered.

C. Gross pay, withholdings, deductions, and net pay are correctly computed.

D. Payroll costs and liabilities are appropriately classified and summarized in the proper periods.

E. Appropriate comparisons are made of personnel, payroll, and work records at reasonable intervals.

F. Net pay and related withholdings are remitted to the appropriate employees and agencies.

G. Access to sensitive personnel files and payroll records is limited to authorized personnel.

III. Audit Considerations (Framed by "SCARE") -- The entity's control activities should address the following matters:

A. Segregation of duties

1. The following activities should be performed by different personnel when circumstances permit:
   a. Establishing and maintaining employee files in the personnel department.
   b. Timekeeping.
   c. Payroll preparation and updating the accounting records.
   d. Check distribution.
   e. Reconciling the payroll bank account with the general ledger account.
2. The treasurer should typically sign the payroll checks.
3. An appropriate departmental supervisor should distribute the payroll checks to employees in that department.
4. Unclaimed checks should be controlled. That is, they should be returned to treasury, secured, and eventually destroyed, if not claimed within an appropriate time.

B. Controls (Physical Controls)

1. Access to personnel files (containing sensitive information) should be limited to authorized personnel.
2. Access to payroll checks should be limited to authorized personnel.
3. Personnel with access to payroll checks should be "bonded."

C. Authorization -- The entity's transactions should be executed as authorized by management.

1. Payroll should be authorized by a responsible official.
2. Payroll computations should be verified by an independent person.
3. Overtime payments should be approved by management.
4. Payroll for management should also be appropriately reviewed and approved.

D. Reviews (Performance Reviews)

1. A company should maintain current and accurate payroll information (which should be periodically matched with information in the personnel files).
2. The payroll checks written should be reconciled to the payroll register, serving as the supporting accounting record for each payroll period.
3. Other appropriate reconciliations should be made on a timely basis: for example, in a manufacturing environment, someone should reconcile the job cost time sheets to time clock cards. (For strict internal control purposes, a company should use time clocks where possible.)

E. EDP/IT (Information Processing)

1. Payroll checks should be prenumbered (and the numerical sequence accounted for).
2. A company should maintain a separate checking account specifically for payroll transactions to establish more accountability and control over these important transactions.

Miscellaneous Cycles

After studying this lesson, you should be able to:

1. *Identify the internal-control objectives associated with miscellaneous transaction cycles (manufactured inventory, fixed assets, and investing/financing).*
2. *Understand the primary control activities normally associated with miscellaneous transaction cycles.*

I. Production/Manufacturing Inventory

A. The Major Objectives of Internal Controls -- In this area, the primary objectives are to provide reasonable assurance that:

1. The resources obtained and used in production (including raw materials, work-in-process, and finished goods) are accurately recorded on a timely basis;
2. Transfers of finished products to customers or others are accurately recorded;
3. Related expenditures are appropriately classified;
4. Access to all categories of inventory (and inventory-related documents) is limited to authorized personnel; and
5. Comparisons of actual inventory on hand are made to recorded amounts at least annually.

B. Audit Considerations (Framed by "SCARE") -- The entity's control activities should address the following matters:

1. **Segregation of duties**
    a. To the extent possible, the company should separate the authorization of inventory-related transactions, the custody of (or access to) inventory, and the accounting record keeping activities.
    b. Sales returns (inventory) should be immediately counted by the receiving clerk and a "receiver" (that is, a receiving document) prepared to verify the quantity and condition of the goods received.
2. **Controls (Physical Controls)**
    a. Access to the inventory should be limited to authorized personnel (the inventory should be physically secured with access restricted to personnel having authorized keys or passcodes).
    b. Access to the important accounting documents, including applicable shipping documents, should be limited to authorized personnel.
3. **Authorization --** The entity's transactions should be executed as authorized by management.
    a. The acquisition and distribution of inventory should be consistent with management's authorization.
    b. Management should establish general approvals of transactions within specified limits, and specifically approve transactions above those limits.
    c. Any adjusting journal entries (including sales returns and allowances, or adjustments to inventory, such as write-downs) should be approved by management.

4. **Reviews (Performance Reviews)**
    a. Actual inventory should be compared periodically to recorded inventory (and any unusual differences should be investigated).
    b. In a manufacturing context, appropriate reconciliations should be made of underlying accounting records (including applicable job order cost sheets or process cost worksheets) to the applicable inventory-related general ledger accounts.
5. **EDP/IT (Information Processing)**
    a. The company should use prenumbered purchase orders for raw materials and components of production, along with prenumbered "receivers," the receiving document. (The numerical sequence of these documents should be properly accounted for.)
    b. The company should consider using a perpetual inventory system for items with high cost per unit.
    c. The company should maintain adequate support for related general ledger control accounts.

II. **Fixed Assets Cycle --** The major objectives of internal controls in this area are to provide reasonable assurance that:

A. Transactions involving property, plant, and equipment are accurately recorded and classified; and are in accordance with management's authorization.

B. Estimates used in the determination of depreciation, depletion, and amortization of the assets' cost basis are reasonable and consistent over time; any changes should be properly approved.

C. Fixed assets are reasonably secure from loss with appropriate property insurance in force.

D. Supporting detailed records are maintained and periodically compared to the assets on hand.

E. Any adjusting journal entries related to fixed assets are approved by the management.

III. **Investing/Financing Cycle --** The major objectives of internal controls in this area are to provide reasonable assurance that:

A. Transactions involving investments and financing are accurately recorded and classified on a timely basis; and as authorized by management.

1. **"Investing" --** As used here, this refers to decisions related to the composition of the company's portfolio of investment assets, both current and noncurrent.
2. **"Financing" --** This refers to decisions related to the structure of the company's noncurrent liabilities and stockholders' equity sections of the balance sheet.

B. Investment assets should be reasonably secure from loss with procedures established to monitor the associated risks. Access should be limited to authorized personnel with appropriate segregation of duties.

C. Supporting detailed records should be maintained and compared periodically to actual investment-related assets of the company.

D. Any adjusting journal entries related to investment-related assets, liabilities, or stockholders' equity are approved by management.

Audit Evidence - Concepts and Standards

Overview of Substantive Procedures

After studying this lesson, you should be able to:

1. *Know the meaning of the term analytical procedures, the 3 general purposes served by analytical procedures, and the 4 considerations that determine the efficiency and effectiveness of analytical procedures that are used for substantive purposes.*
2. *Know the 2 categories of "substantive" audit procedures (and the 2 categories of "tests of details").*
3. *Familiarize yourself with the fundamental ratios that are most often associated with the auditor's substantive analytical procedures.*

I. **The Audit Risk Model --** Recall the "audit risk model" that applies to the assertion level for classes of transactions, account balances, and disclosures. (Note that this audit risk model does not apply at the overall financial statement level.): **AR = IR × CR × DR**; where detection risk is the only component within the auditor's direct influence and which is essentially "set" by specifying the nature, timing, and extent of the auditor's substantive audit procedures.

   A. **Nature --** The auditor has to decide what specific substantive procedures to perform. This includes determining how much emphasis should be placed on "tests of details" (which tend to be labor intensive and expensive, but which provide a relatively stronger basis for conclusions for most financial statement assertions) versus substantive "analytical procedures" (which tend to be less labor intensive and less expensive, but which provide a relatively weaker basis for conclusions for most financial statement assertions).

   B. **Timing --** The auditor has to decide whether to perform the important substantive procedures, at an "interim" date (meaning any date prior to year-end and before the books are closed) or at "final" (at year-end and after the books are closed).

   C. **Extent --** The auditor has to decide how large the samples sizes should be. Since the audit work is performed on a "test basis," should the sample sizes be relatively large or can smaller ample sizes be justified?

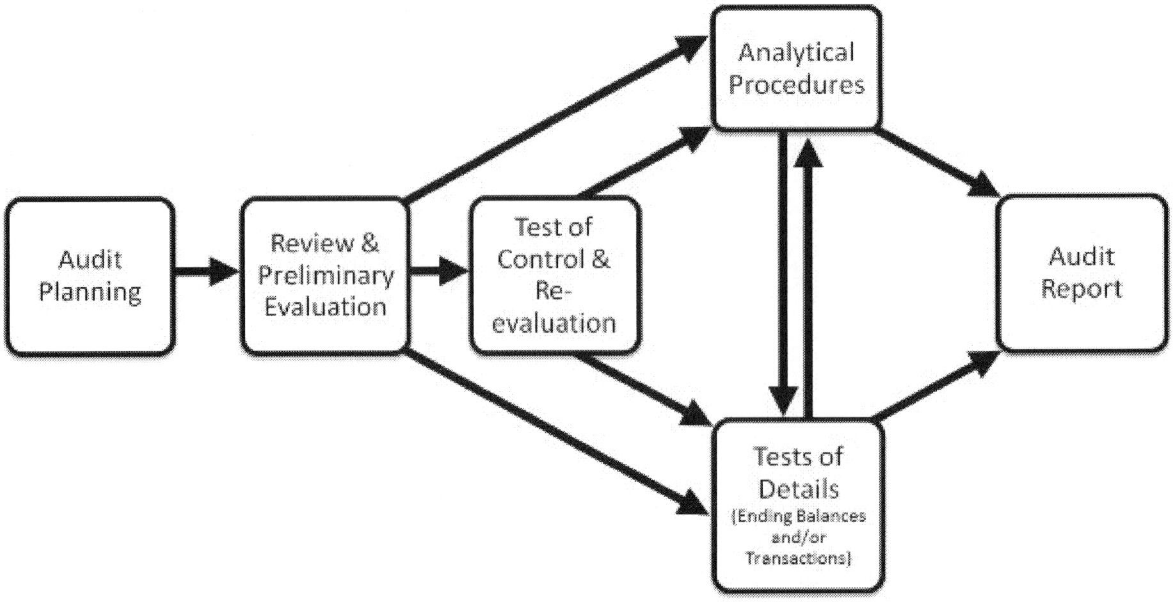

D. **AU 330 --** "Performing Audit Procedures in Response to Assessed Risks and Evaluating the Audit Evidence Obtained," states:

> "In some cases, the auditor may find it impossible to design effective substantive procedures that, by themselves, provide sufficient appropriate audit evidence at the relevant assertion level. This may occur when an entity conducts its business using IT and no documentation of transactions is produced or maintained, other than through the IT system."
>
> In such cases, the auditor would be required to perform tests of the relevant controls, in addition to the planned substantive procedures.

> **Question:**
> Under these circumstances, what would be the consequences if the required tests of controls indicate that internal control is ineffective and cannot be relied on?
>
> **Answer:**
> If the auditor's substantive procedures by themselves are insufficient and if internal control is ineffective, the auditor would not have obtained sufficient appropriate evidence to afford a reasonable basis for the opinion. In other words, these circumstances would constitute a scope limitation!

II. **Substantive Audit Procedures --** These are audit procedures that are directly related to the financial statement elements and disclosures. Recall that the word *substantive* is derived from *substantiate*, which means "to verify that substantive procedures are those audit procedures designed to verify the entity's financial statement elements and disclosures" or, in other words, "to search for material misstatements if there are any."

A. **Tests of Details --** These are the relatively precise (but usually rather expensive, labor-intensive) procedures (that suggest whether the client's recorded amounts are right or not).

> **Definitions:**
> *Tests of Ending Balances*: Verifying the client's recorded amounts by directly testing the composition making up the ending account balance.
>
> *Tests of Transactions:* Verifying the client's recorded amounts by testing those relative few debits and credits (the transactions) that caused the account balance to change from last year's audited balance to this year's recorded balance.

B. **Analytical Procedures --** Recall the AICPA definition of *analytical procedures* -- "evaluations of financial information through analysis of plausible relationships among both financial and nonfinancial data."

> **Note:**
> These tests of reasonableness involve analyzing trends and interrelationships -- the "key" is developing a meaningful expectation by which to judge the reasonableness of the client's recorded amount.

1. **Analytical procedures serve three distinct purposes**

   a. They are useful as a risk assessment procedure for planning purposes;

   b. They are useful (but not required) as a form of substantive evidence (and, in this context, are referred to as "substantive analytical procedures"); and

   c. The auditor is required to perform analytical procedures as near the end of the audit to assist the auditor when forming an overall conclusion about the financial statements.

2. The AICPA states that the effectiveness and efficiency of substantive analytical procedures depends on the following 4 factors or considerations:
   a. **Nature of the assertion --** Substantive analytical procedures may be particularly effective in testing for omissions of transactions that would be hard to detect with procedures that focus on recorded amounts. In other words, the skillful use of analytical procedures may be more effective than tests of details in addressing the "completeness" assertion, since there may be no supporting documents to examine for transactions that were not recorded in the first place!
   b. **Plausibility and predictability of the relationship --** Developing a meaningful expectation to compare to the client's recorded balance is critical to the skillful use of analytical procedures, so the predictability of the relationship is very important.
      i. Relationships in a stable environment are usually more predictable than those in a dynamic environment.
      ii. Relationships involving income statement accounts tend to be more predictable than those involving balance sheet accounts (since the income statement deals with a period of time rather than a single moment in time).
      iii. Relationships involving transactions subject to management discretion tend to be less predictable.
   c. **Availability and reliability of data used --** The reliability of the expectation increases when the data used is (1) obtained from independent outside sources; (2) when it is subject to audit testing (either currently or in the past); or (3) is developed under conditions of effective internal control.
   d. **Precision of the expectation --** The likelihood of detecting a misstatement decreases as the level of aggregation of the data increases. (That is, procedures would be less effective for "high altitude" global comparisons than for more focused, specific comparisons. In other words, relationships of interest to the auditor might be obscured by the noise in the data at a high level of aggregation, whereas those relationships might be more identifiable at a lower level of aggregation. For example, the auditor could focus on sales by month broken down by product line instead of simply comparing current annual sales currently to the prior year.)
3. **Selected Ratios --** Such ratios may be tested in Auditing & Attestation as "analytical procedures" or in Financial Accounting & Reporting as "financial statement analysis."

> **Definition:**
> *Liquidity ratios (also known as solvency ratios)*: Measures of an entity's short-term ability to meet its obligations.

   a. *Working capital* = current assets - current liabilities. This is a definition, not a ratio.
   b. *Current ratio* = current assets/current liabilities.
   c. *Quick ratio* (acid-test ratio) = (cash + marketable securities + A/R)/ current liabilities.
   d. *Current cash to debt ratio* = net cash from operations/ average current liabilities.

> **Definition:**
> *Activity ratios (also known as turnover or efficiency ratios)*: Measures of an entity's effectiveness putting its assets to use.

   e. *Asset turnover* = net sales/ average total assets.
   f. *Receivable turnover* = net (credit) sales/ average trade receivable (net).
   g. *Number of days sales in receivables* = 365 days/ receivable turnover.

h. *Inventory turnover* = cost of goods sold/ average inventory.

i. *Number of days sales in inventory* = 365 days/ inventory turnover.

> **Definition:**
> *Profitability ratios*: Measures of an entity's operating success (failure) for a period of time.

j. *Profit margin on sales* = net income/ net sales.

k. *Gross profit percentage* = (sales - cost of goods sold)/ sales.

l. *Rate of return on assets* = net income/ average total assets.

m. *Rate of return on common stockholders' equity* = (net income - dividends attributable to preferred stockholders)/ average common stockholders' equity.

n. *Earnings per share* = (net income - preferred dividends)/average number of common shares outstanding.

o. *Price earnings ratio* ("P-E ratio") = market price of stock/ earnings per share.

> **Definition:**
> *Coverage ratios (also known as leverage ratios)*: Measures of the entity's ability to meet its obligations over time. (That is, measures of long-term risk to creditors and the extent to which the entity has borrowed up to its available capacity.)

p. *Debt to total assets ratio* = total liabilities/ total assets.

q. *Debt to equity ratio* = total liabilities/ total stockholders' equity.

r. *Times interest earned* = income before interest expense and income taxes/ interest expense.

s. *Cash to debt coverage ratio* = net cash from operations/ average total liabilities.

Nature of Evidence 1

After studying this lesson, you should be able to:

1. *Understand the meaning of the terms sufficient and appropriate.*
2. *Know what constitutes "audit evidence."*
3. *Identify the financial statement assertions specified in AICPA Professional Standards (separately by category of assertion: account balances at period end; transactions and events during the period; and presentation and disclosure), which can be used as broad audit objectives for which evidence must be obtained.*

I. **Responsibilities under AICPA Professional Standards --** The relevant AICPA guidance is provided by AU 500: "Audit Evidence." This pronouncement states that the auditor's objective is to "obtain sufficient appropriate audit evidence to be able to draw reasonable conclusions on which to base the auditor's opinion."

> This SAS provides guidance regarding the third Standard of Fieldwork of GAAS: "The auditor must obtain sufficient appropriate audit evidence by performing audit procedures to afford a reasonable basis for an opinion regarding the financial statements under audit."
>
> That requirement is now embedded in one of the "Performance Principles": "To obtain reasonable assurance, which is a high but not absolute level of assurance, the auditor
>
> -obtains sufficient appropriate audit evidence about whether material misstatements exist, through designing and implementing appropriate responses to the assessed risks."

II. **Audit Evidence**

> **Definitions:**
> *Audit Evidence*: Information used by the auditor in arriving at the conclusions on which the auditor's opinion is based. Audit evidence includes both information contained in the accounting records underlying the financial statements and other information.
>
> *Accounting records:* The records of initial accounting entries and supporting records, such as checks and records of electronic fund transfers, invoices, contracts, the general and subsidiary ledgers, journal entries and other adjustments to the financial statements that are not reflected in journal entries, and records, such as work sheets and spreadsheets, supporting cost allocations, computations, reconciliations and disclosures.
>
> *Other information constituting audit evidence:* Includes minutes of meetings, confirmations, industry analysts' reports, internal control manuals, and any other information obtained by inquiry, observation, and inspection.

> **Note**:The auditor should obtain audit evidence by testing the accounting records, by analysis, review, and reconciling related information; however, the accounting records by themselves do not provide sufficient appropriate audit evidence.

III. **Sufficient Appropriate Audit Evidence --** "Sufficient" refers to the quantity of evidence, whereas "appropriate" refers to the quality of evidence in terms of its relevance and reliability.

A. The quantity of evidence required (related to "sufficient") is directly related to the risk of misstatement (the greater the risk, the more evidence is needed) and inversely related to the quality of evidence (the higher the quality, the less evidence is needed).

B. "Reliability" is affected by the source and nature of evidence and depends upon individual circumstances -- however, the SAS offers the following guidelines:

1. Evidence obtained directly by the auditor is more reliable than evidence obtained indirectly or by inference (e.g., observation of the application of a control is more reliable than inquiry of entity personnel about the application of a control).
2. Evidence is more reliable when obtained from independent (knowledgeable) sources outside the entity;
3. Evidence generated internally is more reliable when the related controls are effective;
4. Evidence is more reliable when it exists in documentary form (whether paper or electronic); and
5. Evidence provided by original documents is more reliable than evidence based on photocopies/facsimiles (faxes).

C. The auditor should consider the reliability of information used, but the auditor is not normally responsible for authenticating the entity's documents. The auditor should obtain evidence about the accuracy and completeness of information used to perform further audit procedures (either in connection with the actual audit procedure or by testing controls related to the information).

D. More assurance is obtained from consistent audit evidence obtained from different sources or of a different nature ("corroborating" information) than from evidence considered individually. When evidence from different sources is inconsistent, the auditor should determine what audit procedures are needed to resolve the inconsistency.

E. Professional judgment is required for "reasonable assurance," and the auditor does not examine all available evidence. The auditor may appropriately consider the cost of information relative to its usefulness, although cost alone is not a valid basis for omitting an audit procedure. Audit evidence is usually "persuasive" (or suggestive) and is rarely "conclusive" (or compelling). The auditor should not be satisfied with evidence that is less than persuasive.

IV. **Using "Assertions" to Obtain Audit Evidence --** In stating that the financial statements are consistent with GAAP, management makes several "assertions" (which are implicit or explicit statements of fact).

A. Historically, the auditing standards discussed 5 traditional financial statement assertions:

1. Existence/occurrence;
2. Completeness;
3. Rights and obligations;
4. Valuation and allocation; and
5. Presentation and disclosure.

B. U.S. professional standards now classify assertions in three separate categories for the auditor's consideration, related to:

1. Account balances;
2. Presentation and disclosure; and
3. Classes of transactions and events.

C. **There are four assertions specific to "account balances at period end"**

1. **Existence --** That the assets, liabilities, and equity interests exist.
2. **Completeness --** That all assets, liabilities, and equity interests that should have been recorded have been recorded. There are no omissions.
3. **Rights and obligations --** That the entity holds or controls the rights to its assets, and the liabilities are the obligations of the entity. Any restrictions on the rights to the assets or obligations for the liabilities must be disclosed.
4. **Valuation and allocation --** That assets, liabilities, and equity interests are included in the financial statements at appropriate amounts (relative to the requirements of GAAP) and any resulting valuation or allocation adjustments are appropriately recorded.

D. **There are four assertions about "presentation and disclosure"**

1. **Occurrence and rights and obligations --** That the disclosed events and transactions have occurred and pertain to the entity.
2. **Completeness --** That all disclosures that should have been included have been included. There are no omissions of required disclosures.
3. **Classification and understandability --** That financial information is appropriately presented, described, and clearly expressed.
4. **Accuracy and valuation --** That financial and other information are disclosed fairly and at appropriate amounts.

E. **There are five assertions about "classes of transactions and events during the period"**

1. **Accuracy --** That amounts and other data have been recorded appropriately.
2. **Occurrence --** That transactions and events that have been recorded have occurred. In other words, they are properly recorded and valid.
3. **Completeness --** That all transactions and events that should have been recorded have been recorded. There are no omissions.
4. **Cutoff --** That transactions and events have been recorded in the correct accounting period. Note that there are only two ways to record a transaction in the wrong period. One is by recorded a transaction prematurely, which violates the "occurrence" assertion; and the other is to record a transaction belatedly, which violates the "completeness" assertion.

> **Note:** "Cutoff" is actually redundant in this context, since establishing "occurrence" (that the recorded transactions are properly recorded) and "completeness" (that there are no omissions of transactions that should have been recorded) together establish that the transactions, in fact, have been recorded in the correct accounting period ("cutoff"). However, "cutoff" is an important issue that auditors must address, so this redundancy emphasizes an important auditing concept.

5. **Classification --** That transactions and events have been recorded in the proper accounts.

See the following example.

Categories of Assertions			
	Account Balances at End of Period	**Presentation & Disclosure**	**Transactions & Events During the Period**
Existence/Occurrence	Applicable	Applicable	Applicable
Completeness	Applicable	Applicable	Applicable
Rights & obligations	Applicable	N/A separately (included with Occurrence)	N/A
Accuracy & Valuation; or Valuation & Allocation	Applicable	Applicable	Applicable
Classification; or Classification & Understandability	N/A	Applicable	Applicable
Cutoff	N/A -- implicit	N/A	Applicable

F. This SAS points out that the auditor may use the assertions as presented above or express them differently as long as the relevant issues have been addressed -- for example, the auditor may combine the assertions about transactions and events with those about account balances; and the auditor may decline to identify a separate assertion about "cutoff" if occurrence and completeness have been established.

G. The auditor should use "relevant assertions" (those that have a meaningful bearing on whether the account is fairly stated) to assess the risk of material misstatement -- the auditor should evaluate the nature of the assertion, the volume of transactions or data involved, and the complexity of the systems (including IT) by which the entity processes and controls the information related to the assertion.

Nature of Evidence 2

After studying this lesson, you should be able to:

1. *Understand the auditor's responsibility to plan and perform substantive procedures in order to be responsive to the assessed risks of material misstatement, according to AICPA Professional Standards.*
2. *Know the three categories of audit procedures.*

I. **Audit Procedures for Obtaining Evidence --** The auditor's basis for conclusion is comprised of three categories of procedures:

   A. Risk assessment procedures;

   B. Tests of controls; and

   C. Substantive procedures.

> **Definitions:**
> *Risk assessment procedures:*: The audit procedures performed to obtain an understanding of the entity and its environment, including the entity's internal control, to identify and assess the risks of material misstatement, whether due to fraud or error, at the financial statement and relevant assertion levels.
>
> *Tests of control*: An audit procedure designed to evaluate the operating effectiveness of controls in preventing, or detecting and correcting, material misstatements at the assertion level. (Note that the auditor must perform tests of controls when the risk assessment includes an expectation of the operating effectiveness of controls or when the substantive procedures alone do not provide sufficient appropriate audit evidence.)
>
> *Substantive procedures: An audit procedure designed to detect material misstatements at the assertion level. Substantive procedures comprise (a) tests of details (classes of transactions, account balances, and disclosures) and (b) substantive analytical procedures.*

II. **Menu of Specific Substantive Audit Procedures --** The auditor may use computer-assisted audit techniques (CAATs) to assist the auditor when information is in electronic form:

   A. **Inspection of records/documents --** Examining records or documents, whether internal or external, whether paper or electronic, or other media;

   B. **Inspection of tangible assets --** Physical examination of the assets;

   C. **Observation --** Looking at a process or procedure being performed by others;

   D. **Inquiry --** Seeking information of knowledgeable persons inside or outside the entity and evaluating their responses. Note that inquiry alone does not provide sufficient appropriate audit evidence either for substantive purposes or for tests of controls.

   E. **Confirmation --** Obtaining a representation directly from a knowledgeable third party;

   F. **Recalculation --** Checking the mathematical accuracy of documents;

   G. **Reperformance --** The auditor's execution of procedures or controls originally performed as part of the entity's internal controls;

> **Note:**
> Analytical procedures are defined as "evaluations of financial information through analysis of plausible relationships among both financial and nonfinancial data."

H. **Analytical procedures --** Includes "scanning" to review accounting data to identify unusual items to be tested further. CAATs may be especially useful in identifying significant or unusual items.

III. **The Auditor Should Plan and Perform Substantive Procedures --** The auditor should design the substantive procedures to be responsive to the assessed risks of material misstatements. The purpose of substantive procedures is to detect material misstatements at the relevant assertion level.

A. The auditor should perform some substantive procedures for all relevant assertions related to each material class of transactions, account balance, and disclosure (regardless of the assessed risk of material misstatement), since there are inherent limitations to internal control and the assessment of risk is judgmental.

B. The auditor's substantive procedures should include the following related to the financial reporting process:

1. Agree the financial statement information to the underlying accounting records; and

2. Examine material journal entries and other adjustments made during the preparation of the financial statements.

C. **Nature of substantive procedures --** These should be responsive to the planned level of detection risk; they consist of:

1. Tests of details and

2. Substantive analytical procedures (should consider testing the controls over the preparation of information used in connection with analytical procedures).

D. **Timing of substantive procedures --** May be performed at an interim date (before year-end) or at final (at or after year-end)

1. Performing substantive procedures at an interim date increases detection risk. The auditor should perform additional substantive procedures (or substantive procedures combined with tests of control) to mitigate the increased risk and provide a reasonable basis for extending the audit conclusions from the interim date to year-end.

2. It is not necessary to rely on internal controls (that is, test the operating effectiveness of controls) to extend the audit conclusions from the interim date to year-end. However, the auditor should consider whether only performing additional substantive procedures is sufficient.

3. When planning to perform substantive analytical procedures for the period following the interim date, the auditor should consider whether the period-end balances are reasonably predictable as to amount, relative significance, and composition.

E. **Extent of substantive procedures --** Determine the implications to sample sizes (considering the planned level of detection risk, materiality, tolerable misstatement, expected misstatement, and the nature of the population).

F. **Evaluating the sufficiency and appropriateness of the audit evidence obtained**

1. **Consider all relevant audit evidence --** The auditor should consider whether the audit evidence appears to corroborate or to contradict the relevant assertions in the financial statements.

2. The sufficiency and appropriateness of audit evidence as a basis for the auditor's conclusions are matters of professional judgment. The auditor's judgment may be influenced by factors such as the following:

a. The significance of the potential misstatement and the likelihood that it may have a material effect;

b. The understanding of the entity and its environment, including internal control;

c. The effectiveness of management's responses and controls to address the risks;

d. The results of the audit procedures performed (including whether the procedures identified instances of fraud or error);

e. The persuasiveness of the audit evidence obtained;

f. The source and reliability of available information; and

g. The experience gained in previous audits with such misstatements.

3. **Documentation --** As covered in the course materials on Internal Controls, the auditor should document the following matters:

   a. The overall responses to address the assessed risk of misstatement at the financial statement level;

   b. The nature, timing, and extent of the further audit procedures;

   c. The linkage of those procedures with the assessed risks at the relevant assertion level;

   d. The results of the audit procedures; and

   e. The conclusions reached in the current audit about the operating effectiveness of controls tested in a prior audit.

Evaluation of Misstatements Identified During the Audit

After studying this lesson you should be able to :

1. *Identify the specific matters related to misstatements that the auditor is required to document.*
2. *Understand the auditor's responsibility to communicate identified misstatements to management, and the auditor's responsibility when management refuses to correct some (or all) of the identified misstatements.*
3. *Understand the auditor's responsibility to accumulate and evaluate the effect of identified misstatements on the audit and to evaluate the effects of uncorrected misstatements on the financial statements.*

I. **Responsibilities under AICPA Professional Standards --** The relevant AICPA guidance is provided by AU 450: "Evaluation of Misstatements Identified During the Audit." This pronouncement states that the auditor's objectives are to evaluate the effect of (1) identified misstatements on the audit; and (2) uncorrected misstatements, if any, on the financial statements.

Definitions:
Misstatement: A difference between the amount, classification, presentation, or disclosure of a reported financial statement item and the amount, classification, presentation, or disclosure that is required for the item to be in accordance with the applicable reporting framework. (Misstatements also involve matters deemed necessary for the financial statements to be presented fairly, in all material respects.)

Uncorrected misstatements: Misstatements that the auditor has accumulated during the audit and that have not been corrected.

II. **Expectations Regarding Identified Misstatements and Uncorrected Misstatements**

A. **Accumulation of identified misstatements --** The auditor should accumulate all misstatements identified during the audit (except for those that are *clearly trivial*, which means *inconsequential*). The auditor may wish to distinguish among the following 3 types of misstatements:

1. **Factual misstatements --** Misstatements for which there is no doubt.
2. **Judgmental misstatements --** Differences due to the judgments of management that the auditor considers unreasonable or to the selection of accounting policies that the auditor views as inappropriate.
3. **Projected misstatements --** The auditor's best estimate of misstatements in populations as suggested by audit sampling.

B. **Consideration of identified misstatements as the audit progresses --** The auditor should determine whether the overall audit strategy and audit plan need to be revised as a result of the identified misstatements. That would be necessary if the aggregate of accumulated misstatements (and other misstatements that may exist) approaches what is considered to be material.

C. **Communication and the correction of misstatements --** The auditor should communicate all misstatements accumulated during the audit on a timely basis with the *appropriate level* of management and request they correct the misstatements. The appropriate level is the one that has the authority to evaluate the misstatements and take necessary action.

1. If management has examined a class of transactions or account balance at the auditor's request (for example, as a result of an audit sample that indicates a misstatement) and has made a correction -- The auditor should perform additional procedures to determine whether any misstatements remain.

2. If management refuses to correct some (or all) of the misstatements -- The auditor should obtain an understanding of management's reasons and take that into consideration when evaluating whether the financial statements are materially misstated.

D. **Evaluating the effect of uncorrected misstatements**

1. **Reassess materiality --** The auditor should reassess materiality to verify that it is appropriate in view of the entity's actual financial results.

2. **Determine whether uncorrected misstatements are material --** The auditor should consider (a) the size and nature of the misstatements; and (b) the effect of uncorrected misstatements related to prior periods.

3. Other (undetected) misstatements may exist when a misstatement results from a break down in internal control, or when inappropriate assumptions or valuation methods have been widely used. The auditor should consider whether the detected and undetected misstatements might exceed materiality.

4. Circumstances affecting the evaluation of materiality include the following: (a) compliance and regulatory requirements; (b) debt covenants; (c) the effect on future periods' financial statements; (d) the effects on changes in earnings (such as changing income to a loss or vice versa) or other trends; (e) the impact on ratios; (f) the effects on segment information; (g) an effect that increases management compensation; (h) the omission of information important to users' understanding; and (i) the misclassification between operating/non-operating items or recurring/non-recurring items.

E. **Documentation of misstatements --** The auditor should document the following 3 matters in the audit documentation: (1) the amount below which misstatements would be viewed as *clearly trivial*; (2) all misstatements accumulated during the audit and whether they have been corrected; and (3) the auditor's conclusion (and the basis for that conclusion) about whether the uncorrected misstatements are material, individually or in the aggregate.

Audit Documentation

After studying this lesson, you should be able to:

1. *Know the major differences between AICPA Professional Standards and PCAOB Auditing Standards with respect to documentation "completion" requirements and "retention" requirements.*
2. *Know the distinction between the auditor's "permanent file" and the current year's audit documentation.*
3. *Understand the auditor's responsibilities to prepare and obtain documentation, in accordance with AICPA Professional Standards.*

I. **Responsibilities under AICPA Professional Standards --** The relevant AICPA guidance is provided by AU 230: "Audit Documentation." This pronouncement states that the auditor's objective is "to prepare documentation that provides:

  A. A sufficient and appropriate record of the basis for the auditor's report; and

  B. Evidence that the audit was planned and performed in accordance with (GAAS) and applicable legal and regulatory requirements."

> **Definition:**
> *Audit documentation*: This is the record of audit procedures performed, relevant audit evidence obtained, and conclusions reached (terms such as *working papers* or *workpapers* are also sometimes used).

II. **Purposes of Audit Documentation**

  A. Provides the principal support for the auditor's report (regarding the procedures performed and the conclusions reached).

  B. Documents the auditor's compliance with GAAS and any applicable legal and regulatory requirements;

    1. That the work was adequately planned and supervised;
    2. That an understanding of the entity and its environment, including internal control, was obtained and evaluated as necessary to assess the risks of material misstatement and to design the audit to be responsive to those risks; and
    3. That the procedures applied and the evidence obtained provide a reasonable basis for the opinion expressed.

  C. The audit documentation assists in controlling the audit work - that is, breaking the overall audit project into manageable tasks that can be delegated to the various members of the audit team (while documenting the work performed and the conclusions reached, and identifying the work yet to be completed).

III. **Ownership and Custody Issues**

  A. **Ownership --** Audit documentation is the auditor's property (the auditor should safeguard it and establish a formal retention policy).

  B. **Confidentiality --** The audit documentation is subject to the restrictions imposed by AICPA ethics rules on confidentiality. (The auditor should prevent unauthorized access to the audit documentation, since it contains entity-specific confidential information.)

C. Auditors should apply appropriate controls over the audit documentation to protect the integrity of the information at all stages of the audit, to prevent unauthorized changes, and to limit access to authorized personnel.

IV. AICPA Requirements

A. Audit documentation should permit an experienced auditor without prior connection to the audit to understand the following:

1. The nature, timing, and extent of procedures performed;
2. The results of those procedures;
3. The conclusions reached on significant matters; and
4. Whether the accounting records agree or reconcile with the audited financial statements.

B. Audit documentation should include abstracts or copies of significant contracts or agreements examined -- if needed by an experienced auditor to understand the basis for conclusions.

C. Audit documentation should identify the specific items tested by the auditor (or the "identifying characteristics" of items tested in connection with the substantive procedures and any tests of control so that the items tested can be determined as necessary).

D. The auditor should also document audit findings or issues that are "significant" (including actions taken to address them and the basis for conclusions reached), and should also document discussions of significant findings or issues with management (including issues discussed, and when and with whom). Such findings and issues include:

1. Significant matters regarding the selection, application, and consistency of accounting principles;
2. Circumstances causing difficulty in applying necessary audit procedures;
3. Results of audit procedures indicating a possible material misstatement;
4. Findings that could result in modification of the audit report; and
5. Audit adjustments (whether or not recorded by management) that could have a material effect individually or when aggregated.

E. If information is identified that contradicts or is inconsistent with the auditor's final conclusions -- the auditor should document how the auditor addressed the contradiction or inconsistency in forming the conclusions.

F. Identification of preparer and reviewer -- the auditor should document who performed the audit work and who reviewed the specific audit documentation.

G. Should document the "report release date" -- That is defined as the date the auditor grants the entity permission to use the auditor's report on the audited financial statements.

V. Revisions -- Any revisions to audit documentation after the date of the auditor's report should comply with the following requirements:

A. **"Documentation completion date" --** The auditor should complete the assembly of the final audit file no later than 60 days after the "report release date." The PCAOB specifies a limit of 45 days for audits of public companies.

B. **Before the documentation completion date --** The auditor may add information received after the report date or delete unnecessary documentation up to the documentation completion date.

C. **After the documentation completion date --** T he auditor must not delete any audit documentation before the end of the retention period; the auditor may add to the documentation, but must document any materials added, by whom, when, reasons for the change, and the effect, if any, on the auditor's conclusions.

D. **Retention requirements --** The AICPA requires that the audit documentation be retained for at least five years from the report release date. (The PCAOB requires retention for at least 7 years for audits of public companies.

VI. **Additional Documentation --** Other Statements on Auditing Standards require additional specific documentation, including, for example, the following:

A. **Aggregated misstatements --** The auditor must document:

1. The nature and effect of misstatements that the auditor aggregates, and
2. The auditor's conclusions as to whether the aggregated misstatements are material to the financial statements.

B. **Analytical procedures --** The auditor must document:

1. The expectation and factors (sources) considered in developing it, when not otherwise apparent;
2. The results of the comparison of that expectation to the recorded amounts (or to ratios based on recorded amounts); and
3. Any additional procedures performed (and the results of those procedures) to investigate unexpected differences from that comparison.

C. **Going concern issues --** The auditor must document:

1. The conditions giving rise to the going concern issue;
2. The elements of management's plan considered important to overcoming the situation;
3. Evidence obtained to evaluate the significant elements of management's plans;
4. The auditor's conclusion as to whether "substantial doubt" remains; and
5. The auditor's conclusion as to whether an explanatory paragraph should be added to the auditor's report.

VII. **Quantity of Content --** The quantity, type, and content of the audit documentation depends on the auditor's professional judgment and may include consideration of the following matters:

A. The risk of material misstatement in the area involved;

B. The amount of judgment involved in performing the work and interpreting the results (including the nature of the audit procedures involved);

C. The nature and extent of any exceptions identified;

D. The significance of the evidence to the assertion involved; and

E. The need to document a conclusion not readily determinable from the documentation of the work performed.

VIII. **Types of "Files" Related to Audit Working Papers**

A. **Permanent file --** Involves matters having ongoing audit significance and may include:

1. Description of the client's industry, a brief history of client, and a description of the client's facilities;
2. Abstracts or copies of important legal documents and important long-term contracts -- documents such as the company's articles of incorporation and bylaws and contracts such as debt agreements, leases, and labor contracts (including pension plans and profit-sharing agreements);
3. Documentation of the auditor's understanding of internal control for the major transaction cycles; and

4. **Historical financial information --** Such as ratio analysis of the client's operations or other data having ongoing usefulness.

B. **Current year's audit files --** The current year's audit files include the auditor's documentation of important administrative matters (such as the audit team's time budget) along with the supporting working papers related to the financial statement items.

   1. Audit plan (sometimes called the "audit program").
   2. Memoranda (documenting planning activities, consideration of fraud, assessment of internal control, etc.).
   3. Abstracts or copies of relevant client documents (including minutes of board of directors' meetings or meetings of those charged with governance).
   4. Letters (confirmations, attorney letters, management representation letter, engagement letter, etc.).
   5. Analyses and schedules (either prepared by client personnel or by the audit team).

C. **Bulk file --** Where documentation that is too voluminous can be stored (for example, magnetic tapes, extensive computer printouts, etc.).

D. **Correspondence file --** Where letters and e-mail messages to and from clients are organized so that the audit team can conveniently review communications related to each client organization.

E. **Report file --** Where prior years' audit reports and management letters are organized (by client) so that the audit team can conveniently review formal reports previously issued for each client.

Confirmation

After studying this lesson, you should be able to:

1. *Understand the auditor's responsibility to perform "alternative procedures" for when no response has been received for a positive confirmation attempt.*
2. *Know the distinction between a "positive" and a "negative" confirmation.*

I. **Responsibilities under AICPA Professional Standards --** The relevant AICPA guidance is provided by AU 505: "External Confirmations." This pronouncement states that the auditor's objective is "to design and perform external confirmations to obtain relevant and reliable audit evidence."

> **Definitions:**
> *External confirmation*: Audit evidence obtained as a direct written response to the auditor from a third party ("the confirming party"), either in paper form or by electronic or other medium (for example, through the auditor's direct access to information held by a third party).
>
> *Positive confirmation request:* A request that the confirming party respond directly to the auditor by providing the requested information or indicating whether the confirming party agrees or disagrees with the information in the request.
>
> *Negative confirmation request:* A request that the confirming party respond directly to the auditor only if the confirming party disagrees with the information provided in the request.

II. **Tailor Objectives/Assertions --** The auditor should tailor the confirmations to the specific audit objectives/assertions. Confirmations are most useful in addressing the existence/occurrence assertion. There are two basic types of confirmation requests:

   A. **Positive confirmation request --** Where a response is requested whether or not the other party agrees with the client's recorded amount. A nonresponse is viewed as a "loose end" that must be addressed.

      1. When individual accounts are large.
      2. Requires second (or possibly third) requests as a follow-up procedure for nonresponses.
      3. If no response is obtained, the auditor must perform "alternative procedures."

   B. **Negative confirmation request --** Where a response is only requested in the event of **disagreement**. A nonresponse is viewed as evidence of agreement by the recipient:

      1. Could easily misinterpret a nonresponse as suggesting "agreement" when, instead, the other party did not even open the envelope!
      2. Therefore, negative confirmations usually require a larger sample size than would positive confirmations.
      3. The auditor may justify using negative confirmations when:
         a. The population consists of a large number of small, rather homogeneous items;
         b. The assessed risk of material misstatement is low, and the relevant controls are operating effectively; and
         c. Recipients are expected to pay attention to the request, and a low rate of exceptions is expected.

C. **Alternative procedures --** Alternative (sometimes called "alternate") audit procedures are usually required when no response is received for a positive confirmation request:

1. **Receivables --** The auditor would first look to see whether cash was received subsequent to the date of the confirmation request. Second best, the auditor would examine the documents underlying the apparent validity of the recorded transaction.

2. **Payables --** The auditor would usually verify subsequent cash disbursements as evidence of payment of the account.

III. **Control of Requests and Responses --** The auditor should "maintain control over the confirmation requests and responses." If the response is by fax, the auditor should consider a direct call to the respondent; and if the response is verbal, encourage a written reply.

IV. **Responding to Risks of Material Misstatement --** AU 330, "Performing Audit Procedures in Response to Assessed Risks and Evaluating the Audit Evidence Obtained," states, " "The auditor should use external confirmation procedures for accounts receivable, except when one or more of the following is applicable:

A. The overall account balance is immaterial.

B. External confirmation procedures for accounts receivable would be ineffective.

C. The auditor's assessed level of risk of material misstatement at the relevant assertion level is low, and the other planned substantive procedures address the assessed risk. In many situations, the use of external confirmation procedures for accounts receivable and the performance of other substantive procedures are necessary to reduce the assessed risk of material misstatement to an acceptably low level."

> AU 330 also states, "If the auditor has determined that an assessed risk of material misstatement at the relevant assertion level is a significant risk, the auditor should perform substantive procedures that are specifically responsive to that risk."

> **Example:**
> If the auditor identified that management is under pressure to meet earnings expectations, there may be a risk that management is inflating sales by improperly recognizing revenue related to sales agreements with terms that preclude revenue recognition or by invoicing sales before shipment. In these circumstances, the auditor may, for example, design external written confirmation requests not only to confirm outstanding amounts, but also to confirm the details of the sales agreements, including date, any rights of return, and delivery terms. In addition, the auditor may find it effective to supplement such external written confirmations with inquiries of nonfinancial personnel in the entity regarding any changes in sales agreements and delivery terms.

Accounting Estimates

After studying this lesson, you should be able to:

1. *Know the auditor's responsibilities when an accounting estimate results in a "significant risk."*
2. *Know the definition of "estimation uncertainty" and how that concept may result in a "significant risk."*
3. *Understand the auditor's responsibilities to apply a risk-based audit approach to evaluate the reasonableness of accounting estimates in accordance with AICPA Professional Standards.*

I. **Responsibilities under AICPA Professional Standards --** The relevant AICPA guidance is provided by AU 540: "Auditing Accounting Estimates, Including Fair Value Accounting Estimates and Related Disclosures." This pronouncement states that the auditor's objective is to obtain sufficient appropriate audit evidence about whether the accounting estimates (including fair value accounting estimates) are reasonable and whether the related disclosures are adequate in view of the applicable financial reporting framework.

Definitions:
Accounting estimate: An approximation of a monetary amount in the absence of a precise means of measurement.

Auditor's point estimate (or auditor's range): The amount (or range of amounts) derived from audit evidence for use in evaluating the recorded or disclosed amount(s).

Estimation uncertainty: The susceptibility of an accounting estimate and related disclosures to an inherent lack of precision in its measurement.

Management's point estimate: The amount selected by management for recognition or disclosure as an accounting estimate.

Outcome of an accounting estimate: The actual monetary amount that results from resolution of the underlying matter addressed by the accounting estimate.

II. **The Risk-Based Audit Approach**

A. **Basis for risk assessment --** The auditor should obtain an understanding of the following:

1. The requirements of the applicable financial reporting framework;
2. How management makes the accounting estimates and the data used, including how management has assessed the effect of estimation uncertainty.

B. **Identifying and assessing risks of material misstatement --** The auditor should evaluate the degree of estimation uncertainty involved, and determine whether any of those accounting estimates result in "significant risks." (Recall that significant risks require the auditor to obtain an understanding of whether relevant controls mitigate such risks.)

C. **Responding to the assessed risks of material misstatement**

1. The auditor should determine whether management has complied with the requirements of the applicable financial reporting framework, and whether the methods used to make the estimate are appropriate and consistently applied.

2. In responding to the assessed the risks, the auditor should do one (or more) of the following:
    a. Determine whether events occurring up to the date of the auditor's report provide evidence about the accounting estimate;
    b. Test how management made the estimate, along with the data used;
    c. Test the operating effectiveness of applicable controls, along with performing appropriate substantive procedures; and/or
    d. Develop a point estimate (or range) to evaluate management's point estimate.
3. The auditor should consider the need for specialized skills or knowledge.

D. **Further substantive procedures to respond to "significant risks" --** The auditor should evaluate the following:
1. How management addressed estimation uncertainty in making the accounting estimate;
2. Whether management's significant assumptions are reasonable; and
3. When relevant, whether management has the intent and ability to carry out specific actions.

E. **Evaluating the reasonableness of the accounting estimates --** The auditor should evaluate whether the accounting estimates are reasonable (or are misstated) relative to the applicable financial reporting framework. The auditor is not responsible for predicting future conditions, transactions, or events, however.

F. **Disclosures --** The auditor should obtain sufficient appropriate audit evidence as to whether the disclosures meet the requirements of the applicable financial reporting framework. For accounting estimates resulting in "significant risks," the auditor should evaluate the adequacy of the disclosure of estimation uncertainty.

G. **Indicators of possible management bias --** The auditor should consider whether the accounting estimates might indicate possible management bias.

H. **Documentation --** The auditor should include documentation regarding (1) the basis for the auditor's conclusions about the reasonableness of accounting estimates resulting in "significant risks" and their disclosure; and (2) any indications of possible management bias. The auditor usually obtains written representations as to whether management believes assumptions used in making accounting estimates are reasonable.

III. **Additional guidance regarding "estimation uncertainty"**

A. **Nature of estimation uncertainty --** The nature of estimation uncertainty varies with the nature of the accounting estimate, the extent to which there is an accepted method (or model) to be used, and the subjectivity of any assumptions or the degree of judgment involved. The risks of material misstatement increase when there is high estimation uncertainty.

B. **Understanding management's assessment --** In obtaining an understanding of whether and how management has assessed estimation uncertainty, the auditor might consider whether management has performed a "sensitivity analysis" and monitors outcomes of prior accounting estimates.

C. **When the estimation uncertainty is high --** The auditor may consider a combination of responses to the assessed risks, including reviewing outcomes, testing how management made its estimate, testing applicable controls, and developing a point estimate (or range) to evaluate management's point estimate.

D. **Narrowing a range --** The auditor's range should encompass all "reasonable" outcomes, not all possible outcomes. A high estimation uncertainty (significant risk) may be indicated if it is not possible to narrow the range to less than or equal to performance materiality.

E. **Reporting --** When there is significant uncertainty, the auditor may add an emphasis-of-matter paragraph to the auditor's report.

Fair Value Estimates

After studying this lesson, you should be able to:

1. *Recognize the role of "observable inputs" and "unobservable inputs" in evaluating estimation uncertainty for fair value accounting estimates.*
2. *Understand the auditor's responsibilities to apply a risk-based audit approach to evaluate the reasonableness of fair value accounting estimates in accordance with AICPA Professional Standards.*

I. **Responsibilities under AICPA Professional Standards --** The relevant AICPA guidance is provided by AU 540: "Auditing Accounting Estimates, Including Fair Value Accounting Estimates and Related Disclosures." This pronouncement states that the auditor's objective is to obtain sufficient appropriate audit evidence about whether the accounting estimates (including fair value accounting estimates) are reasonable and whether the related disclosures are adequate in view of the applicable financial reporting framework.

> **Note:**
> The prior discussion related to auditing "accounting estimates" is also applicable to the discussion here related to auditing "fair value accounting estimates," which is based on the same Statement on Auditing Standards. The focus here is on audit considerations that are specific to fair value measurements and disclosures.

II. **The Risk-Based Audit Approach**

A. **Basis for risk assessment --** The auditor should obtain an understanding of the applicable financial reporting requirements, and how management makes the fair value accounting estimate (and data used), including how management assessed the effect of estimation uncertainty.

B. **Identifying and assessing risks of material misstatement --** The auditor should evaluate the degree of estimation uncertainty involved and determine whether any of those fair value accounting estimates result in "significant risks."

C. **Responding to the assessed risks of material misstatement --** The auditor should determine whether management complied with the applicable financial reporting requirements, and whether the methods used to make the fair value accounting estimate are appropriate and are consistently applied. The auditor should consider the need for specialized skills or knowledge.

D. **Further substantive procedures to respond to "significant risks" --** The auditor should evaluate how management addressed estimation uncertainty; whether management's significant assumptions are reasonable; and, when relevant, whether management has the intent and ability to carry out specific actions.

E. **Evaluating the reasonableness of the estimates --** The auditor should evaluate whether the fair value accounting estimates are reasonable relative to the requirements of the applicable financial reporting framework.

F. **Disclosures --** The auditor should obtain sufficient appropriate audit evidence as to whether the disclosures meet the requirements of the applicable financial reporting framework. The auditor should also evaluate the adequacy of disclosure of the estimation uncertainty for any identified "significant risks."

G. **Indicators of possible management bias --** The auditor should consider whether the fair value accounting estimates might indicate possible management bias.

H. **Documentation --** The auditor should document the following:

1. The basis for the auditor's conclusions about the reasonableness of fair value accounting estimates resulting in "significant risks" and their disclosure, and
2. Any indications of possible management bias.

III. Additional guidance regarding "estimation uncertainty" particularly for fair value accounting estimates

A. **Nature of estimation uncertainty --** High estimation uncertainty results in an increased risk of material misstatement when, for example:

1. Fair value accounting estimates for derivative instruments are not publicly traded; and
2. Fair value accounting estimates are based on a highly specialized entity-developed model or when the assumptions (inputs) cannot be observed in the marketplace.

> "... the existence of published price quotations ordinarily is the best audit evidence of fair value."

B. **Examples of fair value accounting estimates --** complex financial instruments (not traded in an open market); share-based payments; property held for disposal; certain assets or liabilities acquired in a business combination, including intangibles; and nonmonetary exchange of assets.

C. For fair value accounting estimates, assumptions (inputs) affect estimation uncertainty and vary as follows:

1. **"Observable inputs" --** Assumptions that market participants would use in pricing an asset or liability based on market data from sources independent of the reporting entity or
2. **"Unobservable inputs" --** An entity's own judgments about what assumptions market participants would use. Estimation uncertainty increases when the fair value estimates are based on unobservable inputs.

D. **Testing how management makes the estimate --** The auditor may decide to test how management made their estimate (and the data used) when the accounting estimate is a fair value accounting estimate using observable and unobservable inputs.

E. **Evaluating the method of measurement --** Determining whether the method or model used by management is appropriate requires professional judgment.

F. **Evaluating the use of models for fair value accounting estimates --** Matters the auditor may consider in testing the model include the following:

1. Whether the model is validated for suitability prior to usage;
2. Whether appropriate controls exist over changes;
3. Whether the model is periodically tested for validity (when inputs are subjective);
4. Whether adjustments are made to the model's outputs; and
5. Whether the model is adequately documented, including key parameters and limitations.

G. **Considering specialized skills or knowledge --** In considering the need for specialized skills or knowledge, the auditor may consider whether any complex calculations or models are involved in making fair value accounting estimates when no observable market exists.

H. **Indicators of possible management bias --** An example of an indicator of possible management bias would be the use of an entity's own assumptions for fair value accounting estimates that are inconsistent with observable market conditions.

I. **Communication with those charged with governance --** Another SAS requires the auditor to communicate the auditor's views about the qualitative aspects of the entity's significant accounting practices, including accounting estimates. The auditor should determine that they are informed about the process used by management in developing sensitive accounting estimates, as well as the auditor's basis for conclusions about those matters.

Lawyer's Letters

After studying this lesson, you should be able to:

1. *Understand the agreement between the AICPA and American Bar Association regarding matters that can be communicated to the auditor in the "lawyer's letter" in response to a "letter of inquiry" (with emphasis on "asserted" and "unasserted claims").*
2. *Be familiar with the language used in a typical "letter of inquiry to legal counsel."*
3. *Understand procedures the auditor would perform related to legal liability issues.*

I. **Responsibilities under AICPA Professional Standards --** The relevant AICPA guidance is provided by AU 501: "Audit Evidence -- Specific Considerations for Selected Items." This pronouncement states that the auditor's objective is "to obtain sufficient appropriate audit evidence regarding the completeness of litigation, claims, and assessments involving the entity" (among other matters specifically addressed by the SAS).

II. **Audit Procedures Related to Legal Contingencies**

A. Management is the primary source of information about these legal contingencies. The auditor should make appropriate inquiries of management.

B. The auditor should read the minutes of all meetings of those charged with governance where significant issues, including matters related to legal liability, affecting the financial statements likely would be discussed.

C. To corroborate management's responses to the auditor's inquiries about the identity of lawyers who have rendered significant legal services to the client (and to whom a letter of inquiry should be sent) -- the auditor should examine the charges to the related expense account and then examine (vouch to) the appropriate underlying invoices.

D. The auditor should draft "a letter of inquiry" for management to send to those lawyers who have rendered litigation-related services to the entity. The lawyer's response to the letter of inquiry is simply called the " lawyer's letter" (or "attorney's letter"). The primary purpose of the lawyer's letter is to corroborate management's responses to the auditor's inquiries about legal-related contingencies. When the entity's in-house counsel has responsibility for such litigation-related matters, the auditor should send a similar letter of inquiry to the in-house counsel and obtain a written response.

E. One or more "lawyer's letters" are expected to be included in the audit documentation. However, the SAS allows for the possibility that the entity may not have any relevant "litigation, claims, or assessments" having financial reporting significance. In that case, the auditor would include a specific statement of fact in the management representations letter stating that the entity had no legal counsel to address current or potential litigation issues.

III. **Inquiries of the Client's Lawyer(s) --** The letter of inquiry normally includes the entity's listing of pending legal matters that the lawyer is handling (classified separately as "Asserted Claims" and "Unasserted Claims") to facilitate the lawyer's response.

IV. **Asserted Claims --** With respect to asserted claims and active litigation "asserted" means that someone has already filed a claim or has at least announced the intention to make such a claim, which is synonymous with the AICPA's term "pending or threatened litigation." According to the American Bar Association, the lawyer should inform the auditor directly about any omissions of asserted claims in the lawyer's letter responding to the letter of inquiry.

V. **Unasserted Claims --** With respect to unasserted claims and potential litigation, "unasserted" means that the entity has exposure to litigation, but no one has yet announced an intention to sue.

- **A.** The lawyer cannot (according to the American Bar Association's "Statement of Policy Regarding Lawyers' Responses to Auditors' Requests for Information") inform the auditor directly about any omission of unasserted claims as identified in the letter of inquiry.
- **B.** However, lawyers must tell their client about any such omissions and request that client management then inform the auditors.
- **C.** Note that this issue (whether the entity's lawyer has informed management of any omission of an unasserted claim that management should discuss with their auditors) is specifically addressed in the management representations letter.
- **D.** An unasserted claim must be disclosed according to GAAP if the following two conditions exist:
  1. It is probable that a claim will be asserted, and
  2. It is at least reasonably possible that a material unfavorable outcome will occur.

VI. Scope Limitation -- A limitation in the lawyer's response is a scope limitation sufficient to preclude an unqualified opinion (a nonresponse would likely result in a disclaimer of opinion owing to a major scope limitation).

VII. Sample Letter of Inquiry to Legal Counsel

Illustrative Letter of Inquiry to Legal Counsel

(Prepared on Client's Letterhead)

(*Date*[1])

(*Name of Lawyer*)

(*Address of Lawyer*)

Dear__________________:

In connection with an audit of our financial statements at (*balance-sheet date*) and for the (*period*) then ended, management of the Company has prepared, and furnished to our auditors (*state name and address of auditors*), a description and evaluation of certain contingencies, including those set forth below involving matters with respect to which you have been engaged and to which you have devoted substantive attention on behalf of the Company in the form of legal consultation or representation. These contingencies are regarded by management of the Company as material for this purpose.[2] Your response should include matters that existed at (*balance-sheet date*) and during the period from that date to the date of your response.

Pending or Threatened Litigation (excluding unasserted claims)

(Ordinarily, the information would include the following: (1) the nature of the litigation; (2) the progress of the case to date; (3) how management is responding or intends to respond to the litigation (for example, to contest the case vigorously or to seek an out-of-court settlement); and (4) an evaluation of the likelihood of an unfavorable outcome and an estimate, if one can be made, of the amount or range of potential loss.)

Please furnish to our auditors such explanation, if any, that you consider necessary to supplement the foregoing information, including an explanation of those matters as to which your views may differ from those stated and an identification of the omission of any pending or threatened litigation, claims, and assessments or a statement that the list of such matters is complete.

Unasserted Claims and Assessments (considered by management to be probable of assertion, and that, if asserted, would have at least a reasonable possibility of an unfavorable outcome)

(Ordinarily, the information would include the following: (1) the nature of the litigation; (2) how management intends to respond if the claim is asserted; and (3) an evaluation of the likelihood of an unfavorable outcome and an estimate, if one can be made, of the amount or range of potential loss.)

Please furnish to our auditors such explanation, if any, that you consider necessary to supplement the foregoing information, including an explanation of those matters as to which your views may differ from those stated.

We understand that whenever, in the course of performing legal services for us with respect to a matter recognized to involve an unasserted possible claim or assessment that may call for financial statement disclosure, if you have formed a professional conclusion that we should disclose or consider disclosure concerning such possible claim or assessment, as a matter of professional responsibility to us, you will so advise us and will consult with us concerning the question of such disclosure and the applicable requirements of Statement of Financial Accounting Standards No. 5. Please specifically confirm to our auditors that our understanding is correct.

Please specifically identify the nature of and reasons for any limitation on your response.

(The auditor may request the client to inquire about additional matters, for example, unpaid or unbilled charges or specified information on certain contractually assumed obligations of the company, such as guarantees of indebtedness of others.)

Very truly yours,

(*Authorized Signature for Client*)[3]

---

[1]The sending of this letter should be timed so that the lawyer's response is dated as close as practicable to the date of the auditor's report. However, the auditor and client should consider early mailing of a draft inquiry as a convenience for the lawyer in preparing a timely response to the formal letter of inquiry.

[2]Management may indicate a specific materiality limit if an understanding has been reached with the auditor.

[3]If a client has not needed to retain legal counsel, the auditors may express an unqualified opinion on the financial statements even though they have not obtained a letter from legal counsel of the Company. In these circumstances, the auditors should obtain written representation from the Company that legal counsel has not been retained for matters concerning business operations that may involve current or prospective litigation.

Management Representations Letters

After studying this lesson you should be able to :

1. *Understand the auditor's responsibility to obtain a required management representations letter in accordance with AICPA Professional Standards.*
2. *Familiarize yourself with the language used in a typical management representations letter.*

I. Responsibilities under AICPA Professional Standards -- The relevant AICPA guidance is provided by AU 580: "Written Representations." This pronouncement states that the auditor's objectives are "to

- **A.** obtain written representations from management that they believe they have fulfilled their responsibility for the preparation and fair presentation of the financial statements and for the completeness of information provided to the auditor;
- **B.** support other audit evidence relevant to the financial statements by means of written representations determined necessary by the auditor; and
- **C.** respond appropriately to written representations provided by management . . . or if management . . .(does) not provide the written representations requested by the auditor."

II. Document Verbal Responses to Auditor's Inquiries

- **A.** An auditor is required to obtain written representations from management to corroborate management's verbal responses to important inquiries by the auditor.
- **B.** This letter from management is addressed directly to the auditors.
- **C.** The letter should be signed by those members of management with overall responsibility for financial and operating matters - ordinarily the chief executive officer (CEO) and the chief financial officer (CFO).
  - **1.** Their unwillingness to sign the management representations letter would be a scope limitation probably resulting in a disclaimer of opinion or withdrawal from the engagement.
  - **2.** If any such representations are contradicted by other evidence -- the auditor should investigate the circumstances and evaluate the implications to reliance on other management representations.
- **D.** The representations letter should cover all periods encompassed by the auditor's report. If current management was not present for all periods covered, tailor the representations to the circumstances.
- **E.** Date of the management representations letter -- the representations letter should be dated the same as the date of the auditor's report.

III. The Specific Content of the Representations Depend on the Circumstances -- Usually include the following provisions as applicable.

- **A. Regarding the financial statements**
  - **1.** That management is responsible for the fairness of the financial statements.
  - **2.** That management is responsible for internal control over financial reporting.
  - **3.** That management is responsible for internal control to prevent and detect fraud.
  - **4.** That significant assumptions used for any accounting estimates are reasonable.
  - **5.** That related party transactions have been properly accounted for and disclosed.

6. That subsequent events have been properly accounted for and disclosed.
7. That any uncorrected misstatements are immaterial.
8. That the effects of litigation and claims have been properly accounted for and disclosed.

B. Regarding the information provided that

1. All relevant financial records and unrestricted access to personnel were made available to the auditor.
2. All transactions have been recorded.
3. Management has made available the results of their assessment of fraud risks.
4. Regarding fraud, there is no fraud involving management or employees having significant internal control responsibilities, or others where the financial statement effect could be material.
5. Management has no knowledge of suspected fraud communicated by employees, former employees, or others.
6. Management has disclosed all instances of noncompliance with laws and regulations relevant to financial reporting.
7. There are no (undisclosed) litigations, claims, and assessments relevant to the financial statements.
8. Management has disclosed all known related party relationships and transactions.

IV. Sample Management Representations Letter

Illustrative Management Representation Letter

(Prepared on the Entity's Letterhead)

(To Auditor)

(Date)

This representation letter is provided in connection with your audit of the financial statements of ABC Company, which comprise the balance sheet as of December 31, 20XX, and the related statements of income, changes in stockholders' equity, and cash flows for the year then ended, and the related notes to the financial statements, for the purpose of expressing an opinion on whether the financial statements are presented fairly, in all material respects, in accordance with accounting principles generally accepted in the United States (U.S. GAAP).

Certain representations in this letter are described as being limited to matters that are material. Items are considered material, regardless of size, if they involve an omission or misstatement of accounting information that, in the light of surrounding circumstances, makes it probable that the judgment of a reasonable person relying on the information would be changed or influenced by the omission or misstatement.

Except where otherwise stated below, immaterial matters less than $[insert amount] collectively are not considered to be exceptions that require disclosure for the purpose of the following representations. This amount is not necessarily indicative of amounts that would require adjustment to or disclosure in the financial statements.

We confirm that (*, to the best of our knowledge and belief, having made such inquiries as we considered necessary for the purpose of appropriately informing ourselves) [as of (date of auditor's report),*]:

Financial Statements

- We have fulfilled our responsibilities, as set out in the terms of the audit engagement dated (insert date), for the preparation and fair presentation of the financial statements in accordance with U.S. GAAP.

- We acknowledge our responsibility for the design, implementation, and maintenance of internal control relevant to the preparation and fair presentation of financial statements that are free from material misstatement, whether due to fraud or error.

- We acknowledge our responsibility for the design, implementation, and maintenance of internal control to prevent and detect fraud.

- Significant assumptions used by us in making accounting estimates, including those measured at fair value, are reasonable.

- Related party relationships and transactions have been appropriately accounted for and disclosed in accordance with the requirements of U.S. GAAP.

- All events subsequent to the date of the financial statements and for which U.S. GAAP requires adjustment or disclosure have been adjusted or disclosed.

- The effects of uncorrected misstatements are immaterial, both individually and in the aggregate, to the financial statements as a whole. A list of the uncorrected misstatements is attached to the representation letter.

- The effects of all known actual or possible litigation and claims have been accounted for and disclosed in accordance with U.S. GAAP.

(Any other matters that the auditor may consider appropriate.)

Information Provided

- We have provided you with:
    - Access to all information, of which we are aware that is relevant to the preparation and fair presentation of the financial statements such as records, documentation and other matters;
    - Additional information that you have requested from us for the purpose of the audit; and
    - Unrestricted access to persons within the entity from whom you determined it necessary to obtain audit evidence.

- All transactions have been recorded in the accounting records and are reflected in the financial statements.

- We have disclosed to you the results of our assessment of the risk that the financial statements may be materially misstated as a result of fraud.

- We have (*no knowledge of any*) (*disclosed to you all information that we are aware of regarding*) fraud or suspected fraud that affects the entity and involves:
    - Management;
    - Employees who have significant roles in internal control; or
    - Others when the fraud could have a material effect on the financial statements

- We have (*no knowledge of any*) (*disclosed to you all information that we are aware of regarding*) allegations of fraud, or suspected fraud, affecting the entity's financial statements communicated by employees, former employees, analysts, regulators or others.

- We have disclosed to you all known instances of noncompliance or suspected noncompliance with laws and regulations whose effects should be considered when preparing financial statements.
- We (*have disclosed to you all known actual or possible*) (*are not aware of any pending or threatened*) litigation, claims, and assessments whose effects should be considered when preparing the financial statements [and we have not consulted legal counsel concerning litigation, claims, or assessments].
- We have disclosed to you the identity of the entity's related parties and all the related party relationships and transactions of which we are aware.

(*Any other matters that the auditor may consider necessary.*)

(*Name of Chief Executive Officer and Title*)

(*Name of Chief Financial Officer and Title*)

Related Party Issues

After studying this lesson, you should be able to:

1. *Know the definition of the term "elated parties.*
2. *Understand the auditor's responsibility to address related-party issues in accordance with AICPA Professional Standards.*

I. Responsibilities under AICPA Professional Standards -- The relevant AICPA guidance is provided by AU 580: "Related Parties." This pronouncement states that the auditor's objectives are:

A. to obtain an understanding of related party relationships and transactions to address fraud risk factors and evaluate whether the financial statements achieve fair presentation and

B. to obtain sufficient appropriate audit evidence about whether related party relationships and transactions are properly accounted for and adequately disclosed in the financial statements.

II. FASB Definition of Related Parties

> **Definition:**
> *Related parties*: "Affiliates of the enterprise; entities for which investments are accounted for by the equity method by the enterprise; trusts for the benefit of employees, such as pension and profit-sharing trusts that are managed by or under the trusteeship of management; principal owners of the enterprise; its management; members of the immediate families of principal owners of the enterprise and its management; and other parties with which the enterprise may deal if one party controls or can significantly influence the management or operating policies of the other to an extent that one of the transacting parties might be prevented from fully pursuing its own separate interests." The essence of this definition is that one party has the ability to influence the conduct of the other party.

A. Definition (from the SAS)

> **Definition:**
> *Arm's-length transaction*: A transaction conducted on such terms and conditions between a willing buyer and a willing seller who are unrelated and are acting independently of each other and pursuing their own best interests.

III. The Historical Cost Principle -- The historical cost principle in accounting is based on the notion of an exchange price negotiated in an "arms-length" transaction, which results in an accurate measure of the value exchanged. However, related parties could potentially set the transaction price at whatever value they wish, without regard to the "real" economic value. Auditors are generally not in a position to provide reliable, independent appraisals of transaction prices between related parties. As a result, auditors are particularly concerned with the adequacy of disclosure about transactions between related parties.

IV. The Auditor's Responsibilities Under the SAS

A. Risk assessment -- The auditor should assess the risk of material misstatement that could result from the entity's related party relationships and transactions. The auditor should view any significant related party transactions outside the entity's normal course of business as "significant risks."

1. The auditor should inquire of management about

a. The identity of the entity's related parties;

b. The nature of the relationships involved; and

c. Whether the entity engaged in any transactions with those related parties during the period, and, if so, the purpose of the transactions.

2. The auditor should also inquire about (and perform other risk assessment procedures) to obtain an understanding of the applicable controls established to (a) identify and account for such related party relationships and transactions; (b) authorize and approve significant transactions with related parties, as well as those that are outside the normal course of business. (The risk of management override of controls is higher when management has significant influence with parties with whom the entity does business.)

   a. Examples of arrangements that may indicate undisclosed related party relationships

      i. Participation in partnerships with other parties;

      ii. Agreements with other parties having conditions outside the normal course of business; or

      iii. Guarantees involving other parties.

   b. Examples of transactions outside the normal course of business

      i. Complex equity transactions (restructurings or acquisitions);

      ii. Transactions with offshore entities;

      iii. Sales transactions with unusually large discounts; or

      iv. Transactions with circular arrangements (such as repurchase agreements).

3. The auditor should stay alert for any indications of related party relationships or transactions that management has failed to disclose to the auditor. The auditor should be attentive to such matters when

   a. reviewing bank confirmations and other records or documents; and

   b. reading the minutes of meetings of those charged with governance.

4. Relevant information about the related parties should be shared with the members of the engagement team.

B. **Response to risk assessment --** The auditor should obtain sufficient appropriate audit evidence about the assessed risks of material misstatement due to related party relationships and transactions.

1. **When there is a significant risk about related party transactions --** The auditor may perform substantive procedures such as the following:

   a. Confirm specific terms of the transactions with the related parties;

   b. Inspect evidence in the possession of the entity or the related party;

   c. Confirm (or discuss) information with intermediaries, such as banks or others;

   d. Review audited financial statements, income tax returns, or reports issued by regulatory agencies to assess the financial condition of the other party.

2. Procedures to obtain an understanding of the business relationships involving a related party (and to determine the need for further substantive procedures) include the following:

   a. Inquiries of management and those charged with governance;

   b. Inquiries of the related parties;

   c. Inspection of contracts with the related party;

   d. Review of employee whistle-blowing reports, if available; and
   e. Background research, perhaps using the Internet.

C. **Evaluation --** The auditor should evaluate whether the identified related party relationships and transactions have been appropriately accounted for and properly disclosed and whether the financial statements achieve "fair presentation" regarding those related party relationships and transactions. The substance of the transactions is normally more important that their legal form.

   1. If the auditor identifies related party transactions not previously disclosed by management -- The auditor should
      a. Communicate relevant information to members of the engagement team;
      b. Ask management to identify all transactions with the newly identified related party;
      c. Inquire about why the entity's controls did not identify the related party relationship;
      d. Perform appropriate substantive audit procedures;
      e. Reconsider the risk that there may be other undisclosed related party relationships; and
      f. Evaluate whether management's failure to disclose the matter might have been intentional.
   2. If the auditor identifies significant related party transactions outside the entity's normal course of business -- The auditor should determine whether those transactions have been appropriately authorized. The auditor should also inspect any underlying agreements to evaluate whether the terms are consistent with management's explanations or whether the business rationale might suggest fraud.

D. **Communication --** The auditor should communicate with those charged with governance any significant matters involving the entity's related parties.

E. **Documentation --** The auditor should include in the audit documentation the names of the identified related parties and the nature of the related party relationships and transactions.

V. **In Summary --** Procedures to identify the existence of related parties:

A. Inquire of management as to the existence of any related party relationships.

B. Review prior year's audit documentation for continuing engagements.

C. Might inquire of the predecessor auditors for a first-year engagement (if applicable).

D. Review any applicable SEC filings (for public companies) that list related parties.

E. Review stockholder listings of closely held companies to identify major stockholders.

VI. **In Summary --** Procedures to Identify transactions with the related parties

A. Inquire of management about any such transactions. Review any conflict-of-interest statements furnished to the company by management;

B. Review minutes of board of directors' meetings for mention of significant activities with related parties;

C. Review the accounting records for any large, unusual, or nonrecurring transactions, especially near the end of the reporting period;

D. Examine underlying documents for unusual or large transactions (such as investment transactions) and transactions that have terms or conditions that are inconsistent with prevailing market conditions (such as loans with abnormal interest rates or without stated maturity dates):

   1. Guarantees of loans (either payable or receivable) might be identified on confirmations of such loans;

2. Transactions with major customers, suppliers, borrowers, or lenders might indicate undisclosed relationships; and
3. Invoices from law firms might indicate work performed for related parties or related party transactions.

Subsequent Events and Related Issues

After studying this lesson, you should be able to:

1. *Know what is meant by the term subsequent events, and distinguish between those that require adjustments to the financial statement and those that require disclosure without adjustment.*
2. *Understand the auditing procedures associated with identifying subsequent events issues.*
3. *Recognize the effect that subsequent events issues may have on dating the auditor's report.*
4. *Understand the auditor's responsibilities when subsequently discovered facts become known to the auditor before (and after) the report release date.*
5. *Understand the predecessor auditor's responsibility when considering the reissuance of the auditor's report on prior period financial statements.*

I. Responsibilities under AICPA Professional Standards -- The relevant AICPA guidance is provided by AU 560: "Subsequent Events and Subsequently Discovered Facts." This pronouncement states that the auditor's objectives are

A. To obtain sufficient appropriate audit evidence about whether subsequent events are properly reflected in the financial statements;

B. To respond appropriately to subsequently discovered facts; and

C. For a predecessor auditor who is requested to reissue a previously issued report, to perform specified procedures to determine whether the previously issued report is still appropriate.

> **Definitions:**
> *Subsequent events*: Events occurring between the date of the financial statements and the date of the auditor's report.
>
> *Subsequent discovered facts:* Facts that become known to the auditor after the date of the auditor's report that, had they been known to the auditor at that date, may have caused the auditor to revise the auditor's report.

II. Subsequent Events Requiring Adjustment -- Where such an event provides new or better information about circumstances in existence as of the balance sheet date.

> **Example:**
> A lawsuit that could only be estimated at the balance sheet date was settled for a fixed amount prior to the issuance of the audit report; with the benefit of this new information, there is no need to estimate the financial statement consequences, since the actual consequence is now known and can be used to adjust the income statement and balance sheet.

III. Subsequent Events Requiring Disclosure Only -- Where disclosure of a material event or transaction is necessary so that the financial statements will not be misleading, even though the subsequent events issue is unrelated to circumstances existing at the balance sheet date.

> **Example:**
> After the balance sheet date, a tornado wiped out the company's facilities and the company had no casualty insurance; disclosure would be required to prevent financial statement readers from being misled about the entity's circumstances, but adjustment would not be required since the financial statement presentation was appropriate at year-end.

IV. Audit Procedures Regarding Subsequent Events

- **A.** Inquire of management. Include an appropriate reference to such subsequent events in the management representations letter. The auditor should also obtain an understanding of management's procedures to identify subsequent events, as appropriate.
- **B.** Review the minutes of meetings of those charged with governance. (Include all meetings up to the date of the audit report.)
- **C.** The lawyer's letter may be relevant to this issue (regarding legal contingencies).
- **D.** Scan journals and ledgers subsequent to year-end (through fieldwork) for any "unusual" items.

V. Facts Known Before the Report Release Date -- Subsequently discovered facts that became known to the auditor before the report release date

- **A.** The auditor should discuss the matter with management (and possibly those charged with governance) and determine whether the financial statements require revision. If so, the auditor should inquire as to how management will address the matter.
- **B. If management revises the financial statements --** The auditor should perform appropriate audit procedures on the revision.
- **C. If management does not revise the financial statements --** If the auditor believes that revision is necessary, the auditor should appropriately modify the opinion.

VI. Facts Known After the Report Release Date -- Subsequently discovered facts that became known to the auditor after the report release date

- **A.** The auditor should discuss the matter with management (and possibly those charged with governance) and determine whether the financial statements require revision. If so, the auditor should inquire as to how management will address the matter.
- **B. If management revises the financial statements --** The auditor should
  1. Perform appropriate audit procedures on the revision;
  2. Assess whether management's actions are timely and appropriate to ensure that users are informed; and
  3. If the opinion on the revised financial statements differs from that previously expressed; add an emphasis-of-matter or other matter paragraph (that identifies the date of the previous report, the opinion previously expressed, and the reason for the different opinion now expressed).
- **C. If management does not revise the financial statements --** If the auditor believes that revision is necessary, the auditor should determine whether those financial statements have already been made available to third parties.
  1. If the financial statements have not been made available to third parties -- the auditor should notify management and those charged with governance that the financial statements should not be made available to third parties before making necessary revisions and a new audit report has been provided.

2. If the financial statements have been made available -- the auditor should determine whether management has taken timely and appropriate steps to ensure that users have been informed not to rely on those financial statements.

3. If management does not take the necessary steps to inform the users -- the auditor should notify management and those charged with governance that the auditor will try to prevent users' reliance on the auditor's report.

VII. If a Predecessor Auditor Reissues the Auditor's Report

A. The predecessor should perform the following procedures to determine whether the previously issued auditor's report is still appropriate:

1. Read the financial statements of the subsequent period (and compare those financial statements with the ones previously audited and reported on to identify any significant changes);

2. Inquire of and request written representations from management about any issues, including subsequent events, that might affect the previous representations from management; and

3. Obtain a representation letter from the successor auditor about any known matters affecting the financial statements audited by the predecessor.

B. **If a subsequently discovered fact becomes known to the predecessor**

1. The predecessor auditor should discuss the matter with management (and possibly those charged with governance) and determine whether the financial statements require revision. If so, the auditor should inquire as to how management will address the matter.

2. If management revises the financial statements and the predecessor auditor plans to issue a new auditor's report -- the predecessor should:

a. Perform the procedures necessary to evaluate the revision (and date the audit report appropriately or dual-date the report for the revision);

b. Assess steps taken by management to ensure that users do not rely on the erroneous financial statements; and

c. If the opinion on the revised financial statements differs from that previously expressed, add an emphasis-of-matter or other matter paragraph (that identifies the date of the previous report, the opinion previously expressed, and the reason for the different opinion now expressed).

VIII. Dating the Auditor's Report -- Applicable to subsequent events, as well as to subsequently discovered facts involving the auditor or the predecessor auditor.

A. **Dating the auditor's report --** The auditor's report should not be dated earlier than the date on which the auditor has obtained "sufficient appropriate audit evidence to support the opinion."

1. Earlier auditing standards used to emphasize the "completion of fieldwork" as the relevant date for the audit report.

2. Current standards emphasize that the audit report should not be dated before the completion of fieldwork, and may be dated later than that. For example, management must take responsibility for the financial statement presentation, including footnotes; and the auditor must review and evaluate the audit documentation before having "sufficient appropriate evidence" both of which may follow the so-called completion of fieldwork.

B. **Subsequent events --** Dating the auditor's report when a subsequent event occurs after the completion of fieldwork but prior to the issuance of the auditor's report

1. If the financial statements are adjusted without any accompanying disclosure, the report should be dated whenever the auditor has obtained "sufficient appropriate audit

evidence" (which may be the completion of fieldwork or later). In this case, there is no need to consider "dual dating."

2. If the financial statements are (a) adjusted along with additional footnote disclosure; or (b) disclosure is added without adjustment - the audit report may be either "dual dated" (using one date for the overall audit report and a later date to address a specific subsequent event) or the entire audit report may be dated as of the later date (which makes the auditor responsible, in general, for all subsequent events up to that later date).

Example:
"Dual dating" the audit report: "February 16, 20X1, except for Note XY, as to which the date is March 1, 20X1"

C. **Subsequently discovered facts --** If management revised the financial statements

1. **Before the report release date --** The auditor should either date the auditor's report as of a later date (and extend the audit procedures to the new date and obtain an updated management representations letter as of the new date) or dual-date the auditor's report for the revision.

2. **After the report release date (also applicable to a predecessor auditor) --** The auditor should date the audit report appropriately or dual-date the report for the revision.

Going Concern Issues

After studying this lesson, you should be able to:

1. *Know the indicators that would cause the auditor to have "substantial doubt about an entity's ability to continue as a going concern" (and the audit procedures that would likely detect such issues).*
2. *Understand the audit reporting implications of going-concern issues.*
3. *Understand the additional evidence-gathering responsibilities (and documentation requirements) the auditor has when substantial doubt about the entity's ability to continue occurs.*

I. **Responsibilities under AICPA Professional Standards --** The relevant AICPA guidance is provided by AU 570: "The Auditor's Consideration of an Entity's Ability to Continue as a Going Concern." This pronouncement states that the auditor's objectives are to

  A. Evaluate and conclude whether there is substantial doubt about the entity's ability to continue as a going concern for a reasonable period of time;

  B. Assess the possible financial statement effects, including the adequacy of disclosure about the entity's ability to continue as a going concern for a reasonable period of time; and

  C. Determine the implications for the auditor's report.

> **Definition:**
> *Reasonable period of time*: A period of time not to exceed one year beyond the date of the financial statements being audited.

II. **Audit Procedures to Identify Whether There is "Substantial Doubt" --** The auditor's usual audit procedures would ordinarily be sufficient to identify circumstances related to a going-concern issue. In other words, the auditor normally does not need to design audit procedures to specifically search for going concern issues. Such procedures would include:

  A. Analytical procedures;

  B. Review for subsequent events;

  C. Review compliance with terms of loan agreements. (Noncompliance with debt covenants usually results in that debt becoming immediately due and payable!);

  D. Read the minutes of meetings of those charged with governance for any discussion of significant issues; and

  E. Inquire of the entity's attorney(s) about lawsuits by requesting a "lawyer's letter."

III. **Indicators of "Substantial Doubt"**

  A. **Negative trends --** recurring losses, negative cash flows, or working capital deficiencies.

  B. **Other indicators --** defaults on debt, violations of debt covenants, disposals of major assets, or restructuring of debt.

  C. **Internal matters --** labor problems, dependence on single projects or customers, or harmful long-term commitments.

  D. **External matters --** lawsuits, catastrophic losses, harmful legislation, a downturn in the economy causing many companies in an adversely affected industry to fail, or a loss of major customers or suppliers.

IV. Additional Evidence-Gathering Responsibilities -- When the auditor has "substantial doubt about the entity's ability to continue as a going concern," the auditor's reporting responsibilities extend to one year after the balance sheet date.

> **Note:**
> The auditor cannot be expected to predict the future, however!

- **A.** Inquire about management's strategy to overcome the financial difficulties for example, to dispose of assets, to borrow or restructure existing debt, to delay expenditures, or to issue additional stock. These are "mitigating factors" that might be expected to generate meaningful cash inflows or reduce the entity's cash outflows. The auditor should assess whether management's plans would likely mitigate the adverse effects of the entity's circumstances.
- **B.** Plan and perform audit procedures to evaluate the feasibility of those elements of management's plans deemed most important. For example, the auditor should evaluate the feasibility of management's plans to obtain additional financing or to dispose of certain assets.
- **C. Written representations --** The auditor should obtain written representations from management about two matters:
  1. Management's plans designed to mitigate the adverse effects of such conditions and the likelihood that those plans can be executed; and
  2. Management's belief that the financial statements disclose all relevant matters about the going-concern issue of which management is aware.

V. Reporting Responsibilities -- When the auditor continues to have substantial doubt about the entity's ability to continue as a going concern, despite management's plans to mitigate the adverse effects of such conditions:.

- **A.** Evaluate the adequacy of disclosure relative to the requirements of the applicable financial reporting framework. (If the auditor believes that this "substantial doubt" has been mitigated as a result of the perceived effectiveness of management's plans, the auditor should also consider the adequacy of the disclosure of those matters that initially caused the auditor to have substantial doubt, along with the appropriate disclosure of the mitigating factors.)
- **B.** The auditor should add an "emphasis-of-matter" (after the opinion paragraph) to draw the reader's attention to the going-concern uncertainties if the management's disclosure of these uncertainties is adequate and the auditor intends to issue an unqualified opinion. However, if the disclosures are inadequate, then the auditor should appropriately modify the opinion.
- **C.** The auditor could possibly disclaim an opinion if sufficient appropriate evidence cannot be obtained to evaluate the adequacy of the entity's financial statement treatment of these uncertainties in relation to GAAP (as a scope limitation). If disclaiming an opinion, the auditor should not include the emphasis-of-matter paragraph.
- **D.** The SAS points out that the auditor should not use "conditional language" in expressing a conclusion regarding the existence of substantial doubt about the entity's ability to continue as a going concern. As an example of inappropriate conditional language that is prohibited, the SAS offered the following: "The Company has been unable to renegotiate its expiring credit agreements. Unless the Company is able to obtain financial support, there is substantial doubt about its ability to continue as a going concern."

> Sample emphasis-of-matter paragraph (presented after the opinion paragraph):
>
> The accompanying financial statements have been prepared assuming that the Company will continue as a going concern. As discussed in Note X to the financial statements, the Company has suffered recurring losses from operations and has a net capital deficiency that raises substantial doubt about its ability to continue as a going concern. Management's plans in regard to these matters are also described in Note X. The financial statements do not include any adjustments that might result from the outcome of this uncertainty. Our opinion is not modified with respect to this matter.

VI. Documentation Requirements -- The auditor should document the following matters related to going-concern issues:

A. The conditions that caused the auditor to believe that there is substantial doubt about the entity's ability to continue as a going concern.

B. The elements of management's plans considered particularly important.

C. The procedures the auditor performed to evaluate those significant elements of management's plans, and the evidence obtained.

D. The auditor's conclusion as to whether substantial doubt about the entity's ability to continue as a going concern for a reasonable period of time remains or is alleviated by management's strategy.

E. The consideration and effect of that conclusion on the auditor's report.

VII. Required Communication with Those Charged with Governance -- When substantial doubt about the entity's ability to continue as a going concern remains, the auditor should communicate:

A. The nature of the conditions identified;

B. The possible effect on the financial statements and disclosures; and

C. The effects on the auditor's report.

Audit Evidence - Specific Audit Areas

Introduction to Auditing Individual Areas

After studying this lesson, you should be able to:

1. *Identify the four assertions for account balances at the end of the period as broad audit objectives applicable to balance sheet line items for which the auditor must gather evidence as a basis for evaluation.*
2. *Identify certain audit procedures that are generally applicable to each of these assertions and other audit procedures that are generally applicable to every individual audit area.*

I. **Audit Procedures Generally Applicable to the 4 "Assertions" for Account Balances --** Note that these assertions represent broad audit objectives for which the auditor must gather evidence to determine whether the financial statement elements are fairly presented in accordance with the applicable accounting framework (e.g., GAAP).

A. **Existence --** Related to the validity of recorded items.

1. **Confirmation --** (especially when concerned about overstatements.) For example, cash, accounts receivable, inventory held by others, and investments held by others.
2. **Observation --** especially for inventory or investment securities held by the entity.
3. **Agree (vouch) to underlying documents --** Agree items from the accounting record to the supporting source documents to evaluate the appropriateness of recorded items: for example, as an alternate procedure for accounts receivable; to verify additions to property, plant, and equipment accounts; and for various liabilities, such as notes payable.

B. **Completeness --** related to omissions of amounts that should have been recorded.

1. **Cutoff tests --** trace from supporting source documents back to the accounting records looking for omissions. For example, trace from shipping documents to cost of goods sold or to the sales journal, or perform a "search for unrecorded liabilities."
2. **Analytical procedures --** these are applicable to every audit area, but be specific: calculate a particular ratio or compare something specific to another specific thing!

C. **Rights and obligations --** related to any restrictions to the entity's rights to their assets or to the obligations for their liabilities.

1. **Inquire of applicable client personnel --** Inquire about compensating balances with banks, the use of specific assets as collateral for debts, review debt agreements for collateral, etc.; the management representation letter should document these inquiries regarding important matters.
2. **Examine authorization of transactions --** to ascertain whether any unusual conditions apply.

D. **Valuation and allocation --** related to the appropriateness of dollar measurements.

1. **Recalculate account balances --** (verify the client's calculations), for example, for depreciation expense and prepaid insurance.
2. **Trace to subsequent cash receipts or disbursements --** includes tracing to cash receipts or cash disbursements journal and to the applicable bank statement.
3. **Analytical procedures --** review the aged trial balance for accounts receivable to evaluate the allowance for uncollectibles. Test the accuracy of the aged categories by examining underlying invoices; review "receivers" for returns of sales.

4. **Examine published price quotations for fair value measurements, when applicable** -- verify mathematical accuracy. Verify that the supporting ledgers or other accounting records agree to the reported balance per the general ledger before performing other audit procedures on those supporting accounting records for purposes of reaching a conclusion about the fairness of the general ledger account balance involved. "Foot" and "cross-foot" the underlying records to verify that they, in fact, add up.

II. Audit Procedures Generally Applicable to Every Individual Audit Area

A. **Consider the implications of internal control** -- Remember the acronym **"SCARE"** [for "segregation of duties, controls (as in, physical controls), authorization, reviews (as in, performance reviews), and EDP (for information processing)]" discussed in connection with "Internal Control Concepts") to identify control activities of interest to the auditor relevant to planning the **nature, timing, and extent of substantive procedures** that underlie detection risk, based on the assessed level of control risk.

B. **Substantive procedures usually performed in every individual audit area**

1. Agree the financial statement elements (or the trial balance from which the financial statement elements are derived) to the underlying accounting records (i.e., to the general ledger).
2. Scan the entity's journals and ledgers for any "unusual" items.
3. Make appropriate inquiries of management and other personnel (and document those important inquiries and management's responses in the management representations letter).
4. Perform specific analytical procedures - consider historical trends and events within the industry.

Cash

After studying this lesson, you should be able to:

1. *Be familiar with the content of the standard bank confirmation form.*
2. *Verify the appropriateness of each of the items on an entity's bank reconciliation, supporting the entity's reported cash balance.*
3. *Understand what is meant by the term kiting and how the auditor might address this issue.*

I. Review the Client's Bank Reconciliation for Each Cash Account

A. Request a **"cutoff" bank statement** approximately 10 days after year-end, to test the reconciling items on the year-end bank reconciliation: (This request must come from management to the entity's financial institution to provide information directly to the entity's auditors.):

1. **Deposits in-transit --** Verify that items listed as deposits in transit on the bank reconciliation have been processed as deposits on the cutoff bank statement (testing for "existence/occurrence" regarding the validity of those reconciling items); these should appear in chronological order on the cutoff bank statement.
2. **Outstanding checks --** Look for checks processed with the cutoff bank statement and having a date prior to year-end; trace those items to the client's list of outstanding checks for "completeness." (Note that checks outstanding at year-end will not necessarily clear the bank in order or within the period encompassed by the cutoff bank statement.)

B. **Confirm** directly with the bank the balance according to the bank statement (Usually confirm 2 separate bank-related matters: (1) cash balances with emphasis on the "existence" assertion; and (2) liabilities to the bank with emphasis on the "completeness" assertion) -- Note that such evidence obtained from independent sources outside the client organization is viewed as very reliable evidence.

See the following example.

Sample Bank Reconciliation As of 12/31/X1:

Balance per bank @ 12/31/X1	$X[1]
Add: Deposits in Transit	X[2]
Less: Outstanding checks	(X)[3]
Adjusted balance as of 12/31/X1	$X
Balance per books @ 12/31/X1	X[4]
Add: Credits directly by bank (e.g., interest)	X[5]
Less: Charges by bank (service charges, etc.)	(X)[5]
Adjusted balance as of 12/31/X1	$X

Legend:

[1] Confirmed as of 12/31/X1... (A-3).

[2] Agreed to bank cutoff statement (A-4).

[3] Reviewed canceled checks (dated December or earlier and processed in January) returned with bank cutoff statement (A-4); no omissions from the outstanding check listing were noted.

[4] Agreed to General Ledger as of 12/31/X1.

[5] Agreed to client's December bank statement.

See the following Standard Form.

Standard Form to Confirm Account Balance Information with Financial Institutions

Customer Name

Financial Institution's Name and Address [ ] [ ]

We have provided to our accountants the following information as of the close of business on ________, 20___, regarding our deposit and loan balances. Please confirm the accuracy of the information, noting any exceptions to the information provided. If the balances have been left blank, please complete this from by furnishing the balance in the appropriate space below.* Although we do not request nor expect you to conduct a comprehensive, detailed search of your records, if during the process of completing this confirmation additional information about other deposit and loan accounts we may have with you comes to your attention, please include such information below. Please use the enclosed envelope to return the form directly to our accountants.

1. At the close of business on the date listed above, our records indicated the following deposit balance(s):

Account Name	Account No.	Interest Rate	Balance

2. We were directly liable to the financial institution for loans at the close of business on the date listed above as follows:

Account No./Description	Balance	Due Date	Interest Rate	Date through which interest is paid	Description of Collateral

Customer's Authorized Signature — Date

The information presented above by the customer is in agreement with our records. Although we have not conducted a comprehensive, detailed search of our records, no other deposit or loan accounts have come to our attention except as noted below.

Financial Institution Authorized Signature / Title — Date

Exceptions and/or comments

Please return this form directly to our accountants: [ ]

*Ordinarily, balances are intentionally left blank if they are not available at the time the form is prepared.

[ ] D 451 5951

Approved 1990 by American Bankers Association, American Institute of Certified Public Accountants, and Bank Administration Institute. Additional forms available from: AICPA - Order Department, P.O. Box 1003, NY, NY 10108-1003

II. Multiple Checking Accounts with Transfers Among Them

A. Prepare a schedule of interbank (or intercompany) transfers to verify that both sides of the transfer are properly accounted for (that is, verify that the cash receipts journal and the cash disbursements journal both reflect the transfer in the same proper period) and to detect any **"kiting."**

B. Kiting is an overstatement of the true cash balance at year-end caused by recording the receipt, while failing to record the disbursement, associated with a transfer between cash accounts. (Note that recording the disbursement, while failing to record the receipt part of a transfer between cash accounts would result in a misstatement -- however, it would be an understatement of the cash balance and, therefore, would be inconsistent with kiting, which results specifically in an overstatement.)

III. **If Fraud (Misappropriation) is Suspected --** The auditor may prepare a **"proof of cash"** -- This compares the beginning balance per the bank plus deposits minus checks clearing the bank versus the beginning balance per the books plus receipts minus disbursements according to the books.

IV. **Petty Cash --** May count cash on hand at the client's request. (If the auditor chooses to perform any specific audit procedures for an immaterial account, such as petty cash, analytical procedures are usually sufficient, such as simply comparing the current year's general ledger balance to the prior year's general ledger balance.)

V. **Inquire of Management --** About any **restrictions on cash balances.** If there is a minimum balance requirement for cash, then that restriction should be disclosed.

> **Note:**
> The "management representations letter" usually addresses any "compensating balances" (minimum balance requirements) that constitute a restriction on spendable cash. (The usual management representations comment that addresses all general restrictions on the entity's rights to its assets is: "The company has satisfactory title to all owned assets, and there are no liens or encumbrances on such assets nor has any asset been pledged as collateral.")

Accounts Receivable

After studying this lesson, you should be able to:

1. *Know how to identify the appropriate substantive audit procedures to address each of those assertions when auditing accounts receivable.*
2. *Recognize that the 4 assertions for account balances at the end of the period represent a framework for preparing an audit plan to evaluate the fairness of accounts receivable.*

I. **Recall the 4 Assertions --** That Professional Standards identify for account balances at the end of the period: (1) existence; (2) completeness; (3) rights and obligations; and (4) valuation and allocation.

A. Related to the **Existence/Occurrence Assertion** -- Confirm selected individual customers' accounts.

B. Verify that the subsidiary A/R ledger agrees or reconciles with the A/R general ledger balance:

1. Recall that the "accounting records" constitute one category of evidence. The second category is "other information" according to SAS No. 106 and is covered in the review module on Audit Evidence.
2. It is important to establish the logical connection between the detailed accounting records being used for the audit procedure (in this case, the subsidiary ledger of individual customer accounts) and that which is the object of the auditor's intended conclusions (specifically, the general ledger balance for A/R).

C. **Confirm all accounts --** That are determined to be individually material and confirm selected other accounts on a test basis.

1. **Positive confirmations --** Request a response whether the individual customer agrees or disagrees with the stated balance. A nonresponse indicates a situation that should be followed up by the auditor.
2. **Negative confirmations --** Request a response only if the individual customer disagrees with the stated balance.
   a. A nonresponse is taken as evidence supporting the client's representation.
   b. The risk is that the recipient of the request might have thrown it away without even verifying the balance owed.
   c. Accordingly, negative confirmations are usually used only for rather small balances under conditions of effective internal control (that is, low control risk).

D. **Investigate all "exceptions" (disagreements) received --** Determine whether the client's records are accurate and, if not, whether the financial statements are materially misstated.

E. If no response is received to a **positive confirmation** request, the auditor should send a second confirmation request, and perform **"alternate procedures"** if still no response is received.

1. **Subsequent cash receipts (the preferred alternate procedure) --** Trace collections on the account subsequent to the date of the confirmation to the cash receipts journal and to the bank statement (suggests the balance was valid if it was subsequently collected).
2. **Vouch to (inspect) the underlying documents (the last resort if the account has not been collected) --** Examine the documents (customer's purchase order, client's sales invoice, and shipping documents) supporting the validity ("occurrence") of the transactions comprising the account balance.

II. **Related to the Valuation Assertion --** Evaluate the reasonableness of management's estimates of "allowance for uncollectibles" and the "allowance for sales returns."

A. Note that confirmations may contribute, in part, to the auditor's conclusions about the **fairness of the dollar valuation**; however, that contribution relates to establishing the reasonableness of the gross A/R and additional procedures are required to assess the net realizable value of the A/R.

B. **Review the client's aged trial balance of accounts receivable**

1. Inquire about any large, delinquent items.

2. Estimate the percentage of uncollectible accounts within each category of age (based on prior year's working papers tempered by current economic conditions).

C. Review **"receivers" (documents used by the entity's receiving department to capture deliveries) after year-end** for sales returns; consider prior years' returns in view of current economic conditions.

D. Review **adjusting journal entries** (e.g. write-offs) for appropriate authorization.

III. **Related to the Completeness Assertion**

A. Perform a **"cutoff" test** of sales. Examine the shipping documents for the last few shipments before year-end and the first few shipments after year-end; compare these shipping documents with the related sales invoices to assess whether the sales were recorded in the appropriate period.

B. Compare these shipping documents around the end of the period with the related sales invoices (related to the sales journal) to assess whether the sales were recorded in the appropriate period.

C. Proper "cutoff" involves two assertions ("existence/occurrence" and "completeness"). Usually the auditor performs certain specific audit procedures directed at testing the validity of recorded transactions (i.e., existence/occurrence) but "completeness" is primarily addressed by these cutoff procedures (along with applicable analytical procedures).

IV. **Related to the Rights and Obligations Assertion --** Inquire of management:

A. About receivables pledged as collateral for debts (and review loan agreements to identify such collateral).

B. About shipments on consignment that are not actual sales.

C. About any receivables due from employees or management that should be classified separately from ordinary trade receivables.

D. Document such inquiries (and management's response) in the management representations letter.

> **Note:**
> Lapping is an attempt to cover up a theft of receipts, where a clerk might try to apply a later receipt to the prior customer's account (and so on) until the scam ends by writing off someone's account as uncollectible. Lapping is a type of fraud (specifically, misappropriation of assets) that is associated with an improper segregation of duties whereby someone with access to the customer's payment also has the authority to make entries in the accounting records to cover up the theft.

Inventory

After studying this lesson, you should be able to:

1. *Identify appropriate substantive audit procedures to address each of those assertions when auditing inventory.*
2. *Recognize that the 4 assertions for account balances at the end of the period represent a framework for preparing an audit plan to evaluate the fairness of inventory.*

> Recall the four "assertions" that that Professional Standards identify for account balances at the end of the period: (1) existence; (2) completeness; (3) rights and obligations; and (4) valuation and allocation.

I. **Relevant AICPA Guidance --** The relevant AICPA guidance is provided by AU 501: "Audit Evidence - Specific Considerations for Selected Items." Part of this standard focuses specifically on inventory, which is summarized here. The standard states that the auditor's objective is to obtain sufficient appropriate audit evidence about the **existence and condition** of inventory.

II. **Existence Assertion** -- Related to the "existence" assertion -- The auditor participates in the client's physical count of inventory (the observation of inventory):

   A. **Note --** The **client counts** the entire inventory and the **auditor observes** the client's taking of the inventory (while taking independent "test counts"). The auditor participates in this process for two primary reasons, referred to as "dual purpose" tests.

      1. **Internal Control Objectives --** The auditor should study the client's written procedures and instructions given to the employees or others counting the inventory to assess the adequacy of the design of these procedures in achieving an accurate physical count; the auditor's focus here is assessing control risk related to inventory reporting.

      2. **Substantive Audit Objectives --** The auditor should take a sample of inventory items and verify the physical existence of quantities reflected in the client's detailed records supporting the ending inventory; the auditor's focus here is assessing the fairness of the reported inventory.

   B. **Related audit procedures --** Emphasizing quantities:

      1. **Auditor's attendance at physical inventory counting --** Involves (a) inspecting the inventory to ascertain its existence and evaluate its condition (and performing test counts); (b) observing compliance with managements instructions and the performance of procedures for recording and controlling the results of the physical count; and (c) obtaining audit evidence about the reliability of management's count procedures;

      2. Review the client's written inventory-taking procedures to determine that the physical count will be complete and accurate (regarding dates, locations, personnel involved, and instructions about accounting for the prenumbered inventory tags, cutoff procedures, and error resolution procedures);

      3. Assessing the accuracy of the client's reported inventory **quantities**. The auditor should perform test counts for a sample of the prenumbered inventory tags, trace these counts into the client's count sheets (to verify the accuracy of the client's counts on a test basis) and to the client's final inventory listing that supports the general ledger balance. Note that the entity's final inventory listing (reflecting both quantities and dollar amounts) serves as the "subsidiary ledger" for inventory and represents the dollar amount for inventory to which the general ledger account will be adjusted;

4. Focus on the client's prenumbered inventory tags. Determine that all tags have been properly accounted for (that is, all tags are used, unused and returned, or have been voided and returned to a responsible official);

5. The auditor should be alert for and inquire about obsolete or damaged items (for example, dusty or damaged cartons) related to the valuation assertion; the auditor should also be alert for empty containers or hollow spaces.

C. If the physical count of inventory occurs on a date other than the date of the financial statements -- The auditor should perform audit procedures to determine whether changes in inventory between those dates are properly recorded.

D. If the auditor is unable to attend physical inventory counting due to unforeseen circumstances -- The auditor should make some physical counts on an alternative date and perform audit procedures on intervening transactions.

E. If attendance at physical inventory counting is impracticable -- The auditor should perform alternative audit procedures to obtain sufficient appropriate audit evidence regarding the existence and condition of inventory. If that is not possible, then the auditor should appropriately modify the auditor's opinion.

F. If there is a material amount of inventory stored in a **public warehouse,** the auditor can confirm such inventory with the custodian (or could consider physical observation).

III. **Valuation Assertion --** Related to the "Valuation" assertion:

A. **"Price tests" --** Regarding the **unit costs** (not selling prices!) attributed to inventory items:

1. Affected by the client's inventory methods (perpetual versus periodic inventory system) and cost flow assumptions (LIFO, FIFO, average);

2. For merchandising (nonmanufacturing) inventory: examine the appropriate underlying invoices;

3. For manufactured inventory -- Review the supporting job order cost records (or the process cost worksheets) and test to underlying documents.

B. **Test extensions --** Recalculate the product of quantity times cost/unit for selected items:

1. Add up these extensions to verify that the items tested are reflected in the total of the detailed inventory listing supporting the client's general ledger balance. This can be described as "verifying the mathematical accuracy" to establish the connection between the general ledger balance and the supporting detailed listing;

2. Scan the detailed inventory listing for any unusual items;

3. Review the client's reconciliation (or the adjusting journal entry) of the general ledger balance to the detailed inventory listing.

C. **Lower of cost or market considerations --** Inquire of management as to the existence of any damaged, obsolete, or excess inventory items that might require a write-down from historical cost to net realizable value; be attentive to these issues when participating in the observation of inventory.

IV. **Completeness Assertion --** Related to the "completeness" assertion. Procedures that might identify material omissions of inventory:

A. Test **inventory cutoff** (recall "FOB-shipping point" versus "FOB-destination" as a technical issue determining when title to goods is transferred):

1. **Related to increases in inventory --** Review "receivers" (receiving documents used by the entity's receiving department to capture deliveries) for a few days before and after year-end (part of "purchases" cutoff test);

2. **Related to decreases to inventory --** Review shipping documents for a few days before and after year-end (related to "sales" and, hence, "cost of goods sold" cutoff test).

B. **Analytical procedures (perhaps by location or by product-line) --** Compare the current year to the prior year and inquire about any significant differences in:

1. Gross profit rates;
2. Inventory turnover (primarily applicable to the "valuation" assertion regarding slow-moving inventory);
3. Shrinkage rates;
4. Total inventory.

V. Rights and Obligations Assertion

A. Inquire of management about any inventory that might be held on consignment or pledged as collateral for borrowings (and review loan agreements to identify such collateral).

B. Document such inquiries (and management's response) in the management representations letter.

VI. Other Issues Related to Auditing Inventory

A. **Use of specialists --** An auditor may need to engage an outside expert if the determination of **quantities** and/or **quality** is too complex (for example, electronics, precious jewels).

B. If an auditor is unable to verify the **beginning** inventory for a first-year audit, but is able to verify the **ending** inventory:

1. The auditor may render an opinion on the balance sheet and disclaim an opinion on the income statement, statement of retained earnings, and the statement of cash flows (due to the inability to verify cost of goods sold and, hence, net income).
2. It may be possible to establish the reasonableness of a new client's beginning inventory from alternate procedures -- through the use of analytical procedures or by reviewing a predecessor auditor's working papers.

Investments in Securities and Derivative Instruments

Derivative instruments, hedging activities, and investments in securities. In September 2000, the AICPA issued a new Statement on Auditing Standards (SAS 92) to clarify the auditor's responsibilities with respect to: (1) derivative instruments; (2) hedging activities; and (3) investments in securities (that is, all debt and equity securities, including those accounted for using the "equity method"). Note: In view of the recent issuance of this pronouncement, some degree of testing of this topic seems likely!

After studying this lesson, you should be able to:

1. *Understand the auditor's responsibilities under AICPA Professional Standards when auditing investments (including derivative instruments and hedging activities).*
2. *Recognize that the four assertions for account balances at the end of the period represent a framework for preparing an audit plan to evaluate the fairness of investments.*
3. *Identify appropriate substantive audit procedures to address each of those assertions when auditing investments.*

> **Note:**
> The Statements on Auditing Standards that preceded the clarified standards tended to address GAAP issues specifically, whereas the clarified standards are intended to be neutral with respect to the applicable financial reporting framework. Accordingly, the clarified standard no longer addresses FASB-specific issues related to investments and derivatives. The AICPA has indicated that more technical guidance about auditing derivatives will be provided in an AICPA Audit Guide on this topic.

I. **Relevant AICPA Guidance** -- The relevant AICPA guidance is provided by AU 501: "Audit Evidence — Specific Considerations for Selected Items." Part of this standard focuses specifically on investments in securities and derivative instruments, which is summarized here. The standard states that the auditor's objective is to obtain sufficient appropriate audit evidence about the **valuation** of investments in securities and derivative instruments.

II. **Auditing Investments in Securities** -- including derivatives, measured at fair value

 A. The auditor should determine whether the applicable financial reporting framework specifies the method to be used to determine fair value (and evaluate whether the stated fair value is consistent with that method).

 B. Quoted market prices (obtained from financial publications, national exchanges, or NASDAQ) usually provide sufficient evidence of fair value.

 C. If estimates of fair value are obtained from third-party sources (such as broker-dealers)—the auditor should obtain an understanding of their methods used.

 D. If management uses a valuation model—the auditor should obtain sufficient appropriate audit evidence about the fair value based on that model. It might be good to use more than one pricing source to see if there is any consensus when the valuation is subjective or sensitive to changes in the underlying assumptions.

 E. Impairment losses—the auditor should evaluate management's conclusion about the need to recognize an impairment loss, and obtain sufficient appropriate audit evidence supporting any impairment recorded. Determining whether a decline in fair value is other than temporary requires professional judgment, including consideration of the following:

1. Whether the fair value is significantly below the carrying value (and the period of time for which that has been the case);
2. Whether the financial condition of the issuer has deteriorated;
3. Whether the security has been downgraded by a rating agency;
4. Whether dividends have been reduced or eliminated or scheduled interest payments have not been made; or
5. Whether the entity recorded losses from the security after the period-end.

F. Unrealized appreciation or depreciation due to the ineffectiveness of a hedge—the auditor should obtain an understanding of the methods used to determine whether the hedge is effective, including the portion that is ineffective.

III. **Investments in Securities When Valuations Are Based on Cost --** The usual auditing procedures may include inspection of documentation of the purchase price, confirmation with outside parties, and testing the amortization of any discount or premium.

IV. **Investments in Securities When Valuations are Based on the Investee's Financial Results --** (Another SAS addresses investments accounted for using the equity method.)

A. **Reading the audited financial statements of the investee may provide sufficient appropriate audit evidence --** if unable to obtain sufficient appropriate audit evidence, the auditor should determine the effect on the auditor's report.

B. **May need to obtain additional audit evidence --** When there are significant differences in fiscal year-ends or in accounting principles used, the auditor may make inquiries of investor management about the investee. The auditor may need to obtain evidence about any related party transactions between the investor and investee to evaluate the adequacy of disclosure about related party issues. If there is a lack of comparability, owing to different fiscal year-ends, the auditor may need to add an emphasis-of-matter paragraph to the auditor's report.

V. **Summary of Procedures with Emphasis on 4 Balance-sheet-related Assertions --** Summary of procedures used in auditing traditional investment securities (that is, stocks and bonds) with emphasis on the 4 balance-sheet-related assertions.

A. **Related to the Existence Assertion --** the auditor mainly uses inspection and confirmation.

1. Physically inspect any securities in the possession of the client entity.
2. Confirm any stocks and bonds held by an independent custodian.

B. **Related to the Completeness Assertion --** the auditor primarily uses analytical procedures to address the risk of omissions.

1. Evaluate investment income or loss accounts:
   a. Verify revenue through confirmation when investments are held by an independent custodian;
   b. May trace cash receipts to a bank statement; and
   c. May recalculate the interest income on debt instruments or dividends received on stock investments.
2. Compare dividends, interest, or other investment income (loss) to prior year's working papers for reasonableness; dividends can be verified by consulting dividend record books produced by commercial investment advisory services.
3. Review the minutes of the meetings of those charged with governance for approval of any large transactions.

C. **Related to the Valuation Assertion --** The appropriate audit procedures will vary with the nature of the securities involved.

1. For bonds—verify the interest earned by calculations (based on the face value, interest yield, and period held); review the amortization of any premium or discount; inquire about management's intention to hold the security to maturity (and document that inquiry in the management representations letter).
2. For investments (in stocks or bonds) that are marked to market as required by the applicable accounting standards:
    a. Compare the carrying value at the beginning of the period to the prior year's working papers; agree to underlying documents, examine canceled checks for any current year additions to investments and trace the proceeds of any sales to a bank statement.
    b. Verify the year-end fair value (trace to an independent outside source, such as the *Wall Street Journal* or other appropriate quotation) — evaluate the adequacy of disclosure as required by the applicable accounting standards.
    c. Inquire of management about any impairments that may be other than temporary.
3. For investments in stock accounted for by the equity method
    a. Compare the carrying value at the beginning of the period to the prior year's audit working papers; agree (vouch) transactions to underlying documents and examine canceled checks for any current year's additions to investments.
    b. Examine the investee's current year's audited financial statements to verify the investor's percentage share of income (loss) and any dividend distributions.
    c. Inquire of management about any impairments relative to the investment's carrying value.

D. **Related to the Rights and Obligations Assertion --** the auditor primarily uses inquiry and review.

1. Inquire about management's intent and ability affecting investment classifications (and document the inquiry in the management representations letter)—recall the following basic GAAP considerations:
    a. Trading securities
        i. Balance sheet—Reported at fair value (in current assets).
        ii. Income statement—Unrealized holding gains/losses should be reported on the income statement (include interest and dividends, too).
    b. Available-for-sale securities
        i. Balance sheet—should be reported at fair value (either current or noncurrent assets, as appropriate); use unrealized holding gains and losses as a separate component of stockholders' equity.
        ii. Income statement—the unrealized holding gains/losses should be reported in other comprehensive income, not included in net income!
    c. Held-to-maturity (debt) securities
        i. Balance sheet—should be reported at the amortized cost basis (either as current or noncurrent assets, as appropriate).
        ii. Income statement—No recognition of fluctuations in market value should be recorded! Should report interest as revenue.
2. Inquire of management about any restrictions applicable to investments (including any securities pledged as collateral for debt).
3. Review cash receipts and cash disbursements subsequent to year-end for any material transactions affecting investments, perhaps requiring disclosure.

Fixed Assets

Since the composition of the fixed assets' balance is usually substantially carried over from one period to the next, the auditor usually emphasizes substantive tests of transactions (that is, the continuing auditor usually verifies the ending balance by examining the debits and credits that caused the balance to change from the prior year).

After studying this lesson, you should be able to:

1. *Identify the appropriate substantive audit procedures to address each of those assertions when auditing fixed assets.*
2. *Recognize that the four assertions for account balances at the end of the period represent a framework for preparing an audit plan to evaluate the fairness of fixed assets.*

> Recall the four "assertions" that Professional Standards identify for account balances at the end of the period: (1) existence; (2) completeness; (3) rights and obligations; and (4) valuation and allocation.

I. **Existence Assertion --** Related to the "existence" assertion:
   - A. Consider the adequacy of the accounting records -- Verify that the client's detailed fixed asset listing supports the related general ledger account balance.
   - B. **For additions --** Vouch to (inspect) the underlying documents (examine the purchase order, vendor's invoice, and the entity's canceled check if payment has been made); look for approval in the minutes of meetings of those charged with governance if the addition is a "major" one.
   - C. **For disposals --** Trace any proceeds received to the cash receipts journal and bank statement; review for appropriate approval.

> **Note**: Instead of performing tests of ending balances, the continuing auditor will normally verify the appropriateness of the year-end balance of fixed assets by performing substantive tests of transactions. In other words, if there are relatively few transactions that have caused the fixed asset balance to change from last year to this year, the auditor will, in effect, back into the ending balance by taking the beginning balance (audited last year), add any additions, and subtract any disposals. Since there are likely only a few additions and/or disposals, it is more efficient to examine those few transactions, rather than verify a sample of the individual items that comprise the year-end fixed asset balance.

II. **Valuation Assertion --** Related to the "valuation" assertion:
   - A. Review the calculations for depreciation expense -- compare the useful lives and methods used to prior years for consistency, and recalculate on a test basis.
   - B. Consider whether there have been any "impairments" of long-lived assets requiring a write-down from the historical cost-based carrying value - make appropriate inquiries of management (and document such inquiries and management's response in the management representations letter).

III. **Completeness Assertion --** Related to the "completeness" assertion.
   - A. Review the client's "repairs and maintenance expense" account and examine underlying documents for material items to determine whether any of those recorded expenses should instead be capitalized.

B. Review any lease agreements to determine if lease capitalization might be required.

IV. **Rights and Obligations Assertion --** Related to the "rights and obligations" assertion.

A. Inquire of management about any fixed assets pledged as security for borrowings (and review loan agreements to identify such collateral).

B. Document such inquiries (and management's response) in the management representations letter.

Current Liabilities

After studying this lesson, you should be able to:

1. *Recognize that the 4 assertions for account balances at the end of the period represent a framework for preparing an audit plan to evaluate the fairness of current liabilities.*
2. *Know how to identify appropriate substantive audit procedures to address each of those assertions when auditing current liabilities.*

I. **Accounts Payable (or Vouchers Payable) --** Primarily use substantive tests of ending balances.

A. Recall the difference between **accounts payable and vouchers payable** systems described in the review materials related to Internal Control -- Transaction Cycles:

1. **Accounts Payable --** In an accounts payable system, the payables are tracked by the name of the vendor. The total payable to another party, which constitutes a receivable to them, is susceptible to confirmation if desired.
2. **Vouchers Payable --** In a vouchers payable system, the payables are tracked by individual transaction without summarizing the amounts owed by vendor name. The total payable to another party is not susceptible to confirmation, only individual transactions could be confirmed.

B. Recall the four "assertions" that SAS No. 106, "Audit Evidence," identifies for account balances at the end of the period: (1) existence; (2) completeness; (3) rights and obligations; and (4) valuation and allocation.

C. Related to the **"completeness" assertion** (for liabilities, the auditor's primary concern involves "completeness" not "existence"!). Perform a **"search for unrecorded liabilities."** This is done toward the end of fieldwork to provide the best chance of detecting any significant unrecorded liabilities.

1. Review cash disbursements **subsequent to year-end** and, for all disbursements over some specified dollar amount (>$X), examine the related vendors' invoices and the entity's related receiving documents to identify transactions that should have been reported as liabilities as of year-end; compare those apparent liabilities to the details comprising the recorded payables to identify apparent liabilities that are unrecorded.
2. Examine any unpaid invoices on hand at the date of the "search" along with the entity's related receiving documents to identify any transactions that should have been reported as a liability as of year-end.
3. Inquire of management about their knowledge of any unrecorded liabilities and whether all invoices have been made available to the auditor. Document such inquiries and management's response in the management representations letter.

D. Related to the "existence" and "valuation" assertions:

1. Verify the mathematical accuracy of payables by comparing the general ledger balance to the supporting detailed listing of payables.
2. Vouch selected items to the underlying vendor's invoices.
3. Could "confirm" selected payables, but usually do not --Confirmation primarily establishes the validity ("existence") of the recorded items, but there is a relatively low risk that the company would overstate its true liabilities; the far bigger risk is that material liabilities may have been omitted (i.e., "completeness").

4. Usually "valuation" is not a significant audit issue, since there is a presumption that the client will pay 100% of what is owed; the auditor should look to see that the client takes advantage of any available cash discounts for prompt payment.

E. Related to the **"rights and obligations" assertion** -- Inspect the specific terms of the payables and inquire about any related party transactions. Separately classify notes payable for borrowings from accounts payable for ordinary operating activities.

II. **Other Current Liabilities --** The auditor uses analytical procedures extensively to evaluate other miscellaneous payables:

A. **Wages and salaries payable --** The auditor can compute the estimated accrual, in view of the number of days to be accrued relative to a whole pay period.

B. **Dividends payable --** The auditor can compute, in view of the declared dividends/share (per the minutes of meetings of those charged with governance) times the number of shares outstanding.

C. **Interest payable (and the related interest expense) --** The auditor can compute an estimate of accrued interest for the time period involved, based on the interest rate (and payment dates) specified in the underlying debt agreements.

Long-Term Liabilities

After studying this lesson, you should be able to:

1. *Recognize that the 4 assertions for account balances at the end of the period represent a framework for preparing an audit plan to evaluate the fairness of long-term liabilities.*
2. *Identify appropriate substantive audit procedures to address each of those assertions when auditing long-term liabilities.*

> Recall the 4 assertions that Professional Standards identify for account balances at the end of the period: (1) existence; (2) completeness; (3) rights and obligations; and (4) valuation and allocation.

I. Related to the "Completeness" Assertion -- Use substantive tests of transactions (to address decreases in debt):

- **A.** Verify due dates for payments in the loan agreements.
- **B.** Trace cash disbursements from the accounting records to the bank statement.
- **C.** Examine canceled notes if paid in full.
- **D.** Could confirm year-end balances, but confirmations are most applicable to establishing the validity of recorded items (that is, existence).

II. Related to the "Existence/Occurrence" Assertion -- Use substantive tests of transactions (to address increases in debt):

- **A.** Obtain copies of new loan agreements for the auditor's review and documentation.
- **B.** Verify authorization of new debt in minutes of meetings of those charged with governance.
- **C.** Trace receipts from the accounting records to the bank statement.

III. Related to the "Valuation" Assertion -- There are few measurement issues associated with most liabilities, but long-term liabilities should be based on present values:

- **A.** Trace related cash receipts and disbursements from the accounting records to the bank statements.
- **B.** Examine the underlying loan contracts related to the stated dollar amounts.
- **C.** Recalculate the amortization of any premium or discount using the effective interest method.
- **D.** Apply analytical procedures to the related expense accounts (e.g., interest) -- Note that the balance sheet item and the related income statement item are usually addressed on the same audit documentation (working paper).

IV. Related to the "Rights and Obligations" Assertion -- The auditor should make appropriate inquiries of management and review the loan documents:

- **A.** Debt covenants -- Important restrictions should be disclosed. (Note that violations of such covenants can cause the entire balance to become immediately payable.)
- **B.** Collateral -- Any assets pledged as security for the debt should be disclosed.
- **C.** The current portion of long-term debt should be reclassified to current liabilities -- Read the loan documents to identify the principal to be paid within the next year; examine the cash payments for the current-year installment paid if the debt is scheduled to be paid in equal installments.

Stockholders' Equity

After studying this lesson, you should be able to:

1. *Recognize that the 4 assertions for account balances at the end of the period represent a framework for preparing an audit plan to evaluate the fairness of stockholders' equity.*
2. *Identify appropriate substantive audit procedures to address each of those assertions when auditing stockholders' equity.*

> Recall the 4 assertions that Professional Standards identify for account balances at the end of the period: (1) existence; (2) completeness; (3) rights and obligations; and (4) valuation and allocation.

I. **Related to the "Existence" Assertion --** Confirm the outstanding shares of stock if there is an external registrar. (Verify that the stock was issued in accordance with the company's articles of incorporation and with the approval of those charged with governance.)

II. **Related to the "Completeness" Assertion**

   A. Review the minutes of meetings of those charged with governance to identify authorized transactions.

   B. Account for all certificate numbers to establish that no unauthorized shares were issued.

III. **Related to the "Rights and Obligations" Assertion**

   A. Review the minutes of board meetings to verify that any stock and dividend transactions were duly authorized by those charged with governance.

   B. Review contracts with employee stock option plans to verify compliance with such agreements.

   C. Inquire of management about any restrictions that might exist on the availability of retained earnings for purposes of dividend distribution -- the financial statements should disclose any restrictions on retained earnings available for dividend distribution.

IV. **Related to the "Valuation" Assertion**

   A. Review cash receipts and disbursements (and minutes of meetings of those charged with governance) for increases or decreases in stock accounts.

   B. Compare the subsidiary ledger to the general ledger stock accounts. (Examine stock certificates or read the applicable minutes of meetings of those charged with governance to verify the par or stated value per share.)

Payroll

When the auditor chooses to examine the payroll function handled "in-house" by the company (as opposed to an outside payroll service), recall the internal control considerations associated with the payroll transaction cycle covered in the lesson Specific Transaction Cycles.

After studying this lesson, you should be able to:

1. *Recognize that the 5 assertions for transactions and events during the period represent a framework for preparing an audit plan to evaluate the fairness of income statement items, such as payroll expense.*
2. *Identify appropriate substantive audit procedures to address payroll expense.*

> Recall the 5 assertions that Professional Standards identify for "classes of transactions and events for the period under audit": (1) accuracy; (2) occurrence; (3) completeness; (4) cutoff; and (5) classification.

I. Related to the "Accuracy and Occurrence" Assertions

- **A.** Examine personnel records on a test basis, to determine that the levels of compensation and support for all deductions exist for all employees. (Officers' compensation should be documented in the minutes of meetings of those charged with governance.)
- **B.** Trace selected transactions from the payroll register to the general ledger and to the payroll bank account.
- **C.** Recalculate selected entries on the payroll register.

II. Related to the "Completeness" Assertion

- **A.** Review time reports and time cards to verify support for production records.
- **B.** Apply analytical procedures (and recalculation) to verify that the payroll-related accruals at year-end are reasonable.

III. Related to the "Cutoff" Assertion -- Cutoff is effectively addressed when "occurrence" and "completeness" have been addressed; in other words, when the auditor has established that recorded transactions are properly recorded and that there are no omissions of transactions that should have been recorded, the auditor has established that the transactions have been recorded in the correct accounting period.

> AICPA professional standards also state , "... there may not be a separate assertion related to cutoff of transactions and events when the occurrence and completeness assertions include appropriate consideration of recording transactions in the correct accounting period."

IV. Related to the "Classification" Assertion

- **A.** The comments related to accuracy and occurrence apply to recording the transactions in the proper accounts, as well.
- **B.** Review outside reports related to pension, other post-retirement benefits (e.g. insurance), and profit-sharing plans.
- **C.** Verify payroll deductions and taxes, trace cash disbursements for withholdings to appropriate agencies.

D. Note that ordinarily, income statement elements (including revenue and expense items) are primarily audited by analytical procedures. Typically, tests of details will be performed only when the analytical procedures suggest that a risk of material misstatement exists and that a more detailed investigation is warranted. Payroll-related expenses would normally be subject to such analytical procedures, too. The discussion above is presented to provide insights about how such transactions could be tested in detail if the auditor deemed that appropriate.

Audit Sampling

Introduction to Sampling

After studying this lesson, you should be able to:

1. *Understand the distinction between statistical and nonstatistical audit sampling .*
2. *Understand the distinction between sampling risk and nonsampling risk.*
3. *Understand the distinction between false rejection (a Type 1 Error) and false acceptance (a Type 2 Error) comprising sampling risk applicable to tests of control substantive procedures tests .*

> **Definition:**
> *Sampling*: "The selection and evaluation of less than 100 percent of the population of audit relevance such that the auditor expects the items selected to be representative of the population . . ."

I. **Responsibilities under AICPA Professional Standards --** The relevant AICPA guidance is provided by AU 530 "Audit Sampling." This pronouncement states that the auditor's objective is to provide a reasonable basis for the auditor to draw conclusions about the population from which the sample is selected.

II. **There Are Two General Approaches to Sampling --** May depend on the auditor's perceptions of cost/benefit tradeoffs.

   A. **Nonstatistical sampling --** also called "judgmental" sampling

   B. **Statistical --** the benefits relate to objectivity:

      1. Relates to the **sufficiency** of the evidence -- the determination of the sample size in a statistical sampling application establishes how much evidence is required.
      2. The results may seem more defensible to others (such as the courts).
      3. A common misconception is that "statistical sampling" eliminates the need for judgment. Actually, numerous judgments must be made; however, these judgments are made more explicit.
      4. Sampling applications occur in either of 2 contexts:

> **Definitions:**
> *Attributes Sampling*: Sampling for purposes of deciding whether internal controls are working as designed (tests of controls).
>
> *Variables Sampling:* Sampling for purposes of deciding whether account balances (such as inventory or receivables) are fairly stated (substantive tests of details).

III. **Uncertainty and Audit Sampling -- Risk Considerations --** Recall the definition of "Audit Risk" -- The probability that the auditor fails to modify the opinion on financial statements containing a material misstatement. An appendix in SAS No. 111 provides the following model for auditors who want to evaluate the risk components explicitly:

> AR = RMM * AP * TD, where
>
> AR = audit risk;
>
> RMM = risk of material misstatement, consisting of the combined assessments of inherent risk and control risk;
>
> AP = risk that analytical procedures performed for substantive purposes will not detect a material misstatement that occurred; and
>
> TD = risk that tests of details will fail to detect a material misstatement that was not otherwise detected.

IV. **Whether "Nonstatistical" Sampling or "Statistical" Sampling Is Used --** The auditor is fundamentally seeking a sample that is truly representative of the population, so that the auditor gets an accurate signal about the population's characteristics in a highly efficient way.

V. **"Sampling Risk" --** Is the risk that the sample may not be truly representative of the population; in other words, the chance of an erroneous conclusion that the auditor takes by examining a subset of the population, rather than the entire population.

   A. **"Type 1 Errors" (False Rejection)**

      1. Tests of controls => "the risk of **under-reliance** on internal controls" (also known as "risk of assessing control risk too high").
      2. Substantive testing => "the risk of incorrect rejection."
      3. Type 1 errors relate to "efficiency" -- the auditor will probably achieve the appropriate conclusions, although not in the most efficient manner (perhaps taking more than one sample, maybe at the urging of the client who has faith in the effectiveness of the internal control or the fairness of the financial statement element).

   B. **"Type 2 Errors" (False Acceptance)**

      1. Tests of controls => "the risk of **over-reliance** on internal controls" (also known as the "risk of assessing control risk too low").
      2. Substantive testing => "the risk of incorrect acceptance".
      3. Type 2 errors relate to "effectiveness" -- now the auditor may have failed to meet the overall objective, which is to limit audit risk to an acceptably low level. (The client will have no incentive to argue about this conclusion, so the auditors will not have any reason to take a second look.)

> **Note:**
> If there were no variation within a population (that is, if all items were homogeneous), the auditor would only need a sample of one item to assess the whole population! The variability of the population causes the sample size to increase and is responsible for the sampling risk.

VI. **Nonsampling Risk --** Refers to any other mistakes by the auditor (that is, other than sampling risk), not a direct consequence of using a sampling approach:

   A. Inappropriate auditing procedures.

   B. Failure to correctly identify "errors" or amounts sampled, misinterpreting the results, etc.

Attributes Sampling

After studying this lesson, you should be able to:

1. *Understand the meaning of the term "attributes sampling."*
2. *Know the eight steps that comprise an attributes sampling application.*
3. *Know how to determine the sample size for an attributes sampling application using AICPA tables.*

I. **Attributes Sampling --** Statistical sampling for the purpose of identifying the percentage frequency of a characteristic in a population of interest to the auditor; this term is usually used to refer to audit sampling to ascertain the operating effectiveness of internal control (where, for each transaction in the sample, the control procedure of interest was either performed or not performed - there are only two outcomes, similar to 'hit or miss' or "heads or tails")

II. **Eight Steps Comprise an Attributes Sampling**

A. **Identify the Sampling Objective --** That is, the purpose of the test.

B. **Define what Constitutes an "Occurrence" --** Sometimes called a "deviation" or "error" when a control procedure of interest was not properly performed.

C. **Identify the Relevant Population**

1. Specify the relevant time period.
2. Specify the "sampling unit" -- what it is that the auditor is selecting (e.g., sales transactions).

D. **Determine the Sampling Method --** How the specific items (or transactions) are to be selected for the sample.

1. **Statistical Sampling Approaches**

a. **Random Number --** Each transaction has the same probability of being selected (the best approach).

b. **Systematic --** For example, selecting every 100th item.

2. **Judgmental Sampling Approaches --** not appropriate for attributes sampling!

a. **Block --** A group of contiguous items (e.g., the sales transactions for the entire month of June).

b. **"Haphazard" --** Arbitrary selection, with no "conscious" biases. Subconscious biases may exist without the auditor's awareness, however.

E. **Determine the Sample Size --** (Based on AICPA tables.)

Factor (holding all others constant)	Relationship
Expected error rate (related to the variation in population)	**Direct**
Tolerable (deviation) rate (related to precision)	**Inverse**
Risk of over-reliance	**Inverse**
Risk of under-reliance (implicit)	**Inverse**
Population size (implicit)	**Direct**

F. **Select the Sample --** Identify the "occurrences" associated with all the items in the sample.

G. **"Evaluate" the sample results --** This means make a decision as to whether the auditor can rely on the effectiveness of the internal control procedure under consideration.

1. Calculate the **observed deviation rate** = (# errors)/n.
2. Determine the "point estimate," the best single indicator of the percentage of times that the control procedure was performed as designed in the population (ignoring, for the moment, the uncertainty surrounding whether the sample is truly representative of the population).
3. Calculate a "confidence interval" for the **achieved upper precision limit** (in view of the actual errors observed). There are AICPA tables to determine the achieved upper precision limit. (*The topic determination of confidence intervals is not likely to be tested on the CPA exam!*)
4. Compare the achieved upper precision limit to the stated **tolerable rate**; the auditor can only rely on the internal control procedure if the error rate, based on the upper bound of the confidence interval (the "achieved upper precision limit" from the tables) is less than or equal to the stated tolerable rate.
5. Consider the **qualitative characteristics** of the internal control deviations for any implication to the rest of the audit.
6. Make the appropriate decision -- Should the auditor rely on the specific control procedure (that is, **assess control risk at less than the maximum**) or not?

H. **Document the auditor's sampling procedures**

III. Attributes Sampling Example

Statistical Sample Sizes for Tests of Controls						
Five-Percent Risk of Over-reliance						
Expected Population	**Tolerable Rate**					
Deviation Rate	**2%**	**3%**	**4%**	**5%**	**6%**	**7%**
.25	236	157	117	93	78	66
.50	*	157	117	93	78	66
.75	*	208	117	93	78	66
1.00	*	*	156	**93**	78	66
1.25	*	*	156	124	78	66
1.50	*	*	192	124	103	66
1.75	*	*	227	153	103	88
2.00	*	*	*	181	127	88
* Sample size is too large to be cost-effective for most audit applications.						

Note:
This table has been adapted from material copyrighted by the American Institute of Certified Public Accountants, Inc.

IV. Attributes Sampling - Numerical Example

A. Suppose that an auditor specified the following parameters for a statistical sampling application related to internal controls in the revenue/receipts transaction cycle:

Acceptable risk of over-reliance on Internal Control (a Type II error)	**5%**
(The auditor is willing to rely on the control procedure if the statistical test indicates that the control is working as prescribed at least 95% of the time.)	
Estimated population deviation rate	**1%**
Tolerable deviation rate	**5%**

B. Requirement -- Identify the required sample size using the AICPA tables for attributes sampling.

C. Solution -- The 5% **risk of over-reliance** (Type II Error) determines the applicable page of the AICPA tables; the 5% **tolerable rate** determines the applicable column of the AICPA table; and the 1% **estimated population deviation rate** determines the applicable row of the AICPA table.

1. The resulting sample size is **93**.

Variables Sampling

After studying this lesson, you should be able to:

1. *Understand the meaning of the term "variables sampling" and the various specific approaches (difference estimation, ratio estimation, mean-per-unit estimation, and probability-proportionate-to-size sampling).*
2. *Know the eight steps that comprise a variables sampling application.*
3. *Know the factors that affect sample size for a variables sampling application.*
4. *Understand the role of "stratification" in audit sampling.*

I. **Relies Heavily on the Classic "Normal Distribution" --** (With the bell-shaped curve.)

   A. This distribution is determined by two parameters:

      1. The **mean**, related to central tendency; and
      2. **Variance** (or its square root, standard deviation), related to dispersion or variability.

> **Note:**
> If 68% of the area is under the bell-shaped curve, it is within one standard deviation of the mean; if 95.5% of the area is under the bell-shaped curve, is within two standard deviations of the mean.

II. **Basic Steps --** The **eight basic steps in a variables sampling plan** are practically the same as in the attributes sampling case:

   A. Identify the **sampling objective** -- the purpose of "variables sampling" is to determine the inferred audit value of a population of interest (e.g., for accounts receivable or inventory).

> **Note:**
> Auditors should examine all the items that are individually material (i.e., we are not "sampling" these).

   B. Identify the relevant population:

      1. Specify what constitutes the sampling unit;
      2. Be careful to assure that conclusions are properly extended to the appropriate population (i.e., completeness of the population).

   C. **Select the specific sampling technique --** The choices are difference estimation, ratio estimation, mean-per-unit estimation, or probability-proportionate-to-size sampling.

   D. **Calculate the sample size --** Since tables do not exist for this in variables sampling. Recall the **five factors and relationships** to sample size identified for attributes sampling applications -- These factors are still applicable to variables sampling.

   See the following example.

Factor (holding all others constant)	Relationship
Estimated population standard deviation (related to the variation in population)	**Direct**
Allowance for sampling risk (also called "tolerable misstatement") [related to precision]	**Inverse**
Risk of incorrect acceptance (Type II)	**Inverse**
Population size (explicitly considered for variables sampling)	**Direct**
Risk of incorrect rejection (Type I error, only implicitly considered)	**Inverse**

The **basic formula**, based on classical statistics:

n = (S * Z-coefficient * N /A)^2

where:

n represents the sample size to be determined;

S represents the estimated population standard deviation (related to the variability of the population);

Z-coefficient represents a measure of reliability for some level of specified "confidence" (typically about 2);

N represents the size of the population (number of accounts or items of inventory, etc.);

A represents the specified allowance for sampling risk, related to the statistical concept of "precision."

Note: It is very unlikely that the AICPA will require calculations of sample size! However, they frequently test these **concepts**. In particular, they might ask questions related to the factors that influence the sample size and whether that influence is directly or inversely related. The formula identified above is a useful way to keep these relationships straight.

E. Determine the **method of selection** -- **random** (the preferred approach) or systematic.

F. **Conduct the sample**

G. **Evaluate the sample** and project to population:

1. Calculate a point estimate (the implied audit value) for the population based on the sample's audited values.
2. Construct a confidence interval to determine whether to accept or reject the client's recorded balance as consistent with the audit evidence.

Note:The AICPA has rarely tested calculations in this area. On a few occasions, they have required calculations of a "point estimate" for a population; however, calculations of the confidence interval surrounding a point estimate are beyond the scope of the CPA examination!

H. **Document the auditor's sampling procedures** and judgments.

> **Definition:**
> *Stratification*: The auditor may reduce the overall variability within a population by classifying similar items into "sub-populations" (within each group, the variability may be much smaller); the resulting aggregate sample size may be smaller as a result of reducing the combined effects of variability.

III. **Variables Sampling - Specific Sampling Techniques --** Note that the CPA exam has rarely emphasized calculations related to statistical sampling; however, the exam has historically tested the concepts related to sampling.

A. **Difference estimation --** This approach involves identifying the dollar differences between the sample's audit values and applicable book values.

1. **Sample size --** As previously described. Note that we usually need at least 30 differences between audit and book values in our sample when using "difference estimation."
2. Estimate the population's implied audit value.

a. Calculate the average difference between the audit value and book value for items in the sample:

> d = (av - bv)/n

b. Extend that average difference to the population by multiplying it by the number of items in the population:

> D = d * N

c. Calculate the implied population audit value (the "point estimate") by adding the calculated difference for the population to the population's book value:

> AV = BV + D, where D can be either positive or negative

3. Construct a confidence (precision) interval around the population's audit value to compare to the client's recorded balance - beyond the scope of the CPA Examination.

B. **Ratio estimation --** This approach involves identifying the ratio of the audit values and book values for the sampled items.

1. Note that this approach is useful when the dollar amount of the differences between the audit and the book values is expected to be proportional to the book values.
2. Sample size - as previously described.
3. Estimate the population's implied audit value:

a. Calculate the "ratio" for the sample, where the ratio has the sample's audit value in the numerator and the sample's book value in the denominator:

> R = av/bv

b. Estimate the population's audit value (a "point estimate") by multiplying the population's book value by that "ratio:"

> AV = R * BV

4. Construct a confidence (precision) interval around the population's audit value to compare to the client's recorded balance - beyond the scope of the CPA Examination.

C. Mean-per-unit estimation (MPU)

1. Useful when difference or ratio estimation cannot be used - for example, for inventory when perpetual records do not exist (that is, there is no "book" value for each individual sample item).
2. Sample size - as previously described.
3. Estimate the population's implied audit value.
    a. Calculate the average audit value for items in the sample:

MPU = av/n

    b. Multiply that average (MPU) times the number of items in the population:

AV = MPU * N

4. Construct a confidence (precision) interval around the population's audit value to compare to the client's recorded balance - beyond scope of CPA Exam!

D. Probability-proportional-to-size (PPS) sampling -- An introduction.

1. The "sampling unit" is an individual dollar (when a given dollar is selected for the sample, it attaches to the related account or item which is then examined in its entirety); note that individually material items are automatically selected.
2. Useful if there are relatively few differences between audit and book values; otherwise, the sample size can become very large and the PPS application then becomes inefficient.
3. The main advantage is efficiency - it can achieve the maximum possible stratification (which then minimizes the effects of variability on sample size).
4. The main disadvantage is that PPS does not work very well in auditing negative balances (understatements) or zero (unrecorded) balances. Applies best to audit concerns involving overstatements (for example, accounts receivable or inventory when few misstatements are expected).

PPS sampling will be addressed in more depth in the next lesson.

Probability-Proportional-to-Size (PPS) Sampling

After studying this lesson you should be able to :

1. *Understand the relevant sampling unit for probability-proportionate-to-size sampling.*
2. *Determine the sample size and the sampling interval for a probability-proportionate-to-size sampling application.*
3. *Determine the projected misstatement for a probability-proportionate-to-size sampling application.*

I. **PPS "Sampling Unit" --** PPS sampling defines the "sampling unit" to be an individual dollar associated with the financial statement element involved. (Variations of this approach are referred to as dollar-unit sampling or monetary unit sampling.) For example, suppose accounts receivable consists of 7500 customer accounts having a total balance of $3,000,000. The population is viewed as consisting of 3,000,000 individual items (dollars) rather than 7500 accounts. However, when an individual dollar is selected as part of the sample, it attaches to the related account or logical record, which is then examined in its entirety. Accordingly, the probability than an individual account will be selected is "proportional" to that individual account's balance relative to the total for all accounts.

II. **Primary Advantage of PPS Sampling --** The main advantage of PPS sampling is efficiency. If there are few differences between audit and book values, PPS sampling may result in smaller sample sizes than the other sampling methods. If there are many differences, however, PPS sample sizes can become too large to be practical.

III. **Primary Disadvantage of PPS Sampling --** The main disadvantage of PPS sampling is that it does not work very well in auditing negative balances (understatements) or zero (unrecorded) balances. It applies best to audit circumstances involving concerns about overstatements, such as for accounts receivable or inventory; and, then, only when few misstatements are expected.

IV. **Basic Steps in a PPS Sampling Application**

A. Determine the sample size—based on 3 considerations:

1. The "reliability factor" (from an AICPA table based on the risk of incorrect acceptance and the number of overstatements permitted—see the table below);
2. The population book value; and
3. The tolerable misstatement (net of any expected misstatements).

$$n = \frac{\text{Reliability factor (from tables)} \times \text{Book value}}{\text{Tolerable misstatement, net of expected misstatements}}$$

Alternatively, **n = Book Value/sampling interval**, where:

Sampling interval = tolerable misstatement (net of expected misstatements)/reliability factor

See the following illustration.

RELIABILITY FACTORS:

Number of Overstatements	Risk of Incorrect Acceptance 1%	5%	10%	15%	20%
0	4.61	3.00	2.31	1.90	1.61
1	6.64	4.75	3.89	3.38	3.00
2	8.41	6.30	5.33	4.72	4.28
3	10.05	7.76	6.69	6.02	5.52
4	11.61	9.16	8.00	7.27	6.73
5	13.11	10.52	9.28	8.50	7.91

B. **Select the sample --** PPS samples are usually selected using "systematic selection" with a random starting point and a specified "sample interval."

$$\textbf{Sample interval} = \frac{\text{Population book value}}{\text{Sample size}}$$

C. **Evaluate the recorded book value --** To "evaluate" the entity's recorded balance relative to the implied audit value for the population, the auditor should calculate the "upper limit on misstatement," which corresponds to the upper limit of a confidence interval. Such computations are beyond the scope of CPA Exam, but a few concepts (especially "projected misstatement") may be worth remembering.

See the following illustration

Upper limit on misstatement

= [Basic precision + Projected misstatement + Incremental allowance]

where:

Basic Precision:

Basic precision = Reliability Factor × sample interval

(for 0 misstatements)

Projected misstatement:

For accounts having a book value greater than or equal to the sample interval, the actual misstatement should be used to determine the "projected misstatement."

For accounts having book values less than the sample interval, the auditor would have to apply the "tainting percentage" to the sample interval from which that account was selected. Suppose that the sample interval is $2000 and that an account having a book value of $250 has an audit value of $200. The "tainting" is $50/$250 = .20; and, since the account's book value is less than the sample interval, the projected misstatement for this account would be .20 × $2000 = $400.

When there are no misstatements in the sample, the projected misstatement is zero.

Incremental allowance:

The incremental allowance is zero if there are no misstatements of accounts having book values less than the sample interval. The concept is only relevant when there are misstatements of accounts having book values less than the sample interval, but the calculation itself is a technical issue that is beyond the scope of the CPA Exam.

Example Problems

Difference Estimation Problem

I. **Calculating a "Point Estimate" --** Using statistical sampling to assist in verifying the year-end accounts payable balance, an auditor has accumulated the following data (based on a 1984 AICPA Exam question):

	No. of Accounts	Book Balance	Audit Value
Population	4100	$5,000,000	??
Sample	200	$250,000	$300,000

II. **Required --** Using **difference estimation**, calculate the implied value for the year-end accounts payable balance.

Difference Estimation Solution

I. **Calculating a "Point Estimate" --** Using statistical sampling to assist in verifying the year-end accounts payable balance, an auditor has accumulated the following data (based on a 1984 AICPA Exam question):

	No. of Accounts	Book Balance	Audit Value
Population	4100	$5,000,000	??
Sample	200	$250,000	$300,000

II. **Required --** Using **difference estimation**, calculate the implied value for the year-end accounts payable balance.

A. First, calculate the average difference for items in the sample:

d = (av - bv)/n => ($300,000 - $250,000)/ 200 = $250

B. Second, extend that average difference to the population by multiplying it by the number of items in the population:

D = d * N => $250 * 4100 = $1,025,000

C. Third, estimate the population's audit value by adding that difference to the population's book value:

AV = BV + D => $5,000,000 + $1,025,000 = **$6,025,000**

Exam Tip: Even though ratio estimation and difference estimation calculate different "point estimates," that does not mean that the auditor would reach different conclusions about the fairness of the client's book balance. The calculation of the applicable confidence intervals would also differ accordingly. However, the calculation of confidence intervals is currently beyond the scope of the CPA exam.

Ratio Estimation Problem

I. **Calculating a "Point Estimate" --** Using statistical sampling to assist in verifying the year-end accounts payable balance, an auditor has accumulated the following data (based on a 1984 CPA Exam question):

	No. of Accounts	Book Balance	Audit Value
Population	4100	$5,000,000	??
Sample	200	$250,000	$300,000

II. **Required --** Using **ratio estimation**, calculate the implied value for the year-end accounts payable balance.

Ratio Estimation Solution

I. **Calculating a "Point Estimate" --** Using statistical sampling to assist in verifying the year-end accounts payable balance, an auditor has accumulated the following data (based on a 1984 CPA Exam question):

	No. of Accounts	Book Balance	Audit Value
Population	4100	$5,000,000	??
Sample	200	$250,000	$300,000

II. **Required --** Using **ratio estimation**, calculate the implied value for the year-end accounts payable balance.

"Ratio" = av/bv => $300,000/$250,000 = 1.2

A. Estimated population Audit Value = "ratio" * population Book Value

=> 1.2 * $5,000,000 = **$6,000,000**

MPU Estimation Problem

I. **Calculating a "Point Estimate" --** Using statistical sampling to assist in verifying the year-end accounts payable balance, an auditor has accumulated the following data (based on a 1984 CPA Exam question):

	No. of Accounts	Book Balance	Audit Value
Population	4100	$5,000,000	??
Sample	200	$250,000	$300,000

II. **Required --** Using **mean-per-unit estimation**, calculate the implied value for the year-end accounts payable balance.

MPU Estimation Solution

I. **Calculating a "Point Estimate" --** Using statistical sampling to assist in verifying the year-end accounts payable balance, an auditor has accumulated the following data (based on a 1984 CPA Exam question):

	No. of Accounts	**Book Balance**	**Audit Value**
Population	4100	$5,000,000	??
Sample	200	$250,000	$300,000

II. **Required --** Using **mean-per-unit estimation**, calculate the implied value for the year-end accounts payable balance.

A. First, calculate the "mean-per-unit" (that is, the average audit value for items in the sample):

MPU = av/n => $300,000/200 = $1500 per unit

B. Second, calculate the implied audit value for the population by multiplying that MPU times the number of items in the population:

av = MPU * N => $1500 * 4100 = **$6,150,000**

Exam Tip: Even though MPU estimation calculates a different "point estimate" than ratio estimation or difference estimation, it does not mean that the auditor would reach different conclusions about the fairness of the client's book balance. The calculation of the applicable confidence intervals would also differ accordingly. However, the calculation of confidence intervals is currently beyond the scope of the CPA exam.

PPS Sampling Problem

I. **A Numerical Problem -- Sample Size for PPS Sampling**

II. Hill has decided to use probability-proportional-to-size (PPS) sampling, sometimes called dollar-unit sampling, in the audit of a client's accounts receivable balances. Hill plans to use the following PPS sampling table:

Reliability Factors for Errors of Overstatement					
Number of Overstatements	**Risk of Incorrect Acceptance**				
	1%	**5%**	**10%**	**15%**	**20%**
0	4.61	3.00	2.31	1.90	1.61
1	6.64	4.75	3.89	3.38	3.00
2	8.41	6.30	5.33	4.72	4.28
3	10.05	7.76	6.69	6.02	5.52
4	11.61	9.16	8.00	7.27	6.73

Additional Information	
Tolerable misstatement (net of effect of expected misstatement)	$ 24,000
Risk of incorrect acceptance	20%
Number of misstatements allowed	1
Recorded amount of accounts receivable	$240,000
Number of accounts	360

III. **Required --** What sample size should Hill use?

PPS Sampling Solution

I. A Numerical Problem -- Sample Size for PPS Sampling

II. Hill has decided to use probability-proportional-to-size (PPS) sampling, sometimes called dollar-unit sampling, in the audit of a client's accounts receivable balances. Hill plans to use the following PPS sampling table:

Reliability Factors for Errors of Overstatement					
Number of Overstatements	**Risk of Incorrect Acceptance**				
	1%	**5%**	**10%**	**15%**	**20%**
0	4.61	3.00	2.31	1.90	1.61
1	6.64	4.75	3.89	3.38	3.00
2	8.41	6.30	5.33	4.72	4.28
3	10.05	7.76	6.69	6.02	5.52
4	11.61	9.16	8.00	7.27	6.73

Additional Information	
Tolerable misstatement (net of effect of expected misstatement)	$ 24,000
Risk of incorrect acceptance	20%
Number of misstatements allowed	1
Recorded amount of accounts receivable	$240,000
Number of accounts	360

III. Required -- What sample size should Hill use?

A. n = reliability factor from tables* Book Value / tolerable error

B. => (3.0 * $240,000) / $24,000 = **30**

IT (Computer) Auditing

IT Controls - General Controls

After studying this lesson, you should be able to:

1. *Understand the meaning of the term "general controls" relevant to an IT (computerized) environment.*
2. *Know the five categories of such general controls.*

I. **The Study and Evaluation of Internal Control --** This is somewhat different in a computerized environment:

   A. **The basic control objectives are the same, however!**

   B. Particular considerations in an Electronic Data Processing (EDP) (often referred to as an Information Technology (IT)) environment:

      1. A **disadvantage** is that the **segregation of duties** may be undermined -- If someone gets unauthorized access to the computer system, it may be difficult to separate incompatible activities.

      2. Another **disadvantage** is that the usual **audit trail may be lacking.** There may be no "paper trail" auditors are accustomed to following.

      3. An **advantage** is that **computer processing is uniform** -- Computers don't have "good" days and "bad" days; if a particular transaction is processed correctly one time, an identical transaction will be processed correctly, too.

   C. The **specific evidence gathering procedures** may differ.

II. **General Controls --** Controls that have pervasive effects on all the specific applications; there are five categories of "general controls:"

   A. **Organization and Operation**

      1. **Segregation of duties --** Especially within the EDP department; also between the EDP and various user departments.

      2. Focus on the **primary areas of responsibility** -- As much as possible, try to separate the following activities within the EDP department:

         a. **Systems analyst --** Responsible for designing the system.

         b. **Programmer --** Responsible for writing the code that makes up the programs.

         c. **Operator --** Responsible for running the system.

         d. **Librarian --** Responsible for keeping track of the programs and files and verifying that access is limited to authorized personnel.

         e. **Security --** Responsible for protecting the programs and data files and implementing procedures to safeguard the system.

   B. **Systems development and documentation --** Regarding the appropriate authorization and documentation of new systems; any changes should be appropriately documented.

   C. **Hardware and Systems Software**

      1. **"Built In" Controls**

         a. **Parity check --** Especially related to transmissions of information between system hardware components. A "bit" added to each character so that the loss of any portion of the data might be detected.

b. **Echo check --** Especially related to transmissions of information over the phone lines. A signal that what was "sent" was, in fact, "received."

c. **Diagnostic routines --** That check internal operations of hardware components (usually when booting up the system).

d. **Boundary protection --** For running multiple jobs concurrently.

2. **Operating system --** Controls and instructions built into the software that runs the hardware.

D. **Access --** The access to data, software, and the hardware should be limited to authorized personnel.

E. **Data and procedures --** Including physical safeguards that can protect the data files:

1. **File labels --** Internal and external labels that might prevent using a file for an unintended or inappropriate use.

2. **File protection rings --** A processing control related to magnetic tapes that prevents critical data from being overwritten (similar to a "read only" switch on a floppy disk).

3. **File protection plans --** Duplicates or prior generations. "Grandfather" and "father" versions that can be used to recreate a current file by updating earlier files with current transaction data.

IT Controls - Application Controls

After studying this lesson, you should be able to:

1. *Understand the meaning of the term application controls relevant to an IT (computerized) environment.*
2. *Know the 3 categories of application controls (input, processing, and output) and specific examples of controls associated with each such category.*

I. **Application Controls --** Related to the specific computer processing applications; now the emphasis is placed on the specific input, processing, and output activities.

A. **Input**

1. **Objectives --** That the input of data is accurate and as authorized.
2. **Examples**

a. **Preprinted forms --** So that employees will know exactly where to look for particular items of information.

b. **Keypunch --** Verification/duplication.

c. **Control totals --** Where useful comparisons are made to verify that all of the data were input properly.

i. **"Batch totals" --** Totals that actually mean something (for example, the day's cash withdrawals at an ATM location).

ii. **"Hash totals" --** Totals that have no meaningful interpretation per se, even though a total can be arithmetically determined (for example, adding up employees' social security numbers to verify that no employees were dropped from a payroll application).

iii. **Record count --** Keeping track of the number of records processed to determine that the appropriate number was accounted for.

d. **Logic checks --** Refers to certain computer edit routines that might signal when erroneous data have been input.

i. **Limit tests --** Are the data all within some predetermined range? For example, a payroll program may specify an upper limit for how many hours can be legitimately worked.

ii. **Validity checks --** Are the data recognized as legitimate possibilities (for example, gender codes could only be "M" or "F")?

iii. **Missing data checks --** Are there any omissions from any fields in which data should have been present?

iv. **Check digits --** A check digit is an arithmetic manipulation of a numerical field that captures the information content of that field and then gets "tacked" onto the end of that numeric field.

e. **Error resolution procedures --** Whenever the control procedures flag a data input problem, there should be procedures to pull out the item, fix the problem, and then put the item back in line for data entry.

B. **Processing**

1. **Objectives --** That the processing of data is accurate and as authorized.
2. **Examples**

a. **Control totals --** Same as for the corresponding section under "Input" above.

b. **Checkpoint/restart --** For particularly long processing runs, there should be built in "checkpoint/restart" procedures so that, if the program crashes, it does not have to be restarted from the very beginning.

c. **Limit on processing time --** A predetermined limit for computer processing time might be specified; if that time is exceeded, the program can assume an error has occurred and shut down the processing run.

d. **Internal (e.g. "headers") and external labels --** Should be used on all files to reduce the likelihood of mistakes caused by using the wrong files.

e. **Error resolution procedures (the same idea as for "input") --** Whenever the control procedures flag a data processing problem, there should be procedures to pull out the item, fix the problem, and then put the item back in line for the necessary data processing.

C. **Output**

1. **Objectives --** That the output of data (and the distribution of any related reports) is accurate and as authorized.

2. **Examples**

   a. **Control totals (same idea as for "Input" and "Processing")**

   b. **Output limits --** A predetermined page (or time) limit might be specified; if those limits are exceeded, the program can assume an error has occurred and stop the output activity.

   c. **Error resolution procedures --** (the same idea as for "Input" and "Processing"). Whenever the control procedures flag a data output problem, there should be procedures to pull out the item, fix the problem, and then put the item back in line for proper output.

IT Evidence-Gathering Procedures

The auditor's evidence gathering procedures may be affected by a computerized environment -- "auditing through the computer" (as opposed to "auditing around the computer").

After studying this lesson, you should be able to:

1. *Understand the costs and benefits associated with developing generalized audit software versus customizing software to a specific entity's circumstances.*
2. *Understand specific procedures that the auditor may perform in an IT environment to test relevant controls.*

I. **Audit Software (focus is on substantive test work) --** Especially to access the client's files, but may also be used to help achieve the audit objectives:

   A. **Generalized software --** Canned audit programs to access and test client's files; initially expensive to develop, but can be efficient if used on numerous engagements.

   B. **Customized software --** Programs specifically written to access the files of a particular client; may be cheaper in the short run, but more expensive in the long run if such costs are incurred for many clients.

   C. **Data mining software --** Commercially available software (such as ACL or Idea) can be easily used to access client's electronic data and perform a broad range of substantive audit tasks (such as performing analytical procedures and sampling for confirmation work).

II. **Procedures Related to Tests of Controls --** When those IT-related controls are internal and unobservable:

   A. **Test data --** Introducing "dummy" transactions under the auditor's control:

      1. Include some known errors to test the client's internal controls by checking whether the client's system catches those known errors.
      2. The auditor need not include every possible type of error; include only those kinds of errors that are of interest to the auditor.
      3. But be careful not to contaminate the client's database.

   B. **Integrated test facility (ITF) --** Create a fictitious division or department within the client and process the "dummy" data along with the client's "live" data; again, be careful not to contaminate the client's actual files.

   C. **Parallel simulation --** Processing the client's actual data on the auditor's software and then comparing auditor's output to client's output for agreement.

   D. **Tagging specific client transactions and tracing them through the client's system --** Such "tagging" is analogous to an electronic tag attached to an animal in the wilderness so that researchers can follow the animal's movement.

> **Note:**
> Test data, ITF, and parallel simulation test how well the client's systems work (after the fact), especially in detecting errors.

   E. **Embedded Audit Modules --** (and audit hooks) - Systems that don't have a permanent audit trail require that any "auditing" occurs while processing take place.

      1. **Embedded audit modules --** Routines that are built into the application program to perform an ongoing audit function.

2. **Audit hooks --** An exit point that is built into the application program where an audit module can be added subsequently.

Note: Tagging, embedding audit modules, and audit hooks test the working of the system while processing takes place.

Note: Inquiry, observation, and inspection can be used to gather evidence about external, observable EDP-related controls that are not otherwise documented.

Other IT Considerations

After studying this lesson, you should be able to:

1. *Understand a variety of other terms and concepts associated with processing and networking in an IT environment.*

I. **Hardware versus Software**

  A. **Hardware --** The central processing unit (CPU) and all the other related equipment.

  B. **Software --** The systems programs and all the applications programs:

    1. **Operating system --** The set of instructions that runs the CPU and the related peripheral equipment.

    2. **Compiler --** Translates the source program into object program:

      a. **Source program --** Written in a specific programming language (for example, FORTRAN, COBOL).

      b. **Object program --** The instructions in machine readable form.

II. **Modes of Operation --** Related to when the transactions are processed:

  A. **Batch processing --** When transactions are collected for periodic processing (for example, daily updates for an ATM machine).

  B. **Online, real-time processing**

    1. **"Online" --** Means that the user is in direct communication with the computer's central processing unit (CPU).

    2. **"Real-time" --** Means that the data files are immediately updated.

III. **Service Organizations --** Independent computer centers may be engaged to process a client's transactional data; using such a service organization is a form of "outsourcing" and represents an alternative to having a company's own IT department.

IV. **Distributed Systems --** Involves a single database, which is literally distributed across multiple computers connected by a communication link. In other words, a network of remote computers connected to the main system (i.e. a "host" server) whereby each location can then have input/output, processing, and printing capabilities.

V. **Database Systems --** A set of interconnected files that eliminates the redundancy associated with maintaining separate files for different subsets of the organization; a key concern is limiting the users' access to the appropriate parts of the database as authorized.

VI. **"Hierarchical" vs. "Relational" Database Structures**

  A. **Hierarchical --** Data elements at one level encompass the data elements immediately below (constructed like a company's "organizational chart"). These structures are largely outdated.

  B. **Relational --** An integrated database having the structure of a spreadsheet (where each row consists of fields related to a particular customer or item and each column consists of a specific information field that is applicable to each customer or item).

VII. **Networks --** Basic definitions

  A. **Local area network (LAN) --** A network of hardware and software interconnected throughout a building or campus (usually limited to a few miles in scope).

  B. **Wide area network (WAN) --** A larger version of a LAN that might span a whole city or country.

C. **Value added network (VAN) --** A network that facilitates "EDI" transactions (see the section on e-commerce below) between the buying and selling companies in such transactions, but the VAN is maintained by an independent company.

D. **Internet --** A worldwide network of privately controlled computers.

E. **Intranet --** A local area network that uses internet technology to facilitate communications throughout a particular organization (perhaps using a "firewall" to insulate the organization's system from unauthorized, outside entry).

F. **Extranet --** Same as "intranet," except that important external constituents (e.g. major customers or suppliers) are also connected.

VIII. Electronic Commerce

A. **Electronic funds transfer (EFT) --** Involves the transfer of monies between financial accounts (usually associated with financial institutions).

B. **Electronic data interchange (EDI) --** Involves an electronic transaction between companies (one is selling, the other is buying).

1. The usual hardcopy documents (e.g. purchase orders, sales invoices) don't exist!
2. The goal is greater efficiency and less paperwork - should result in lower receivable/payable balances.
3. **Point-to-point (point of sale) transactions --** Involve direct computer-to-computer communication between the parties.
4. **Value Added Network --** As indicated above, an independent company may develop the electronic infrastructure to facilitate these electronic business activities (along with support services).

IX. Using the Internet -- Security and information reliability remain major concerns, although no direct investment is specifically required to engage in e-commerce transactions. Note that the AICPA developed "*WebTrust*" as an assurance service to address such concerns for a consumer/buyer.

Audit Reports

Introduction to Audit Reports

After studying this lesson, you should be able to:

1. *State the Reporting Principle under the clarified standards (and how that compares to the now-superseded Reporting Standards of GAAS).*
2. *Know the structure and content of the* ***unmodified*** *auditor's report (and how that compares to what was previously known as the standard* ***unqualified*** *audit report.*
3. *Recognize the various alternative audit reports in addition to the unmodified auditor's report introduced here.*

I. **Relevant AICPA Guidance --** The relevant AICPA guidance is provided by AU 700: "Forming an Opinion and Reporting on Financial Statements." The standard states that the auditor's objectives are to form an opinion on the financial statements based on an evaluation of the audit evidence obtained, and express clearly that opinion through a written report.

II. **Principles --** Recall that the 10 criteria previously known as GAAS have been replaced in the clarified standards by 7 principles. Accordingly, the 4 Reporting Standards of GAAS have been replaced by 1 of those principles dealing with Reporting.

A. The 4 Reporting Standards previously associated with GAAS (and currently still associated with the PCAOB's auditing standards) — Recall the memory aid GCDO representing the key words of the standards: GAAP, Consistency, Disclosure, and Opinion.

> 1. **GAAP**—"The auditor must state in the auditor's report whether the financial statements are presented in accordance with generally accepted accounting principles (GAAP)."
>
> 2. **Consistency**—"The auditor must identify in the auditor's report those circumstances in which such principles have not been consistently observed in the current period in relation to the preceding period."
>
> 3. **Disclosure**—"When the auditor determines that informative disclosures are not reasonably adequate, the auditor must so state in the auditor's report."
>
> 4. **Opinion**—"The auditor must either express an opinion regarding the financial statements, taken as a whole, or state that an opinion cannot be expressed, in the auditor's report. When the auditor cannot express an overall opinion, the auditor should state the reasons therefore in the auditor's report. In all cases where an auditor's name is associated with financial statements, the auditor should clearly indicate the character of the auditor's work, if any, and the degree of responsibility the auditor is taking, in the auditor's report."

B. The 7 principles identified as a framework for audit standard setting in the clarified standards include one principle specifically on Reporting:

> "Based on an evaluation of the audit evidence obtained, the auditor expresses, in the form of a written report, an opinion in accordance with the auditor's findings, or states that an opinion cannot be expressed. The opinion states whether the financial statements are presented fairly, in all material respects, in accordance with the applicable financial reporting framework."

III. "Standard Unqualified Audit Report" -- Prior to the clarified standards, the AICPA auditing standards referred to the "Standard **Unqualified** Audit Report"—Such an audit report consisted of 3 paragraphs known as the introductory, scope, and opinion paragraphs, as shown below.

> **Standard Unqualified Auditor's Report**
>
> Independent Auditor's Report
>
> We have audited the balance sheets of ABC Company at December 31, 20X2 and 20X1, and the related statements of income, retained earnings, and cash flows for the years then ended. These financial statements are the responsibility of the Company's management. Our responsibility is to express an opinion on these financial statements based on our audits.
>
> We conducted our audits in accordance with auditing standards generally accepted in the United States of America. Those standards require that we plan and perform the audit to obtain reasonable assurance about whether the financial statements are free of material misstatement. An audit includes examining, on a test basis, evidence supporting the amounts and disclosures in the financial statements. An audit also includes assessing the accounting principles used and significant estimates made by management, as well as evaluating the overall financial statement presentation. We believe that our audits provide a reasonable basis for our opinion.
>
> In our opinion, the financial statements referred to above present fairly, in all material respects, the financial position of ABC Company at December 31, 20X2 and 20X1, and the results of their operations and their cash flows for the years then ended, in conformity with accounting principles generally accepted in the United States of America.
>
> /s/ CPA firm (signed by audit engagement partner)
>
> Date (The auditor's report should not be dated earlier than the date on which the auditor has obtained sufficient appropriate audit evidence to support the opinion.)

> In the clarified standards, the AICPA has replaced the previous term unqualified with unmodified.

IV. Clarified Standards -- Under the AICPA's Clarified Standards, the auditor's unmodified report has been reformatted and expanded to reflect 4 main sections:

- **A.** The first section ordinarily has no label, and merely identifies the nature of the engagement and the entity's financial statements involved (consisting of 1 sentence). However, if the auditor's report includes a section after the opinion paragraph labeled **"Report on Other Legal and Regulatory Requirements**," then the introductory paragraph should be labeled **"Report on the Financial Statements**." (Samples of both versions of audit reports are provided below.)
- **B.** The second section is labeled **"Management's Responsibility for the Financial Statements"**—(1 sentence) States that management is responsible for the fair presentation of the financial statements and the design and implementation of internal control.
- **C.** The third section is labeled "Auditor's Responsibility," which consists of 3 separate paragraphs.
  1. The first consists of 3 sentences — (1) responsibility to express an opinion; (2) conducted the audit in accordance with (GAAS); and (3) plan and perform the audit to provide reasonable assurance.
  2. The second consists of 5 sentences — (1) perform procedures to obtain audit evidence about the amounts and disclosures; (2) the procedures depend on the auditor's judgment, including assessment of risks of material misstatement, whether due to fraud or error; (3) in making those risk assessments, the auditor considers internal control; (4) auditor expresses no such opinion (on internal control, when not engaged to report on internal control in an integrated audit); and (5) an audit includes evaluating the appropriateness of accounting policies used and the reasonableness of significant accounting estimates.

3. The third consists of 1 sentence — expressing the auditor's belief that the audit evidence is sufficient and appropriate to provide a basis for the opinion.

D. The fourth section is labeled **"Opinion"** — (1 sentence) Expresses the auditor's opinion (in the same wording as that used in the previous AICPA standards).

E. Signature block — The AICPA now requires identification of the CPA's city/state, in addition to the signature and date.

V. **Alternative Audit Reports --** These various auditor's reports will be discussed in detail in subsequent lessons.

A. Auditor's report includes an emphasis-of-matter paragraph.

B. Auditor's report includes an other-matter paragraph.

C. Auditor expresses a qualified opinion—the auditor expresses one or more reservations about (1) the financial statement presentation (owing to a material departure from the requirements of the applicable financial reporting framework); or (2) the audit engagement (owing to a scope limitation about a material matter for which the auditor was unable to obtain sufficient appropriate audit evidence).

D. Auditor expresses an adverse opinion—the auditor states that the financial statements are not fairly stated (as a result of a departure from the requirements of the applicable financial reporting framework that is material and pervasive).

E. Auditor expresses a disclaimer of opinion—a report in which the auditor expresses no conclusion about the fairness of the entity's financial statements (due to a scope limitation that is material and pervasive).

VI. **Comparative Financial Statements --** The continuing auditor should report appropriately on the financial statements of each period presented that the auditor has audited. The type of opinion need not be the same for each period. (Sample reports will be provided in connection with specific lessons on the various modified audit reports.)

A. Prior period financial statements audited by a predecessor auditor whose report is not reissued—The auditor should add an other-matter paragraph stating: (1) that the financial statements of the prior period were audited by a predecessor auditor; (2) the type of opinion given (and the reason for any modification); (3) the nature of any emphasis-of-matter paragraph or other-matter paragraph; and (4) the date of the predecessor's report.

B. Prior period financial statements not audited

1. If those financial statements were compiled or reviewed (and the report on the prior period financial statements is not reissued)—the auditor should included an other-matter paragraph that identifies: (1) the nature of the service performed in the prior period; (2) a description of any modifications noted; (3) a statement that the service does not provide a basis for an opinion; and (4) the date of the report.

2. If the prior period financial statements were not audited, reviewed, or compiled—the auditor's report should include an other-matter paragraph pointing out that fact.

VII. **Sample Auditor's Reports Presented Below**

A. Unmodified auditor's report on the current year (and prior year) comparative financial statements with no reference to legal and regulatory requirements, so the introductory paragraph is not separately labeled.

B. Unmodified auditor's report is presented on a sentence-by-sentence basis to facilitate the review of the contents of such an auditor's report.

C. Unmodified auditor's report on the current year (and prior year) comparative financial statements now including a reference to legal and regulatory requirements, so the introductory paragraph is labeled "Report on the Financial Statements."

Sample Unmodified Auditor's Report Under AICPA Clarified Standards (Without Reference to Legal and Regulatory Requirements):

Independent Auditor's Report

(Appropriate Addressee)

We have audited the accompanying consolidated financial statements of ABC Company and its subsidiaries, which comprise the consolidated balance sheets as of December 31, 20X1 and 20X0, and the related consolidated statements of income, changes in stockholders' equity and cash flows for the years then ended, and the related notes to the financial statements.

Management's Responsibility for the Financial Statements

Management is responsible for the preparation and fair presentation of these consolidated financial statements in accordance with accounting principles generally accepted in the United States of America; this includes the design, implementation, and maintenance of internal control relevant to the preparation and fair presentation of consolidated financial statements that are free from material misstatement, whether due to fraud or error.

Auditor's Responsibility

Our responsibility is to express an opinion on these consolidated financial statements based on our audits. We conducted our audits in accordance with auditing standards generally accepted in the United States of America. Those standards require that we plan and perform the audit to obtain reasonable assurance about whether the consolidated financial statements are free from material misstatement.

An audit involves performing procedures to obtain audit evidence about the amounts and disclosures in the consolidated financial statements. The procedures selected depend on the auditor's judgment, including the assessment of the risks of material misstatement of the consolidated financial statements, whether due to fraud or error. In making those risk assessments, the auditor considers internal control relevant to the entity's preparation and fair presentation of the consolidated financial statements in order to design audit procedures that are appropriate in the circumstances, but not for the purpose of expressing an opinion on the effectiveness of the entity's internal control. Accordingly, we express no such opinion. An audit also includes evaluating the appropriateness of accounting policies used and the reasonableness of significant accounting estimates made by management, as well as evaluating the overall presentation of the consolidated financial statements.

We believe that the audit evidence we have obtained is sufficient and appropriate to provide a basis for our audit opinion.

Opinion

In our opinion, the consolidated financial statements referred to above present fairly, in all material respects, the financial position of ABC Company and its subsidiaries as of December 31, 20X1 and 20X0, and the results of their operations and their cash flows for the years then ended in accordance with accounting principles generally accepted in the United States of America.

(Auditor's signature — firm name, signed by audit engagement partner)

(**Auditor's city and state** — this is a new requirement under the Clarified Standards)

(Date of the auditor's report — when the auditor has obtained sufficient appropriate audit evidence as a reasonable basis for the opinion.)

See the following example.

Unmodified Auditor's Report Under AICPA Clarified Standards (Presented Sentence-By-Sentence):

Independent Auditor's Report

(Introductory Paragraph)

1. We have audited the accompanying consolidated financial statements of ABC Company and its subsidiaries, which comprise the consolidated balance sheets as of December 31, 20X1 and 20X0, and the related consolidated statements of income, changes in stockholders' equity and cash flows for the years then ended, and the related notes to the financial statements.

Management's Responsibility for the Financial Statements

1. Management is responsible for the preparation and fair presentation of these consolidated financial statements in accordance with accounting principles generally accepted in the United States of America; this includes the design, implementation, and maintenance of internal control relevant to the preparation and fair presentation of consolidated financial statements that are free from material misstatement, whether due to fraud or error.

Auditor's Responsibility

(First of 3 paragraphs)

1. Our responsibility is to express an opinion on these consolidated financial statements based on our audits.

2. We conducted our audits in accordance with auditing standards generally accepted in the United States of America.

3. Those standards require that we plan and perform the audit to obtain reasonable assurance about whether the consolidated financial statements are free from material misstatement.

(Second of 3 paragraphs)

4. An audit involves performing procedures to obtain audit evidence about the amounts and disclosures in the consolidated financial statements.

5. The procedures selected depend on the auditor's judgment, including the assessment of the risks of material misstatement of the consolidated financial statements, whether due to fraud or error.

6. In making those risk assessments, the auditor considers internal control relevant to the entity's preparation and fair presentation of the consolidated financial statements in order to design audit procedures that are appropriate in the circumstances, but not for the purpose of expressing an opinion on the effectiveness of the entity's internal control.

7. Accordingly, we express no such opinion.

8. An audit also includes evaluating the appropriateness of accounting policies used and the reasonableness of significant accounting estimates made by management, as well as evaluating the overall presentation of the consolidated financial statements.

(Third of 3 paragraphs)

9. We believe that the audit evidence we have obtained is sufficient and appropriate to provide a basis for our audit opinion.

Opinion

1. In our opinion, the consolidated financial statements referred to above present fairly, in all material respects, the financial position of ABC Company and its subsidiaries as of December 31, 20X1 and 20X0, and the results of their operations and their cash flows for the years then ended in accordance with accounting principles generally accepted in the United States of America.

Sample Unmodified Auditor's Report Under AICPA Clarified Standards (Including Reference to Legal and Regulatory Requirements):

Independent Auditor's Report

(Appropriate Addressee)

Report on the Financial Statements[1]

We have audited the accompanying consolidated financial statements of ABC Company and its subsidiaries, which comprise the consolidated balance sheets as of December 31, 20X1 and 20X0, and the related consolidated statements of income, changes in stockholders' equity and cash flows for the years then ended, and the related notes to the financial statements.

Management's Responsibility for the Financial Statements

Management is responsible for the preparation and fair presentation of these consolidated financial statements in accordance with accounting principles generally accepted in the United States of America; this includes the design, implementation, and maintenance of internal control relevant to the preparation and fair presentation of consolidated financial statements that are free from material misstatement, whether due to fraud or error.

Auditor's Responsibility

Our responsibility is to express an opinion on these consolidated financial statements based on our audits. We conducted our audits in accordance with auditing standards generally accepted in the United States of America. Those standards require that we plan and perform the audit to obtain reasonable assurance about whether the consolidated financial statements are free from material misstatement.

An audit involves performing procedures to obtain audit evidence about the amounts and disclosures in the consolidated financial statements. The procedures selected depend on the auditor's judgment, including the assessment of the risks of material misstatement of the consolidated financial statements, whether due to fraud or error. In making those risk assessments, the auditor considers internal control relevant to the entity's preparation and fair presentation of the consolidated financial statements in order to design audit procedures that are appropriate in the circumstances, but not for the purpose of expressing an opinion on the effectiveness of the entity's internal control.[2] Accordingly, we express no such opinion. An audit also includes evaluating the appropriateness of accounting policies used and the reasonableness of significant accounting estimates made by management, as well as evaluating the overall presentation of the consolidated financial statements.

We believe that the audit evidence we have obtained is sufficient and appropriate to provide a basis for our audit opinion.

Opinion

In our opinion, the consolidated financial statements referred to above present fairly, in all material respects, the financial position of ABC Company and its subsidiaries as of December 31, 20X1 and 20X0, and the results of their operations and their cash flows for the years then ended in accordance with accounting principles generally accepted in the United States of America.

Report on Other Legal and Regulatory Requirements

(The form and content of this section of the auditor's report will vary depending on the nature of the auditor's other reporting responsibilities.)

(Auditor's signature)

(Auditor's city and state)

(Date of the auditor's report)

[1]The subtitle "Report on the Financial Statements" is unnecessary in circumstances when the second subtitle, "Report on Other Legal and Regulatory Requirements," is not applicable.

[2]When the auditor has responsibility for expressing an opinion on the effectiveness of internal control in conjunction with the audit of the entity's financial statements, the sentence would be stated as follows: "In making those risk assessments, the auditor considers internal control relevant to the entity's preparation and fair presentation of the consolidated financial statements in order to design audit procedures that are appropriate in the circumstances." In addition, the next sentence, "Accordingly, we express no such opinion," would be omitted.

Audits of Group Financial Statements

After studying this lesson, you should be able to:

1. *Know how a reference to a component auditor affects the auditor's report.*
2. *Understand the difference between a component and a group, and distinguish between the group's auditor and a component auditor.*

I. **Relevant AICPA Guidance --** The relevant AICPA guidance is provided by AU 600: "Special Considerations — Audits of Group Financial Statements (Including the Work of Component Auditors)." The standard states that the auditor's objectives are to determine whether to act as the auditor of the group financial statements, and, if so, (1) to determine whether to make reference to the audit of the component auditor; (2) to communicate clearly with component auditors; and (3) to obtain sufficient appropriate audit evidence regarding the financial information of the components and the consolidation process to express an opinion on the group financial statements.

II. **Selected Definitions:**

> **Component** — An entity for which group or component management prepares financial information that is required by the applicable financial reporting framework to be included in the group financial statements.
>
> **Component auditor** — An auditor who performs work on the financial information of a component that will be used as audit evidence for the group audit. (**A component auditor may be part of the group engagement partner's firm, a network-affiliated firm, or another unrelated firm.**)
>
> **Group** — All the components whose financial information is included in the group financial statements. A group always has more than one component.
>
> **Group financial statements** — Financial statements that include the financial information of more than one component. This term also refers to combined financial statements aggregating the financial information prepared by components that are under common control.
>
> **Group-wide controls** — Controls designed, implemented, and maintained by group management over group financial reporting.
>
> **Significant component** — A component identified by the group engagement team that (a) is of individual financial significance to the group; or (b) due to its specific nature, is likely to include significant risks of material misstatement of the group financial statements.

III. **Responsibilities of the Group Engagement Partner and the Group Engagement Team**

A. **Group engagement partner --** The group engagement partner is responsible for (1) the supervision and performance of the group audit engagement in compliance with professional standards and applicable regulatory requirements; and (2) determining whether the auditor's report is appropriate in the circumstances.

B. **Acceptance and continuance --** The group engagement team should obtain an understanding of the group, its components, and their environments sufficient to identify the significant components.

1. The group engagement partner should evaluate whether sufficient appropriate audit evidence will be obtained, including the use of the component auditors' work, to act as the auditor of the group financial statements.

2. If sufficient appropriate audit evidence would not be obtained, the auditor should not accept a new engagement or should withdraw from a continuing engagement. (If withdrawal is not permitted, the auditor should disclaim an opinion.)

C. **Assess the risks of material misstatement of the group financial statements --** The auditor should obtain an understanding of the group, its components, and their environments (including group-wide controls) and obtain an understanding of the consolidation process and the instructions issued by group management to components.

D. **Obtain an understanding of the component auditor(s)**

1. Recall that the term component auditor applies to auditors of other offices of the group engagement partner's firm (for an engagement involving multiple offices of the same firm), to a network-affiliated firm, or to another unrelated firm (that is not subject to the quality controls of the group engagement partner's firm).

2. The group engagement team should obtain an understanding of (a) the component auditor's independence and professional competence; (b) the extent to which the group engagement team will be involved in the work of the component auditor; (c) whether the group engagement team will be able to obtain information affecting the consolidation process from the component auditor.

E. The group engagement team should determine materiality (1) for the group financial statements as a whole, (2) for the components to be audited by the group engagement team or by component auditors, and (3) the threshold for determining clearly trivial to the group financial statements.

F. **Responding to assessed risks --** If work to be performed on the consolidation process or the financial information of the components is based on an expectation that group-wide controls are operating effectively, the group engagement team (or the component auditor) should test the operating effectiveness of those controls.

G. **Consolidation process --** The group engagement team should perform further audit procedures on the consolidation process to respond to the assessed risks of material misstatement associated with the consolidation process, including evaluating whether all components have been included and whether there are any indicators of possible management bias or fraud.

H. **Communications with a component auditor --** The group engagement team should communicate its requirements of the component on a timely basis, and request that the component auditor communicate matters relevant to the group engagement team's conclusions.

I. **Involvement in the work of the component auditors --** For a significant component for which the auditor of the group financial statements is assuming responsibility for the component auditor's work, the auditor should (a) discuss with the component auditor the significance of the component to the group and the susceptibility of the component to material misstatement; and (b) review the component auditor's documentation of identified significant risks of material misstatement to the group financial statements.

J. **Documentation --** The group engagement team's audit documentation should include the following:

1. An analysis of components indicating those that are significant (and the type of work performed);

2. Written communications between the group engagement team and the component auditors about the group engagement team's requirements;

3. Those components for which reference to the component auditors' reports were made in the auditor's report; and

4. The financial statements of the component and the report of the component auditor for components referenced in the auditor's report on the group financial statements.

K. Determining whether to reference a component auditor in the auditor's report

1. Reference to the component auditor should not be made unless: (a) the component's financial statements are prepared using the same financial reporting framework used by the group; (b) the component auditor has performed an audit on the component's financial statements in accordance with GAAS (or PCAOB standards, if applicable); and **(c) the component auditor has issued an audit report on the component's financial statements that is not restricted as to use**.
2. If the group engagement partner decides to assume responsibility for the component auditor's work — No reference should be made to the component auditor in the auditor's report.
3. If the group engagement partner decides to name the component auditor in the auditor's report — The component auditor's permission should be obtained and the component auditor's report should be presented along with the auditor's report on the group financial statements.

L. Effect of reference to a component auditor on the auditor's report

1. No effect on the introductory paragraph or management's responsibility section.
2. Auditor's responsibility section — The first paragraph should be modified to identify the component audited by other auditors and the magnitude of the financial statements involved.
3. The opinion paragraph should refer to "In our opinion, **based on our audit and the report of the other auditors, ..."**

M. Sample report that refers to a component auditor

See the following example.

Independent Auditor's Report

(Appropriate Addressee)

Report on the Consolidated Financial Statements

We have audited the accompanying consolidated financial statements of ABC Company and its subsidiaries, which comprise the consolidated balance sheets as of December 31, 20X1 and 20X0, and the related consolidated statements of income, changes in stockholders' equity and cash flows for the years then ended, and the related notes to the financial statements.

Management's Responsibility for the Financial Statements

Management is responsible for the preparation and fair presentation of these consolidated financial statements in accordance with accounting principles generally accepted in the United States of America; this includes the design, implementation and maintenance of internal control relevant to the preparation and fair presentation of consolidated financial statements that are free from material misstatement, whether due to fraud or error.

Auditor's Responsibility

Our responsibility is to express an opinion on these consolidated financial statements based on our audit. **We did not audit the financial statements of B Company, a wholly-owned subsidiary, whose statements reflect total assets and revenues constituting 20 percent and 22 percent, respectively, of the related consolidated totals. Those statements were audited by other auditors, whose report has been furnished to us, and our opinion, insofar as it relates to the amounts included for B Company, is based solely on the report of the other auditors.** We conducted our audits in accordance with auditing standards generally accepted in the United States of America. Those standards require that we plan and perform the audit to obtain reasonable assurance about whether the consolidated financial statements are free from material misstatement.

An audit involves performing procedures to obtain audit evidence about the amounts and disclosures in the consolidated financial statements. The procedures selected depend on the auditor's judgment, including the assessment of the risks of material misstatement of the consolidated financial statements, whether due to fraud or error. In making those risk assessments, the auditor considers internal control relevant to the entity's preparation and fair presentation of the consolidated financial statements in order to design audit procedures that are appropriate in the circumstances, but not for the purpose of expressing an opinion on the effectiveness of the entity's internal control. Accordingly, we express no such opinion. An audit also includes evaluating the appropriateness of accounting policies used and the reasonableness of significant accounting estimates made by management, as well as evaluating the overall presentation of the consolidated financial statements.

We believe that the audit evidence we have obtained is sufficient and appropriate to provide a basis for our audit opinion.

Opinion

In our opinion, **based on our audit and the report of the other auditors**, the consolidated financial statements referred to above presents fairly, in all material respects, the financial position of ABC Company and its subsidiaries as of December 31, 20X1 and 20X2, in accordance with accounting principles generally accepted in the United States of America.

(Auditor's Signature)

(Auditor's City and State)

(Date of the Auditor's Report)

Emphasis-of-Matter and Other-Matter Paragraphs

After studying this lesson, you should be able to:

1. *Know the definition of (and distinction between) emphasis-of-matter and other-matter paragraphs in the auditor's report.*
2. *Know the three matters for which an emphasis-of-matter paragraph is required.*
3. *Know how an emphasis-of-matter and/or other-matter paragraph would be presented in the auditor's report.*

I. **Responsibilities under AICPA Professional Standards --** The relevant AICPA guidance is provided by AU 706 "Emphasis-of-Matter Paragraphs and Other-Matter Paragraphs in the Independent Auditor's Report." This pronouncement states that the auditor's objective is to draw the users' attention, as necessary, to (1) a matter, already appropriately presented/disclosed in the financial statements, that is important to the users' understanding of the financial statements (emphasis-of-matter paragraph); or (2) any other matter that is relevant to the users' understanding of the audit, the auditor's responsibilities, or the auditor's report (other-matter paragraph).

> **Definitions:**
> *Emphasis-of-matter paragraph*: A paragraph that refers to a matter appropriately presented or disclosed in the financial statements that, in the auditor's judgment, is of such importance that it is fundamental to users' understanding of the financial statements.
>
> *Other-matter paragraph*: A paragraph that refers to a matter other than those presented or disclosed in the financial statements that, in the auditor's judgment, is relevant to users' understanding of the audit, the auditor's responsibilities, or the auditor's report.

II. **Emphasis-of-matter paragraph**

- **A.** Matters for which an emphasis-of-matter paragraph is **required**:
  1. When the auditor has substantial doubt about the entity's ability to continue as a going concern;
  2. When there is an inconsistency in accounting principles used; and
  3. When the financial statements are prepared in accordance with special purpose frameworks. (This topic will be discussed in another lesson.)
- **B.** Circumstances for which an auditor may consider it necessary to add an emphasis-of-matter paragraph: (1) an uncertainty as to the outcome of unusually important litigation or regulator action; (2) a major casualty having a significant effect; (3) significant transactions with related parties; or (4) unusually important subsequent events.
- **C.** Presentation of the emphasis-of-matter paragraph
  1. Presented immediately after the opinion paragraph;
  2. Should have an appropriate heading, such as "Emphasis of Matter";
  3. Should reference the specific matter being emphasized and identify where relevant disclosures can be found in the financial statements; and
  4. State that the auditor's opinion is not modified with respect to the matter emphasized.
- **D.** Example of such a paragraph for a going concern issue:

> **Emphasis-of-Matter** (presented after the opinion paragraph):
>
> The accompanying financial statements have been prepared assuming that the Company will continue as a going concern. As discussed in Note X to the financial statements, the Company has suffered recurring losses from operations and has a net capital deficiency that raise substantial doubt about its ability to continue as a going concern. Management's plans in regard to these matters are also described in Note X. The financial statements do not include any adjustments that might result from the outcome of this uncertainty. Our opinion is not modified with respect to this matter.

III. Other-matter paragraph

A. Circumstances for which an auditor may consider it necessary to add an other-matter paragraph:

1. Relevant to users' understanding of the audit — In rare situations, the auditor may add an other-matter paragraph to explain why it was not possible for the auditor to withdraw from an engagement in which a scope limitation that was pervasive resulted in a disclaimer of opinion.

2. Relevant to users' understanding of the auditor's responsibilities or the auditor's report — For example, when the opinion expressed on the prior year's financial statements is different than the opinion previously expressed (as a result of management's correction of a material departure from the applicable financial reporting framework).

B. **Presentation of the other-matter paragraph**

1. When the other matter paragraph is intended to draw users' attention to a matter relevant to their understanding of the audit of the financial statements — The other matter paragraph should be presented immediately after the opinion paragraph and after any emphasis-of-matter paragraph(s).

   a. When the other-matter paragraph is intended to draw users' attention to a matter relating to other reporting responsibilities addressed in the auditor's report — The paragraph may be included in the section of the report labeled "Report on Other Legal and Regulatory Requirements."

   b. When relevant to all the auditor's responsibilities or users' understanding of the auditor's report — The other-matter paragraph may also be included as a separate section following the "Report on the Financial Statements" and the "Report on Other Legal and Regulatory Requirements."

2. Should have an appropriate heading, such as "Other Matter."

C. Example of such a paragraph when the opinion expressed on the prior year's financial statements is different than the opinion previously expressed:

> **Other Matter** (presented after the opinion and emphasis-of-matter paragraphs):
>
> In our report dated March 1, 20X1, we expressed an opinion that the 20X0 financial statements did not fairly present the financial position, results of operations, and cash flows of ABC Company in accordance with accounting principles generally accepted in the United States of America because of two departures from such principles: (1) ABC Company carried its property, plant, and equipment at appraisal values, and provided for depreciation on the basis of such values, and (2) ABC Company did not provide for deferred income taxes with respect to differences between income for financial reporting purposes and taxable income. As described in Note X, the Company has changed its method of accounting for these items and restated its 20X0 financial statements to conform with accounting principles generally accepted in the United States of America. Accordingly, our present opinion on the restated 20X0 financial statements, as presented herein, is different from that expressed in our previous report.

IV. Communication with Those Charged with Governance -- The auditor should communicate with those charged with governance about the proposed wording of any expected emphasis-of-matter or other-matter paragraph(s).

Note:
The Statements on Auditing Standards that preceded the clarified auditing standards used the term **explanatory paragraph** in a variety of contexts, including emphasis of a matter and explaining the basis for an opinion that was other than unqualified. Sometimes the explanatory paragraph preceded the opinion, sometimes it followed the opinion, and in some circumstances the auditor had a choice to place the explanatory paragraph either before or after the opinion paragraph. Under the clarified auditing standards, the term explanatory paragraph is no longer used.

Qualified for Scope Limitation

After studying this lesson, you should be able to:

1. *Understand when and how to express a qualified audit opinion for a scope limitation affecting the auditor's basis for conclusions.*

I. Relevant AICPA Guidance

Relevant AICPA Guidance -- The relevant AICPA guidance is provided by AU 705: "Modifications to the Opinion in the Independent Auditor's Report." The standard states that the auditor's objective is to express clearly an appropriately modified opinion when (1) the auditor concludes that the financial statements as a whole are misstated; or (2) **the auditor is unable to obtain sufficient appropriate audit evidence to conclude that the financial statements as a whole are free from material misstatement**. This lesson focuses on the second matter, which is known as a scope limitation.

> **Definitions:**
> *Modified opinion*: A qualified opinion, an adverse opinion, or a disclaimer of opinion.
>
> *Pervasive*: (a) Effects that are not confined to specific elements, accounts or items of the financial statements; (b) effects that, if so confined, represent or could represent a substantial proportion of the financial statements; or (c) regarding disclosures, are fundamental to users' understanding of the financial statements.

II. Opinion Scope Limitation Involves Judgment

A. **Qualified opinion --** The auditor should express a qualified opinion when the auditor is unable to obtain sufficient appropriate audit evidence, and the auditor concludes that the possible effect on the financial statements, if any, could be **material, but not pervasive**. (This lesson focuses on the qualified opinion in connection with a scope limitation.)

B. **Disclaimer of opinion --** The auditor should express a disclaimer of opinion when the auditor is unable to obtain sufficient appropriate audit evidence, and the auditor concludes that the possible effect on the financial statements, if any, could be **material and pervasive**. (A separate lesson focuses on the disclaimer of opinion.)

III. Circumstances Resulting in a Scope Limitation

A. **Circumstances beyond the control of the entity --** for example, the entity's accounting records have been destroyed.

B. **Circumstances related to the nature or timing of the auditor's work --** for example, the auditor determines that substantive procedures alone are not sufficient and the entity's controls are ineffective; the auditor is unable to obtain audited financial statements of an investee (accounted for using the equity method); or the timing of the auditor's appointment does not permit the auditor to observe the physical counting of inventories.

C. **Limitations imposed by management --** for example, management prevents the auditor from requesting external confirmation of certain account balances. The auditor should request that management remove any such limitation.

   1. If management refuses—the auditor should communicate the matter to those charged with governance and determine whether it is possible to perform alternative procedures to obtain sufficient appropriate audit evidence.

   2. If unable to obtain sufficient appropriate audit evidence (and if the effects could be both material and pervasive)—the auditor should withdraw from the audit (when practicable) or issue a disclaimer of opinion.

IV. Effect of a Qualification for a Scope Limitation on the Auditor's Report

A. No effect on the introductory paragraph or management's responsibility section.

B. Auditor's responsibility section—modify the last sentence to state, "We believe that the audit evidence we have obtained is sufficient and appropriate to provide a basis for our **qualified** audit opinion."

C. Add a "Basis for Qualified Opinion" paragraph (with such a label) before the opinion paragraph.

D. Qualify the opinion using appropriate language such as: "In our opinion, **except for the possible effects of the matter described in the Basis for Qualified Opinion paragraph**, the financial statements referred to above present fairly . . ." and label the opinion paragraph "Qualified Opinion."

V. Sample Audit Report Qualified for a Scope Limitation Follows

Independent Auditor's Report

(Appropriate Addressee)

We have audited the accompanying financial statements of ABC Company, which comprise the balance sheet as of December 31, 20X1, and the related statements of income, changes in stockholders' equity and cash flows for the year then ended, and the related notes to the financial statements.

Management's Responsibility for the Financial Statements

Management is responsible for the preparation and fair presentation of these financial statements in accordance with accounting principles generally accepted in the United States of America; this includes the design, implementation, and maintenance of internal control relevant to the preparation and fair presentation of financial statements that are free from material misstatement, whether due to fraud or error.

Auditor's Responsibility

Our responsibility is to express an opinion on these financial statements based on our audit. We conducted our audit in accordance with auditing standards generally accepted in the United States of America. Those standards require that we plan and perform the audit to obtain reasonable assurance about whether the financial statements are free from material misstatement.

An audit involves performing procedures to obtain audit evidence about the amounts and disclosures in the consolidated financial statements. The procedures selected depend on the auditor's judgment, including the assessment of the risks of material misstatement of the consolidated financial statements, whether due to fraud or error. In making those risk assessments, the auditor considers internal control relevant to the entity's preparation and fair presentation of the consolidated financial statements in order to design audit procedures that are appropriate in the circumstances, but not for the purpose of expressing an opinion on the effectiveness of the entity's internal control. Accordingly, we express no such opinion. An audit also includes evaluating the appropriateness of accounting policies used and the reasonableness of significant accounting estimates made by management, as well as evaluating the overall presentation of the financial statements.

We believe that the audit evidence we have obtained is sufficient and appropriate to provide a basis for our qualified audit opinion.

Basis for Qualified Opinion

ABC Company's investment in XYZ Company, a foreign affiliate acquired during the year and accounted for under the equity method, is carried at $xxx on the balance sheet at December 31, 20X1, and ABC Company's share of XYZ Company's net income of $xxx is included in ABC Company's net income for the year then ended. We were unable to obtain sufficient appropriate audit evidence about the carrying amount of ABC Company's investment in XYZ Company as of December 31, 20X1 and ABC Company's share of XYZ Company's net income for the year then ended because we were denied access to the financial information, management, and the auditors of XYZ Company. Consequently, we were unable to determine whether any adjustments to these amounts were necessary.

Qualified Opinion

In our opinion, except for the possible effects of the matter described in the Basis for Qualified Opinion paragraph, the financial statements referred to above present fairly, in all material respects, the financial position of ABC Company as of December 31, 20X1, and the results of its operations and its cash flows for the year then ended in accordance with accounting principles generally accepted in the United States of America.

(Auditor's signature)

(Auditor's city and state)

(Date of the auditor's report)

Qualified for Misstatement

After studying this lesson, you should be able to:

1. *Understand when and how to express a qualified audit opinion for a misstatement (including inadequate disclosure) affecting the fair presentation of an entity's financial statements.*

I. **Relevant AICPA Guidance --** The relevant AICPA guidance is provided by AU 705: "Modifications to the Opinion in the Independent Auditor's Report." The standard states that the auditor's objective is to express clearly an appropriately modified opinion when (1) the auditor concludes that the financial statements as a whole are misstated; or (2) the auditor is unable to obtain sufficient appropriate audit evidence to conclude that the financial statements as a whole are free from material misstatement. (This lesson focuses on the first matter, since the scope limitation is discussed in a separate lesson.)

Definitions:
Modified opinion: A qualified opinion, an adverse opinion, or a disclaimer of opinion.

Pervasive: (a) Effects that are not confined to specific elements, accounts or items of the financial statements; (b) effects that, if so confined, represent or could represent a substantial proportion of the financial statements; or (c) regarding disclosures, are fundamental to users' understanding of the financial statements.

II. **Opinion Choice for a Misstatement (Including Inadequate Disclosure) Involves Judgment**

A. **Qualified opinion --** The auditor should express a qualified opinion when the auditor concludes that misstatements are **material, but not pervasive** to the financial statements.

B. **Adverse opinion --** The auditor should express an adverse opinion when the auditor concludes that misstatements are **material, and pervasive** to the financial statements. (A separate lesson focuses on the adverse opinion.)

III. **Effect of a Qualification for a Misstatement on the Auditor's Report**

A. No effect on the introductory paragraph or management's responsibility section.

B. Auditor's responsibility section—modify the last sentence to state, "We believe that the audit evidence we have obtained is sufficient and appropriate to provide a basis for our **qualified** audit opinion."

C. Add a "Basis for Qualified Opinion" paragraph (with such a label) before the opinion paragraph. The auditor should include a description and quantification of the financial effects of the misstatement (when practicable); likewise, the auditor should include the omitted information (when practicable).

D. Qualify the opinion using appropriate language such as: "In our opinion, **except for the effects of the matter described in the Basis for Qualified Opinion paragraph**, the financial statements referred to above present fairly . . ." and label the opinion paragraph "Qualified Opinion."

IV. **Sample Audit Report Qualified for a Misstatement**

See the following example.

Independent Auditor's Report

(Appropriate Addressee)

We have audited the accompanying financial statements of ABC Company, which comprise the balance sheet as of December 31, 20X1, and the related statements of income, changes in stockholders' equity and cash flows for the year then ended, and the related notes to the financial statements.

Management's Responsibility for the Financial Statements

Management is responsible for the preparation and fair presentation of these financial statements in accordance with accounting principles generally accepted in the United States of America; this includes the design, implementation, and maintenance of internal control relevant to the preparation and fair presentation of financial statements that are free from material misstatement, whether due to fraud or error.

Auditor's Responsibility

Our responsibility is to express an opinion on these financial statements based on our audit. We conducted our audit in accordance with auditing standards generally accepted in the United States of America. Those standards require that we plan and perform the audit to obtain reasonable assurance about whether the financial statements are free from material misstatement.

An audit involves performing procedures to obtain audit evidence about the amounts and disclosures in the consolidated financial statements. The procedures selected depend on the auditor's judgment, including the assessment of the risks of material misstatement of the consolidated financial statements, whether due to fraud or error. In making those risk assessments, the auditor considers internal control relevant to the entity's preparation and fair presentation of the consolidated financial statements in order to design audit procedures that are appropriate in the circumstances, but not for the purpose of expressing an opinion on the effectiveness of the entity's internal control. Accordingly, we express no such opinion. An audit also includes evaluating the appropriateness of accounting policies used and the reasonableness of significant accounting estimates made by management, as well as evaluating the overall presentation of the financial statements.

We believe that the audit evidence we have obtained is sufficient and appropriate to provide a basis for our qualified audit opinion.

Basis for Qualified Opinion

The Company has stated inventories at cost in the accompanying balance sheets. Accounting principles generally accepted in the United States of America require inventories to be stated at the lower of cost or market. If the Company stated inventories at the lower of cost or market, a write down of $xxx and $xxx would have been required as of December 31, 20X1 and 20X0, respectively. Accordingly, cost of sales would have been increased by $xxx and $xxx, and net income, income taxes, and stockholders' equity would have been reduced by $xxx, $xxx, and $xxx, and $xxx, $xxx, and $xxx, as of and for the years then ended in accordance with accounting principles generally accepted in the United States of America.

Qualified Opinion

In our opinion, except for the effects of the matter described in the Basis for Qualified Opinion paragraph, the financial statements referred to above present fairly, in all material respects, the financial position of ABC Company as of December 31, 20X1 and 20X0, and the results of its operations and its cash flows for the years then ended in accordance with accounting principles generally accepted in the United States of America.

(Auditor's signature)

(Auditor's city and state)

(Date of the auditor's report)

Adverse Opinion

After studying this lesson, you should be able to:

1. *Understand how to express an adverse audit opinion when a material and pervasive misstatement causes an entity's financial statement presentation to be misleading.*

I. **Relevant AICPA Guidance --** The relevant AICPA guidance is provided by AU 705: "Modifications to the Opinion in the Independent Auditor's Report." The standard states that the auditor's objective is to express clearly an appropriately modified opinion when (1) **the auditor concludes that the financial statements as a whole are misstated**; or (2) the auditor is unable to obtain sufficient appropriate audit evidence to conclude that the financial statements as a whole are free from material misstatement. (This lesson focuses on the first matter, since the scope limitation is discussed elsewhere.)

> **Definitions:**
> *Modified opinion*: A qualified opinion, an adverse opinion, or a disclaimer of opinion.
>
> *Pervasive*: (a) Effects that are not confined to specific elements, accounts or items of the financial statements; (b) effects that, if so confined, represent or could represent a substantial proportion of the financial statements; or (c) regarding disclosures, are fundamental to users' understanding of the financial statements.

II. **Opinion Choice for a Misstatement (Including Inadequate Disclosure) Involves Judgment**

A. **Qualified opinion --** The auditor should express a qualified opinion when the auditor concludes that misstatements are *material, but not pervasive* to the financial statements. (A separate lesson focuses on the qualified opinion.)

B. **Adverse opinion --** The auditor should express an adverse opinion when the auditor concludes that misstatements are *material, and pervasive* to the financial statements.

III. **Effect of an Adverse Opinion on the Auditor's Report**

A. No effect on the introductory paragraph or management's responsibility section.

B. Auditor's responsibility section—modify the last sentence to state, "We believe that the audit evidence we have obtained is sufficient and appropriate to provide a basis for our **adverse** audit opinion."

C. Add a "Basis for Adverse Opinion" paragraph (with such a label) before the opinion paragraph. The auditor should include a description and quantification of the financial effects of the misstatement (when practicable); likewise, the auditor should include the omitted information (when practicable).

D. Express the adverse opinion using appropriate language such as: "In our opinion, **because of the significance of the matter discussed in the Basis for Adverse Opinion paragraph, the financial statements referred to above do not present fairly** . . ." and label the opinion paragraph "Adverse Opinion."

IV. **Sample Audit Report with an Adverse Opinion for Misstatement**

See the following example.

Independent Auditor's Report

(Appropriate Addressee)

We have audited the accompanying consolidated financial statements of ABC Company and its subsidiaries, which comprise the consolidated balance sheets as of December 31, 20X1, and the related consolidated statements of income, changes in stockholder' equity and cash flows for the year then ended, and the related notes to the financial statements.

Management's Responsibility for the Financial Statements

Management is responsible for the preparation and fair presentation of these consolidated financial statements in accordance with accounting principles generally accepted in the United States of America; this includes the design, implementation, and maintenance of internal control relevant to the preparation and fair presentation of consolidated financial statements that are free from material misstatement, whether due to fraud or error.

Auditor's Responsibility

Our responsibility is to express an opinion on these consolidated financial statements based on our audit. We conducted our audit in accordance with auditing standards generally accepted in the United States of America. Those standards require that we plan and perform the audit to obtain reasonable assurance about whether the financial statements are free from material misstatement.

An audit involves performing procedures to obtain audit evidence about the amounts and disclosures in the consolidated financial statements. The procedures selected depend on the auditor's judgment, including the assessment of the risks of material misstatement of the consolidated financial statements, whether due to fraud or error. In making those risk assessments, the auditor considers internal control relevant to the entity's preparation and fair presentation of the consolidated financial statements in order to design audit procedures that are appropriate in the circumstances, but not for the purpose of expressing an opinion on the effectiveness of the entity's internal control. Accordingly, we express no such opinion. An audit also includes evaluating the appropriateness of accounting policies used and the reasonableness of significant accounting estimates made by management, as well as evaluating the overall presentation of the consolidated financial statements.

We believe that the audit evidence we have obtained is sufficient and appropriate to provide a basis for our adverse audit opinion.

Basis for Adverse Opinion

As described in Note X, the Company has not consolidated the financial statements of subsidiary XYZ Company that it acquired during 20X1 because it has not yet been able to ascertain the fair values of certain of the subsidiary's material assets and liabilities at the acquisition date. This investment is therefore accounted for on a cost basis by the Company. Under accounting principles generally accepted in the United States of America, the subsidiary should have been consolidated because it is controlled by the Company. Had XYZ Company been consolidated, many elements in the accompanying consolidated financial statements would have been materially affected. The effects on the consolidated financial statements of the failure to consolidate have not been determined.

Adverse Opinion

In our opinion, because of the significance of the matter discussed in the Basis for Adverse Opinion paragraph, the consolidated financial statements referred to above do not present fairly the financial position of ABC Company and its subsidiaries as of December 31, 20X1, or the results of their operations or their cash flows for the years then ended.

(Auditor's signature)

(Auditor's city and state)

(Date of the auditor's report)

Disclaimer of Opinion

After studying this lesson, you should be able to:

1. *Understand how to express a disclaimer of opinion for a scope limitation when the possible effects are viewed as material and pervasive.*

I. **Relevant AICPA Guidance --** The relevant AICPA guidance is provided by AU 705: "Modifications to the Opinion in the Independent Auditor's Report." The standard states that the auditor's objective is to express clearly an appropriately modified opinion when (1) the auditor concludes that the financial statements as a whole are misstated; or (2) **the auditor is unable to obtain sufficient appropriate audit evidence to conclude that the financial statements as a whole are free from material misstatement**. This lesson focuses on the second matter, which is known as a *scope limitation*.

> **Definitions:**
> *Modified opinion*: A qualified opinion, an adverse opinion, or a disclaimer of opinion.
>
> *Pervasive* : (a) Effects that are not confined to specific elements, accounts or items of the financial statements; (b) effects that, if so confined, represent or could represent a substantial proportion of the financial statements; or (c) regarding disclosures, are fundamental to users' understanding of the financial statements.

II. **Opinion Choice for a Scope Limitation Involves Judgment**

A. **Qualified opinion --** The auditor should express a qualified opinion when the auditor is unable to obtain sufficient appropriate audit evidence, and the auditor concludes that the possible effect on the financial statements, if any, could be *material, but not pervasive*. (Another lesson focuses on the qualification for a scope limitation.)

B. **Disclaimer of opinion --** The auditor should express a disclaimer of opinion when the auditor is unable to obtain sufficient appropriate audit evidence, and the auditor concludes that the possible effect on the financial statements, if any, could be *material and pervasive*.

III. **Circumstances Resulting in a Scope Limitation**

A. **Circumstances beyond the control of the entity --** for example, the entity's accounting records have been destroyed.

B. **Circumstances related to the nature or timing of the auditor's work --** for example, the auditor determines that substantive procedures alone are not sufficient and the entity's controls are ineffective; the auditor is unable to obtain audited financial statements of an investee (accounted for using the equity method); or the timing of the auditor's appointment does not permit the auditor to observe the physical counting of inventories.

C. **Limitations imposed by management --** for example, management prevents the auditor from requesting external confirmation of certain account balances. The auditor should request that management remove any such limitation.

1. If management refuses -- The auditor should communicate the matter to those charged with governance and determine whether it is possible to perform alternative procedures to obtain sufficient appropriate audit evidence.

2. If unable to obtain sufficient appropriate audit evidence (and if the effects could be both material and pervasive) -- the auditor should withdraw from the audit (when practicable) or issue a disclaimer of opinion.

IV. **Effect of a Disclaimer of Opinion on the Auditor's Report**

A. Minor effect on the introductory paragraph ("We were engaged to audit ...") and no effect on the management's responsibility section.

B. Auditor's responsibility section -- revise this section to consist of the following 2 sentences: "Our responsibility is to express an opinion on these financial statements based on conducting the audit in accordance with auditing standards generally accepted in the United States of America. **Because of the matter described in the Basis for Disclaimer of Opinion paragraph, however, we were not able to obtain sufficient appropriate audit evidence to provide a basis for an audit opinion."**

C. Add a "Basis for Disclaimer of Opinion" paragraph (with such a label) before the opinion paragraph.

D. Disclaim an opinion using appropriate language such as: **"Because of the significance of the matter described in the Basis for Disclaimer of Opinion paragraph, we have not been able to obtain sufficient appropriate audit evidence to provide a basis for an audit opinion. Accordingly, we do not express an opinion on these financial statements."** Add an appropriate title preceding the paragraph, such as "Disclaimer of Opinion."

V. Sample Audit Report with a Disclaimer of Opinion for a Scope Limitation Follows

Independent Auditor's Report

(Appropriate Addressee)

We were engaged to audit the accompanying financial statements of ABC Company, which comprise the balance sheet as of December 31, 20X1, and the related statements of income, changes in stockholders' equity and cash flows for the year then ended, and the related notes to the financial statements.

Management's Responsibility for the Financial Statements

Management is responsible for the preparation and fair presentation of these financial statements in accordance with accounting principles generally accepted in the United States of America; this includes the design, implementation, and maintenance of internal control relevant to the preparation and fair presentation of financial statements that are free from material misstatement, whether due to fraud or error.

Auditor's Responsibility

Our responsibility is to express an opinion on these financial statements based on conducting the audit in accordance with auditing standards generally accepted in the United States of America. **Because of the matter described in the Basis for Disclaimer of Opinion paragraph, however, we were not able to obtain sufficient appropriate audit evidence to provide a basis for an audit opinion.**

Basis for Disclaimer of Opinion

The company's investment in XYZ Company, a joint venture, is carried at $xxx on the Company's balance sheet, which represents over 90 percent of the Company's net assets as of December 31, 20X1. We were not allowed access to the management and the auditors of XYZ Company. As a result, we were unable to determine whether any adjustments were necessary relating to the Company's proportional share of XYZ Company's assets that it controls jointly, its proportional share of XYZ Company's liabilities for which it is jointly responsible, its proportional share of XYZ Company's income and expenses for the year, and the elements making up the statements of changes in stockholders' equity and cash flows.

Disclaimer of Opinion

Because of the significance of the matter described in the Basis for Disclaimer of Opinion paragraph, we have not been able to obtain sufficient appropriate audit evidence to provide a basis for an audit opinion. Accordingly, we do not express an opinion on these financial statements.

(Auditor's signature)

(Auditor's city and state)

(Date of the auditor's report)

Consistency of Financial Statements

After studying this lesson, you should be able to:

1. *Identify how the auditor's report should address a material inconsistency in the financial statements caused by a change in accounting principle or a correction of previously issued financial statements.*

I. **Relevant AICPA Guidance --** The relevant AICPA guidance is provided by AU 708: "Consistency of Financial Statements." The standard states that the auditor's objectives are to (1) evaluate the consistency of the financial statements for the periods presented; and (2) communicate appropriately in the auditor's report when comparability has been materially affected (a) by a change in accounting principle or (b) by adjustments to correct a material misstatement in previously issued financial statements.

II. **Evaluating Consistency**

A. The auditor should evaluate whether the comparability between periods has been affected by either a material change in accounting principle or a material restatement of financial statements.

B. **When the auditor's opinion covers 2 (or more) periods --** the auditor should evaluate the consistency between such periods, as well as the consistency of the earliest period covered by the auditor's opinion with the prior period.

C. **Change in accounting principle**

D. The auditor should evaluate a change in accounting principles about 4 matters:

1. Whether the adopted principle is in accordance with the applicable financial reporting framework;
2. Whether the method of accounting for the effect of the change is in accordance with the applicable financial reporting framework;
3. Whether the disclosures about the change are adequate; and
4. Whether the entity has justified that the alternative adopted is **preferable**. (The issuance of an accounting pronouncement that requires or expresses a preference for an accounting principle is considered sufficient justification for a change in principle.)

E. **When those 4 criteria are met (and the change has a material effect on the financial statements) --** the auditor should include an *emphasis-of-matter* paragraph in the auditor's report to describe the change and reference the footnote disclosure applicable to the change. The auditor should state that the auditor's opinion is not modified regarding the matter.

1. Include the emphasis-of-matter paragraph in subsequent periods until the new principle is applied in all periods presented.
2. If the change is accounted for by retrospective application to the financial statements, the emphasis-of-matter paragraph is only needed in the period of the change.

F. **When those 4 criteria have not all been met (and the change has a material effect on the financial statements) --** The auditor should evaluate whether the change results in a material misstatement and consider whether the auditor's report should be modified.

G. **When a change in the reporting entity results in financial statements that are essentially those of a different reporting entity --** The auditor should include an emphasis-of-matter paragraph in the auditor's report describing the change in the entity and referencing the entity's disclosure. However, that is unnecessary when the change in entity results from a transaction or event, such as the purchase or disposition of a subsidiary.

H. **Correction of a material misstatement in previously issued financial statements**

1. **When the financial statements are restated to correct a prior material misstatement** -- the auditor should include an emphasis-of-matter paragraph in the auditor's report. (That paragraph need not be included in subsequent periods.) The auditor should state that the auditor's opinion is not modified regarding the matter.
2. **If the financial statement disclosures relating to the restatement are not adequate** -- the auditor should evaluate the inadequacy of disclosure and consider whether the auditor's report should be modified.
3. A change from an accounting principle that is not in accordance with the applicable financial reporting framework to one that is in accordance is a correction of a misstatement.

III. Effect on the Auditor's Report

A. The auditor need not refer to consistency, unless there is an inconsistency due to a material change in accounting principle or restatement.

B. Sample emphasis-of-matter paragraph for a voluntary change in principle:

> Emphasis-of-Matter:
>
> As discussed in Note X to the financial statements, the entity has elected to change its method of accounting for (*describe accounting method change*) in (*insert year(s) of financial statements that reflect the accounting method change*). Our opinion is not modified with respect to this matter.

C. Sample emphasis-of-matter paragraph for a restatement:

> Emphasis-of-Matter:
>
> As discussed in Note X to the financial statements, the 20X2 financial statements have been restated to correct a misstatement. Our opinion is not modified with respect to this matter.

Opening Balances - Initial Audits

After studying this lesson, you should be able to:

1. *Know how the inability to verify beginning inventory would impact the auditor's report when the effect is material and pervasive.*
2. *Know that the auditor cannot refer to the predecessor as providing a partial basis for the auditor's report.*
3. *Describe the auditor's responsibility for verifying opening balances (and consistency) in an initial audit engagement.*

I. **Relevant AICPA Guidance --** The relevant AICPA guidance is provided by AU 510: "Opening Balances — Initial Audit Engagements, Including Reaudit Engagements." The standard states that the auditor's objective is to obtain sufficient audit evidence about whether (a) opening balances contain misstatements that materially affect the current period's financial statements; and (b) appropriate accounting policies reflected in the opening balances have been consistently applied in the current period (or changes are appropriately accounted for and adequately presented and disclosed).

II. **Selected Definitions**

> **Definitions:**
> *Initial audit engagement*: An engagement in which (a) the financial statements for the prior period were not audited; or (b) the financial statements for the prior period were audited by a predecessor auditor.
>
> *Opening balances*: Those account balances that exist at the beginning of the period. (also include matters requiring disclosure that existed at the beginning of the period, such as contingencies and commitments).
>
> *Predecessor auditor*: The auditor from a different audit firm who has reported on the most recent audited financial statements (or was engaged to perform, but did not complete, an audit of the financial statements).
>
> *Reaudit*: An initial audit engagement to audit financial statements that have been previously audited by a predecessor auditor.

III. **Audit Procedures**

A. The auditor should read the most recent financial statements and any predecessor's audit report for information relevant to opening balances.

B. The auditor should request management to authorize the predecessor to respond fully to inquiries by the auditor and to allow the auditor to review the predecessor auditor's audit documentation.

1. The predecessor may request a *consent and acknowledgment letter* from the entity to document the authorization regarding the communication with the auditor. Such a letter is not required, but the SAS provides an example.
2. The predecessor may also request a *successor auditor acknowledgment letter* to document the auditor's agreement regarding the use of the predecessor auditor's audit documentation before permitting access to it. Such a letter is not required, but the SAS provides an example.

3. The extent to which the predecessor permits access to the audit documentation is a matter of professional judgment.

4. The auditor's use of the predecessor's information is influenced by the auditor's assessment of the predecessor's competence and independence.

C. **Evaluate the entity's opening balances**

1. Obtain sufficient appropriate audit evidence as to whether opening balances contain misstatements affecting the current period financial statements by (a) determining whether the prior closing balances have been properly brought forward; (b) determining whether the opening balances reflect the application of appropriate accounting policies; and (c) evaluating whether current period audit procedures provide evidence relevant to the opening balances (such as reviewing the predecessor's audit documentation).

2. If the opening balances contain material misstatements affecting the current period, the auditor should determine the effect on the current period's financial statements and communicate the misstatements to the appropriate level of management and those charged with governance.

D. **Evaluate the consistency of accounting policies --** the auditor should obtain sufficient appropriate audit evidence as to whether the accounting policies reflected in the opening balances have been consistently applied in the current period (and whether any changes have been properly reported).

E. Discovery of possible material misstatements in financial statements reported on by a predecessor auditor.

1. The auditor should request management to inform the predecessor of the situation and arrange a 3-way meeting to resolve the matter.

2. If management does not cooperate (or if the auditor is not satisfied with the resolution of the matter), the auditor should evaluate the implications to the current engagement and whether to withdraw. The auditor may also wish to consult with legal counsel for guidance.

IV. **Audit Reporting Considerations**

A. **Reference to predecessor --** The auditor should **not** refer to the predecessor's work or report as a partial basis for the auditor's opinion.

B. **Opening balances**

1. If unable to obtain sufficient appropriate audit evidence regarding the opening balances, the auditor should either express a qualified opinion or disclaim an opinion, as appropriate.

2. If there is a material misstatement in the opening balances, the auditor should either express a qualified or adverse opinion, as appropriate.

C. **Consistency of accounting policies --** The auditor should either express a qualified or adverse opinion (as appropriate) if the current period's accounting policies are not consistently applied in relation to the opening balances (or if any material changes are not properly reported).

V. **Sample Report --** A sample report follows with a disclaimer of opinion on results of operations and cash flows and an unmodified opinion on financial position (owing to the inability to verify opening inventory such that the effect is deemed to be material and pervasive).

A. Modify introductory sentence — ". . . and were engaged to audit . . ."

B. Do not change to Management's Responsibility section.

C. Modify Auditor's Responsibility section—modify the first 2 paragraphs and comment on the "basis for unmodified opinion on financial position" at the end.

D. Add a "Basis for Disclaimer" paragraph on results of operations and cash flows.

E. Disclaim an opinion on results of operations and cash flows.

F. Provide an opinion only on financial position.

G. **Sample report with a disclaimer of opinion on results of operations and cash flows and an unmodified opinion on financial position (owing to the inability to verify opening inventory)**

Independent Auditor's Report

(Appropriate Addressee)

We have audited the accompanying balance sheet of ABC Company, as of December 31, 20X1, and were engaged to audit the related statements of income, changes in stockholders' equity and cash flows for the year then ended, and the related notes to the financial statements.

Management's Responsibility for the Financial Statements

Management is responsible for the preparation and fair presentation of these financial statements in accordance with accounting principles generally accepted in the United States of America; this includes the design, implementation, and maintenance of internal control relevant to the preparation and fair presentation of financial statements that are free from material misstatement, whether due to fraud or error.

Auditor's Responsibility

Our responsibility is to express an opinion on these financial statements based on conducting the audit in accordance with auditing standards generally accepted in the United States of America. Because of the matters described in the Basis for Disclaimer of Opinion paragraph, however, we were not able to obtain sufficient appropriate audit evidence to provide a basis for an audit opinion on the income statement and the cash flow statement.

We conducted our audit of the balance sheet in accordance with auditing standards generally accepted in the United States of America. Those standards require that we plan and perform the audit to obtain reasonable assurance about whether the balance sheet is free of material misstatement.

An audit involves performing procedures to obtain audit evidence about the amounts and disclosures in the consolidated financial statements. The procedures selected depend on the auditor's judgment, including the assessment of the risks of material misstatement of the consolidated financial statements, whether due to fraud or error. In making those risk assessments, the auditor considers internal control relevant to the entity's preparation and fair presentation of the consolidated financial statements in order to design audit procedures that are appropriate in the circumstances, but not for the purpose of expressing an opinion on the effectiveness of the entity's internal control. Accordingly, we express no such opinion. An audit also includes evaluating the appropriateness of accounting policies used and the reasonableness of significant accounting estimates made by management, as well as evaluating the overall presentation of the financial statements.

We believe that the audit evidence we have obtained is sufficient and appropriate to provide a basis for our unmodified opinion on the financial position.

Basis for Disclaimer of Opinion on the Results of Operations and Cash Flows

We were not appointed as auditors of the company until after December 31, 20X0, and thus did not observe the counting of the physical inventories at the beginning of the year. We were unable to satisfy ourselves by alternative means concerning inventory quantities held at December 31, 20X0. Since opening inventories enter into the determination of the net income and cash flows, we were unable to determine whether adjustments might have been necessary relating to the profit for the year reported in the income statement and the net cash flows from operating activities reported in the cash flow statement.

Disclaimer of Opinion on the Results of Operations and Cash Flows

Because of the significance of the matter described in the Basis for Disclaimer of Opinion paragraph, we have not been able to obtain sufficient appropriate audit evidence to provide a basis for an audit opinion on the income statement and the cash flow statement. Accordingly, we do not express an opinion on the results of operations and cash flows for the year ended December 31, 20X1.

Opinion on the Financial Position

In our opinion, the balance sheet presents fairly, in all material respects, the financial position of ABC Company, as of December 31, 20X1, in accordance with accounting principles generally accepted in the United States of America.

(Auditor's signature)

(Auditor's city and state)

(Date of the auditor's report)

Other Information Along with Financial Statements

After studying this lesson, you should be able to:

1. *Identify the auditor's responsibility for other information included in a document containing the audited financial statements.*

I. Relevant AICPA Guidance

Relevant AICPA Guidance -- The relevant AICPA guidance is provided by AU 720: "Other Information in Documents Containing Audited Financial Statements." The standard states that the auditor's objective is to respond appropriately when the auditor becomes aware that documents containing audited financial statements and the auditor's report include other information that could undermine the credibility of those financial statements and the auditor's report.

Definitions:
Other information: Information other than the financial statements and the auditor's report that is included in a document containing audited financial statements and the auditor's report (can be financial and nonfinancial information, but excludes *required supplementary information*).

Inconsistency: Other information that conflicts with information contained in the audited financial statements (may raise doubt about the auditor's conclusions and the basis for the auditor's opinion).

Misstatement of fact: Other information that is unrelated to matters appearing in the audited financial statements that is incorrectly presented (may undermine the credibility of the document containing the audited financial statements).

II. Auditor Responsibilities

A. When the audited financial statements and auditor's report is included in a document containing *other information*, the auditor should read the other information to identify any material inconsistencies with the financial statements.

   1. **Examples of** *other information* **--** Financial summaries or highlights, management reports on operations, employment data, financial ratios, selected quarterly data, employment data, names of officers/directors, etc.
   2. Other information does not include press releases, cover letters accompanying documents containing the audited financial statements, information in analyst briefings, or information posted to the entity's Web site.

B. **Material inconsistencies identified *prior* to the report release date**

   1. Request that management make appropriate revision.
   2. **If management refuses --** inform those charged with governance and (a) include an *other-matter* paragraph to the auditor's report, (b) withhold the auditor's report, or (c) withdraw from the engagement (when permitted).

C. **Material inconsistencies identified *after* the report release date**

   1. **If management agrees to make the revision --** the auditor may review steps taken by management to ensure that users of the financial statements and other information are informed of the need for revision.
   2. **If management refuses --** inform those charged with governance and take appropriate action (such as seeking advice from the auditor's legal counsel).

D. **Material misstatements of fact --** the auditor should discuss the matter with management and, if there is a material misstatement of fact, the auditor should request management to consult with a qualified third party (such as the entity's legal counsel). If management refuses to correct a material misstatement of fact, the auditor should communicate the matter to those charged with governance.

III. **Reporting Issues—disclaiming an Opinion on the Other Information**

> **Note**: The auditor is not required to reference the other information in the auditor's report, but may choose to include a disclaimer of opinion on it to avoid any confusion.

> **Other Matter**
>
> Our audit was conducted for the purpose of forming an opinion on the basic financial statements as a whole. The (*identify the other information*) is presented for purposes of additional analysis and is not a required part of the basic financial statements. Such information has not been subjected to the auditing procedures applied in the audit of the basic financial statements, and accordingly, we do not express an opinion or provide any assurance on it.

Supplementary Information Related to Financial Statements

After studying this lesson, you should be able to:

1. *Identify the auditor's responsibilities when engaged to report on supplementary information in relation to the audited financial statements.*
2. *Prepare an appropriate other-matter paragraph when expressing an opinion on the supplementary information in relation to the audited financial statements in a combined report on the audited financial statements.*

I. **Relevant AICPA Guidance --** The relevant AICPA guidance is provided by AU 725: "Supplementary Information in Relation to the Financial Statements as a Whole." The standard states that the auditor's objective is to evaluate the presentation of the supplementary information and report on whether it is fairly stated, in all material respects, in relation to the financial statements as a whole.

II. **Fairly Stated --** When engaged to determine whether supplementary information is fairly stated in relation to the financial statements.

   A. The auditor should determine whether:

      1. The supplementary information was derived from (or directly related to) the underlying records used to prepare the financial statements;
      2. The supplementary information relates to the same period as the financial statements;
      3. The auditor served as the auditor of the financial statements; and
      4. Either an unmodified or qualified opinion was expressed on the financial statements (must not have issued an adverse opinion or disclaimer of opinion); and
      5. The supplementary information will either accompany the entity's audited financial statements or the audited financial statements will be made *readily available* by the entity. (Note: *Readily available* means without further action by the entity. Being available upon the user's request is not considered *readily available*).

   B. The auditor should obtain management's agreement that management has responsibility for:

      1. Preparing the supplementary information in accordance with applicable criteria;
      2. Providing the auditor with written representations;
      3. Including the auditor's report on the supplementary information in any document containing the supplementary information that references the auditor's association with it; and
      4. Presenting the supplementary information with the audited financial statements (or making the audited financial statements *readily available* to the intended users of the supplementary information).

   C. The auditor should perform the following procedures:

      1. Inquire of management about the purpose of the supplementary information and the criteria used to prepare it;
      2. Obtain an understanding about the methods used and whether those methods have changed (and if changed, the reasons for any changes);
      3. Compare and reconcile the supplementary information to the financial statements or to the underlying records used for the financial statements;

4. Inquire of management about any significant assumptions used;
5. Evaluate the appropriateness and completeness of the supplementary information in relationship to the audited financial statements; and
6. Obtain appropriate written representations from management.

III. Reporting on Supplementary Information in Relation to Audited Financial Statements

A. **Form of report --** The auditor may issue a separate report on the supplementary information (in addition to the report on the audited financial statements) or combine the report on the supplementary information with the report on the financial statements. (If the latter, then add an other-matter paragraph regarding the supplementary information.)

B. If the auditor expressed an adverse opinion or a disclaimer of opinion on the financial statements, the auditor is prohibited from reporting on the supplementary information.

C. If the supplementary information is materially misstated in relation to the financial statements, the auditor should discuss the matter with management and propose appropriate revision. If management does not revise the supplementary information, the auditor should either appropriately modify the opinion on the supplementary information or withhold the separate report on it.

D. Sample other-matter paragraph when the auditor expresses an unmodified opinion on the financial statements and on the supplementary information in a combined report:

> **Other Matter**
>
> Our audit was conducted for the purpose of forming an opinion on the financial statements as a whole. The (*identify accompanying supplementary information*) is presented for purposes of additional analysis and is not a required part of the financial statements. Such information is the responsibility of management and was derived from and relates directly to the underlying accounting and other records used to prepare the financial statements. The information has been subjected to the auditing procedures applied in the audit of the financial statements and certain additional procedures, including comparing and reconciling such information directly to the underlying accounting and other records used to prepare the financial statements or to the financial statements themselves, and other additional procedures in accordance with auditing standards generally accepted in the United States of America. In our opinion, the information is fairly stated in all material respects in relation to the financial statements as a whole.

Required Supplementary Information

After studying this lesson you should be able to:

1. *Prepare an appropriate emphasis-of-matter or other-matter paragraph when commenting on required supplementary information (or its omission) in connection with audited financial statements.*
2. *Identify the auditor's responsibilities when required supplementary information is associated with audited financial statements.*

I. Relevant AICPA Guidance

Relevant AICPA Guidance -- The relevant AICPA guidance is provided by AU 730: "Required Supplementary Information." The standard states that the auditor's objectives are to (1) describe in the auditor's report whether required supplementary information is presented, and (2) communicate when the supplementary information has not been presented in accordance with the established guidelines (or when material modification is necessary).

Definitions:
Required supplementary information: Information that a designated accounting standard setter requires to accompany an entity's basic financial statements (the information is not part of the basic financial statements, but authoritative guidelines for measurement and presentation have been established).

Designated accounting standard setter: A body designated by the AICPA council to establish GAAP pursuant to Rule 202, *Compliance With Standards*.

II. Procedures to Be Performed by the Auditor

A. Inquire of management about the methods used to prepare the information, including (1) whether it is measured and presented in accordance with prescribed guidelines; (2) whether the methods of measurement or presentation have been changed relative to prior period; and (3) whether any significant assumptions affect the measurement or presentation of it.

B. Compare the information for consistency with (1) management's responses to the auditor's inquiries; (2) the basic financial statements; and (3) other knowledge obtained during the audit of the basic financial statements.

III. Reporting Implications

A. The auditor should include an other-matter paragraph in the auditor's report commenting appropriately on the required supplementary information. The supplementary information cannot affect the auditor's opinion on the financial statements, since it is outside of those financial statements.

B. The specific language to be used depends upon the particular circumstances.

1. Whether the required supplementary information is included and the auditor has applied the procedures described above (no material departures);
2. Whether the required supplementary information is omitted;
3. Whether some required supplementary information is missing and some is presented in accordance with prescribed guidelines;
4. Whether the auditor has identified any material departures from prescribed guidelines;
5. Whether the auditor is unable to complete required procedures; or
6. Whether the auditor has unresolved doubts as to whether the required supplementary information is presented in accordance with prescribed guidelines.

Example language when the required supplementary information is included and the auditor has performed the applicable procedures without identifying any material departures:

[*Identify the applicable financial reporting framework (for example, accounting principles generally accepted in the United States of America*)] require that the (*identify the required supplementary information*) on page XX be presented to supplement the basic financial statements. Such information, although not a part of the basic financial statements is required by (*identify designated accounting standard setter*) who considers it to be an essential part of financial reporting for placing the basic financial statements in an appropriate operational, economic, or historical context. We have applied certain limited procedures to the required supplementary information in accordance with auditing standards generally accepted in the United States of America, which consisted of inquiries of management about the methods of preparing the information and comparing the information for consistency with management's responses to our inquiries, the basic financial statements, and other knowledge we obtained during our audit of the basic financial statements. We do not express an opinion or provide any assurance on the information because the limited procedures do not provide us with sufficient evidence to express an opinion or provide any assurance.

Alert to Restrict Report

After studying this lesson you should be able to:

1. *Identify the appropriate wording associated with an alert to restrict the use of the auditor's written communication.*
2. *Identify the circumstances for which the auditor should include an alert to restrict the use of the auditor's written communication.*

I. **Relevant AICPA Guidance --** The relevant AICPA guidance is provided by AU 905: "Alert That Restricts the Use of the Auditor's Written Communication." The standard states that the auditor's objective is to restrict the use of the auditor's written communication by including an alert when the potential exists for that communication to be misunderstood if taken out of the context of its intended use.

II. **Using an *Alert* to Restrict the Use of the Auditor's Report**

A. Such an alert should be included as a separate paragraph of the report when:

1. The subject matter is based on criteria that are only suitable for (or available to) a limited number of users; or
2. The matters are presented in a *by-product report* that is not the primary objective of the engagement.

B. **Including an alert --** The auditor is not prohibited from including such an alert in any other auditor's report or written communication.

C. **Purpose of the alert --** The purpose of the alert is to restrict the use of the auditor's written communication because of the potential for misunderstanding if taken out of the context for which the written communication is intended.

D. **Content of the alert --** The auditor should state that the written communication is intended solely for the use of the specified parties (and either identify or refer to those parties). .

E. **Adding other specified parties --** The auditor should obtain acknowledgment in writing from such other parties as to their understanding of the nature of the engagement, the criteria used, and the auditor's written communication. They can be added after the release of the auditor's written communication (by amending the written communication to add them, but without changing the original date of the auditor's written communication).

F. **Distribution of the auditor's written communication --** The auditor is not responsible for enforcing the distribution of the auditor's written communication after its release. The purpose of the alert is to appropriately communicate such restricted distribution.

III. **Sample Reporting Language for an Alert to Restrict the Use of the Auditor's Report**

A. *A typical alert consists of one sentence at the end of the auditor's report:*

> This (*report, letter, presentation, or communication*) is intended solely for the information and use of (*list or refer to the specified parties*) and is not intended to be and should not be used by anyone other than these specified parties.

B. *Alert for engagements performed in accordance with Government Auditing Standards:*

The purpose of this (*report, letter, presentation, or communication*) is solely to (*describe the purpose of the auditor's written communication, such as to describe the scope of our testing of internal control over financial reporting and compliance, and the results of that testing, and not to provide an opinion on the effectiveness of the entity's internal control over financial reporting or on compliance*). This (*report, letter, presentation, or communication*) is an integral part of an audit performed in accordance with Government Auditing Standards in considering (*describe the results that are being assessed, such as the entity's internal control over financial reporting and compliance*). Accordingly, this (*report, letter, presentation, or communication*) is not suitable for any other purpose.

Financial Statements Using Another Country's Framework

After studying this lesson you should be able to:

1. *Identify the reporting language that would be appropriate when issuing an audit report on financial statements prepared in accordance with a financial reporting framework generally accepted in another country.*
2. *Identify the auditor's responsibilities when engaged to report on financial statements prepared in accordance with a financial reporting framework generally accepted in another country.*

I. **Relevant AICPA Guidance --** The relevant AICPA guidance is provided by AU 910: "Financial Statements Prepared in Accordance With a Financial Reporting Framework Generally Accepted in Another Country." The standard states that the auditor's objective, when engaged to report on financial statements prepared in accordance with a financial reporting framework generally accepted in another country, is to address appropriately the special considerations that are relevant to: (1) the acceptance of the engagement; (2) the planning and performance of the engagement; and (3) the formation of an opinion and reporting on the financial statements.

II. **Acceptance of the Engagement**

   A. **Considerations --** The auditor should obtain an understanding of (1) the purpose for which the financial statements are prepared; (2) the intended users of the financial statements; and (3) steps taken by management to determine that the framework is acceptable in the circumstances.

   B. **Users --** The auditor should consider whether the intended users are likely to be familiar with the applicable financial reporting framework.

III. **Performance of the Engagement**

   A. **Use solely outside the U.S. --** When auditing financial statements intended for use solely outside the U.S., the auditor should comply with GAAS, except for requirements related to the form and content of the auditor's report. The auditor should obtain an understanding of the entity's selection and application of accounting policies.

   B. **Consultation with others --** The auditor may wish to consult with others having expertise in applying that country's reporting framework.

IV. **Reporting**

   A. **For use only outside the U.S.A --** The auditor should report either using (1) a U.S. form of report (including a statement that refers to the note to the financial statements that describes the basis of presentation, including the country involved); or (2) the report form and content of the other country (identify the other country in the report).

   B. **For use both outside and inside the U.S.A --** If the financial statements are also intended for use in the U.S.A, the auditor should report using the U.S. form of report, including an emphasis-of-matter paragraph that (1) identifies the financial reporting framework used; (2) refers to the note to the financial statements describing that framework; and (3) indicates that such a framework differs from U.S. GAAP.

   C. **Summary of the differences in the audit reporting language relative to U.S. form.**

      1. The first sentence would be changed as follows: ". . .financial statements, which, as described in note X to the financial statements, have been prepared on the basis of (*specify the financial reporting framework generally accepted*) in (*name of the country*)."
      2. The sentence describing management's responsibilities would be changed as follows: "Management is responsible for the preparation and fair presentation of these financial

statements in accordance with (*specify the financial reporting framework generally accepted*) in (*name of country*);"

3. The second sentence in the section on the auditor's responsibility would be changed as follows: "We conducted our audit in accordance with auditing standards generally accepted in the United States of America (and [*in name of country*])."
4. The opinion would be changed as follows: "In our opinion, the financial statements referred to above present fairly, in all material respects, . . . in accordance with (*specify the financial reporting framework generally accepted*) in (*name of country*)."

V. Sample Report -- U.S. Form of Independent Auditor's Report to Report on Financial Statements Prepared in Accordance With a Financial Reporting Framework Generally Accepted in Another Country That Are *Intended for Use Only Outside the United States*:

Independent Auditor's Report

(Appropriate Addressee)

We have audited the accompanying financial statements of ABC Company, which comprise the balance sheet as of December 31, 20X1, and the related statements of income, changes in stockholders' equity, and cash flows for the year then ended, and the related notes to the financial statements, which, as described in note X to the financial statements, have been prepared on the basis of (*specify the financial reporting framework generally accepted*) in (*name of country*).

Management's Responsibility for the Financial Statements

Management is responsible for the preparation and fair presentation of these financial statements in accordance with (*specify the financial reporting framework generally accepted*) in (*name of country*); this includes the design, implementation, and maintenance of internal control relevant to the preparation and fair presentation of financial statements that are free from material misstatement, whether due to fraud or error.

Auditor's Responsibility

Our responsibility is to express an opinion on these financial statements based on our audit. We conducted our audit in accordance with auditing standards generally accepted in the United States of America (and [*in name of country*]). Those standards require that we plan and perform the audit to obtain reasonable assurance about whether the financial statements are free from material misstatement.

An audit involves performing procedures to obtain audit evidence about the amounts and disclosures in the financial statements. The procedures selected depend on the auditor's judgment, including the assessment of the risks of material misstatement of the financial statements, whether due to fraud or error. In making those risk assessments, the auditor considers internal control relevant to the entity's preparation and fair presentation of the financial statements in order to design audit procedures that are appropriate in the circumstances, but not for the purpose of expressing an opinion on the effectiveness of the entity's internal control. Accordingly, we express no such opinion. An audit also includes evaluating the appropriateness of accounting policies used and the reasonableness of significant accounting estimates made by management, as well as evaluating the overall presentation of the financial statements.

We believe that the audit evidence we have obtained is sufficient and appropriate to provide a basis for our audit opinion.

Opinion

In our opinion, the financial statements referred to above present fairly, in all material respects, the financial position of ABC Company as of December 31, 20X1, and the results of its operations and its cash flows for the year then ended in accordance with (*specify the financial reporting framework generally accepted*) in (*name of country*).

(Auditor's signature)

(Auditor's city and state)

(Date of the auditor's report)

Reporting on Summary Financial Statements

After studying this lesson you should be able to:

1. *Identify the reporting language that would be appropriate when issuing an audit report on summary financial statements.*
2. *Identify the auditor's responsibilities when engaged to report on an entity's summary financial statements.*

I. Relevant AICPA Guidance

Relevant AICPA Guidance -- The relevant AICPA guidance is provided by AU 810: "Engagements to Report on Summary Financial Statements." The standard states that the auditor's objectives are (1) to determine whether it is appropriate to accept the engagement to report on summary financial states; and (2) if engaged, to perform the necessary procedures, to form an opinion on whether the summary financial statements are consistent with the audited financial statements from which they have been derived, and to clearly express that opinion (and the basis for it) through a written report.

> **Definitions:**
> *Applied criteria*: The criteria applied by management in the preparation of the summary financial statements.
>
> *Summary financial statements*: Historical financial information that is derived from financial statements but that contains less detail than the financial statements, while still providing a structured representation consistent with that provided by the financial statements.

II. Engagement Acceptance

A. The auditor must have been engaged to audit the financial statements as a whole in order to accept an engagement to report on summary financial statements.

B. Before accepting an engagement to report on summary financial statements — The auditor should (1) determine whether the applied criteria are acceptable; and (2) obtain a written agreement from management acknowledging their responsibilities and accepting the expected form and content of the auditor's report.

III. Procedures to Be Performed by the Auditor

A. Evaluate whether the summary financial statements adequately disclose their summarized nature and identify the audited financial statements;

B. When unaccompanied by the audited financial statements, evaluate whether the audited financial statements are **readily available** to users;

C. Evaluate whether the summary financial statements adequately disclose the applied criteria;

D. Compare the summary financial statements with the related audited financial statements;

E. Evaluate whether the summary financial statements are prepared in accordance with the applied criteria;

F. Evaluate whether the summary financial statements contain necessary information at an appropriate level of aggregation so they are not misleading; and

G. Obtain a written representations letter that addresses the following matters:

> **Note:**
> Audited financial statements are viewed as *readily available* if users can obtain them without any further action by the entity. Management's statement that they are available upon request, would **not** be considered readily available

1. Management has prepared the summary financial statements in accordance with the applied criteria (and that the applied criteria are acceptable);
2. Management has made the audited financial statements readily available to the intended users;
3. If the date of the report on the summary financial information is later than the date of the report on the audited financial statements, include a statement as to whether management believes any of its previous representations need to be modified and whether any subsequent events require adjustment to or disclosure in the audited financial statements.
4. The representation letter should be dated the same as the auditor's report.

IV. Form of the Auditor's Opinion

A. **Only an unmodified or adverse opinion is permitted --** The summary financial statements are either **consistent** or **not consistent** with the audited financial statements; accordingly, a qualified opinion is not permitted.

1. **Unmodified opinion --** When issuing an unmodified opinion on the summary financial statements, the opinion should state that they are consistent, in all material respects, with the audited financial statements from which they have been derived, in accordance with the applied criteria.
2. **Adverse opinion --** When issuing an adverse opinion on the summary financial statements, the opinion should state that the financial statements are not consistent, in all material respects, with the audited financial statements in accordance with the applied criteria.

B. **Adverse opinion or disclaimer of opinion --** When the auditor's report on the audited financial statements contains an adverse opinion or a disclaimer of opinion, the auditor should either withdraw from the engagement to report on the summary financial statements (when withdrawal is possible) or disclaim an opinion on the summary financial statements.

V. Auditor's Report on Summary Financial Statements -- Include the following elements:

A. A title that includes the word *independent*;

B. Addressee;

C. Introductory paragraph that (1) identifies the summary financials; (2) identifies the audited financial statements from which the summary financials were derived; (3) refers to the auditor's report on the financial statements and the date; and (4) states that the summary financials do not include all the disclosures required for complete financial statements;

D. Description of management's responsibility;

E. Statement about the auditor's responsibility;

F. A paragraph that clearly describes an opinion;

G. The auditor's signature, city and state, and date of the report.

VI. Sample Audit Report on Summary Financial Statements

See the following example.

Independent Auditor's Report on Summary Financial Statements

(Appropriate Addressee)

The accompanying summary financial statements, which comprise the summary balance sheet as of December 31, 20X1, the summary income statement, summary statement of changes in stockholders' equity and summary cash flow statement for the year then ended, and the related notes, are derived from the audited financial statements of ABC Company as of and for the year ended December 31, 20X1. We expressed an unmodified audit opinion on those audited financial statements in our report dated February 15, 20X2. The audited financial statements, and the summary financial statements derived therefrom, do not reflect the effects of events, if any, that occurred subsequent to the date of our report on the audited financial statements.

The summary financial statements do not contain all the disclosures required by (*describe financial reporting framework applied in the preparation of the financial statements of ABC Company*). Reading the summary financial statements, therefore, is not a substitute for reading the audited financial statements of ABC Company.

Management's Responsibility for the Summary Financial Statements

Management is responsible for the preparation of the summary financial statements on the basis described in Note X.

Auditor's Responsibility

Our responsibility is to express an opinion about whether the summary financial statements are consistent, in all material respects, with the audited financial statements based on our procedures, which were conducted in accordance with auditing standards generally accepted in the United States of America. The procedures consisted principally of comparing the summary financial statements with the related information in the audited financial statements from which the summary financial statements have been derived, and evaluating whether the summary financial statements are prepared in accordance with the basis described in Note X. We did not perform any audit procedures regarding the audited financial statements after the date of our report on those financial statements.

Opinion

In our opinion, the summary financial statements of ABC Company as of and for the year ended December 31, 20X1 referred to above are consistent, in all material respects, with the audited financial statements from which they have been derived, on the basis described in Note X.

(Auditor's signature)

(Auditor's city and state)

(Date of the auditor's report)

Interim Financial Information

After studying this lesson you should be able to :

1. *Identify the reporting language that would be appropriate when issuing a review report on an audit entity's interim financial information.*
2. *Identify the auditor's responsibilities when engaged to report on an entity's interim financial information.*

I. **Relevant AICPA Guidance --** The relevant AICPA guidance is provided by AU 930: "Interim Financial Information." The standard states that the auditor's objective is to obtain a basis for reporting whether the auditor is aware of any material modifications that should be made to the interim financial information for it to be in accordance with the applicable financial reporting framework through performing limited procedures.

> **Definition:**
> *Interim financial information*: Financial information prepared and presented in accordance with an applicable financial reporting framework that comprises either a complete or condensed set of financial statements covering a period(s) less than one full year or covering a 12-month period ending on a date other than the entity's fiscal year end.

II. **Engagement Acceptance**

A. Before accepting an engagement to review the interim financial information, the auditor should (1) determine whether the financial reporting framework to be applied is acceptable; and (2) obtain the agreement of management regarding the engagement terms.

B. Agreement on engagement terms -- The auditor should agree upon the terms of the engagement with management (or those charged with governance) and record those terms in an engagement letter that includes: (1) the objectives and scope of the engagement; (2) the responsibilities of management; (3) the responsibilities of the auditor; (4) the limitations of a review engagement; and (5) identification of the applicable financial reporting framework.

III. **Engagement Performance**

A. Obtain an understanding of the entity and its environment, including internal control related to the preparation of annual and interim financial information -- Should be sufficient to (1) identify the types of potential misstatements (and likelihood of occurrence) and (2) select the inquiries and analytical procedures for the auditor's basis for conclusions.

B. Analytical procedures, inquiries, and other review procedures.

1. **Analytical procedures --** The auditor should apply analytical procedures to the interim information to identify unusual items that may indicate a material misstatement, including the following:

    a. Comparing the interim financial information with comparable information for the immediately preceding period and with the corresponding period(s) in the previous year;

    b. Comparing recorded amounts or ratios developed from recorded amounts to expectations; and

    c. Comparing disaggregated revenue data.

2. **Inquiries and other review procedures --** The auditor should make the following inquiries and perform the following other procedures in a review of interim financial information.

a. Read the available minutes of meetings of stockholders, directors, and appropriate committees;

b. Obtain reports from any component auditors related to reviews of significant components or inquire of those auditors if reports have not been issued;

c. Inquire of management about the matters normally associated with a management representations letter;

d. Obtain evidence that the interim financial information agrees to (or reconciles with) the accounting records;

e. Read the interim financial information; and

f. Read other information in documents containing the interim financial information to see if any of it is materially inconsistent.

3. **Inquiry concerning litigation, claims, and assessments --** The auditor should inquire of legal counsel if information about litigation, claims, and assessments does not appear to be presented in accordance with the applicable financial reporting framework.

4. **Going concern issues --** If information indicates that there may be substantial doubt about an entity's ability to continue as a going concern, the auditor should inquire of management about plans for dealing with adverse effects and consider the adequacy of disclosure about such matters.

5. The auditor should consider the reasonableness and consistency of management's responses, but the auditor is not required to corroborate management's responses with other evidence.

C. **Evaluating the results of interim review procedures --** The auditor should evaluate, individually and in the aggregate, misstatements to determine whether material modification should be made to the interim financial information.

D. **Written representations from management --** The auditor should obtain written representations from management for all interim financial information presented as of the date of the auditor's review report. If management does not provide the written representation requested, the auditor should withdraw from the engagement to review the interim financial information.

IV. Reporting on a Review of Interim Financial Information

A. **Form of the review report --** The report should be in writing and include the following:

1. Title;
2. Addressee;
3. An introductory paragraph;
4. A section on "Management's Responsibility for the Financial Statements";
5. A section on "Auditor's Responsibility";
6. A concluding section that expresses conclusions (negative assurance); and
7. The signature, city and state, and date of the review report.

B. Each page of the interim financial information should be clearly marked *unaudited.*

C. **If comparative information is presented that has not been reviewed --** The report should indicate that the auditor assumes no responsibility for it.

D. **Modification of the auditor's review report --** When the interim financial information has not been prepared in accordance with the applicable financial reporting framework in all material respects, the auditor should consider whether modification of the review report is sufficient to address the matter.

1. **If modification is sufficient --** The auditor should modify the review report by describing the nature of the departure, and stating the effects on the interim financial information (or providing the appropriate information when disclosure is inadequate), if practicable.
2. **If modification is not sufficient --** The auditor should withdraw from the review engagement.

E. **Interim financial information accompanying audited financial statements --** The auditor should include an *other-matter paragraph* in the report on audited financial statements when the following conditions exist:

1. The interim financial information that has been reviewed is included in a document containing the audited financial statements;
2. The interim information accompanying the audited financial statements does **not** appear to be presented in accordance with the applicable financial reporting framework; and
3. The auditor's separate review report, which refers to the departure, is not presented with the interim financial information.

V. Sample Review Report of the Entity's Auditor

Independent Auditor's Review Report

(Appropriate Addressee)

Report on the Financial Statements

We have reviewed the accompanying (*describe the interim financial information or statements reviewed*) of ABC Company and subsidiaries as of September 30, 20X1, and for the three-month and none-month periods then ended.

Management's Responsibility

The Company's management is responsible for the preparation and fair presentation of the interim financial information in accordance with (*identify the applicable financial reporting framework; for example, accounting principles generally accepted in the United States of America*); this responsibility includes the design, implementation, and maintenance of internal control sufficient to provide a reasonable basis for the preparation and fair presentation of interim financial information in accordance with the applicable financial reporting framework.

Auditor's Responsibility

Our responsibility is to conduct our review in accordance with auditing standards generally accepted in the United States of America applicable to reviews of interim financial information. A review of interim financial information consists principally of applying analytical procedures and making inquiries of persons responsible for financial and accounting matters. It is substantially less in scope than an audit conducted in accordance with auditing standards generally accepted in the United States of America, the objective of which is the expression of an opinion regarding the financial information. Accordingly, we do not express such an opinion.

Conclusion

Based on our review, we are not aware of any material modifications that should be made to the accompanying interim financial information for it to be in accordance with (*identify the applicable financial reporting framework; for example, accounting principles generally accepted in the United States of America*).

(Auditor's signature)

(Auditor's city and state)

(Date of the auditor's report)

VI. Filings with the SEC Under Federal Securities Statutes

A. Relevant AICPA Guidance -- The relevant AICPA guidance is provided by AU 925: "Filings with the U.S. SEC Under the Securities Act of 1933." The standard states that the auditor's objective is to perform specified procedures at or shortly before the effective date of the registration statement to sustain the burden of proof that the auditor has performed a reasonable investigation [under Section 11(b)(3)(B)].

> *Auditor's consent*: A statement signed and dated by the auditor giving consent to use the auditor's report in a registration statement.
>
> *Awareness letter*: A letter signed and dated by the auditor to acknowledge the auditor's awareness that the review report on interim financial information is being used in a registration statement (also known as an *acknowledgment letter*).
>
> *Effective date of the registration*: The date on which the registration statement becomes effective for purposes of evaluating the auditor's liability under Section 11 of the Securities Act of 1933.

B. Responsibilities under Federal securities statutes - the Securities Act of 1933 -- promotes fair disclosure and prohibits fraud in initial public offerings of securities.

1. **Management's** responsibilities are the same as with the financial statements used for other purposes - that is, the financial statements are the representations of management.
2. The **independent accountant's** responsibilities are similar to other types of reporting - Section 11 of the 1933 Act prohibits false or misleading statements (or material omissions) in registration statements.
    a. Section 11 defense - after a reasonable investigation, the independent accountant had reasonable grounds to believe that the financial statements were fairly stated (but the CPA has the burden of proof).
    b. Statutory responsibility is determined in light of the circumstances on the effective date of the registration statement.
    c. The CPA should read the relevant parts of any prospectus filed under the 1933 Act to verify that the independent accountant's name is not being used inappropriately. (Note that a *prospectus* is an informational document required to be filed with the SEC in connection with a registration statement to offer securities for sale; the prospectus cannot be used to finalize sales of such securities until the registration statement is declared effective by the SEC.)
    d. When the registration statement references the interim financial information reviewed by the accountant - the prospectus should clearly indicate that the review report is not part of the registration statement within the meaning of the 1933 Act. The auditor's review report is only required if the registration statement indicates that the unaudited interim information has been reviewed.

C. Subsequent events procedures in connection with filings under the Securities Act of 1933

1. Extend the procedures regarding subsequent events from the audit report date up to (or as near as practicable) to the effective date of the registration statement.
2. Following fieldwork, the auditor may usually rely on inquiries of appropriate client personnel - obtain written representations from management regarding those financial and accounting matters.

3. An auditor who has reported on the financial statements from prior periods, but not the most recent audited financial statements included in the registration statement, is responsible for events subsequent to the date of the prior-period's audited financial statements. The auditor should:

   a. Read the applicable portions of the prospectus and registration statement.

   b. Obtain a letter of representations from the successor auditor as to whether the successor's audit identified any matters that might have a material effect on the prior period's financial statements.

Sample Reports

Unmodified Opinion (Reference to Legal Requirements)

Independent Auditor's Report

(Appropriate Addressee)

Report on the Financial Statements[1]

We have audited the accompanying consolidated financial statements of ABC Company and its subsidiaries, which comprise the consolidated balance sheets as of December 31, 20X1 and 20X0, and the related consolidated statements of income, changes in stockholders' equity and cash flows for the years then ended, and the related notes to the financial statements.

Management's Responsibility for the Financial Statements

Management is responsible for the preparation and fair presentation of these consolidated financial statements in accordance with accounting principles generally accepted in the United States of America; this includes the design, implementation, and maintenance of internal control relevant to the preparation and fair presentation of consolidated financial statements that are free from material misstatement, whether due to fraud or error.

Auditor's Responsibility

Our responsibility is to express an opinion on these consolidated financial statements based on our audits. We conducted our audits in accordance with auditing standards generally accepted in the United States of America. Those standards require that we plan and perform the audit to obtain reasonable assurance about whether the consolidated financial statements are free from material misstatement.

An audit involves performing procedures to obtain audit evidence about the amounts and disclosures in the consolidated financial statements. The procedures selected depend on the auditor's judgment, including the assessment of the risks of material misstatement of the consolidated financial statements, whether due to fraud or error. In making those risk assessments, the auditor considers internal control relevant to the entity's preparation and fair presentation of the consolidated financial statements in order to design audit procedures that are appropriate in the circumstances, but not for the purpose of expressing an opinion on the effectiveness of the entity's internal control.[2] Accordingly, we express no such opinion. An audit also includes evaluating the appropriateness of accounting policies used and the reasonableness of significant accounting estimates made by management, as well as evaluating the overall presentation of the consolidated financial statements.

We believe that the audit evidence we have obtained is sufficient and appropriate to provide a basis for our audit opinion.

Opinion

In our opinion, the consolidated financial statements referred to above present fairly, in all material respects, the financial position of ABC Company and its subsidiaries as of December 31, 20X1 and 20X0, and the results of their operations and their cash flows for the years then ended in accordance with accounting principles generally accepted in the United States of America.

Report on Other Legal and Regulatory Requirements

(Auditor's signature)

(Auditor's city and state)

(Date of the auditor's report)

[1] The subtitle "Report on the Financial Statements" is unnecessary in circumstances when the second subtitle, "Report on Other Legal and Regulatory Requirements," is not applicable.

[2] When the auditor has responsibility for expressing an opinion on the effectiveness of internal control in conjunction with the audit of the entity's financial statements, the sentence would be stated as follows: "In making those risk assessments, the auditor considers internal control relevant to the entity's preparation and fair presentation of the consolidated financial statements in order to design audit procedures that are appropriate in the circumstances." In addition, the next sentence, "Accordingly, we express no such opinion," would be omitted.

Unmodified Opinion (No Reference to Legal Requirements)

Independent Auditor's Report

(Appropriate Addressee)

We have audited the accompanying consolidated financial statements of ABC Company and its subsidiaries, which comprise the consolidated balance sheets as of December 31, 20X1 and 20X0, and the related consolidated statements of income, changes in stockholders' equity and cash flows for the years then ended, and the related notes to the financial statements.

Management's Responsibility for the Financial Statements

Management is responsible for the preparation and fair presentation of these consolidated financial statements in accordance with accounting principles generally accepted in the United States of America; this includes the design, implementation, and maintenance of internal control relevant to the preparation and fair presentation of consolidated financial statements that are free from material misstatement, whether due to fraud or error.

Auditor's Responsibility

Our responsibility is to express an opinion on these consolidated financial statements based on our audits. We conducted our audits in accordance with auditing standards generally accepted in the United States of America. Those standards require that we plan and perform the audit to obtain reasonable assurance about whether the consolidated financial statements are free from material misstatement.

An audit involves performing procedures to obtain audit evidence about the amounts and disclosures in the consolidated financial statements. The procedures selected depend on the auditor's judgment, including the assessment of the risks of material misstatement of the consolidated financial statements, whether due to fraud or error. In making those risk assessments, the auditor considers internal control relevant to the entity's preparation and fair presentation of the consolidated financial statements in order to design audit procedures that are appropriate in the circumstances, but not for the purpose of expressing an opinion on the effectiveness of the entity's internal control.[1] Accordingly, we express no such opinion. An audit also includes evaluating the appropriateness of accounting policies used and the reasonableness of significant accounting estimates made by management, as well as evaluating the overall presentation of the consolidated financial statements.

We believe that the audit evidence we have obtained is sufficient and appropriate to provide a basis for our audit opinion.

Opinion

In our opinion, the consolidated financial statements referred to above present fairly, in all material respects, the financial position of ABC Company and its subsidiaries as of December 31, 20X1 and 20X0, and the results of their operations and their cash flows for the years then ended in accordance with accounting principles generally accepted in the United States of America.

(Auditor's signature)

(Auditor's city and state)

(Date of the auditor's report)

[1] When the auditor has responsibility for expressing an opinion on the effectiveness of internal control in conjunction with the audit of the entity's financial statements, the sentence would be stated as follows: "In making those risk assessments, the auditor considers internal control relevant to the entity's preparation and fair presentation of the consolidated financial statements in order to design audit procedures that are appropriate in the circumstances." In addition, the next sentence, "Accordingly, we express no such opinion," would be omitted.

Unmodified Opinion (Sentence-by-Sentence)

Independent Auditor's Report

(Appropriate Addressee)

(Introductory Paragraph)

We have audited the accompanying consolidated financial statements of ABC Company and its subsidiaries, which comprise the consolidated balance sheets as of December 31, 20X1 and 20X0, and the related consolidated statements of income, changes in stockholders' equity and cash flows for the years then ended, and the related notes to the financial statements.

Management's Responsibility for the Financial Statements

Management is responsible for the preparation and fair presentation of these consolidated financial statements in accordance with accounting principles generally accepted in the United States of America; this includes the design, implementation, and maintenance of internal control relevant to the preparation and fair presentation of consolidated financial statements that are free from material misstatement, whether due to fraud or error.

Auditor's Responsibility

(First of 3 paragraphs)

1. Our responsibility is to express an opinion on these consolidated financial statements based on our audits.

2. We conducted our audits in accordance with auditing standards generally accepted in the United States of America.

3. Those standards require that we plan and perform the audit to obtain reasonable assurance about whether the consolidated financial statements are free from material misstatement.

(Second of 3 paragraphs)

4. An audit involves performing procedures to obtain audit evidence about the amounts and disclosures in the consolidated financial statements.

5. The procedures selected depend on the auditor's judgment, including the assessment of the risks of material misstatement of the consolidated financial statements, whether due to fraud or error.

6. In making those risk assessments, the auditor considers internal control relevant to the entity's preparation and fair presentation of the consolidated financial statements in order to design audit procedures that are appropriate in the circumstances, but not for the purpose of expressing an opinion on the effectiveness of the entity's internal control.

7. Accordingly, we express no such opinion.

8. An audit also includes evaluating the appropriateness of accounting policies used and the reasonableness of significant accounting estimates made by management, as well as evaluating the overall presentation of the consolidated financial statements.

(Third of 3 paragraphs)

9. We believe that the audit evidence we have obtained is sufficient and appropriate to provide a basis for our audit opinion.

Opinion

In our opinion, the consolidated financial statements referred to above present fairly, in all material respects, the financial position of ABC Company and its subsidiaries as of December 31, 20X1 and 20X0, and the results of their operations and their cash flows for the years then ended in accordance with accounting principles generally accepted in the United States of America.

(Auditor's signature)

(Auditor's city and state)

(Date of the auditor's report)

Unmodified in Current Year, Balance Sheet in Prior Year

Independent Auditor's Report

(Appropriate Addressee)

We have audited the accompanying financial statements of ABC Company, which comprise the balance sheet as of December 31, 20X2 and 20X1, and the related statements of income, changes in stockholders' equity and cash flows for the years then ended, and the related notes to the financial statements.

Management's Responsibility for the Financial Statements

Management is responsible for the preparation and fair presentation of these financial statements in accordance with accounting principles generally accepted in the United States of America; this includes the design, implementation, and maintenance of internal control relevant to the preparation and fair presentation of financial statements that are free from material misstatement, whether due to fraud or error.

Auditor's Responsibility

Our responsibility is to express an opinion on these financial statements based on our audits. Except as explained in the Basis for Disclaimer of Opinion paragraph, we conducted our audits in accordance with auditing standards generally accepted in the United States of America. Those standards require that we plan and perform the audit to obtain reasonable assurance about whether the financial statements are free from material misstatement.

An audit involves performing procedures to obtain audit evidence about the amounts and disclosures in the consolidated financial statements. The procedures selected depend on the auditor's judgment, including the assessment of the risks of material misstatement of the consolidated financial statements, whether due to fraud or error. In making those risk assessments, the auditor considers internal control relevant to the entity's preparation and fair presentation of the consolidated financial statements in order to design audit procedures that are appropriate in the circumstances, but not for the purpose of expressing an opinion on the effectiveness of the entity's internal control. Accordingly, we express no such opinion. An audit also includes evaluating the appropriateness of accounting policies used and the reasonableness of significant accounting estimates made by management, as well as evaluating the overall presentation of the financial statements.

We believe that the audit evidence we have obtained is sufficient and appropriate to provide a basis for our audit opinions on the balance sheets as of December 31, 20X2 and 20X1, and the statements of income, changes in stockholders' equity and cash flows for the year ended December 31, 20X2.

Basis for Disclaimer of Opinion on 20X1 Operations and Cash Flows

We did not observe the taking of the physical inventory as of December 31, 20X0, since that date was prior to our appointment as auditors for the Company, and we were unable to satisfy ourselves regarding inventory quantities by means of other auditing procedures. Inventory amounts as of December 31, 20X0 enter into the determination of net income and cash flows for the year ended December 31, 20X1.

Disclaimer of Opinion on 20X1 Operations and Cash Flows

Because of the significance of the matter described in the Basis for Disclaimer of Opinion paragraph, we have not been able to obtain sufficient appropriate audit evidence to provide a basis for an audit opinion on the results of operations and cash flows for the year ended December 31, 20X1. Accordingly, we do not express an opinion on the results of operations and cash flows for the year ended December 31, 20X1.

Opinion

In our opinion, the balance sheets of ABC Company as of December 31, 20X2 and 20X1, and the statements of income, changes in stockholders' equity and cash flows for the year ended December 31, 20X2, present fairly, in all material respects, the financial position of ABC Company as of December 31, 20X2 and 20X1, and the results of its operations and its cash flows for the year ended December 31, 20X2 in accordance with accounting principles generally accepted in the United States of America.

(Auditor's signature)

(Auditor's city and state)

(Date of the auditor's report)

Unmodified in Prior Year, Qualified in Current Year

Independent Auditor's Report

(Appropriate Addressee)

We have audited the accompanying financial statements of ABC Company, which comprise the balance sheet as of December 31, 20X1 and 20X0, and the related statements of income, changes in stockholders' equity and cash flows for the years then ended, and the related notes to the financial statements.

Management's Responsibility for the Financial Statements

Management is responsible for the preparation and fair presentation of these financial statements in accordance with accounting principles generally accepted in the United States of America; this includes the design, implementation, and maintenance of internal control relevant to the preparation and fair presentation of financial statements that are free from material misstatement, whether due to fraud or error.

Auditor's Responsibility

Our responsibility is to express an opinion on these financial statements based on our audits. We conducted our audits in accordance with auditing standards generally accepted in the United States of America. Those standards require that we plan and perform the audit to obtain reasonable assurance about whether the financial statements are free from material misstatement.

An audit involves performing procedures to obtain audit evidence about the amounts and disclosures in the consolidated financial statements. The procedures selected depend on the auditor's judgment, including the assessment of the risks of material misstatement of the consolidated financial statements, whether due to fraud or error. In making those risk assessments, the auditor considers internal control relevant to the entity's preparation and fair presentation of the consolidated financial statements in order to design audit procedures that are appropriate in the circumstances, but not for the purpose of expressing an opinion on the effectiveness of the entity's internal control. Accordingly, we express no such opinion. An audit also includes evaluating the appropriateness of accounting policies used and the reasonableness of significant accounting estimates made by management, as well as evaluating the overall presentation of the financial statements.

We believe that the audit evidence we have obtained is sufficient and appropriate to provide a basis for our qualified audit opinion.

Basis for Qualified Opinion

The Company has excluded, from property and debt in the accompanying 20X1 balance sheet, certain lease obligations that were entered into in 20X1 which, in our opinion, should be capitalized in accordance with accounting principles generally accepted in the United States of America. If these lease obligations were capitalized property would be increased by $xxx, long-term debt by $xxx, and retained earnings by $xxx as of December 31, 20X1, and net income and earnings per share would be increased (decreased) by $xxx and $xxx, respectively, for the year then ended.

Qualified Opinion

In our opinion, except for the effects on the 20X1 financial statements of not capitalizing certain lease obligations as described in the Basis for Qualified Opinion paragraph, the financial statements referred to above present fairly, in all material respects, the financial position of ABC Company as of December 31, 20X1 and 20X0, and the results of its operations and its cash flows for the years then ended in accordance with accounting principles generally accepted in the United States of America.

(Auditor's signature)

(Auditor's city and state)

(Date of the auditor's report)

Qualified for Scope

Independent Auditor's Report

(Appropriate Addressee)

Report on the Financial Statements[i]

We have audited the accompanying financial statements of ABC Company, which comprise the balance sheet as of December 31, 20X1, and the related statements of income, changes in stockholders' equity and cash flows for the year then ended, and the related notes to the financial statements.

Management's Responsibility for the Financial Statements

Management is responsible for the preparation and fair presentation of these financial statements in accordance with accounting principles generally accepted in the United States of America; this includes the design, implementation, and maintenance of internal control relevant to the preparation and fair presentation of financial statements that are free from material misstatement, whether due to fraud or error.

Auditor's Responsibility

Our responsibility is to express an opinion on these financial statements based on our audit. We conducted our audit in accordance with auditing standards generally accepted in the United States of America. Those standards require that we plan and perform the audit to obtain reasonable assurance about whether the financial statements are free from material misstatement.

An audit involves performing procedures to obtain audit evidence about the amounts and disclosures in the consolidated financial statements. The procedures selected depend on the auditor's judgment, including the assessment of the risks of material misstatement of the consolidated financial statements, whether due to fraud or error. In making those risk assessments, the auditor considers internal control relevant to the entity's preparation and fair presentation of the consolidated financial statements in order to design audit procedures that are appropriate in the circumstances, but not for the purpose of expressing an opinion on the effectiveness of the entity's internal control. Accordingly, we express no such opinion. An audit also includes evaluating the appropriateness of accounting policies used and the reasonableness of significant accounting estimates made by management, as well as evaluating the overall presentation of the financial statements.

We believe that the audit evidence we have obtained is sufficient and appropriate to provide a basis for our qualified audit opinion.

Basis for Qualified Opinion

ABC Company's investment in XYZ Company, a foreign affiliate acquired during the year and accounted for under the equity method, is carried at $xxx on the balance sheet at December 31, 20X1, and ABC Company's share of XYZ Company's net income of $xxx is included in ABC Company's net income for the year then ended. We were unable to obtain sufficient appropriate audit evidence about the carrying amount of ABC Company's investment in XYZ Company as of December 31, 20X1 and ABC Company's share of XYZ Company's net income for the year then ended because we were denied access to the financial information, management, and the auditors of XYZ Company. Consequently, we were unable to determine whether any adjustments to these amounts were necessary.

Qualified Opinion

In our opinion, except for the possible effects of the matter described in the Basis for Qualified Opinion paragraph, the financial statements referred to above present fairly, in all material respects, the financial position of ABC Company as of December 31, 20X1, and the results of its operations and its cash flows for the year then ended in accordance with accounting principles generally accepted in the United States of America.

Report on Other Legal and Regulatory Requirements

(Form and content of this section of the auditor's report will vary depending on the nature of the auditor's other reporting responsibilities.)

(Auditor's signature)

(Auditor's city and state)

(Date of the auditor's report)

[i] The subtitle "Report on the Financial Statements" is unnecessary in circumstances when the second subtitle, "Report on Other Legal and Regulatory Requirements," is not applicable.

Qualified for Material Misstatement

Independent Auditor's Report

(Appropriate Addressee)

Report on the Financial Statements[i]

We have audited the accompanying financial statements of ABC Company, which comprise the balance sheet as of December 31, 20X1 and 20X0, and the related statements of income, changes in stockholders' equity and cash flows for the years then ended, and the related notes to the financial statements.

Management's Responsibility for the Financial Statements

Management is responsible for the preparation and fair presentation of these financial statements in accordance with accounting principles generally accepted in the United States of America; this includes the design, implementation, and maintenance of internal control relevant to the preparation and fair presentation of financial statements that are free from material misstatement, whether due to fraud or error.

Auditor's Responsibility

Our responsibility is to express an opinion on these financial statements based on our audits. We conducted our audits in accordance with auditing standards generally accepted in the United States of America. Those standards require that we plan and perform the audit to obtain reasonable assurance about whether the financial statements are free from material misstatement.

An audit involves performing procedures to obtain audit evidence about the amounts and disclosures in the consolidated financial statements. The procedures selected depend on the auditor's judgment, including the assessment of the risks of material misstatement of the consolidated financial statements, whether due to fraud or error. In making those risk assessments, the auditor considers internal control relevant to the entity's preparation and fair presentation of the consolidated financial statements in order to design audit procedures that are appropriate in the circumstances, but not for the purpose of expressing an opinion on the effectiveness of the entity's internal control. Accordingly, we express no such opinion. An audit also includes evaluating the appropriateness of accounting policies used and the reasonableness of significant accounting estimates made by management, as well as evaluating the overall presentation of the financial statements.

We believe that the audit evidence we have obtained is sufficient and appropriate to provide a basis for our qualified audit opinion.

Basis for Qualified Opinion

The Company has stated inventories at cost in the accompanying balance sheets. Accounting principles generally accepted in the United States of America require inventories to be stated at the lower of cost or market. If the Company stated inventories at the lower of cost or market, a write down of $xxx and $xxx would have been required as of December 31, 20X1 and 20X0, respectively. Accordingly, cost of sales would have been increased by $xxx and $xxx, and net income, income taxes, and stockholders' equity would have been reduced by $xxx, $xxx, and $xxx, and $xxx, $xxx, and $xxx, as of and for the years then ended in accordance with accounting principles generally accepted in the United States of America.

Qualified Opinion

In our opinion, except for the effects of the matter described in the Basis for Qualified Opinion paragraph, the financial statements referred to above present fairly, in all material respects, the financial position of ABC Company as of December 31, 20X1 and 20X0, and the results of its operations and its cash flows for the years then ended in accordance with accounting principles generally accepted in the United States of America.

Report on Other Legal and Regulatory Requirements

(Form and content of this section of the auditor's report will vary depending on the nature of the auditor's other reporting responsibilities.)

(Auditor's signature)

(Auditor's city and state)

(Date of the auditor's report)

[i] The subtitle "Report on the Financial Statements" is unnecessary in circumstances when the second subtitle, "Report on Other Legal and Regulatory Requirements," is not applicable.

Qualified for Inadequate Disclosure

Independent Auditor's Report

(Appropriate Addressee)

We have audited the accompanying financial statements of ABC Company, which comprise the balance sheet as of December 31, 20X1 and 20X0, and the related statements of income, changes in stockholders' equity and cash flows for the years then ended, and the related notes to the financial statements.

Management's Responsibility for the Financial Statements

Management is responsible for the preparation and fair presentation of these financial statements in accordance with accounting principles generally accepted in the United States of America; this includes the design, implementation, and maintenance of internal control relevant to the preparation and fair presentation of financial statements that are free from material misstatement, whether due to fraud or error.

Auditor's Responsibility

Our responsibility is to express an opinion on these financial statements based on our audits. We conducted our audits in accordance with auditing standards generally accepted in the United States of America. Those standards require that we plan and perform the audit to obtain reasonable assurance about whether the financial statements are free from material misstatement.

An audit involves performing procedures to obtain audit evidence about the amounts and disclosures in the consolidated financial statements. The procedures selected depend on the auditor's judgment, including the assessment of the risks of material misstatement of the consolidated financial statements, whether due to fraud or error. In making those risk assessments, the auditor considers internal control relevant to the entity's preparation and fair presentation of the consolidated financial statements in order to design audit procedures that are appropriate in the circumstances, but not for the purpose of expressing an opinion on the effectiveness of the entity's internal control. Accordingly, we express no such opinion. An audit also includes evaluating the appropriateness of accounting policies used and the reasonableness of significant accounting estimates made by management, as well as evaluating the overall presentation of the financial statements.

We believe that the audit evidence we have obtained is sufficient and appropriate to provide a basis for our qualified audit opinion.

Basis for Qualified Opinion

The company's financial statements do not disclose (*describe the nature of the omitted information that is not practicable to present in the auditor's report*). In our opinion, disclosure of this information is required by accounting principles generally accepted in the United States of America.

Qualified Opinion

In our opinion, except for the omission of the information described in the Basis for Qualified Opinion paragraph, the financial statements referred to above present fairly, in all material respects, the financial position of ABC Company as of December 31, 20X1 and 20X0, and the results of its operations and its cash flows for the years then ended in accordance with accounting principles generally accepted in the United States of America.

(Auditor's signature)

(Auditor's city and state)

(Date of the auditor's report)

Adverse Opinion

Independent Auditor's Report

(Appropriate Addressee)

We have audited the accompanying consolidated financial statements of ABC Company and its subsidiaries, which comprise the consolidated balance sheets as of December 31, 20X1, and the related consolidated statements of income, changes in stockholders' equity and cash flows for the year then ended, and the related notes to the financial statements.

Management's Responsibility for the Financial Statements

Management is responsible for the preparation and fair presentation of these consolidated financial statements in accordance with accounting principles generally accepted in the United States of America; this includes the design, implementation, and maintenance of internal control relevant to the preparation and fair presentation of consolidated financial statements that are free from material misstatement, whether due to fraud or error.

Auditor's Responsibility

Our responsibility is to express an opinion on these consolidated financial statements based on our audit. We conducted our audit in accordance with auditing standards generally accepted in the United States of America. Those standards require that we plan and perform the audit to obtain reasonable assurance about whether the financial statements are free from material misstatement.

An audit involves performing procedures to obtain audit evidence about the amounts and disclosures in the consolidated financial statements. The procedures selected depend on the auditor's judgment, including the assessment of the risks of material misstatement of the consolidated financial statements, whether due to fraud or error. In making those risk assessments, the auditor considers internal control relevant to the entity's preparation and fair presentation of the consolidated financial statements in order to design audit procedures that are appropriate in the circumstances, but not for the purpose of expressing an opinion on the effectiveness of the entity's internal control. Accordingly, we express no such opinion. An audit also includes evaluating the appropriateness of accounting policies used and the reasonableness of significant accounting estimates made by management, as well as evaluating the overall presentation of the consolidated financial statements.

We believe that the audit evidence we have obtained is sufficient and appropriate to provide a basis for our adverse audit opinion.

Basis for Adverse Opinion

As described in Note X, the Company has not consolidated the financial statements of subsidiary XYZ Company that it acquired during 20X1 because it has not yet been able to ascertain the fair values of certain of the subsidiary's material assets and liabilities at the acquisition date. This investment is therefore accounted for on a cost basis by the Company. Under accounting principles generally accepted in the United States of America, the subsidiary should have been consolidated because it is controlled by the Company. Had XYZ Company been consolidated, many elements in the accompanying consolidated financial statements would have been materially affected. The effects on the consolidated financial statements of the failure to consolidate have not been determined.

Adverse Opinion

In our opinion, because of the significance of the matter discussed in the Basis for Adverse Opinion paragraph, the consolidated financial statements referred to above do not present fairly the financial position of ABC Company and its subsidiaries as of December 31, 20X1, or the results of their operations or their cash flows for the years then ended.

(Auditor's signature)

(Auditor's city and state)

(Date of the auditor's report)

Disclaimer of Opinion for Scope

Independent Auditor's Report

(Appropriate Addressee)

Report on the Financial Statements[i]

We were engaged to audit the accompanying financial statements of ABC Company, which comprise the balance sheet as of December 31, 20X1, and the related statements of income, changes in stockholders' equity and cash flows for the year then ended, and the related notes to the financial statements.

Management's Responsibility for the Financial Statements

Management is responsible for the preparation and fair presentation of these financial statements in accordance with accounting principles generally accepted in the United States of America; this includes the design, implementation, and maintenance of internal control relevant to the preparation and fair presentation of financial statements that are free from material misstatement, whether due to fraud or error.

Auditor's Responsibility

Our responsibility is to express an opinion on these financial statements based on conducting the audit in accordance with auditing standards generally accepted in the United States of America. Because of the matter described in the Basis for Disclaimer of Opinion paragraph, however, we were not able to obtain sufficient appropriate audit evidence to provide a basis for an audit opinion.

Basis for Disclaimer of Opinion

The company's investment in XYZ Company, a joint venture, is carried at $xxx on the Company's balance sheet, which represents over 90 percent of the Company's net assets as of December 31, 20X1. We were not allowed access to the management and the auditors of XYZ Company. As a result, we were unable to determine whether any adjustments were necessary relating to the Company's proportional share of XYZ Company's assets that it controls jointly, its proportional share of XYZ Company's liabilities for which it is jointly responsible, its proportional share of XYZ Company's income and expenses for the year, and the elements making up the statements of changes in stockholders' equity and cash flows.

Disclaimer of Opinion

Because of the significance of the matter described in the Basis for Disclaimer of Opinion paragraph, we have not been able to obtain sufficient appropriate audit evidence to provide a basis for an audit opinion. Accordingly, we do not express an opinion on these financial statements.

Report on Other Legal and Regulatory Requirements

(Form and content of this section of the auditor's report will vary depending on the nature of the auditor's other reporting responsibilities.)

(Auditor's signature)

(Auditor's city and state)

(Date of the auditor's report)

[i] The subtitle "Report on the Financial Statements" is unnecessary in circumstances when the second subtitle, "Report on Other Legal and Regulatory Requirements," is not applicable.

Unmodified on B/S, Disclaimer on I/S and Cash Flows

Sample report with a disclaimer of opinion on results of operations and cash flows and an unmodified opinion on financial position (due to inability to verify opening inventory):

Independent Auditor's Report

(Appropriate Addressee)

We have audited the accompanying balance sheet of ABC Company, as of December 31, 20X1, and were engaged to audit the related statements of income, changes in stockholders' equity and cash flows for the year then ended, and the related notes to the financial statements.

Management's Responsibility for the Financial Statements

Management is responsible for the preparation and fair presentation of these financial statements in accordance with accounting principles generally accepted in the United States of America; this includes the design, implementation, and maintenance of internal control relevant to the preparation and fair presentation of financial statements that are free from material misstatement, whether due to fraud or error.

Auditor's Responsibility

Our responsibility is to express an opinion on these financial statements based on conducting the audit in accordance with auditing standards generally accepted in the United States of America. Because of the matters described in the Basis for Disclaimer of Opinion paragraph, however, we were not able to obtain sufficient appropriate audit evidence to provide a basis for an audit opinion on the income statement and the cash flow statement.

We conducted our audit of the balance sheet in accordance with auditing standards generally accepted in the United States of America. Those standards require that we plan and perform the audit to obtain reasonable assurance about whether the balance sheet is free of material misstatement.

An audit involves performing procedures to obtain audit evidence about the amounts and disclosures in the consolidated financial statements. The procedures selected depend on the auditor's judgment, including the assessment of the risks of material misstatement of the consolidated financial statements, whether due to fraud or error. In making those risk assessments, the auditor considers internal control relevant to the entity's preparation and fair presentation of the consolidated financial statements in order to design audit procedures that are appropriate in the circumstances, but not for the purpose of expressing an opinion on the effectiveness of the entity's internal control. Accordingly, we express no such opinion. An audit also includes evaluating the appropriateness of accounting policies used and the reasonableness of significant accounting estimates made by management, as well as evaluating the overall presentation of the financial statements.

We believe that the audit evidence we have obtained is sufficient and appropriate to provide a basis for our unmodified opinion on the financial position.

Basis for Disclaimer of Opinion on the Results of Operations and Cash Flows

We were not appointed as auditors of the company until after December 31, 20X0, and thus did not observe the counting of the physical inventories at the beginning of the year. We were unable to satisfy ourselves by alternative means concerning inventory quantities held at December 31, 20X0. Since opening inventories enter into the determination of the net income and cash flows, we were unable to determine whether adjustments might have been necessary relating to the profit for the year reported in the income statement and the net cash flows from operating activities reported in the cash flow statement.

Disclaimer of Opinion on the Results of Operations and Cash Flows

Because of the significance of the matter described in the Basis for Disclaimer of Opinion paragraph, we have not been able to obtain sufficient appropriate audit evidence to provide a basis for an audit opinion on the income statement and the cash flow statement. Accordingly, we do not express an opinion on the results of operations and cash flows for the year ended December 31, 20X1.

Opinion on the Financial Position

In our opinion, the balance sheet presents fairly, in all material respects, the financial position of ABC Company, as of December 31, 20X1, in accordance with accounting principles generally accepted in the United States of America.

(Auditor's signature)

(Auditor's city and state)

(Date of the auditor's report)

Emphasis-of-Matter Paragraph

Independent Auditor's Report

(Appropriate Addressee)

Report on the Financial Statements

We have audited the accompanying financial statements of ABC Company, which comprise the balance sheet as of December 31, 20X1, and the related statements of income, changes in stockholders' equity and cash flows for the year then ended, and the related notes to the financial statements.

Management's Responsibility for the Financial Statements

Management is responsible for the preparation and fair presentation of these financial statements in accordance with accounting principles generally accepted in the United States of America; this includes the design, implementation, and maintenance of internal control relevant to the preparation and fair presentation of financial statements that are free from material misstatement, whether due to fraud or error.

Auditor's Responsibility

Our responsibility is to express an opinion on these financial statements based on our audit. We conducted our audit in accordance with auditing standards generally accepted in the United States of America. Those standards require that we plan and perform the audit to obtain reasonable assurance about whether the financial statements are free from material misstatement.

An audit involves performing procedures to obtain audit evidence about the amounts and disclosures in the financial statements. The procedures selected depend on the auditor's judgment, including the assessment of the risks of material misstatement of the financial statements, whether due to fraud or error. In making those risk assessments, the auditor considers internal control relevant to the entity's preparation and fair presentation of the financial statements in order to design audit procedures that are appropriate in the circumstances, but not for the purpose of expressing an opinion on the effectiveness of the entity's internal control.[i] Accordingly, we express no such opinion. An audit also includes evaluating the appropriateness of accounting policies used and the reasonableness of significant accounting estimates made by management, as well as evaluating the overall presentation of the financial statements.

We believe that the audit evidence we have obtained is sufficient and appropriate to provide a basis for our audit opinion.

Opinion

In our opinion, the financial statements referred to above present fairly, in all material respects, the financial position of ABC Company as of December 31, 20X1, and the results of its operations and its cash flows for the year then ended in accordance with accounting principles generally accepted in the United States of America.

Emphasis of Matter

As discussed in Note X to the financial statements, the Company is a defendant in a lawsuit (*briefly describe the nature of the litigation consistent with the Company's description in the note to the financial statements*). Our opinion is not modified with respect to this matter.

Report on Other Legal and Regulatory Requirements

(Form and content of this section of the auditor's report will vary depending on the nature of the auditor's other reporting responsibilities.)

(Auditor's signature)

(Auditor's city and state)

(Date of the auditor's report)

[i] When the auditor has responsibility for expressing an opinion on the effectiveness of internal control in conjunction with the audit of the entity's financial statements, the sentence would be stated as follows: "In making those risk assessments, the auditor considers internal control relevant to the entity's preparation and fair presentation of the consolidated financial statements in order to design audit procedures that are appropriate in the circumstances." In addition, the next sentence, "Accordingly, we express no such opinion," would be omitted.

Other-Matter Paragraph

Independent Auditor's Report

(Appropriate Addressee)

Report on the Financial Statements

We have audited the accompanying financial statements of ABC Company, which comprise the balance sheet as of December 31, 20X1 and 20X0, and the related statements of income, changes in stockholders' equity and cash flows for the years then ended, and the related notes to the financial statements.

Management's Responsibility for the Financial Statements

Management is responsible for the preparation and fair presentation of these financial statements in accordance with accounting principles generally accepted in the United States of America; this includes the design, implementation, and maintenance of internal control relevant to the preparation and fair presentation of financial statements that are free from material misstatement, whether due to fraud or error.

Auditor's Responsibility

Our responsibility is to express an opinion on these financial statements based on our audits. We conducted our audits in accordance with auditing standards generally accepted in the United States of America. Those standards require that we plan and perform the audit to obtain reasonable assurance about whether the financial statements are free from material misstatement.

An audit involves performing procedures to obtain audit evidence about the amounts and disclosures in the financial statements. The procedures selected depend on the auditor's judgment, including the assessment of the risks of material misstatement of the financial statements, whether due to fraud or error. In making those risk assessments, the auditor considers internal control relevant to the entity's preparation and fair presentation of the financial statements in order to design audit procedures that are appropriate in the circumstances, but not for the purpose of expressing an opinion on the effectiveness of the entity's internal control. Accordingly, we express no such opinion. An audit also includes evaluating the appropriateness of accounting policies used and the reasonableness of significant accounting estimates made by management, as well as evaluating the overall presentation of the financial statements.

We believe that the audit evidence we have obtained is sufficient and appropriate to provide a basis for our audit opinion.

Opinion

In our opinion, the financial statements referred to above present fairly, in all material respects, the financial position of ABC Company as of December 31, 20X1 and 20X0, and the results of its operations and its cash flows for the years then ended in accordance with accounting principles generally accepted in the United States of America.

Other Matter

In our report dated March 1, 20X1, we expressed an opinion that the 20X0 financial statements did not fairly present the financial position, results of operations, and cash flows of ABC Company in accordance with accounting principles generally accepted in the United States of America because of two departures from such principles: (1) ABC Company carried its property, plant, and equipment at appraisal values, and provided for depreciation on the basis of such values, and (2) ABC Company did not provide for deferred income taxes with respect to differences between income for financial reporting purposes and taxable income. As described in Note X, the Company has changed its method of accounting for these items and restated its 20X0 financial statements to conform with accounting principles generally accepted in the United States of America. Accordingly, our present opinion on the restated 20X0 financial statements, as presented herein, is different from that expressed in our previous report.

Report on Other Legal and Regulatory Requirements

(Form and content of this section of the auditor's report will vary depending on the nature of the auditor's other reporting responsibilities.)

(Auditor's signature)

(Auditor's city and state)

(Date of the auditor's report)

Reference to Component Auditor

Independent Auditor's Report

(Appropriate Addressee)

Report on the Consolidated Financial Statements

We have audited the accompanying consolidated financial statements of ABC Company and its subsidiaries, which comprise the consolidated balance sheets as of December 31, 20X1 and 20X0, and the related consolidated statements of income, changes in stockholders' equity and cash flows for the years then ended, and the related notes to the financial statements.

Management's Responsibility for the Financial Statements

Management is responsible for the preparation and fair presentation of these consolidated financial statements in accordance with accounting principles generally accepted in the United States of America; this includes the design, implementation and maintenance of internal control relevant to the preparation and fair presentation of consolidated financial statements that are free from material misstatement, whether due to fraud or error.

Auditor's Responsibility

Our responsibility is to express an opinion on these consolidated financial statements based on our audit. We did not audit the financial statements of B Company, a wholly-owned subsidiary, whose statements reflect total assets and revenues constituting 20 percent and 22 percent, respectively, of the related consolidated totals. Those statements were audited by other auditors, whose report has been furnished to us, and our opinion, insofar as it relates to the amounts included for B Company, is based solely on the report of the other auditors. We conducted our audits in accordance with auditing standards generally accepted in the United States of America. Those standards require that we plan and perform the audit to obtain reasonable assurance about whether the consolidated financial statements are free from material misstatement.

An audit involves performing procedures to obtain audit evidence about the amounts and disclosures in the consolidated financial statements. The procedures selected depend on the auditor's judgment, including the assessment of the risks of material misstatement of the consolidated financial statements, whether due to fraud or error. In making those risk assessments, the auditor considers internal control relevant to the entity's preparation and fair presentation of the consolidated financial statements in order to design audit procedures that are appropriate in the circumstances, but not for the purpose of expressing an opinion on the effectiveness of the entity's internal control. Accordingly, we express no such opinion. An audit also includes evaluating the appropriateness of accounting policies used and the reasonableness of significant accounting estimates made by management, as well as evaluating the overall presentation of the consolidated financial statements.

We believe that the audit evidence we have obtained is sufficient and appropriate to provide a basis for our audit opinion.

Opinion

In our opinion, based on our audit and the report of the other auditors, the consolidated financial statements referred to above presents fairly, in all material respects, the financial position of ABC Company and its subsidiaries as of December 31, 20X1 and

20X2, in accordance with accounting principles generally accepted in the United States of America.

(Auditor's signature)

(Auditor's city and state)

(Date of the auditor's report)

F/S Prepared on Cash Basis

Independent Auditor's Report

(Appropriate Addressee)

We have audited the accompanying financial statements of ABC Partnership, which comprise the statement of assets and liabilities arising from cash transactions as of December 31, 20X1, and the related statement of revenue collected and expenses paid for the year then ended, and the related notes to the financial statements.

Management's Responsibility for the Financial Statements

Management is responsible for the preparation and fair presentation of these financial statements in accordance with the cash basis of accounting described in Note X; this includes determining that the cash basis of accounting is an acceptable basis for the presentation of the financial statements in the circumstances. Management is also responsible for the design, implementation and maintenance of internal control relevant to the preparation and fair presentation of financial statements that are free from material misstatement, whether due to fraud or error.

Auditor's Responsibility

Our responsibility is to express an opinion on these financial statements based on our audit. We conducted our audit in accordance with auditing standards generally accepted in the United States of America. Those standards require that we plan and perform the audit to obtain reasonable assurance about whether the financial statements are free from material misstatement.

An audit involves performing procedures to obtain audit evidence about the amounts and disclosures in the financial statements. The procedures selected depend on the auditor's judgment, including the assessment of the risks of material misstatement of the financial statements, whether due to fraud or error. In making those risk assessments, the auditor considers internal control relevant to the partnership's preparation and fair presentation of the financial statements in order to design audit procedures that are appropriate in the circumstances, but not for the purpose of expressing an opinion on the effectiveness of the partnership's internal control. Accordingly, we express no such opinion. An audit also includes evaluating the appropriateness of accounting policies used and the reasonableness of significant accounting estimates made by management, as well as evaluating the overall presentation of the financial statements.

We believe that the audit evidence we have obtained is sufficient and appropriate to provide a basis for our audit opinion.

Opinion

In our opinion, the financial statements referred to above present fairly, in all material respects, the assets and liabilities arising from cash transactions of ABC Partnership as of December 31, 20X1, and its revenue collected and expenses paid during the year then ended in accordance with the cash basis of accounting described in Note X.

Basis of Accounting

We draw attention to Note X of the financial statements, which describes the basis of accounting. The financial statements are prepared on the cash basis of accounting, which is a basis of accounting other than accounting principles generally accepted in the United States of America. Our opinion is not modified with respect to this matter.

(Auditor's signature)

(Auditor's city and state)

(Date of the auditor's report)

F/S Prepared on Regulatory Basis (for General Use)

Independent Auditor's Report

(Appropriate Addressee)

We have audited the accompanying financial statements of XYZ City, Any State, which comprise cash and unencumbered cash for each fund as of December 31, 20X1, and the related statements of cash receipts and disbursements and disbursements-budged and actual for the year then ended, and the related notes to the financial statements.

Management's Responsibility for the Financial Statements

Management is responsible for the preparation and fair presentation of these financial statements in accordance with the financial reporting provisions of Section Y of Regulation Z of Any State. Management is also responsible for the design, implementation and maintenance of internal control relevant to the preparation and fair presentation of financial statements that are free from material misstatement, whether due to fraud or error.

Auditor's Responsibility

Our responsibility is to express an opinion on these financial statements based on our audit. We conducted our audit in accordance with auditing standards generally accepted in the United States of America. Those standards require that we plan and perform the audit to obtain reasonable assurance about whether the financial statements are free from material misstatement.

An audit involves performing procedures to obtain audit evidence about the amounts and disclosures in the financial statements. The procedures selected depend on the auditor's judgment, including the assessment of the risks of material misstatement of the financial statements, whether due to fraud or error. In making those risk assessments, the auditor considers internal control relevant to the partnership's preparation and fair presentation of the financial statements in order to design audit procedures that are appropriate in the circumstances, but not for the purpose of expressing an opinion on the effectiveness of the partnership's internal control. Accordingly, we express no such opinion. An audit also includes evaluating the appropriateness of accounting policies used and the reasonableness of significant accounting estimates made by management, as well as evaluating the overall presentation of the financial statements.

We believe that the audit evidence we have obtained is sufficient and appropriate to provide a basis for our audit opinions.

Basis for Adverse Opinion on U.S. Generally Accepted Accounting Principles

As described in Note X of the financial statements, the financial statements are prepared by XYZ City on the basis of the financial reporting provisions of Section Y of Regulation Z of Any State, which is a basis of accounting other than accounting principles generally accepted in the United States of America, to meet the requirements of Any State.

The effects on the financial statements of the variances between the regulatory basis of accounting described in Note X and accounting principles generally accepted in the United States of America, although not reasonably determinable, are presumed to be material.

Adverse Opinion on U.S. Generally Accepted Accounting Principles

In our opinion, because of the significance of the matter discussed in the "Basis for Adverse Opinion on U.S. Generally Accepted Accounting Principles" paragraph, the financial statements referred to above do not present fairly, in accordance with accounting principles generally accepted in the United States of America, the financial position of each fund of XYZ City as of December 31, 20X1, or changes in financial position or cash flows thereof for the year then ended.

Opinion on Regulatory Basis of Accounting

In our opinion, the financial statements referred to above present fairly, in all material respects, the cash and unencumbered cash of each fund of XYZ City as of December 31, 20X1, and their respective cash receipts and disbursements, and budgetary results for the year then ended in accordance with the financial reporting provisions of Section Y of Regulation Z of Any State described in Note X.

(Auditor's signature)

(Auditor's city and state)

(Date of the auditor's report)

Single Financial Statement

Independent Auditor's Report

(Appropriate Addressee)

We have audited the accompanying balance sheet of ABC Company as of December 31, 20X1, and the related notes (the financial statement).

Management's Responsibility for the Financial Statements

Management is responsible for the preparation and fair presentation of the financial statement in accordance with accounting principles generally accepted in the United States of America; this includes the design, implementation and maintenance of internal control relevant to the preparation and fair presentation of the financial statement that is free from material misstatement, whether due to fraud or error.

Auditor's Responsibility

Our responsibility is to express an opinion on the financial statement based on our audit. We conducted our audit in accordance with auditing standards generally accepted in the United States of America. Those standards require that we plan and perform the audit to obtain reasonable assurance about whether the financial statement is free from material misstatement.

An audit involves performing procedures to obtain audit evidence about the amounts and disclosures in the financial statement. The procedures selected depend on the auditor's judgment, including the assessment of the risks of material misstatement of the financial statement, whether due to fraud or error. In making those risk assessments, the auditor considers internal control relevant to the entity's preparation and fair presentation of the financial statement in order to design audit procedures that are appropriate in the circumstances, but not for the purpose of expressing an opinion on the effectiveness of the entity's internal control. Accordingly, we express no such opinion. An audit also includes evaluating the appropriateness of accounting policies used and the reasonableness of significant accounting estimates made by management, as well as evaluating the overall presentation of the financial statement.

We believe that the audit evidence we have obtained is sufficient and appropriate to provide a basis for our audit opinion.

Opinion

In our opinion, the financial statement referred to above presents fairly, in all material respects, the financial position of ABC Company as of December 31, 20X1, in accordance with accounting principles generally accepted in the United States of America.

(Auditor's signature)

(Auditor's city and state)

(Date of the auditor's report)

Specific Element (Special Purpose Framework)

Independent Auditor's Report

(Appropriate Addressee)

We have audited the accompanying schedule of royalties applicable to engine production of the Q Division of ABC Company for the year ended December 31, 20X1, and the related notes (the schedule).

Management's Responsibility for the Financial Statements

Management is responsible for the preparation and fair presentation of the schedule in accordance with the financial reporting provisions of Section Z of the license agreement between ABC Company and XYZ Corporation dated January 1, 20X1 (the contract). Management is also responsible for the design, implementation and maintenance of internal control relevant to the preparation and fair presentation of financial statements that are free from material misstatement, whether due to fraud or error.

Auditor's Responsibility

Our responsibility is to express an opinion on the schedule based on our audit. We conducted our audit in accordance with auditing standards generally accepted in the United States of America. Those standards require that we plan and perform the audit to obtain reasonable assurance about whether the schedule is free from material misstatement.

An audit involves performing procedures to obtain audit evidence about the amounts and disclosures in the schedule. The procedures selected depend on the auditor's judgment, including the assessment of the risks of material misstatement of the schedule, whether due to fraud or error. In making those risk assessments, the auditor considers internal control relevant to the entity's preparation and fair presentation of the schedule in order to design audit procedures that are appropriate in the circumstances, but not for the purpose of expressing an opinion on the effectiveness of the entity's internal control. Accordingly, we express no such opinion. An audit also includes evaluating the appropriateness of accounting policies used and the reasonableness of significant accounting estimates made by management, as well as evaluating the overall presentation of the schedule.

We believe that the audit evidence we have obtained is sufficient and appropriate to provide a basis for our audit opinion.

Opinion

In our opinion, the schedule referred to above presents fairly, in all material respects, the royalties applicable to engine production of the Q Division of ABC Company for the year ended December 31, 20X1, in accordance with the financial reporting provisions of Section Z of the contract.

Basis of Accounting

We draw attention to Note X of the schedule, which describes the basis of accounting. The schedule was prepared by ABC Company on the basis of the financial reporting provisions of Section Z of the contract, which is a basis of accounting other than accounting principles generally accepted in the United States of America, to comply with the financial reporting of the contract referred to above. Our opinion is not modified with respect to this matter.

Restriction on Use

Our report is intended solely for the information and use of ABC Company and XYZ Corporation and is not intended to be and should not be used by anyone other than these specified parties.

(Auditor's signature)

(Auditor's city and state)

(Date of the auditor's report)

Incomplete Presentation

Independent Auditor's Report

(Appropriate Addressee)

We have audited the accompanying Historical Summaries of Gross Income and Direct Operating Expenses of ABC Apartments for each of the three years in the period ended December 31, 20X1, and the related notes (the historical summaries).

Management's Responsibility for the Financial Statements

Management is responsible for the preparation and fair presentation of these historical summaries in accordance with accounting principles generally accepted in the United States of America; this includes the design, implementation and maintenance of internal control relevant to the preparation and fair presentation of the financial statement that is free from material misstatement, whether due to fraud or error.

Auditor's Responsibility

Our responsibility is to express an opinion on the historical summaries based on our audit. We conducted our audit in accordance with auditing standards generally accepted in the United States of America. Those standards require that we plan and perform the audit to obtain reasonable assurance about whether the historical summaries are free from material misstatement.

An audit involves performing procedures to obtain audit evidence about the amounts and disclosures in the historical summaries. The procedures selected depend on the auditor's judgment, including the assessment of the risks of material misstatement of the historical summaries, whether due to fraud or error. In making those risk assessments, the auditor considers internal control relevant to the entity's preparation and fair presentation of the historical summaries in order to design audit procedures that are appropriate in the circumstances, but not for the purpose of expressing an opinion on the effectiveness of the entity's internal control. Accordingly, we express no such opinion. An audit also includes evaluating the appropriateness of accounting policies used and the reasonableness of significant accounting estimates made by management, as well as evaluating the overall presentation of the historical summaries.

We believe that the audit evidence we have obtained is sufficient and appropriate to provide a basis for our audit opinion.

Opinion

In our opinion, the historical summaries referred to above present fairly, in all material respects, the gross income and direct operating expenses described in Note X of ABC Apartments for each of the three years in the period ended December 31, 20X1, in accordance with accounting principles generally accepted in the United States of America.

Emphasis of Matter

We draw attention to Note X to the historical summaries, which describes that the accompanying historical summaries were prepared for the purpose of complying with the rules and regulations of Regulator DEF (for inclusion in the filing of Form Z of ABC Company) and are not intended to be a complete presentation of the company's revenues and expenses. Our opinion is not modified with respect to this matter.

(Auditor's signature)

(Auditor's city and state)

(Date of the auditor's report)

Application of Accounting Principles (Second Opinion)

Written Report to the Requesting Party about the Application of Accounting Principles (Sometimes called a *Second Opinion*):

Introduction

We have been engaged to report on the appropriate application of the requirements of accounting principles generally accepted in the United States of America to the specific transaction described below. This report is being issued to ABC Company for assistance in evaluating accounting policies for the described specific transaction. Our engagement has been conducted in accordance with Statement on Auditing Standards Reports on Application of Requirements of an Applicable Financial Reporting Framework.

Description of Transactions

The facts, circumstances, and assumptions relevant to the specific transaction as provided to us by the management of ABC Company are as follows:

(*Include text discussing the facts, circumstances, and assumptions relevant to the specific transaction.*)

Appropriate Accounting Principles

(*Include text discussing accounting principles generally accepted in the United States of America and how they apply to the described transaction.*)

Concluding Comments

The ultimate responsibility for the decision on the appropriate application of the requirements of accounting principles generally accepted in the United States of America for an actual transaction rests with the preparers of financial statements, who should consult with their continuing accountant. Our conclusion on the appropriate application of the requirements of accounting principles generally accepted in the United States of America for the described specific transaction is based solely on the facts provided to us as previously described; should these facts and circumstances differ, our conclusion may change.

Restricted Use

This report is intended solely for the information and use of those charged with governance and management of ABC Company and is not intended to be and should not be used by anyone other than these specified parties.

Report on Summary Financial Statements

Independent Auditor's Report

(Appropriate Addressee)

The accompanying summary financial statements, which comprise the summary balance sheet as of December 31, 20X1, the summary income statement, summary statement of changes in stockholders' equity and summary cash flow statement for the year then ended, and the related notes, are derived from the audited financial statements of ABC Company as of and for the year ended December 31, 20X1. We expressed an unmodified audit opinion on those audited financial statements in our report dated February 15, 20X2. The audited financial statements, and the summary financial statements derived therefrom, do not reflect the effects of events, if any, that occurred subsequent to the date of our report on the audited financial statements.

The summary financial statements do not contain all the disclosures required by (*describe financial reporting framework applied in the preparation of the financial statements of ABC Company*). Reading the summary financial statements, therefore, is not a substitute for reading the audited financial statements of ABC Company.

Management's Responsibility for the Summary Financial Statements

Management is responsible for the preparation of the summary financial statements on the basis described in Note X.

Auditor's Responsibility

Our responsibility is to express an opinion about whether the summary financial statements are consistent, in all material respects, with the audited financial statements based on our procedures, which were conducted in accordance with auditing standards generally accepted in the United States of America. The procedures consisted principally of comparing the summary financial statements with the related information in the audited financial statements from which the summary financial statements have been derived, and evaluating whether the summary financial statements are prepared in accordance with the basis described in Note X. We did not perform any audit procedures regarding the audited financial statements after the date of our report on those financial statements.

Opinion

In our opinion, the summary financial statements of ABC Company as of and for the year ended December 31, 20X1 referred to above are consistent, in all material respects, with the audited financial statements from which they have been derived, on the basis described in Note X.

(Auditor's signature)

(Auditor's city and state)

(Date of the auditor's report)

Review Report on Interim Financial Statements

Independent Auditor's Report

(Appropriate Addressee)

Report on the Financial Statements

We have reviewed the accompanying (*describe the interim financial information or statements reviewed*) of ABC Company and subsidiaries as of September 30, 20X1, and for the three-month and none-month periods then ended.

Management's Responsibility

The Company's management is responsible for the preparation and fair presentation of the interim financial information in accordance with (*identify the applicable financial reporting framework; for example, accounting principles generally accepted in the United States of America*); this responsibility includes the design, implementation, and maintenance of internal control sufficient to provide a reasonable basis for the preparation and fair presentation of interim financial information in accordance with the applicable financial reporting framework.

Auditor's Responsibility

Our responsibility is to conduct our review in accordance with auditing standards generally accepted in the United States of America applicable to reviews of interim financial information. A review of interim financial information consists principally of applying analytical procedures and making inquiries of persons responsible for financial and accounting matters. It is substantially less in scope than an audit conducted in accordance with auditing standards generally accepted in the United States of America, the objective of which is the expression of an opinion regarding the financial information. Accordingly, we do not express such an opinion.

Conclusion

Based on our review, we are not aware of any material modifications that should be made to the accompanying interim financial information for it to be in accordance with (*identify the applicable financial reporting framework; for example, accounting principles generally accepted in the United States of America*).

(Auditor's signature)

(Auditor's city and state)

(Date of the auditor's report)

Other Types of Reports

Reports on Application of Requirements of Framework

After studying this lesson, you should be able to:

1. *Identify the reporting accountant's responsibilities when engaged to provide a second opinion on the requirements of the applicable financial reporting framework.*
2. *Identify the reporting language that would be appropriate when issuing a written report on the requirements of the applicable financial reporting framework.*

I. **Relevant AICPA Guidance --** The relevant AICPA guidance is provided by AU 915: "Reports on Application of Requirements of an Applicable Financial Reporting Framework." The standard states that the auditor's objective, when engaged to issue a written report or provide oral advice on the application of the requirements of an applicable financial reporting framework to a specific transaction or on the type of report that may be issued on a specific entity's financial statements, is to appropriately address: (1) the acceptance of the engagement; (2) the planning and performance of the engagement; and (3) reporting on the specific transaction or type of report.

> **Definitions:**
> *Hypothetical transaction*: A transaction or financial reporting issue that does not involve facts or circumstances of a specific entity.
>
> *Reporting accountant*: An accountant, other than a continuing accountant, who prepares a written report or provides oral advice on the application of the requirements of an applicable financial reporting framework to a specific transaction or on the type of report that may be issued on a specific entity's financial statements. (A reporting accountant who is also engaged to provide accounting advice to a specific entity on a recurring basis is commonly referred to as an *advisory accountant*.)
>
> *Specific transaction*: A completed or proposed transaction or group of related transaction or a financial reporting issue involving facts and circumstances of a specific entity.

II. **Engagement Acceptance**

A. The reporting accountant should consider the following: (1) the circumstances under which the written report or oral advice is requested; (2) the purpose of the request; and (3) the intended use of the written report or oral advice.

B. The reporting accountant should not accept any engagement involving a *hypothetical transaction*.

C. If it is appropriate to accept an engagement under this SAS, the reporting accountant should establish an understanding with the requesting party that: (1) management is responsible for the proper accounting treatment and should consult with the continuing accountant; (2) management acknowledges that the reporting accountant may need to consult with the continuing accountant and, if requested, that management will authorize the continuing accountant to respond to the reporting accountant's inquiries; and (3) management will notify those charged with governance and the continuing accountant about the engagement.

III. **Engagement Panning and Performance**

A. The reporting accountant should:

1. Obtain an understanding of the specific transaction(s) or the conditions relevant to the type of report that may be issued;
2. Review the requirements of the applicable financial reporting framework;
3. Consult with other professionals or others, if appropriate;
4. Consider existing relevant precedents or analogies;
5. Request permission from management to consult with the continuing accountant and request that management authorize the continuing accountant to respond fully to the reporting accountant's inquiries; and
6. Consult with the continuing accountant regarding the facts.

B. **Consulting with the continuing accountant --** The reporting accountant (who is engaged to issue a written report or provide oral advice on the application of the requirements of an applicable financial reporting framework to a specific transaction) should consult with the continuing accountant **unless**:

1. The reporting accountant is engaged to provide recurring accounting and reporting advice and (a) **does not believe that a second opinion is being requested**; (b) has full access to management; and (c) believes that the relevant information has been obtained.
2. **Documentation --** If the reporting accountant deems it unnecessary to consult with the continuing accountant, the reporting accountant should document the justification for not consulting.

C. **Continuing accountant's responses --** The continuing accountant's responsibilities for responding to inquiries of the reporting accountant are the same as those of a predecessor auditor responding to an auditor's inquiries. The continuing accountant may indicate whether the method of accounting recommended by the continuing accountant is disputed by management and convey the continuing accountant's conclusion on the application of the requirements of an applicable financial reporting framework.

IV. Written Report

A. The report should be addressed to the requesting party and include the following:

1. A description of the engagement and reference to this SAS;
2. Identification of the specific entity, a description of any specific transaction(s), and a statement about the source of information;
3. A statement describing the application of the requirements of an applicable financial reporting framework (and country involved);
4. A statement that management is responsible for the proper accounting treatment and they should consult with their continuing accountants;
5. A statement that any differences in the facts or circumstances may change the report;
6. A restriction that the report is intended solely for the specified parties. (The restricted distribution of the report does not prevent distribution of the report to the continuing accountant.)

B. The requirements associated with written report may be useful when providing oral advice, too.

V. Sample Written Report to the Requesting Party

See the following example.

Introduction

We have been engaged to report on the appropriate application of the requirements of accounting principles generally accepted in the United States of America to the specific transaction described below. This report is being issued to ABC Company for assistance in evaluating accounting policies for the described specific transaction. Our engagement has been conducted in accordance with Statement on Auditing Standards Reports on Application of Requirements of an Applicable Financial Reporting Framework.

Description of Transactions

The facts, circumstances, and assumptions relevant to the specific transaction as provided to us by the management of ABC Company are as follows:

(*Include text discussing the facts, circumstances, and assumptions relevant to the specific transaction.*)

Appropriate Accounting Principles

(*Include text discussing accounting principles generally accepted in the United States of America and how they apply to the described transaction.*)

Concluding Comments

The ultimate responsibility for the decision on the appropriate application of the requirements of accounting principles generally accepted in the United States of America for an actual transaction rests with the preparers of financial statements, who should consult with their continuing accountant. Our conclusion on the appropriate application of the requirements of accounting principles generally accepted in the United States of America for the described specific transaction is based solely on the facts provided to us as previously described; should these facts and circumstances differ, our conclusion may change.

Restricted Use

This report is intended solely for the information and use of those charged with governance and management of ABC Company and is not intended to be and should not be used by anyone other than these specified parties.

F/S with Special Purpose Frameworks

After studying this lesson, you should be able to:

1. *Identify the 4 specific bases of accounting associated with the term special purpose framework.*
2. *Identify the reporting language that would be appropriate when issuing an audit report on financial statements prepared using a special purpose framework, and the differences in such reporting language depending upon the particular basis of accounting involved.*

I. **Relevant AICPA Guidance --** The relevant AICPA guidance is provided by AU 800: "Special Considerations — Audits of Financial Statements Prepared In Accordance With Special Purpose Frameworks." The standard states that the auditor's objectives are to (1) the acceptance of the engagement; (2) the planning and performance of that engagement; and (3) forming an opinion and reporting on the financial statements.

> **Definition:**
> *Special purpose framework*: A financial reporting framework other than GAAP that is one of the following bases of accounting: (1) cash basis, (2) tax basis, (3) regulatory basis, or (4) contractual basis. (A later SAS amended this definition to further include: (5) "A basis of accounting that uses a definite set of logical, reasonable criteria that is applied to all material items appearing in financial statements.")

II. **Engagement Acceptance**

A. **Acceptability of the financial reporting framework --** The auditor should obtain an understanding of (a) the purpose for which the financial statements are prepared; (b) the intended users; and (c) the steps taken by management to determine that the applicable financial reporting framework is acceptable in the circumstances.

B. **Preconditions for an audit --** The auditor should obtain the agreement of management that it understands its responsibility to include all informative disclosures that are appropriate for the special purpose framework used, including (a) a description of the special purpose framework; (b) informative disclosures similar to those required by GAAP; (c) a description of any significant interpretations of the contract on which the special purpose financial statements are based, when applicable; and (d) additional disclosures beyond those specifically required that may be necessary to achieve fair presentation.

III. **Engagement Planning and Performance**

A. **When the engagement is based on an underlying contract --** The auditor should obtain an understanding of any *significant interpretations* of the contract that management made.

B. An interpretation is significant when adoption of another reasonable interpretation would have produced a material difference.

IV. **Forming an Opinion and Reporting Considerations**

A. **Description of the applicable financial reporting framework --** The auditor should consider whether the financial statements are appropriately titled (should not use financial statement names that imply GAAP), include a summary of significant accounting policies, and adequately describe how the special purpose framework differs from GAAP. These differences do not have to be quantified, however.

B. **Fair presentation --** The auditor should determine whether informative disclosures are included similar to those required by GAAP, and whether additional disclosures are needed to achieve fair presentation.

C. **Auditor's report** -- The report should describe the *purpose for which the financial statements are prepared* (**if regulatory basis or contractual basis**) or reference a note containing that information about the special purpose framework used.

D. **Alerting readers in an emphasis of matter paragraph** -- The auditor's report on special purpose financial statements should include an *emphasis of matter* ("Basis of Accounting") paragraph that (1) indicates that the financial statements are prepared in accordance with the applicable special purpose framework; (2) refers to the note that describes that framework; and (3) states that the special purpose framework is a basis of accounting other than GAAP. (The only exception to such an alert involves *regulatory basis financial statements intended for general use* for which no such alert is needed.)

E. **Restricting the use of the auditor's report to the intended users** -- The auditor's report should also include an *other matter* paragraph that restricts the use of the auditor's report to those within the entity, the parties to the contract/agreement, or the regulatory agencies to whom the entity is subject **when the financial statements are prepared in accordance with either** (1) a contractual basis of accounting; or (2) a regulatory basis of accounting. (The only exception to such a restriction involves *regulatory basis financial statements intended for general use* for which no such restriction is needed. And no such restriction applies to cash basis or tax basis.)

F. **Regulatory basis financial statements intended for** *general use* -- If the financial statements are prepared in accordance with a regulatory basis of accounting and are intended for general use, the auditor should not include the *emphasis of matter* or *other matter* paragraphs. Instead, the auditor should express (1) an opinion as to whether the financial statements are prepared in accordance with GAAP (which they are not); and (2) an opinion in a separate paragraph as to whether the financial statements are prepared in accordance with the special purpose framework.

G. **Auditors report prescribed by law or regulation** -- If the prescribed specific layout, form, or wording of the auditor's report is not acceptable (or would cause the auditor to make an inappropriate statement), the auditor should either reword the prescribed form or attach separately an appropriately worded audit report.

Question:
Which special purpose frameworks require a *description of purpose for which such financial statements are prepared*?

Answer:
Only regulatory basis (whether intended for general use or not) and contractual basis. (Cash basis and tax basis do not!)

Question:
Which special purpose frameworks require an *emphasis of matter* paragraph alerting readers to the special purpose framework?

Answer:
Cash basis, tax basis, regulatory basis (if restricted), and contractual basis do. (Only regulatory basis intended for general use does not require such an alert!)

Question:
Which special purpose frameworks require an *other matter* paragraph to restrict the distribution of the auditor's report to specified users?

Answer:
Only regulatory basis (if restricted) and contractual basis do. (Cash basis, tax basis, and regulatory basis intended for general use do not require such a restriction!)

V. Sample Audit Report for Financial Statements Prepared on a *Cash Basis*

Independent Auditor's Report

(Appropriate Addressee)

We have audited the accompanying financial statements of ABC Partnership, which comprise the statement of assets and liabilities arising from cash transactions as of December 31, 20X1, and the related statement of revenue collected and expenses paid for the year then ended, and the related notes to the financial statements.

Management's Responsibility for the Financial Statements

Management is responsible for the preparation and fair presentation of these financial statements in accordance with the cash basis of accounting described in Note X; this includes determining that the cash basis of accounting is an acceptable basis for the presentation of the financial statements in the circumstances. Management is also responsible for the design, implementation and maintenance of internal control relevant to the preparation and fair presentation of financial statements that are free from material misstatement, whether due to fraud or error.

Auditor's Responsibility

Our responsibility is to express an opinion on these financial statements based on our audit. We conducted our audit in accordance with auditing standards generally accepted in the United States of America. Those standards require that we plan and perform the audit to obtain reasonable assurance about whether the financial statements are free from material misstatement.

An audit involves performing procedures to obtain audit evidence about the amounts and disclosures in the financial statements. The procedures selected depend on the auditor's judgment, including the assessment of the risks of material misstatement of the financial statements, whether due to fraud or error. In making those risk assessments, the auditor considers internal control relevant to the partnership's preparation and fair presentation of the financial statements in order to design audit procedures that are appropriate in the circumstances, but not for the purpose of expressing an opinion on the effectiveness of the partnership's internal control. Accordingly, we express no such opinion. An audit also includes evaluating the appropriateness of accounting policies used and the reasonableness of significant accounting estimates made by management, as well as evaluating the overall presentation of the financial statements.

We believe that the audit evidence we have obtained is sufficient and appropriate to provide a basis for our audit opinion.

Opinion

In our opinion, the financial statements referred to above present fairly, in all material respects, the assets and liabilities arising from cash transactions of ABC Partnership as of December 31, 20X1, and its revenue collected and expenses paid during the year then ended in accordance with the cash basis of accounting described in Note X.

Basis of Accounting

We draw attention to Note X of the financial statements, which describes the basis of accounting. The financial statements are prepared on the cash basis of accounting, which is a basis of accounting other than accounting principles generally accepted in the United States of America. Our opinion is not modified with respect to this matter.

(Auditor's signature)

(Auditor's city and state)

(Date of the auditor's report)

Audits of Single F/S and Specific Elements, Accounts, or Items

After studying this lesson you should be able to:

1. *Identify the auditor's responsibilities when engaged to report on a single financial statement or specific element of a financial statement.*
2. *Identify the reporting language that would be appropriate when issuing an audit report on a single financial statement or specific element of a financial statement.*

I. **Relevant AICPA Guidance --** The relevant AICPA guidance is provided by AU 805 "Special considerations — Audits of Single Financial Statements and Specific Elements, Accounts, or Items of a Financial Statement." The standard states that the auditor's objective is to appropriately address the special considerations that are relevant to (1) the acceptance of the engagement; (2) the planning and performance of the engagement; and (3) reporting on the single financial statement or the specific element.

II. **Engagement Acceptance**

   A. **Application of GAAS --** If not engaged to audit the complete set of financial statements, the auditor should determine whether the audit of a single financial statement or a specific element of those financial statements in accordance with GAAS is practicable.

   B. **Acceptability of the financial reporting framework --** The auditor should obtain an understanding of (a) the purpose for which the single financial statement or specific element of a financial statement is prepared; (b) the intended users; and (c) the steps taken by management to determine that the application of the financial reporting framework is acceptable and that disclosure is adequate.

III. **Engagement Planning and Performance**

   A. **If the specific element is based on stockholders' equity --** The auditor should obtain sufficient appropriate evidence to enable the auditor to express an opinion about financial position. (This effectively means that the auditor should have audited the whole balance sheet in order to report on an element based on stockholders' equity.)

   B. **If the specific element is based upon the entity's net income or the equivalent --** The auditor should obtain sufficient appropriate evidence to enable the auditor to express an opinion about both financial position and results of operations. (This effectively means that the auditor should have audited the complete set of financial statements in order to report on an element based on net income.)

   C. **Considerations when planning and performing the audit --** Written representations from management about the complete set of financial statements would be replaced by representations about the single financial statement or the specific element in accordance with the applicable financial reporting framework.

IV. **Forming an Opinion and Reporting Considerations**

   A. Reporting on the entity's complete set of financial statements and a single financial statement or a specific element of those financial statements.

      1. If the auditor is engaged to audit a single financial statement or a specific element of a financial statement in connection with an audit of the complete set of financial statements -- The auditor should (1) issue a separate report and express a separate opinion for each engagement, and (2) indicate in the report on a specific element of a financial statement the date of the auditor's report on the complete set of financial statements and the nature of that opinion under an appropriate heading.

2. An audited single financial statement or an audited specific element of a financial statement may normally be published along with the entity's audited complete set of financial statements if the single financial statement or specific element is sufficiently differentiated from the complete set of financial statements.

3. If the presentation does not sufficiently differentiate the single financial statement or specific element from the audited financial statements -- The auditor should ask management to address the situation; and the auditor should not release the auditor's report until satisfied with the resolution.

B. Modified opinion, emphasis-of-matter paragraph, or other-matter paragraph in the auditor's report on the entity's financial statements.

1. If the modified opinion on the set of financial statements is relevant to the audit of the specific element (that is, the modification is material and pervasive with respect to the specific element) -- The auditor should (a) express an adverse opinion on the specific element when the modification applicable to the set of financial statements is a result of a material misstatement in the financial statements; or (b) disclaim an opinion on the specific element when the modification applicable to the set of financial statements is a result of a scope limitation. (Note: Otherwise that would be equivalent to expressing a *piecemeal opinion*, which is prohibited.)

2. If the modified opinion on the set of financial statements is relevant to the audit of the specific element and the auditor still considers it appropriate to express an unmodified opinion on that specific element -- The auditor should only do that if (a) that opinion is expressed in a report that does not accompany the report containing the adverse opinion or disclaimer of opinion, and (b) the specific element does not constitute a major portion of the entity's complete set of financial statements or the specific element is not based on stockholders' equity or net income or equivalent.

3. A single statement constitutes a major portion of a complete set of financial statements, so the auditor should not express an unmodified opinion on the single financial statements when an adverse opinion or disclaimer of opinion is expressed on the complete set of financials.

4. If the report on the complete set of financial statements includes an emphasis-of-matter or other-matter paragraph relevant to the single financial statement or the specific element -- The auditor should include a similar emphasis-of-matter or other-matter paragraph in the report on the single financial statement or specific element.

C. Reporting on an incomplete presentation (that is otherwise in accordance with GAAP) -- The auditor should include an emphasis-of-matter paragraph in the auditor's report that (1) states the purpose for which the presentation is prepared and refers to a note in the financial statements that describes the basis of presentation; and (2) indicates that the presentation is not intended to be a complete presentation.

V. Sample Report on a Single Financial Statement (Based on a General Purpose Framework)

See the following example.

Independent Auditor's Report

(Appropriate Addressee)

We have audited the accompanying balance sheet of ABC Company as of December 31, 20X1, and the related notes (the financial statement).

Management's Responsibility for the Financial Statements

Management is responsible for the preparation and fair presentation of the financial statement in accordance with accounting principles generally accepted in the United States of America; this includes the design, implementation and maintenance of internal control relevant to the preparation and fair presentation of the financial statement that is free from material misstatement, whether due to fraud or error.

Auditor's Responsibility

Our responsibility is to express an opinion on the financial statement based on our audit. We conducted our audit in accordance with auditing standards generally accepted in the United States of America. Those standards require that we plan and perform the audit to obtain reasonable assurance about whether the financial statement is free from material misstatement.

An audit involves performing procedures to obtain audit evidence about the amounts and disclosures in the financial statement. The procedures selected depend on the auditor's judgment, including the assessment of the risks of material misstatement of the financial statement, whether due to fraud or error. In making those risk assessments, the auditor considers internal control relevant to the entity's preparation and fair presentation of the financial statement in order to design audit procedures that are appropriate in the circumstances, but not for the purpose of expressing an opinion on the effectiveness of the entity's internal control. Accordingly, we express no such opinion. An audit also includes evaluating the appropriateness of accounting policies used and the reasonableness of significant accounting estimates made by management, as well as evaluating the overall presentation of the financial statement.

We believe that the audit evidence we have obtained is sufficient and appropriate to provide a basis for our audit opinion.

Opinion

In our opinion, the financial statement referred to above presents fairly, in all material respects, the financial position of ABC Company as of December 31, 20X1, in accordance with accounting principles generally accepted in the United States of America.

(Auditor's signature)

(Auditor's city and state)

(Date of the auditor's report)

Reporting on Compliance with Requirements in a F/S Audit

After studying this lesson you should be able to:

1. *Identify the auditor's responsibilities when engaged to report on an entity's compliance with contractual or regulatory requirements in connection with an audit of the entity's financial statements.*
2. *Identify the reporting language that would be appropriate when issuing a report on compliance with contractual or regulatory requirements either in a separate report on compliance or a combined report on the audited financial statement and on compliance issues.*

I. **Relevant AICPA Guidance --** The relevant AICPA guidance is provided by AU 806 "Reporting on Compliance with Aspects of Contractual Agreements or Regulatory Requirements in Connection With Audited Financial Statements." The standard states that the auditor's objective, when requested to report on an entity's compliance with aspects of contractual agreements or regulatory requirements in connection with the audit of financial statements, is to report appropriately on such matters.

II. **Reports on Compliance with Aspects of Contractual Agreements or Regulatory Requirements**

   A. The auditor should include a statement that nothing came to the auditor's attention to cause the auditor to believe that the entity failed to comply with the specified aspects of the contractual agreements or regulatory requirements only if: (1) the auditor did not identify any such noncompliance; (2) the auditor expressed an unmodified or qualified opinion on the financial statements involved; and (3) the covenants or regulatory requirements related to accounting matters that have been subjected to procedures applied in the audit.

   B. When instances of noncompliance have been identified -- the auditor's report on compliance should describe that noncompliance. Note: If the entity has obtained a waiver for such noncompliance, the auditor may include a statement that a waiver has been obtained; but, all instances of noncompliance must be described in the report, including those for which a waiver has been obtained.

   C. When the auditor has issued an adverse opinion or disclaimed an opinion -- the auditor should issue a report on compliance only when instances of noncompliance were identified.

   D. The report on compliance should be in writing and should be presented either as a separate report or may be combined with the auditor's report on the financial statements.

   E. Include a paragraph conveying an *appropriate alert* that restricts the distribution of the report on compliance issues to the specified users.

III. **A Separate Report on Compliance with Aspects of Contractual Agreements When No Instances of Noncompliance Are Identified**

   See the following example.

Independent Auditor's Report

(Appropriate Addressee)

We have audited, in accordance with auditing standards generally accepted in the United States of America, the financial statements of XYZ Company, which comprise the balance sheet as of December 31, 20X2, and the related statements of income, changes in stockholders' equity, and cash flows for the year then ended, and the related notes to the financial statements, and have issued our report thereon dated February 16, 20X3.

In connection with our audit, nothing came to our attention that caused us to believe that XYZ Company failed to comply with the terms, covenants, provisions, or conditions of sections XX to YY, inclusive, of the Indenture dated July 21, 20X0, with ABC Bank, insofar as they relate to accounting matters. However, our audit was not directed primarily toward obtaining knowledge of such noncompliance. Accordingly, had we performed additional procedures, other matters may have come to our attention regarding the Company's noncompliance with the above-referenced terms, covenants, provisions, or conditions of the Indenture, insofar as they relate to accounting matters.

This report is intended solely for the information and use of the board of directors and management of XYZ Company and ABC Bank and is not intended to be and should not be used by anyone other than these specified parties.

(Auditor's signature)

(Auditor's city and state)

(Date of the auditor's report)

IV. A Separate Report on Compliance with Aspects of Contractual Agreements When Instances of Noncompliance Are Identified

Independent Auditor's Report

(Appropriate Addressee)

We have audited, in accordance with auditing standards generally accepted in the United States of America, the financial statements of XYZ Company, which comprise the balance sheet as of December 31, 20X2, and the related statements of income, changes in stockholders' equity, and cash flows for the year then ended, and the related notes to the financial statements, and have issued our report thereon dated March 5, 20X3.

In connection with our audit, we noted that XYZ Company failed to comply with the Working Capital provision of section XX of the Loan Agreement dated March 1, 20X2, with ABC Bank. Our audit was not directed primarily toward obtaining knowledge as to whether XYZ Company failed to comply with the terms, covenants, provisions, or conditions of sections XX to YY, inclusive, of the Loan Agreement, insofar as they relate to accounting matters. Accordingly, had we performed additional procedures, other matters may have come to our attention regarding noncompliance with the above-referenced terms, covenants, provisions, or conditions of the Loan Agreement, insofar as they relate to accounting matters.

This report is intended solely for the information and use of the board of directors and management of XYZ Company and ABC Bank and is not intended to be and should not be used by anyone other than these specified parties.

(Auditor's signature)

(Auditor's city and state)

(Date of the auditor's report)

V. A Combined Report on Audited Financial Statements and Compliance with Aspects of Contractual Agreements When No Instances of Noncompliance Are Identified

Independent Auditor's Report

(Appropriate Addressee)

We have audited the accompanying financial statements of ABC Company, which comprise the balance sheet as of December 31, 20X1, and the related statements of income, changes in stockholders' equity, and cash flows for the year then ended, and the related notes to the financial statements.

Management's Responsibility for the Financial Statements

Management is responsible for the preparation and fair presentation of these financial statements in accordance with accounting principles generally accepted in the United States of America; this includes the design, implementation, and maintenance of internal control relevant to the preparation and fair presentation of financial statements that are free from material misstatement, whether due to fraud or error.

Auditor's Responsibility

Our responsibility is to express an opinion on these financial statements based on our audit. We conducted our audit in accordance with auditing standards generally accepted in the United States of America. Those standards require that we plan and perform the audit to obtain reasonable assurance about whether the financial statements are free from material misstatement.

An audit involves performing procedures to obtain audit evidence about the amounts and disclosures in the financial statements. The procedures selected depend on the auditor's judgment, including the assessment of the risks of material misstatement of the financial statements, whether due to fraud or error. In making those risk assessments, the auditor considers internal control relevant to the entity's preparation and fair presentation of the financial statements in order to design audit procedures that are appropriate in the circumstances, but not for the purpose of expressing an opinion on the effectiveness of the entity's internal control. Accordingly, we express no such opinion. An audit also includes evaluating the appropriateness of accounting policies used and the reasonableness of significant accounting estimates made by management, as well as evaluating the overall presentation of the financial statements.

We believe that the audit evidence we have obtained is sufficient and appropriate to provide a basis for our audit opinion.

Opinion

In our opinion, the financial statements referred to above present fairly, in all material respects, the financial position of ABC Company as of December 31, 20X1, and the results of its operations and its cash flows for the year then ended in accordance with accounting principles generally accepted in the United States of America.

Other Matter

In connection with our audit, nothing came to our attention that caused us to believe that ABC Company failed to comply with the terms, covenants, provisions, or conditions of sections XX to YY, inclusive, of the Indenture dated July 21, 20X0 with XYZ Bank, insofar as they relate to accounting matters. However, our audit was not directed primarily toward obtaining knowledge of such noncompliance. Accordingly, had we performed additional procedures, other matters may have come to our attention regarding the Company's noncompliance with the above-referenced terms, covenants, provisions, or conditions of the Indenture, insofar as they relate to accounting matters.

Restricted Use Relating to the Other Matter

The communication related to compliance with the aforementioned Indenture described in the Other Matter paragraph is intended solely for the information and use of the boards of directors and management of ABC Company and XYZ Bank and is not intended to be and should not be used by anyone other than these specified parties.

(Auditor's signature)

(Auditor's city and state)

(Date of the auditor's report)

Service Organizations - User Auditors

After studying this lesson you should be able to:

1. *Identify the user auditor's responsibilities when auditing a user entity that has outsourced some degree of transaction processing to a service organization.*
2. *Understand the implications that a service auditor's report may have to the user auditor's report on the user entity's financial statement.*

I. Relevant AICPA Guidance -- The relevant AICPA guidance is provided by AU 402: "Audit Considerations Relating to an Entity Using a Service Organization." The standard states that the user auditor's objectives, when the user entity uses the services of a service organization, are to: (1) obtain an understanding of the nature and significance of the services provided and their effect on the user entity's internal control relevant to the audit sufficient to assess the risks of material misstatement, and (2) design and perform audit procedures that are responsive to those risks.

> **Definitions:**
> *Complementary user entity controls*: Controls that management of the service organization assumes, in the design of its service, will be implemented by user entities, and which, if necessary to achieve the control objectives stated in management's description of the service organization's system, are identified as such in that description.
>
> *Service auditor*: A practitioner who reports on controls at a service organization
>
> *Service organization*: A service organization used by another service organization to perform some of the services provided to user entities that are relevant to those user entities' internal control over financial reporting. (This SAS also applies to subservice organizations.)
>
> *Type 1 report*: Report on management's description of a service organization's system and the **suitability of the design** of controls.
>
> *Type 2 report*: Report on management's description of a service organization's system and the **suitability of the design and operating effectiveness of controls**.
>
> *User auditor*: An auditor who audits and reports on the financial statements of a user entity.
>
> *User entity*: An entity that uses a service organization and whose financial statements are being audited.

II. User Auditor Responsibilities

A. Obtain an understanding of the services provided by a service organization, including internal controls.

1. The services of a service organization are relevant to the audit of a user entity when those services (and the controls over those services) affect the user entity's information system related to financial reporting and safeguarding assets.
2. The user auditor should evaluate the design and implementation of relevant controls at the user entity related to the service organization's services.
3. The user auditor should determine whether a sufficient understanding of the nature and significance of the service organization's services and their effect on the user entity's internal control relevant to the audit have been obtained to assess the risks of material misstatement.

4. If the user auditor is unable to obtain a sufficient understanding from the user entity -- the user auditor should obtain that understanding by
    a. Obtaining and reading the service auditor's type 1 or type 2 report;
    b. Contacting the service organization (through the user entity) to obtain specific information, or visiting the service organization and performing necessary procedures about relevant controls; or
    c. Using another auditor to perform procedures to provide the necessary information about controls at the service organization.
5. Using a type 1 or type 2 report to support the user auditor's understanding.
    a. The user auditor should be satisfied about (1) the service auditor's professional competence and independence and (2) the standards that the service auditor followed in issuing the report.
    b. The user auditor should (1) evaluate whether the report provides sufficient appropriate evidence for understanding the user entity's relevant internal controls and (2) determine whether any *complementary user entity controls* identified by the service organization are relevant in assessing the risks of material misstatement.

B. Responding to the assessed risks of material misstatement

1. **Evidence at the user entity --** The user auditor should determine whether sufficient appropriate audit evidence is available at the user entity; and, if not, perform further audit procedures at the service organization.
2. **Tests of controls --** When the user auditor's risk assessment includes an expectation that controls at the service organization are operating effectively, the user auditor should obtain evidence about such operating effectiveness by either obtaining a type 2 report or performing appropriate tests of controls at the service organization (or using another auditor to perform those tests of controls).
3. **A user entity may outsource some or all of its finance function to a service organization --** In that case, a significant portion of the audit evidence resides at the service organization. Necessary substantive procedures may be performed at the service organization by the user auditor or by the service auditor on the user auditor's behalf. The user auditor is still responsible for obtaining sufficient appropriate audit evidence.

C. Inquiry about fraud, noncompliance, and uncorrected misstatements -- The user auditor should inquire of the user entity's management as to whether they are aware of any fraud, noncompliance with laws and regulations, or uncorrected misstatements at the service organization affecting the financial statements of the user entity.

III. Reporting Issues to the User Auditor

A. Modified opinion

1. **Scope limitation --** If the user auditor is unable to obtain sufficient appropriate audit evidence about the services provided by the service organization relevant to the user entity's financial statements, the user auditor should modify the opinion for a scope limitation.
2. **Reference to service auditor --** The user auditor may refer to the service auditor in the user auditor's report containing a modified opinion if that reference would be relevant to understanding the user auditor's modification. The user auditor should indicate that such reference does not change the user auditor's responsibility for that opinion.

B. Unmodified opinion -- The user auditor should not refer to the service auditor in the user auditor's report containing an unmodified opinion. The user auditor is responsible for the opinion expressed, and no *division of responsibility* is permitted.

Service Organizations - Service Auditors

After studying this lesson, you should be able to:

1. *Understand the service auditor's requirements under AICPA Attestation Standards when engaged to report on internal control over financial reporting at a service organization.*
2. *Identify the nature of the two different types of reports on internal control that a service auditor may be engaged to issue.*

I. **Relevant AICPA Guidance --** The relevant AICPA guidance applicable to the *service auditor* is provided by AT 801 (SSAE No. 16), "Reporting on control at a Service Organization."

II. **Distinction Between the *Service Auditor* and the *User Auditor***

> **Definitions:**
> *Service Auditor*: Practitioner who reports on controls at a service organization.
>
> *User Auditor:* An auditor who audits and reports on the financial statements of a user entity. (In other words, the auditor of an entity that has outsourced the processing of its transactions to the service organization for whom such processing may be more efficient; the user auditor must consider relevant internal controls of the service organization in auditing the financial statements of such a user entity.)

III. **Applicability**

A. **The attestation standards apply to internal control reporting by the service auditor --** The service auditor may be engaged to issue either of two types of reports on internal control applicable to a service organization.

1. **On the adequacy of the design of internal control --** (called a "type 1 engagement" by AICPA Professional Standards) Whether the control policies and procedures are suitably designed and placed in operation.
2. **On the operating effectiveness of internal control (based on tests of controls) --** (called a "type 2 engagement" by AICPA Professional Standards) Whether the policies and procedures are suitably designed and working effectively to provide reasonable assurance of achieving the stated control objectives.

B. **Examples of such services --** Bank trust departments, mortgage banks that service mortgages for others, IT centers (for example, processing checks for financial institutions or handling the details of subscriptions for magazine publishers).

C. Management of the service organization is required to provide the service auditor with a written assertion (1) about the fairness of the presentation of the description of the system and (2) about the suitability of the design; and, in a *type 2 engagement*, management is also required to provide a written assertion (3) about the operating effectiveness of the controls. Those assertions should either accompany the service auditor's report or be included in the service organization's description of the system of internal control.

IV. **Responsibilities of Service Auditors (governed by SSAEs) --** Must be independent of **service** organization, but **not** necessarily independent of all **user** entities.

A. **Procedures**

1. **Inquiry --** of service organization management and other personnel.
2. **Inspection --** of documentation (flowcharts, narrative memoranda, or questionnaires).

3. **Observation --** of internal control activities.
4. Obtainment of management's written representations as deemed appropriate.
5. Performance of test of control -- If reporting on the operating effectiveness of internal control, the service auditor must perform appropriate **tests of controls.**

B. **Reporting on the adequacy of the design of internal control --** (That is, reporting on the internal control policies and procedures placed in operation, which are also known as a "type 1" engagement) - the service auditor's report ordinarily consists of the following sections:

1. **Scope --** identify the nature of the engagement and the **specific date** involved.
2. Service organization's responsibilities.
3. Service auditor's responsibilities - reference the attestation standards established by the AICPA and describe an examination; also, **disclaim an opinion on operating effectiveness.**
4. Inherent limitations of internal control.
5. Opinion - (1) that the description fairly presents the system that was designed and implemented as of the specific date; and (2) that the controls related to the stated control objectives were suitably designed to provide reasonable assurance that the control objectives would be achieved if the controls operated effectively as of the specific date.
6. Restricted use - distribution should be restricted to the service organization, user entities, and the user entities' independent auditors.

C. **Reporting on the operating effectiveness of internal control --** (That is, reporting on the policies and procedures placed in operation **and** on their operating effectiveness, which are also known as a "type 2" engagement) - the service auditor's report ordinarily consists of the following sections:

1. Scope - identify the nature of the engagement and the period involved.
2. Service organization's responsibilities.
3. Service auditor's responsibilities - reference the attestation standards established by the AICPA and describe an examination.
4. Inherent limitations of internal control.
5. Opinion - (1) that the description fairly presents the system that was designed and implemented throughout the period; (2) that the controls related to the stated control objectives were suitably designed to provide reasonable assurance that the control objectives would be achieved if the controls operated effectively throughout the period; and (3) that the controls tested operated effectively throughout the period.
6. Description of tests of controls - reference the pages of the service auditor's report identifying the specific controls tested and the nature, timing, and results of those tests.
7. Restricted use - distribution should be restricted to the service organization, user entities, and the user entities' independent auditors.

Note:
Management specifies the control objectives to be tested - Should cover a reporting period of **at least six months.**

Comfort Letters

After studying this lesson, you should be able to:

1. *Understand the purpose of comfort letters provided by accountants to underwriters and other financial intermediaries in connection with an entity's stock issuance.*
2. *Understand the basic structure of comfort letters and the nature of the assurance specifically provided by the entity's accountants/auditors.*

I. **Relevant AICPA Guidance --** The relevant AICPA guidance is provided by AU 920: "Letters for Underwriters and Certain Other Requesting Parties." The standard states that the auditor's objectives, when engaged to issue a letter to a requesting party in connection with an entity's financial statements included in a securities offering, are to appropriately address: (1) the acceptance of the engagement and the scope of services, and (2) issue a letter with the appropriate form and content.

II. **Purpose --** Section 11 of the Securities Act of 1933 provides for liability to underwriters and certain others (such as a broker-dealer or a financial intermediary) when there is a material omission or misstatement to a registration statement.

   A. A *comfort letter* from the independent accountants may help underwriters or others having a statutory due diligence defense under Section 11 of the Act establish a *reasonable investigation* (that is, *due diligence*).

   B. Comfort letters are not required and are not filed with the SEC.

   C. The scope is specified in the underwriting agreement (between the client and the underwriters or others); a copy of the agreement should be given to the accountants.

   D. The accountants should meet with the underwriters (or certain other requesting parties) to establish their specific needs and give them a *draft* of the comfort letter in advance to avoid misunderstandings.

   E. The accountants should avoid implying that the procedures performed were adequate for the underwriter's (or other parties') purposes.

III. **A Typical Comfort Letter --** Usually consists of the following:

   A. An introductory paragraph that identifies the particular registration statement and the audited financial statements and schedules with which the accountant is associated;

   B. A statement as to the independence of the accountants;

   C. **Positive expression of opinion --** Whether the **audited** financial statements and schedules **comply as to form** with the requirements of the Act and the SEC;

   D. **Negative assurance --** Whether the **unaudited** condensed interim financial information complies as to form with the requirements of the Act and the SEC;

   E. **Negative assurance --** Whether any material modifications should be made to the unaudited condensed consolidated financial statements;

   F. **Negative assurance --** Whether there has been any change during a specified period in capital stock, increase in long-term debt, or any decrease in other specified financial statement items;

   G. A concluding paragraph that limits the distribution of the comfort letter to specified parties for the purposes stated;

IV. Other Reporting Considerations

A. Dating of the letter -- usually dated on or shortly before the effective date of the registration.

B. Addressee -- should only be addressed to the client, named underwriters, broker-dealer, or the financial intermediary related to the securities.

C. Comment on the previously audited financial statements referred to in the registration statement.

1. Give **positive assurance** (opinion) as to whether the audited financial statements comply with the **form** and content required by the SEC.

2. Use the following language: "In our opinion (include the phrase 'except as disclosed in the registration statement,' if applicable) the consolidated financial statements and financial statement schedules audited by us and included in the registration statement comply as to form in all material respects with the applicable accounting requirements of the Act and the related published rules and regulations."

D. Commenting on the **unaudited financial statements, condensed interim financial information, or capsule financial information** -- must first have knowledge of internal control over financial reporting.

1. **Unaudited financial statements and schedules and unaudited condensed interim financial information --** Can give negative assurance that such information complies as to form with SEC requirements.

2. **Capsule financial information --** (Unaudited summarized interim information in narrative or tabular form) -- At most, can give negative assurance; in some cases, may be required to structure comments as procedures and findings.

E. Commenting on financial **forecasts; subsequent changes**; or **tables, statistics, and other financial information.**

1. **Forecasts --** Must have knowledge of the entity's accounting and financial reporting; can attach the forecast's compilation report, if applicable.

2. **Subsequent changes --** Comments usually relate to any changes in capital stock, increase in long-term debt, or decreases in other specified financial statement items (subsequent to latest financial statements included in registration).

3. Can give negative assurance if within 135 days of the most recent period for which an audit or review was performed -- procedures are usually limited to reading the minutes and making inquiries of management.

4. **Tables, statistics, and other financial information --** Limited to matters related to accounting records and subject to controls over financial reporting; should not comment on nonaccounting matters, such as square footage of facilities, number of employees, or sales backlog information.

F. Letter should state that the accountants make no representation involving legal interpretations.

Government Auditing Standards

After studying this lesson, you should be able to:

1. *Understand the distinction between "GAAS" and "GAGAS" (issued by the U.S. Government Accountability Office) and the additional responsibilities resulting from those Government Auditing Standards.*
2. *Understand the circumstances causing the Single Audit Act to be applicable.*

I. **Government Auditing Standards --** Government Auditing Standards (also known as Generally Accepted Government Auditing Standards or GAGAS) are issued by the U.S. Government Accountability Office (in GAO's "Yellow Book") under the authority of the Comptroller General of the United States.

> **Note:**
> These additional standards are presented at the end of this study text as excerpted from GAO's 2011 Yellow Book. GAO revises the Yellow Book periodically, and a revision is currently "in process" in 2014.

A. GAGAS must be followed when required by applicable law, regulation, or agreement. These standards may apply to a variety of different governmental engagements, including financial audits, performance audits, and attestation engagements.

B. GAGAS go beyond the 10 criteria formerly known as "GAAS," and include additional general, fieldwork, and reporting standards.

C. Summary of the primary reporting differences associated with GAGAS (relative to engagements under GAAS):

1. **Additional reporting requirements regarding internal control --** Government Auditing Standards require a written report on internal control in every financial audit under GAGAS. This includes commentary about the auditor's understanding of internal control for planning purposes and the assessment of control risk, as well as the scope of the auditor's testing of internal control. When the auditor communicates "significant deficiencies," the auditor should also obtain a response from officials of the entity and include a copy of management's written response (or a summary of management's oral response) in the auditor's report.

2. **Additional reporting requirements regarding compliance with applicable laws and regulations --** Government Auditing Standards require a written report on compliance with applicable laws and regulations. This report should distinguish between (a) "general requirements" that apply to all federal financial programs; and (b) "specific requirements" that apply to a particular program by a specific statutory (legislative) requirement.

   a. The auditor focuses on instances of noncompliance that have a "material and direct effect" on the entity's financial statements.

   b. Management is responsible for identifying laws and regulations that have a direct and material effect on the entity's financial statements, and it is common for auditors to obtain written representations from management that all such laws and regulations have been appropriately identified.

   c. The auditor's report on compliance should comment on the scope of the auditor's testing of the entity's compliance with applicable laws and regulations.

   d. The auditor's report on compliance should also identify (1) fraud that is more than inconsequential; (2) illegal acts identified that are more than inconsequential; (3) other violations of contracts or grants that are material; and (4) instances of "abuse" that are material.

   e. Auditors may have a duty to report instances of fraud, illegal acts, or abuse to authorities outside the entity (such as a federal inspector general, etc.) when (1) management fails to meet its legal requirements to report such matters; or (2) when management fails to appropriately respond to identified instances of fraud, illegal acts, or abuse.

3. **Additional reporting requirements regarding illegal acts --** Government Auditing Standards also require the auditor to report any known instances of illegal acts that could result in **criminal prosecution**.

II. **Single Audit Act of 1984, as Amended --** The Single Audit Act is applicable to state and local governmental entities that have expenditures of federal assistance (grants) now aggregating at least $750,000 in a given year. It imposes certain requirements on such entities and their auditors that go beyond GAAS and even GAGAS.

A. Management's responsibilities under the Single Audit Act include the following:

1. Prepare the financial statements along with a schedule of expenditures of federal assistance.

2. Prepare a "corrective action plan" to respond to any current-year audit findings.

3. Submit certain necessary forms, including the audit report to the designated Federal Audit Clearinghouse on a timely basis.

B. The auditor's responsibilities under the Single Audit Act include the following:

1. The audit should be conducted in accordance with GAGAS;

2. The auditor should identify each "major program" to be audited based on appropriate risk assessment considerations (and materiality should be determined separately for each major program);

3. The auditor should evaluate whether the financial statements and schedule of expenditures of federal assistance are fairly presented using appropriate criteria;

4. The auditor should obtain an appropriate understanding of internal control over the federal assistance programs and perform testing of internal control over designated major programs;

5. The auditor should evaluate the entity's compliance with applicable laws, regulations, or other requirements having a direct and material effect on designated major programs;

6. The auditor should report any identified audit findings, including material instances of noncompliance with applicable laws, regulations, or other requirements involving designated major programs; identified instances of fraud; and significant deficiencies in internal controls over designated major programs.

C. **Summary comments regarding the Single Audit Act**

1. **Efficiency --** A single coordinated audit of the aggregate federal financial assistance provided to a state or local governmental entity (with emphasis on the entity's major programs) is intended to result in greater efficiency compared to the alternative, which would be having multiple audits of the entity conducted on a grant-by-grant basis.

2. **Added requirements --** A single coordinated audit of the aggregate federal financial assistance involves more than just a financial statement audit. Additional testing of internal control is required for major programs, and additional testing is also required for major programs regarding the entity's compliance with applicable laws, regulations, or other requirements applicable to major programs.

3. **Multiple reports --** The auditor should issue reports on (a) the fairness of the entity's financial statements (and schedule of expenditures of federal assistance); (b) internal control over financial reporting (with emphasis on major programs); and (c) compliance with applicable laws, regulations, and other requirements. If audit findings were identified, the auditor should also prepare a "Schedule of Findings and Questioned Costs."

III. **GAGAS—Excerpted from GAO's Yellow Book (2011 Edition)**

General Standards

1. **Independence**—"In all matters relating to the audit work, the audit organization and the individual auditor, whether government or public, must be independent."
2. **Professional Judgment**—"Auditors must use professional judgment in planning and performing audits and in reporting the results."
3. **Competence**—"The staff assigned to perform the audit must collectively possess adequate professional competence needed to address the audit objectives and perform the work in accordance with GAGAS."
4. **Quality Control and Assurance**—"Each audit organization performing audits in accordance with GAGAS must:"
   a. "Establish and maintain a system of quality control that is designed to provide the audit organization with reasonable assurance that the organization and its personnel comply with professional standards and applicable legal and regulatory requirements, and"
   b. "have an external peer review performed by reviewers independent of the audit organization being reviewed at least once every 3 years."

Additional GAGAS Requirements for Performing Financial Audits:

1. **Auditor Communication**—"In addition to the AICPA requirements for auditor communication, when performing a GAGAS financial audit, auditors should communicate pertinent information that in the auditors' professional judgment needs to be communicated to individuals contracting for or requesting the audit, and to cognizant legislative committees when auditors perform the audit pursuant to a law or regulation, or they conduct the work for the legislative committee that has oversight of the audited entity. This requirement does not apply if the law or regulation requiring an audit of the financial statements does not specifically identify the entities to be audited, such as audits required by the Single Audit Act Amendments of 1996."
2. **Previous Audits and Attestation Engagements**—"When performing a GAGAS audit, auditors should evaluate whether the audited entity has taken appropriate corrective action to address findings and recommendations from previous engagements that could have a material effect on the financial statements or other financial data significant to the audit objectives. When planning the audit, auditors should ask management of the audited entity to identify previous audits, attestation engagements, and other studies that directly relate to the objectives of the audit, including whether related recommendations have been implemented. Auditors should use this information in assessing risk and determining the nature, timing, and extent of current audit work, including determining the extent to which testing the implementation of the corrective actions is applicable to the current audit objectives."
3. **Fraud, Noncompliance with Provisions of Laws, Regulations, Contracts, and Grant Agreements, and Abuse**—"In addition to the AICPA requirements concerning fraud and noncompliance with provisions of laws and regulations, when performing a GAGAS financial audit, auditors should extend the AICPA requirements pertaining to the auditors' responsibilities for laws and regulations to also apply to consideration of compliance with provisions of contracts or grant agreements."
4. **Developing Elements of a Finding**—"In a financial audit, findings may involve deficiencies in internal control; noncompliance with provisions of laws, regulations, contracts, or grant agreements; fraud; or abuse. As part of a GAGAS audit, when auditors identify findings, auditors should plan and perform procedures to develop the elements of the findings that are relevant and necessary to achieve the audit objectives."
5. **Audit Documentation**—"In addition to the AICPA requirements for audit documentation, auditors should comply with the following additional requirements when performing a GAGAS financial audit."
   a. "Document supervisory review, before the report release date, of the evidence that supports the findings, conclusions, and recommendations contained in the auditors' report."

b. "Document any departures from the GAGAS requirements and the impact on the audit and on the auditors' conclusions when the audit is not in compliance with applicable GAGAS requirements due to law, regulation, scope limitations, restrictions on access to records, or other issues impacting the audit."

Additional GAGAS Requirements for Reporting on Financial Audits:

1. **Reporting auditors' compliance with GAGAS**—"When auditors comply with all applicable GAGAS requirements for financial audits, they should include a statement in the auditors' report that they performed the audit in accordance with GAGAS. Because GAGAS incorporates by reference the AICPA SASs, GAGAS does not require auditors to cite compliance with the AICPA standards when citing compliance with GAGAS."
2. **Reporting on internal control and compliance with provisions of laws, regulations, contracts, and grant agreements**—"When providing an opinion or a disclaimer on financial statements, auditors should also report on internal control over financial reporting and on compliance with provisions of laws, regulations, contracts, or grant agreements that have a material effect on the financial statements. Auditors report on internal control and compliance, regardless of whether or not they identify internal control deficiencies or instances of noncompliance."
   "Auditors should include either in the same or in separate report(s) a description of the scope of the auditors' testing of internal control over financial reporting and of compliance with provisions of laws, regulations, contracts, or grant agreements."
3. **Communicating deficiencies in internal control, fraud, noncompliance with provisions of laws, regulations, contracts, and grant agreements, and abuse**—"When performing GAGAS financial audits, auditors should communicate in the report on internal control over financial reporting and compliance, based upon the work performed, (1) significant deficiencies and material weaknesses in internal control; (2) instances of fraud and noncompliance with provisions of laws or regulations that have a material effect on the audit and any other instances that warrant the attention of those charged with governance; (3) noncompliance with provisions of contracts or grant agreements that has a material effect on the audit; and (4) abuse that has a material effect on the audit."
4. **Reporting views of responsible officials**—"When performing a GAGAS financial audit, if the auditors' report discloses deficiencies in internal control, fraud, noncompliance with provisions of laws, regulations, contracts, or grant agreements, or abuse, auditors should obtain and report the views of responsible officials of the audited entity concerning the findings, conclusions, and recommendations, as well as any planned corrective actions."
5. **Reporting confidential or sensitive information**—"When performing a GAGAS financial audit, if certain pertinent information is prohibited from public disclosure or is excluded from a report due to the confidential or sensitive nature of the information, auditors should disclose in the report that certain information has been omitted and the reason or other circumstances that make the omission necessary."
6. **Distributing reports**—"Distribution of reports completed in accordance with GAGAS depends on the relationship of the auditors to the audited organization and the nature of the information contained in the report. Auditors should document any limitation on report distribution."

Compliance Audits

After studying this lesson, you should be able to:

1. *Understand the circumstances causing AU 801 (SAS No. 117), "Compliance Audits," to be applicable, along with understanding the auditor's responsibilities under this SAS.*

> SAS No. 117 "Compliance Audits" was originally issued in clarified format. It has been reclassified as AU 935 to be compatible with International Standards on Auditing.

I. Relevant AICPA Guidance -- The relevant AICPA guidance is provided by AU 935: "Compliance Audits." The standard states that the auditor's objectives are to (1) obtain sufficient appropriate audit evidence to form an opinion and report whether the entity complied in all material respects with applicable compliance requirements (at the level specified in the governmental audit requirement), and (2) identify audit and reporting requirements specified in the governmental audit requirements that are supplementary to GAAS and Government Auditing Standards and perform procedures to address those requirements.

II. Applicability -- When an auditor is engaged to perform a *compliance audit* in accordance with (1) generally accepted auditing standards (GAAS), (2) Government Auditing Standards (also called "Generally Accepted Government Auditing Standards" (GAGAS) from GAO's "Yellow Book" issued under the authority of the Comptroller General of the United States), and (3) a governmental audit requirement requiring an expression of opinion on compliance with applicable compliance requirements.

- **A.** This SAS applies to the compliance audit, but not to the financial statement audit part of such an engagement - example engagements for which this SAS applies includes an audit under OMB Circular A-133, "Audits of States, Local Governments, and Non-Profit Organizations;" also includes a department-specific requirement such as "U.S. Department of Housing and Urban Development Audit Requirements Related to Entities Such as Public Housing Agencies, Nonprofit and For-Profit Housing Projects, and Certain Lenders."
- **B. Definition of** *governmental audit requirement* **--** A governmental requirement established by law, regulation, rule, or provision of contracts or grant agreements requiring that an entity undergo an audit of its compliance with applicable compliance requirements related to one or more government programs.

III. Compliance Auditing - Requirements and Guidance

- **A. This SAS incorporated the AICPA's *risk assessment* standards**
    1. The auditor should perform risk assessment procedures to obtain an understanding of the applicable compliance requirements and internal controls over compliance - the nature and extent of the risk assessment procedures may vary with the circumstances (such as the complexity of the compliance requirements and the depth of the auditor's knowledge of internal control over compliance).
    2. The auditor should assess the risks of material noncompliance (whether due to fraud or error) for each applicable compliance requirement and consider whether any of those are *pervasive* to compliance.
    3. The auditor should perform further audit procedures in response to the assessed risks, such as develop an overall response to any risks that are *pervasive* to the entity's compliance; perform appropriate tests of details; and perform tests of controls when there is an expectation of operating effectiveness or when required to do so. (Note that an example of a *pervasive* risk of noncompliance would be financial difficulty that increases the risk that grant funds will be used for unauthorized purposes.)

B. **Supplementary audit requirements --** The auditor should identify *supplementary audit requirements* (beyond GAAS and GAGAS) specified in the governmental audit requirement.

1. Some governmental audit requirements specifically identify the applicable compliance requirements, whereas others provide a framework for the auditor to determine the applicable compliance requirements.
2. OMB Circular A-133, "Audits of States, Local Governments and Non-Profit Organizations," provides a framework ("Compliance Supplement") to determine the compliance requirements.

C. **Written representations --** The auditor should obtain written representations from management tailored to the entity and the governmental audit requirement.

D. **Subsequent events --** The auditor should perform procedures up to the date of the auditor's report to identify subsequent events related to the entity's compliance (e.g., reports from grantors regarding noncompliance or information about noncompliance obtained through other professional engagements for the entity); an example of a subsequent event warranting disclosure is the discovery of noncompliance causing the grantor to stop the funding.

E. **Evaluating the evidence and forming an opinion --** Most governmental audit requirements specify that the auditor's opinion on compliance is at the *program* level (and materiality is usually determined based on the program taken as a whole).

1. The auditor should consider *likely questioned costs* (not just *known questioned costs*) and other noncompliance that may not result in questioned costs.
2. The auditor may include a variety of factors in assessing the risk of noncompliance, including: (a) the complexity of the compliance requirements; (b) how long the entity has been subject to those compliance requirements; (c) the degree of judgment involved in compliance; and (d) the entity's compliance in prior years.

F. **Reporting --** The auditor may issue (1) a separate report on compliance only; (2) a combined report on compliance and on internal control over compliance; or (3) a separate report on internal control over compliance.

Combined Report on Compliance with Applicable Requirements and Internal Control Over Compliance

Independent Auditor's Report

(Addressee)

Compliance

We have audited (entity's name) compliance with the (identify the applicable compliance requirements or reference the document that describes the applicable compliance requirements) applicable to (entity's) (identify the government program(s) audited or refer to a separate schedule that identifies the program(s)) for the year ended June 30, 20X1. Compliance with the requirements referred to above is the responsibility of (entity's) management. Our responsibility is to express an opinion on (entity's) compliance based on our audit.

We conducted our audit of compliance in accordance with auditing standards generally accepted in the United States of America; the standards applicable to financial audits contained in Government Auditing Standards issued by the Comptroller General of the United States; and (name of the governmental audit requirement or program-specific audit guide). Those standards and (name of the governmental audit requirement or program-specific audit guide) require that we plan and perform the audit to obtain reasonable assurance about whether noncompliance with the compliance requirements referred to above that could have a material effect on (identify the government program(s) audited or refer to a separate schedule that identifies the program(s)). An audit includes examining, on a test basis, evidence about (entity's) compliance with those requirements and performing such other procedures as we considered necessary in the circumstances. We believe that our audit provides a reasonable basis for our opinion. Our audit does not provide a legal determination of (entity's) compliance with those requirements.

In our opinion, (entity's name) complied, in all material respects, with the compliance requirements referred to above that are applicable to (identify the government program(s) audited) for the year ended June 30, 20X1.

Internal Control Over Compliance

Management of (entity's name) is responsible for establishing and maintaining effective internal control over compliance with the compliance requirements referred to above. In planning and performing our audit, we considered (entity's) internal control over compliance to determine the auditing procedures for the purpose of expressing our opinion on compliance, but not for the purpose of expressing an opinion on the effectiveness of internal control over compliance. Accordingly, we do not express an opinion on the effectiveness of (entity's) internal control over compliance.

A deficiency in internal control over compliance exists when the design or operation of a control does not allow management or employees, in the normal course of performing their assigned functions, to prevent, or detect and correct, noncompliance on a timely basis. A material weakness in internal control over compliance is a deficiency, or combination of deficiencies in internal control over compliance, such that there is a reasonable possibility that material noncompliance with a compliance requirement will not be prevented, or detected and corrected, on a timely basis.

This report is intended solely for the information and use of management, (identify the body or individuals charged with governance), others within the entity, (identify the legislative or regulatory body), and (identify the grantor agency(ies)) and is not intended to be and should not be used by anyone other than these specified parties.

(Signature)

(Auditor's city and state)

(Date)

G. **Documentation --** The auditor should document the risk assessment procedures performed, responses to the assessed risks of material noncompliance, the basis for materiality levels, and compliance with applicable *supplementary audit requirements*.

H. **Communication --** The auditor should communicate the following matters with those charged with governance: the auditor's responsibilities under GAAS, GAGAS, and the governmental audit requirements; an overview of the planned scope and timing of the compliance audit; and any significant findings.

I. **Reissuance of the compliance report --** When reissuing a compliance report, the auditor should add an explanatory paragraph describing why the report is being reissued and noting any changes from the previously issued report; if additional audit procedures are performed, the auditor's report date should be updated.

SSARSs - Framework

After studying this lesson, you should be able to:

1. *Know the "framework" applicable to SSARSs, consisting of requirements ("unconditional" and "presumptively mandatory") and explanatory material.*
2. *Know the SSARSs, interpretive publications, and other publications' "hierarchy" applicable to compilation and review engagements .*

I. **Statements on Standards for Accounting and Review Services (SSARSs) --** Are issued by the AICPA's "Accounting and Review Services Committee" (ARSC). These standards apply to **reviews** and **compilations** of financial statements for nonpublic entities (referred to as "**nonissuers**").

   A. **Compilation --** Assists management in presenting financial information in the form of financial statements without providing any assurance; "Although a compilation is **not an assurance engagement**, it is an attest engagement." (AR 60.05)

   B. **Review --** The objective is to obtain "limited assurance" that there are no material modifications that should be made to the financial statements; "A review engagement is **an assurance engagement** as well as an attest engagement." (AR 60.07)

II. **Framework for Compilation and Review Engagements --** SSARS contain both "requirements" and "explanatory material."

   A. **Requirements --** There are two categories: "unconditional" and "presumptively mandatory."

      1. **"Unconditional requirements" --** The accountant is required to comply with an unconditional requirement without exception (indicated by the words **"must"** or **"is required"**)

      2. **"Presumptively mandatory requirements" --** Indicated by the word **"should."**

         a. The accountant is also required to comply with a "presumptively mandatory requirement" -- but it allows for the possibility of exception.

         b. In rare circumstances, the accountant may depart from a presumptively mandatory requirement. The accountant must document the justification for the departure and how the alternative procedures performed in the circumstances were sufficient to achieve the objectives of the presumptively mandatory requirement.

III. **Explanatory Material --** Defined as the text within a SSARS (excluding any related appendices or interpretations) that may provide further explanation on the professional requirements or describe other procedures or actions possibly applicable to the auditor (practitioner).

   A. Such explanatory material is intended to be descriptive and does not impose a professional requirement.

   B. Explanatory material is identified by the terms **"may," "might," or "could."**

IV. **Hierarchy of Compilation and Review Standards and Guidance**

   A. **SSARSs --** They provide a measure of quality and the objectives to be achieved in both a compilation and review engagement. (Compliance is enforceable by Rule 202 of the AICPA Code of Professional Conduct, "Compliance With Standards," which requires accountants to adhere to standards promulgated by the ARSC.)

   B. **"Interpretive publications"**

      1. Consist of compilation and review interpretations (and appendices) of the SSARSs, AICPA Audit and Accounting Guides, and AICPA Auditing Statements of Position, to the extent applicable to compilation and review engagements.

2. Accountants should be aware of (and consider) interpretive publications applicable to compilations and reviews. When accountants do not apply such guidance, they should be prepared to explain how they complied with the SSARS provisions related to such interpretive publications.

C. **"Other compilation and review publications" --** Other publications have no authoritative status, but they may help the accountant understand and apply the SSARS (for example, articles in the *Journal of Accountancy* and the AICPA's *CPA Letter*, continuing professional education programs, textbooks).

SSARSs - Compilations

After studying this lesson, you should be able to:

1. *Know what is meant by the term "compilation."*
2. *Understand the accountant's responsibilities for a compilation engagement.*
3. *Know the structure of the accountant's report for a compilation engagement.*

> **Definition:**
> *Compilation*: A compilation is a service, the objective of which is to assist management in presenting financial information in the form of financial statements without undertaking to obtain or provide any assurance that there are no material modifications that should be made. (The accountant functions primarily as an "assembler" of the financial statements using financial data provided by management.)

I. **Establishing an Understanding --** The accountant should establish an understanding (regarding the engagement's objectives, management's responsibilities, the accountant's responsibilities, and the limitations of the engagement, among other matters) with management and document that in writing with an engagement letter.

II. **Compilation Performance Requirements**

  A. Should have or obtain an understanding of the industry and the entity itself, including the accounting principles and practices used;

  B. **Read the financial statements --** The accountant should read the entity's financial statements to see if they are appropriate in form and free of obvious material errors;

  C. **Other compilation procedures --** The accountant is not required to verify the information supplied by the entity, but should obtain additional or revised information when the accountant believes the financial statements are materially misstated;

  D. **Documentation --** The accountant should document the work performed in accordance with SSARSs; the extent of the documentation varies with the circumstances, but should include: (1) the engagement letter; (2) any findings or issues that are considered "significant;" and (3) any communications (whether oral or written) to the appropriate level of management about fraud or illegal acts.

III. **Reporting**

  A. **Elements of the compilation report**

    1. **Title --** "Accountant's Compilation Report" or "Independent Accountant's Compilation Report";
    2. Addressee;
    3. **Introductory paragraph --** Identify the financial statements and the nature of the engagement; include a disclaimer of any level of assurance;
    4. **Management's responsibility --** For the financial statements and related internal control;
    5. **Accountant's responsibility --** To conduct the compilation in accordance with SSARSs issued by the AICPA;
    6. Signature of the accountant (either manual or printed);
    7. Date of the report (the date of completion of the compilation).

Compilation Report on Financial Statements

Accountant's Compilation Report

(Appropriate Salutation)

I (we) have compiled the accompanying balance sheet of XYZ Company as of December 31, 20XX, and the related statements of income, retained earnings, and cash flows for the year then ended. I (we) have not audited or reviewed the accompanying financial statements and, accordingly, do not express an opinion or provide any assurance about whether the financial statements are in accordance with accounting principles generally accepted in the United States of America.

Management (owners) is (are) responsible for the preparation and fair presentation of the financial statements in accordance with accounting principles generally accepted in the United States of America and for designing, implementing, and maintaining internal control relevant to the preparation and fair presentation of the financial statements.

My (our) responsibility is to conduct the compilation in accordance with Statements on Standards for Accounting and Review Services issued by the American Institute of Certified Public Accountants. The objective of a compilation is to assist management in presenting financial information in the form of financial statements without undertaking to obtain or provide any assurance that there are no material modifications that should be made to the financial statements.

(Signature of accounting firm or the accountant, as appropriate)

(Date)

B. **Additional comments about the compilation report**

1. Each page of the financial statements should reference the compilation report (see "Accountant's Compilation Report").
2. The report should not describe any other procedures that were performed;
3. Financial statements that omit substantially all disclosures may be compiled, as long as the omission of disclosures is not intended to mislead readers (must add a paragraph to the compilation report that comments on the omission of substantially all disclosures);
4. If the accountant is not independent -- The accountant is permitted to compile the entity's financial statements since no assurance is provided;
5. Emphasis of a matter -- the accountant may choose to add a paragraph to the compilation report to emphasize a matter (for example, going concern issues, related party transactions, subsequent events, etc.); such a paragraph is not a substitute for proper disclosure, so an emphasis paragraph can only be used for a matter that has been disclosed in the financial statements.

C. **Departures from the applicable accounting framework (for example, GAAP) --** Add a separate paragraph to the compilation report; however, if such modification of the report is not an adequate way to disclose the departure, the accountant should instead withdraw from the engagement.

Note:
If lacking independence, the accountant must add a final paragraph to the report to state that fact. May choose to add a single sentence without any explanation, or may instead choose to disclose the reason(s) for the impairment of independence. If commenting on the reason(s), the accountant must include all of the reasons involved, not just selected reasons.

IV. **Change in an Engagement from an Audit (or Review) to a Compilation --** Before agreeing to such a change, the accountant should consider: (1) the reason for the client's request (e.g., whether a scope limitation is imposed by the client or by circumstances); (2) the additional effort required to complete the audit or review; and (3) the estimated additional cost to complete the audit or review. (If there is a reasonable basis for making such a change, the compilation report should not mention the original engagement or the reason(s) for the change.)

SSARSs - Reviews

After studying this lesson, you should be able to:

1. *Know what is meant by the term "review" for a nonissuer.*
2. *Understand the accountant's responsibilities for a review engagement under SSARSs.*
3. *Know the structure of the accountant's report for a review engagement under SSARSs.*

> **Definition:**
> *Review*: A review is a service, the objective of which is to obtain limited assurance that there are no material modifications that should be made to the financial statements in order for the statements to be in conformity with the applicable financial reporting framework. (Note that "A review is an assurance engagement as well as an attest engagement." The level of assurance for a review is described as "negative assurance.")

I. **Establishing an Understanding --** The accountant should establish an understanding (regarding the engagement's objectives, management's responsibilities, the accountant's responsibilities, and the limitations of the engagement, among other matters) with management and document that in writing with an engagement letter.

II. **Review Performance Requirements**

A. Should have or obtain an understanding of the industry and the entity itself, including the accounting principles and practices used;

B. **Designing and performing review procedures --** A review consists, primarily, of performing analytical procedures and making inquiries of management and other client personnel; (Those procedures constitute "review evidence")

C. **Analytical procedures --** Comparing expectations developed by the accountant to recorded amounts or ratios based on recorded amounts; such procedures may be performed at the financial statement level or at the detailed account level;

D. **Inquiries and other review procedures --** The accountant should direct inquiries to management about a variety of matters; should also read the minutes of board meetings, etc.; should read the financial statements for apparent compliance with the applicable financial reporting framework; and obtain reports from other accountants who have audited or reviewed financial statements of any significant components of the entity;

E. **Incorrect, incomplete, or otherwise unsatisfactory information --** If the accountant believes that the financial statements may be materially misstated, the accountant should perform additional procedures to obtain limited assurance that there are no material modifications that should be made to the financial statements;

F. **Management representations --** Written representations are required from management for all financial statements and periods covered by the accountant's review report. (If current management was not present for all such periods, the accountant should still obtain written representations from current management for all such periods.)

III. **Documentation --** The accountant should document the work performed in accordance with SSARSs; the extent of the documentation varies with the circumstances, but should include: (1) the engagement letter; (2) the analytical procedures performed; (3) additional procedures performed as a follow-up to the analytical procedures; (4) significant matters addressed by inquiries; (5) any findings that are "significant;" (6) any significant "unusual matters" considered and their disposition; (7) communications (whether oral or written) to the appropriate level of management regarding fraud or illegal acts; and (8) the management representation letter.

IV. Reporting

A. Elements of the review report

1. **Title --** "Independent Accountant's Review Report";
2. Addressee;
3. **Introductory paragraph --** Identify the financial statements and the nature of the engagement; state that a review is substantially less in scope than an audit and include a disclaimer of opinion;
4. **Management's responsibility --** For the financial statements and related internal control;
5. **Accountant's responsibility --** To conduct the review in accordance with SSARSs issued by the AICPA;
6. Results of the engagement (expressed as "negative assurance");
7. Signature of the accountant (either manual or printed);
8. Date of the report (not before the date of completion of the review).

Review Report on Financial Statements

Independent Accountant's Review Report

(Appropriate Salutation)

I (we) have reviewed the accompanying balance sheet of XYZ Company as of December 31, 20XX, and the related statements of income, retained earnings, and cash flows for the year then ended. A review includes primarily applying analytical procedures to management's (owners') financial data and making inquiries of company management (owners). A review is substantially less in scope than an audit, the objective of which is the expression of an opinion regarding the financial statements as a whole. Accordingly, I (we) do not express such an opinion.

Management (owners) is (are) responsible for the preparation and fair presentation of the financial statements in accordance with accounting principles generally accepted in the United States of America and for designing, implementing, and maintaining internal control relevant to the preparation and fair presentation of the financial statements.

My (our) responsibility is to conduct the review in accordance with Statements on Standards for Accounting and Review Services issued by the American Institute of Certified Public Accountants. Those standards require me (us) to perform procedures to obtain limited assurance that there are no material modifications that should be made to the financial statements. I (We) believe that the results of my (our) procedures provide a reasonable basis for our report.

Based on my (our) review, I am (we are) not aware of any material modifications that should be made to the accompanying financial statements in order for them to be in conformity with accounting principles generally accepted in the United States of America.

(Signature of accounting firm or the accountant, as appropriate)

(Date)

B. Additional comments about the review report

1. Each page of the financial statements should reference the review report (see "Independent Accountant's Review Report").
2. **An "incomplete review" (scope limitation) --** When the accountant is unable to perform the inquiry and analytical procedures considered necessary; cannot issue a review report under these circumstances;

3. **Emphasis of a matter --** The accountant may choose to add a paragraph to the review report to emphasize a matter (for example, going concern issues, related party transactions, subsequent events, etc.); such a paragraph is not a substitute for proper disclosure, so an emphasis paragraph can only be used for a matter that has been disclosed in the financial statements.

C. **Departures from the applicable accounting framework (for example, GAAP) --** Add a separate paragraph to the review report; however, if such modification of the report is not an adequate way to disclose the departure, the accountant should instead withdraw from the engagement .

V. **Change in an Engagement from an Audit to a Review --** Before agreeing to such a change, the accountant should consider: (1) the reason for the client's request (e.g., whether a scope limitation is imposed by the client or by circumstances); (2) the additional effort required to complete the audit; and (3) the estimated additional cost to complete the audit. (If there is a reasonable basis for making such a change, the review report should not mention the original engagement or the reason(s) for the change.)

SSARSs - Other Topics

After studying this lesson, you should be able to:

1. *Understand the accountant's reporting responsibilities under SSARSs for comparative financial statements (both for a continuing accountant and for a successor accountant).*
2. *Understand the accountant's responsibilities under SSARSs when engaged to compile specified "elements" of a financial statement.*
3. *Understand the accountant's responsibilities under SSARSs when engaged to compile "pro forma" financial information.*
4. *Understand the accountant's responsibilities for other miscellaneous topics under SSARSs, including for communicating with the predecessor, for compilation reports on financial statements in certain prescribed forms, and for the accountant's association with personal financial statements solely for purposes of financial planning.*

I. Review and Compilation Reports on Comparative Financial Statements

A. For a recurring engagement

1. Can review (or compile) both years' financial statements;
2. Can review one year's financial statements and compile the financials of another year - add an additional paragraph at the end of the current year's report (describing the nature and date of the prior year's report);
3. Can remove a prior reference to a GAAP departure for the prior year's financial statements (when that GAAP problem was later resolved) - add an appropriate explanatory paragraph;
4. Can review or compile the current year's financial statements and audit the prior year's financial statements. Note that the Statements on Auditing Standards (SASs) govern the reporting requirements when auditing any given year's financial statements.

B. If not a recurring engagement (i.e., there are new accountants for the current year) and if the prior year's financial statements are presented for comparative purposes:

1. If a predecessor accountant reviewed or compiled the prior year's financial statements - indicate that fact in an explanatory paragraph (specifying the nature and date of the predecessor's report) ;
2. Indicate that the (current) accountant takes no responsibility for the prior year's financial statements.

II. Compilation of Specified Elements -- The accountant may be engaged to compile "specified elements, accounts, or items of a financial statement."

A. Establish an understanding -- (Preferably in writing) as to the services to be performed - describe the nature and limitations of those services and the nature of the report to be issued.

1. The understanding should specifically include that the engagement cannot be relied upon to disclose errors, fraud, or illegal acts.
2. The understanding should also include that the accountant will inform the appropriate level of management of any material errors and of any information coming to the accountant's attention that fraud or an illegal act may have occurred (need not report matters regarding illegal acts that are "clearly inconsequential").

B. **Performance requirements --** Read the compiled elements, accounts, or items and consider whether that information appears to be free of obvious material errors.

C. **Reporting requirements --** Each page of the compiled elements, accounts, or items should include a reference such as "See Accountant's Compilation Report."

   1. **Not required to be independent --** But if not independent, disclose that lack of independence;

   2. The accountant may "assist" with the compilation of specified elements, accounts, or items of a financial statement without issuing a compilation report (if not actually engaged to compile such information) - should consider issuing a compilation report anyway when associated with such information so that users will not attribute unwarranted assurance.

III. **Compilation of Pro Forma Financial Information --** The accountant may be engaged to compile "pro forma financial information." Note that presentations of "pro forma financial information" are not within the definition of "financial statements."

A. **General comments --** Label the pro forma information in a way that distinguishes it from historical financial information.

   1. Objective of pro forma information -- to show the significant effects on historical financial information associated with a transaction (actual or proposed) had the transaction occurred at an earlier date.

   2. To compile the pro forma financial information -- the accountant must have compiled, reviewed, or audited the historical financial statements on which the pro forma information is based.

B. **Establish an understanding --** (Preferably in writing) as to the services to be performed -- describe the nature and limitations of those services and the nature of the report to be issued.

   1. The understanding should specifically include that the engagement cannot be relied upon to disclose errors, fraud or illegal acts.

   2. The understanding should also include that the accountant will inform the appropriate level of management of any material errors and of any information coming to the accountant's attention that fraud or an illegal act may have occurred (need not report matters regarding illegal acts that are "clearly inconsequential").

C. **Performance requirements --** Read the compiled pro forma financial information (including the summary of significant assumptions) and consider whether that information appears to be free of obvious material errors.

D. **Reporting requirements --** Each page of the compiled pro forma financial information should include a reference such as "See Accountant's Compilation Report."

   1. Not required to be independent -- but if not independent, disclose that lack of independence without describing the specific reason for it.

   2. The accountant may "assist" with the compilation of pro forma financial information without issuing a compilation report (if not actually engaged to compile such information) -- should consider issuing a compilation report anyway when associated with such information so that users will not attribute unwarranted assurance.

   3. The report should not describe any other procedures performed by the accountant before or during the compilation engagement.

IV. **When an accountant submits unaudited financial statements to the client that are *not expected to be used by a third party* --** The accountant must either (1) issue a compilation report or, alternatively, (2) document an understanding with the client by an engagement letter and a management representation letter in which, among other things to be addressed, management states that the financial statements are for internal use only and are not to be used by third parties.

> **Note**: In this case, the engagement letter allows the accountant to submit the unaudited financial statements without having to issue a compilation report. Include a reference on each page of the financial statements restricting their use to management only! If unauthorized distribution of these financial statements is discovered, discuss the matter with management and if they are uncooperative, the accountant should notify known third parties not to use the financial statements (and probably should consult with his or her attorney, too).

V. Miscellaneous Issues Related to Reviews and Compilations

- **A.** If there is a change of the public(issuer)/nonpublic(nonissuer) status of a client -- the current status of the entity governs what standards apply to the engagement.
- **B.** Communication between the successor and the predecessor accountants -- not required to communicate with the predecessor, but the successor may certainly choose to:
  - **1.** Requires the client's permission (due to confidentiality considerations).
  - **2.** The successor may also ask to review the predecessor's documentation. (The predecessor is not necessarily obligated to permit such a review, however.)
- **C.** Compilation reports on financial statements in certain prescribed forms:
  - **1.** When unaudited financial statements of a nonissuer are presented in a prescribed form (not GAAP) -- for banks, trade associations, or credit agencies.
  - **2.** Add an explanatory paragraph at the end of the compilation report indicating that the prescribed form differs from GAAP -- the second paragraph should refer to "... in the form prescribed by ..."
  - **3.** Any other known deficiencies should be identified in the report.
- **D.** Personal financial statements included with personal financial plans:
  - **1.** When the accountant helps prepare personal financial statements related to developing an individual's personal financial plans or goals -- a compilation report is not required. (The financial statements must not be used for any other purpose, however.)
  - **2.** The report should state the purpose of these financial statements is intended solely to help develop the financial plan, and note that the financial statements have not been audited, reviewed, or compiled; and indicate that the financial statements may be incomplete.

Sample Reports

Financial Statements Prepared on the Cash Basis

Independent Auditor's Report

We have audited the accompanying statements of assets and liabilities arising from cash transactions of XYZ Company as of December 31, 20x2 and 20x1, and the related statements of revenue collected and expenses paid for the years then ended. These financial statements are the responsibility of the Company's management. Our responsibility is to express an opinion on these financial statements based on our audits.

We conducted our audits in accordance with auditing standards generally accepted in the United States of America. Those standards require that we plan and perform the audit to obtain reasonable assurance about whether the financial statements are free of material misstatement. An audit includes examining, on a test basis, evidence supporting the amounts and disclosures in the financial statements. An audit also includes assessing the accounting principles used and significant estimates made by management, as well as evaluating the overall financial statement presentation. We believe that our audits provide a reasonable basis for our opinion.

As described in Note X, these financial statements were prepared on the basis of cash receipts and disbursements, which is a comprehensive basis of accounting other than generally accepted accounting principles.

In our opinion, the financial statements referred to above present fairly, in all material respects, the assets and liabilities arising from cash transactions of XYZ Company as of December 31, 20x2 and 20x1, and its revenue collected and expenses paid during the years then ended, **on the basis of accounting described in Note X**.

Note:
Notice that the financial statements are named in a way to avoid confusing them with financial statements prepared under GAAP.

Profit Participation

Independent Auditor's Report

We have audited, in accordance with generally accepted auditing standards, the financial statements of XYZ Company for the year ended December 31, 20x1, and have issued our report thereon, dated March 10, 20x2. We have also audited XYZ Company's schedule of Reed Smith's profit participation for the year ended December 31, 20x1. This schedule is the responsibility of the Company's management. Our responsibility is to express an opinion on this schedule based on our audit.

We conducted our audit of the schedule in accordance with auditing standards generally accepted in the United States of America. Those standards require that we plan and perform the audit to obtain reasonable assurance about whether the schedule of profit participation is free of material misstatement. An audit includes examining, on a test basis, evidence supporting the amounts and disclosures in the schedule. An audit also includes assessing the accounting principles used and significant estimates made by management, as well as evaluating the overall schedule presentation. We believe that our audit provides a reasonable basis for our opinion.

We have been informed that the documents that govern the determination of Reed Smith's profit participation are (a) the employment agreement between Reed Smith and XYZ Company dated February 1, 20x0, (b) the production and distribution agreement between XYZ Company and Television Network Incorporated dated March 1, 20x0, and (c) the studio facilities agreement between XYZ Company for the year ended December 31, 20x1, in accordance with the provisions of the agreements referred to above.

In our opinion, the schedule of profit participation referred to above presents fairly, in all material respects, Reed Smith's participation in the profits of XYZ Company for the year ended December 31, 20x1, in accordance with the provisions of the agreements referred to above.

This report is intended solely for the information and use of the board of directors and management of XYZ Company and Reed Smith and should not be used for any other purpose.

Note:
Notice that, since the object of this report is "profit participation" (a bottom-line concept), the auditor also must have audited the entire income statement and make reference to the related audit report.

Sample Review Report on Financial Statements

<u>Independent Accountant's Review Report</u>

I (we) have reviewed the accompanying balance sheet of XYZ Company as of December 31, 20XX, and the related statements of income, retained earnings, and cash flows for the year then ended. A review includes, primarily, applying analytical procedures to management's (owners') financial data and making inquiries of company management (owners). A review is substantially less in scope than an audit, the objective of which is the expression of an opinion regarding the financial statements as a whole. Accordingly, I (we) do not express such an opinion.

Management (owners) is (are) responsible for the preparation and fair presentation of the financial statements in accordance with accounting principles generally accepted in the United States of America and for designing, implementing, and maintaining internal control relevant to the preparation and fair presentation of the financial statements.

My (our) responsibility is to conduct the review in accordance with Statements on Standards for Accounting and Review Services issued by the American Institute of Certified Public Accountants. Those standards require me (us) to perform procedures to obtain limited assurance that there are no material modifications that should be made to the financial statements. I (We) believe that the results of my (our) procedures provide a reasonable basis for our report.

Based on my (our) review, I am (we are) not aware of any material modifications that should be made to the accompanying financial statements in order for them to be in conformity with accounting principles generally accepted in the United States of America.

(Signature of accounting firm or the accountant, as appropriate)

(Date)

Sample Compilation Report on Financial Statements

Sample Compilation Report on Financial Statements of a Nonissuer (Assuming No Known Material GAAP Departures)

Compilation Report on Financial Statements

Accountant's Compilation Report

(Appropriate Salutation)

I (we) have compiled the accompanying balance sheet of XYZ Company as of December 31, 20XX, and the related statements of income, retained earnings, and cash flows for the year then ended. I (we) have not audited or reviewed the accompanying financial statements and, accordingly, do not express an opinion or provide any assurance about whether the financial statements are in accordance with accounting principles generally accepted in the United States of America.

Management (owners) is (are) responsible for the preparation and fair presentation of the financial statements in accordance with accounting principles generally accepted in the United States of America and for designing, implementing, and maintaining internal control relevant to the preparation and fair presentation of the financial statements.

My (our) responsibility is to conduct the compilation in accordance with Statements on Standards for Accounting and Review Services issued by the American Institute of Certified Public Accountants. The objective of a compilation is to assist management in presenting financial information in the form of financial statements without undertaking to obtain or provide any assurance that there are no material modifications that should be made to the financial statements.

(Signature of accounting firm or the accountant, as appropriate)

(Date)

Separate Report on Compliance (No Instances of Noncompliance)

Independent Auditor's Report

(Appropriate Addressee)

We have audited, in accordance with auditing standards generally accepted in the United States of America, the financial statements of XYZ Company, which comprise the balance sheet as of December 31, 20X2, and the related statements of income, changes in stockholders' equity, and cash flows for the year then ended, and the related notes to the financial statements, and have issued our report thereon dated February 16, 20X3.

In connection with our audit, nothing came to our attention that caused us to believe that XYZ Company failed to comply with the terms, covenants, provisions, or conditions of sections XX to YY, inclusive, of the Indenture dated July 21, 20X0, with ABC Bank, insofar as they relate to accounting matters. However, our audit was not directed primarily toward obtaining knowledge of such noncompliance. Accordingly, had we performed additional procedures, other matters may have come to our attention regarding the Company's noncompliance with the above-referenced terms, covenants, provisions, or conditions of the Indenture, insofar as they relate to accounting matters.

This report is intended solely for the information and use of the board of directors and management of XYZ Company and ABC Bank and is not intended to be and should not be used by anyone other than these specified parties.

(Auditor's signature)

(Auditor's city and state)

(Date of the auditor's report)

Separate Report on Compliance (With Noncompliance Identified)

Independent Auditor's Report

(Appropriate Addressee)

We have audited, in accordance with auditing standards generally accepted in the United States of America, the financial statements of XYZ Company, which comprise the balance sheet as of December 31, 20X2, and the related statements of income, changes in stockholders' equity, and cash flows for the year then ended, and the related notes to the financial statements, and have issued our report thereon dated March 5, 20X3.

In connection with our audit, we noted that XYZ Company failed to comply with the "Working Capital" provision of section XX of the Loan Agreement dated March 1, 20X2, with ABC Bank. Our audit was not directed primarily toward obtaining knowledge as to whether XYZ Company failed to comply with the terms, covenants, provisions, or conditions of sections XX to YY, inclusive, of the Loan Agreement, insofar as they relate to accounting matters. Accordingly, had we performed additional procedures, other matters may have come to our attention regarding noncompliance with the above-referenced terms, covenants, provisions, or conditions of the Loan Agreement, insofar as they relate to accounting matters.

This report is intended solely for the information and use of the board of directors and management of XYZ Company and ABC Bank and is not intended to be and should not be used by anyone other than these specified parties.

(Auditor's signature)

(Auditor's city and state)

(Date of the auditor's report)

Combined Report on Audited Financial Statements and Compliance Issues

Independent Auditor's Report

(Appropriate Addressee)

We have audited the accompanying financial statements of ABC Company, which comprise the balance sheet as of December 31, 20X1, and the related statements of income, changes in stockholders' equity, and cash flows for the year then ended, and the related notes to the financial statements.

Management's Responsibility for the Financial Statements

Management is responsible for the preparation and fair presentation of these financial statements in accordance with accounting principles generally accepted in the United States of America; this includes the design, implementation, and maintenance of internal control relevant to the preparation and fair presentation of financial statements that are free from material misstatement, whether due to fraud or error.

Auditor's Responsibility

Our responsibility is to express an opinion on these financial statements based on our audit. We conducted our audit in accordance with auditing standards generally accepted in the United States of America. Those standards require that we plan and perform the audit to obtain reasonable assurance about whether the financial statements are free from material misstatement.

An audit involves performing procedures to obtain audit evidence about the amounts and disclosures in the financial statements. The procedures selected depend on the auditor's judgment, including the assessment of the risks of material misstatement of the financial statements, whether due to fraud or error. In making those risk assessments, the auditor considers internal control relevant to the entity's preparation and fair presentation of the financial statements in order to design audit procedures that are appropriate in the circumstances, but not for the purpose of expressing an opinion on the effectiveness of the entity's internal control. Accordingly, we express no such opinion. An audit also includes evaluating the appropriateness of accounting policies used and the reasonableness of significant accounting estimates made by management, as well as evaluating the overall presentation of the financial statements.

We believe that the audit evidence we have obtained is sufficient and appropriate to provide a basis for our audit opinion.

Opinion

In our opinion, the financial statements referred to above present fairly, in all material respects, the financial position of ABC Company as of December 31, 20X1, and the results of its operations and its cash flows for the year then ended in accordance with accounting principles generally accepted in the United States of America.

Other Matter

In connection with our audit, nothing came to our attention that caused us to believe that ABC Company failed to comply with the terms, covenants, provisions, or conditions of sections XX to YY, inclusive, of the Indenture dated July 21, 20X0 with XYZ Bank, insofar as they relate to accounting matters. However, our audit was not directed primarily toward obtaining knowledge of such noncompliance. Accordingly, had we performed additional procedures, other matters may have come to our attention regarding the Company's noncompliance with the above-referenced terms, covenants, provisions, or conditions of the Indenture, insofar as they relate to accounting matters.

Restricted Use Relating to the Other Matter

The communication related to compliance with the aforementioned Indenture described in the Other Matter paragraph is intended solely for the information and use of the boards of directors and management of ABC Company and XYZ Bank and is not intended to be and should not be used by anyone other than these specified parties.

(Auditor's signature)

(Auditor's city and state)

(Date of the auditor's report)

Other Professional Services

Attestation Standards

After studying this lesson, you should be able to:

1. *Know the definition of "attest engagement" and the three different kinds of attest engagements identified in the definition of "attest engagement" - examination, review, and agreed-upon procedures.*
2. *Know the 11 Attestation Standards.*
3. *Understand the guidance that is applicable to attest engagements, including Statements on Standards for Attestation Engagements (SSAEs), interpretive publications, and other attestation publications.*
4. *Know the two types of professional requirements ("unconditional requirements" and "presumptively mandatory requirements") and the language associated with each.*

Definitions:
Attest Engagement: (Revised by SSAE 10) - When a CPA practitioner is engaged to issue (or does issue) an examination, a review, or an agreed-upon procedures report on subject matter, or an assertion about the subject matter that is the responsibility of another party. (Now the CPA can report directly on the subject matter or on the responsible party's assertion, which previously required a written assertion!)

Assertion: Any declaration about whether the subject matter is in conformity with the criteria selected (previously had to be in writing!).

Responsible Party: The person(s) responsible for the subject matter (or a party who has a reasonable basis for making a written assertion about the subject matter) - being able to identify a responsible party is a prerequisite for an attest engagement.

I. There are 11 Attestation Standards (similar, but not identical, the now superseded 10 GAAS)

A. General Standards (remember: T-K-C-I-D)

1. **T**echnical training in the **attest function**.

"The practitioner must have adequate technical training and proficiency to perform the attestation engagement."

2. **K**nowledge in the **subject matter of assertion** (since the subject matter is now something other than traditional GAAP-based financial statements. . .).

"The practitioner must have adequate knowledge of the subject matter."

3. **C**riteria - measurement criteria are *suitable and available*. (The criteria should be chosen by the client or the responsible party.)

"The practitioner must have reason to believe that the subject matter is capable of evaluation against criteria that are suitable and available to users."

a. **Suitable --** Objective, measurable, complete, and relevant. (Criteria established by *due process* procedures are usually suitable.)

b. **Available --** Can be publicly available: in the presentation of the subject matter or assertion, in the practitioner's report, understood by users; or available to the specified parties.

4. **I**ndependence

> "The practitioner must maintain independence in mental attitude in all matters relating to the engagement."

5. **D**ue professional care

> "The practitioner must exercise due professional care in the planning and performance of the engagement and the preparation of the report."

B. Standards of field work (remember: P-E)

1. **P**lanning and supervision.

> "The practitioner must adequately plan the work and must properly supervise any assistants."

2. **E**vidence.

> "The practitioner must obtain sufficient evidence to provide a reasonable basis for the conclusion that is expressed in the report."

> **Note**: The CPA should usually consider obtaining a written representation letter from the responsible party - the responsible party's refusal to furnish written representations, when deemed necessary, is a scope limitation (modify report for examination; withdraw from a review).

C. Standards of reporting (remember: N-C-R-L)

1. **N**ature of engagement. (In general, whether it is an *examination*, a *review*, or *agreed-upon procedures* engagement - subject to some technical exceptions where the choices may differ!)

> "The practitioner must identify the subject matter or the assertion being reported on and state the character of the engagement in the report."

2. **C**onclusions (whether the assertion is reliable)

> "The practitioner must state the practitioner's conclusion about the subject matter or the assertion in relation to the criteria against which the subject matter was evaluated in the report."

3. **R**eservations.

> "The practitioner must state all of the practitioner's significant reservations about the engagement, the subject matter, and, if applicable, the assertion related thereto in the report."

a. **About the engagement --** As to the criteria used or the scope of work.

b. **About the presentation --** As to the reliability of the assertion.

4. **L**imited use reports. (The distribution of reports for *agreed-upon procedures* engagements must be **restricted to specific users.)**

> "The practitioner must state in the report that the report is intended solely for the information and use of the specified parties under the following circumstances:
>
> 1. When the criteria used to evaluate the subject matter are determined by the practitioner to be appropriate only for a limited number of parties who either participated in their establishment or can be presumed to have an adequate understanding of the criteria;
>
> 2. When the criteria used to evaluate the subject matter are available only to specified parties;
>
> 3. When reporting on subject matter and a written assertion has not been provided by the responsible party; and
>
> 4. When the report is on an attestation engagement to apply agreed-upon procedures to the subject matter."

> **Note**: Add a paragraph at the end of the report to restrict its distribution. The practitioner can negotiate to restrict the distribution of any report, but some reports must be restricted. The practitioner is not responsible for controlling the client's distribution of reports!

II. **Usual Menu of Attestation Engagements under these Standards --** Note that the SSAEs apply to attest engagements that are not otherwise covered by other standards (that is, by SASs or SSARSs); must establish *an understanding* with the client (including the nature of services involved and the parties' respective responsibilities).

III. **Examination --** Expressing a high level of assurance (that is, a positive expression of opinion and, therefore, a low level of *attestation risk*). The report should:

A. Identify any material deficiencies noted:

1. **For a scope limitation --** Issue a qualified or disclaimer of opinion;

2. **Problems with presentation --** Issue a qualified or adverse opinion.

B. Can also add an explanatory paragraph to emphasize other matters as desired.

C. Can be issued for general distribution:

1. Describe the nature of the engagement and the scope of work performed.

2. Refer to the applicable professional standards governing the work.

IV. **Review --** Expressing a lower (sometimes called *moderate*) level of assurance (that is, negative assurance and, therefore, a moderate level of *attestation risk*). The report:

- **A.** Should identify any material deficiencies noted;
- **B.** Can also add an explanatory paragraph to emphasize other matters; and
- **C.** Indicate that the scope of the work was less than an examination and disclaim an opinion.

V. Agreed-Upon Procedures -- Where the practitioner and the *specified parties* agree upon the specific procedures to be performed (and the specified parties take responsibility for the sufficiency of the procedures for their purposes!).

A. Limit the Distribution of the Report -- to the *specified users* who participated in identifying the procedures to be used (and who take responsibility for the sufficiency of the procedures!).

1. Usually communicate directly with specified users in advance to obtain their acknowledgment of the sufficiency of procedures.
2. If unable to communicate directly - this requirement may be met by (a) comparing the procedures to the specified users' written requirements; (b) discussing the procedures with representatives of the specified users; or (c) reviewing contracts or correspondence involving the specified users.
3. Adding *nonparticipant parties* - obtain the party's statement as to the sufficiency of the procedures (usually in writing); can even add parties after the report has been issued. (Practitioner can provide written acknowledgment that the party has been added.)
4. Procedures may evolve or be modified over time - there is flexibility as long as the specified parties take responsibility for the sufficiency of the procedures for their purposes.
5. Avoid vague terminology - don't use terms like general review; limited review; check; or test unless clearly defined by the parties.
6. Involvement of internal auditors and other client personnel - basically the same as for their involvement with an audit. (The practitioners cannot take the internal auditors' work as their own or report in a way that implies *shared responsibility* for that work.)
7. Obtain *an understanding* with the client as to services to be performed and respective responsibilities (should agree upon materiality limits, the involvement of *specialists*, etc.).

B. Basic Agreed-Upon Procedures Reports

1. Identify the subject matter (or assertion); refer specifically to "attestation standards established by the (AICPA)." Note that specified parties are responsible for the sufficiency of procedures.
2. Conclusions should be presented in the form of **"PROCEDURES and FINDINGS"** (either enumerate in the body of the report or refer to the applicable appendix or exhibit where the procedures and findings are identified). Note that no other form of assurance is given.
3. Indicate that this is not an examination and disclaim an opinion.
4. Restrict the distribution of the report to the specified parties.

C. Additional Reporting Considerations

1. *Materiality* does not apply unless defined in advance.
2. Explanatory language can be added as deemed appropriate (to describe the condition of records or control; to explain that the practitioner has no responsibility to update the report, etc.).
3. Scope limitations - try to obtain agreement from the specified parties to modify the agreed-upon procedures; if such agreement cannot be obtained, describe any restrictions in the report (or else withdraw from the engagement).

D. SSAE Hierarchy

1. **Attestation standards --** Practitioners must comply with SSAEs. (These are enforceable under Rule 202 "Compliance With Standards" of the AICPA Code of Professional Conduct.)

2. **Attestation interpretations --** (Consisting of Interpretations of the SSAEs, appendices to the SSAE, etc.) Practitioners should be prepared to explain how they complied with the SSAE provisions involved when such guidance is not applied.

3. **Other attestation publications --** (Consisting of articles in professional journals and newsletters, continuing professional education programs, textbooks, etc.) These have no authoritative status, so practitioners may choose to apply such guidance when they deem it relevant and appropriate, perhaps considering the author's reputation, etc.

E. Categories of Professional Requirements

1. **"Unconditional requirements" --** The practitioner must comply without exception (indicated by "must" in SSAEs).

2. **"Presumptively mandatory requirements" --** In rare circumstances, the practitioner may depart from such a "requirement," but must document the justification for the departure and how the alternate procedures performed were adequate to meet the objective of the "requirement" (indicated by "should" in SSAEs).

> **Note:**
> Descriptive guidance that does not impose a *requirement* (indicated by *may*, *might*, or *could* in SSAEs).

Financial Forecasts and Projections

After studying this lesson, you should be able to:

1. *Know the two different types of prospective financial statements: forecasts and projections.*
2. *Know the three kinds of engagements (and the structure of the reports) examination, compilation, and agreed-upon procedures, associated with prospective financial statements.*
3. *Understand the "partial presentation" of a forecast based on the AICPA's minimum presentation guidelines.*

I. **There are Two Types of "Prospective Financial Statements" --** Note that "prospective" involves a forward-looking, rather than historical, perspective:

   A. **Forecasts --** Represents the predicted financial statement outcome (that is, the "best guess").

   B. **Projections --** Represents the expected financial statement outcome based on certain specified hypothetical assumptions (more of a "what if ...?" scenario).

II. **Examination of Such Prospective Financial Statements**

   A. **Responsibilities --** Evaluate the presentation of the prospective financial statement information and evaluate the underlying assumptions for reasonableness.

   B. **Basic examination report issues --** Usually three paragraphs (four if limiting the distribution of the report to specified users):

      1. **1st paragraph (describe the engagement) --** Identify the prospective financial statements presented; identify management's responsibility and the practitioner's responsibility.
      2. **2nd paragraph (AICPA standards) --** State that examination complied with AICPA standards and express belief about reasonable basis for opinion.
      3. **3rd paragraph (express opinion) --** State that presentation conforms with AICPA guidelines and that underlying assumptions provide a reasonable basis for the prospective financial statement information (caution that the results may not be achieved).

         See the following example.

Examination Report on Forecasted Financial Statements

<u>Independent Accountant's Report</u>

To the Board of Directors and Stockholders

ABC Company

We have examined the accompanying forecasted balance sheet, statements of income, retained earnings, and cash flows of ABC Company as of December 31, 20X1, and for the year then ending. ABC Company's management is responsible for the forecast. Our responsibility is to express an opinion on the forecast based on our examination.

Our examination was conducted in accordance with attestation standards established by the American Institute of Certified Public Accountants and, accordingly, included such procedures as we considered necessary to evaluate both the assumptions used by management and the preparation and presentation of the forecast. We believe that our examination provides a reasonable basis for our opinion.

In our opinion, the accompanying forecast is presented in conformity with guidelines for presentation of a forecast established by the American Institute of Certified Public Accountants, and the underlying assumptions provide a reasonable basis for management's forecast. However, there will usually be differences between the forecasted and actual results, because events and circumstances frequently do not occur as expected, and those differences may be material. We have no responsibility to update this report for events and circumstances occurring after the date of this report.

/s/ CPA firm (signed by engagement partner)

Date (usually the last day of field work)

C. **Additional examination report issues**

1. **Only a "forecast" can be issued for general distribution; the CPA must restrict the distribution of the report for a "projection."** (Add an additional paragraph to limit the distribution of the report.)
2. If the prospective information is presented as a **range**, add an additional paragraph to the report pointing out that fact.
3. May add an explanatory paragraph to emphasize a matter as desired.
4. **Modification of the opinion**
   a. Issue a **qualified** or **adverse opinion** - when the presentation departs from AICPA guidelines.
   b. Issue an **adverse opinion** if the presentation is not in conformity with AICPA guidelines or if the underlying assumptions are not reasonable.
   c. **Disclaim** an opinion if the scope of the examination is insufficient.

III. **Compilation of Prospective Financial Statement Information --** No assurance is given, the CPA is merely assembling the information in prospective form.

A. **Responsibilities --** Disclose all significant assumptions; read the information and consider whether it is consistent with AICPA guidelines; even though no assurance is given for a compilation, consider whether the compiled information is obviously inappropriate.

B. **Reporting --** Usually consists of two paragraphs. (Three if limiting the distribution of the report to specified users.)

1. **1st paragraph --** Identify the prospective financial statement information compiled and state that the compilation was made in accordance with AICPA standards.

2. **2nd paragraph --** Point out that a compilation is limited in scope (and disclaim an opinion); caution that the results may not be achieved; and state that the accountant takes no responsibility for any events after the report date.

C. The CPA must **restrict the distribution of the report on a "projection."** (Add an additional paragraph to limit the distribution of the report.)

D. If the prospective information is presented as a **range**, add an additional paragraph to the report pointing out that fact.

E. May add an explanatory paragraph to emphasize a matter as desired.

F. Any identified **deficiencies and omissions** must be noted.

G. Do not have to be independent to compile prospective financial statements (since not conveying any assurance) - if **lacking independence**, add a sentence at the end of the compilation report pointing out that fact.

IV. **Applying Agreed-Upon Procedures to Prospective Financial Statement Information**

A. Specified users participate in **determining the particular procedures** to be performed -- usually meet with the users to discuss their needs (or to provide them with a draft of the anticipated report in advance to reduce misunderstandings).

B. **Reporting --** Usually consists of five paragraphs:

1. Identify the prospective financial statement information, the specified users, the type of engagement, and refer to AICPA standards.
2. Refer to AICPA's attestation standards.
3. Enumerate the procedures performed and the resulting findings.
4. State that the scope was less than an examination under AICPA guidelines and caution that the results may not be achieved; state that the accountant takes no responsibility for events occurring after the report date and **disclaim an opinion.**
5. **Restrict the distribution of the report to the specified users for all "agreed-upon procedures" engagements!**

V. **Restricted Reports --** The following reports on prospective financial statement information must be restricted:

A. Any type of report on a **projection** (since projections are too easily misunderstood to be appropriate for general distribution!).

B. An **agreed-upon procedures** report on a forecast.

C. Any type of report on a **"partial presentation"** of a forecast (where any omission of the AICPA **minimum presentation guidelines** causes a presentation to be inappropriate for general distribution).

D. **Minimum presentation guidelines**

1. Sales or gross revenues;
2. Gross profit or cost of sales;
3. Unusual or infrequently occurring items;
4. Provision for income taxes;
5. Discontinued operations or extraordinary items;
6. Income from continuing operations;
7. Net income;
8. Basic and diluted earnings per share;

9. Significant changes in financial position;
10. Description of what the responsible party intends the prospective financial statements to represent;
11. Summary of significant assumptions;
12. Summary of significant accounting policies.

VI. Prospective Financial Statements Included in a Document with Other Information

A. **Practitioner-submitted document --** Includes prospective financial information along with historical financial statements (on which the practitioner reports - as an audit, review, or compilation).

1. Must also report on the prospective information (as an examination, compilation, or agreed-upon procedures).
2. The only exception is prospective information that is labeled a "budget" (not extending beyond the end of the fiscal year) - indicate that the budget was not compiled or examined and disclaim an opinion.

B. **Client-prepared document --** Includes prospective financial information and historical financial statements (and the practitioner has reported on one or the other, but not both) - do not consent to the use of the practitioner's name unless the other subject matter is covered by an appropriate report (or there is an indication that the practitioner takes no responsibility for the other subject matter).

Pro Forma Financial Information

After studying this lesson, you should be able to:

1. *Know what is meant by the term "pro forma" financial information.*
2. *Understand the accountant's responsibilities under SSAEs when engaged to examine or review such pro forma financial information.*

I. **"Pro Forma" Financial Information --** Shows the significant effects on historical financial information that might have been had a transaction (actual or proposed) occurred at an earlier date.

II. **Examples --** The effects of a business combination, disposal of a significant segment of the business, change in capitalization, or issuance of securities and application of the proceeds.

III. **Required Conditions for Reporting on Pro Forma Financial Information**

A. The document containing the pro forma information includes or references the complete historical financial statements.

B. The accountant has **audited** or **reviewed** the related historical financial statements. (Note that the level of assurance on the pro forma information cannot exceed the level of assurance on the historical financial statements!)

C. The practitioner should have an appropriate level of knowledge of the accounting and financial reporting practices of the entity involved (having audited or reviewed the entity's financial statements would provide that).

IV. **There are Two Basic Types of Engagements Related to Pro Forma Financial Statements**

A. **Examination of pro forma financial information --** Results in "positive assurance."

See the following page for example.

Examination Report on Pro Forma Financial Information

Independent Accountant's Report

We have examined the pro forma adjustments reflecting the transactions (or event) described in Note 1 and the application of those adjustments to the historical amounts in the accompanying pro forma financial condensed balance sheet of ABC Company as of December 31, 20X1, and the pro forma condensed statement of income for the year then ended. The historical condensed financial statements are derived from the historical financial statements of ABC Company, which were audited by us, and of XYZ Company, which were audited by other accountants, appearing elsewhere herein. Such pro forma adjustments are based upon management's assumptions described in Note 2. ABC Company's management is responsible for the pro forma financial information. Our responsibility is to express an opinion on the pro forma financial information based on our examination.

Our examination was conducted in accordance with attestation standards established by the American Institute of Certified Public Accountants and, accordingly, included such procedures as we considered necessary in the circumstances. We believe that our examination provides a reasonable basis for our opinion.

The objective of this pro forma financial information is to show what the significant effects on the historical financial information might have been had the transaction (or event) occurred at an earlier date. However, the pro forma condensed financial statements are not necessarily indicative of the results of operations or related effects on financial position that would have been attained had the above-mentioned transaction (or event) actually occurred earlier.

In our opinion, management's assumptions provide a reasonable basis for presenting the significant effects directly attributable to the above-mentioned transaction (or event) described in Note 1, the related pro forma adjustments give appropriate effect to those assumptions, and the pro forma column reflects the proper application of those adjustments to the historical financial statement amounts in the pro forma condensed balance sheet as of December 31, 20X1, and the pro forma condensed statement of income for the year then ended.

Note: Additional paragraph(s) may be added before the opinion paragraph to emphasize certain matters relating to the attest engagement or the subject matter.

B. Review of pro forma financial information -- Results in "negative assurance."

See the following page for example.

Review Report on Pro Forma Financial Information

<u>Independent Accountant's Report</u>

We have reviewed the pro forma adjustments reflecting the transactions (or event) described in Note 1 and the application of those adjustments to the historical amounts in the accompanying pro forma financial condensed balance sheet of XYZ Company as of March 31, 20X2, and the pro forma condensed statement of income for the three months then ended. The historical condensed financial statements are derived from the historical unaudited financial statements of XYZ Company, which were reviewed by us, and of ABC Company, which were reviewed by other accountants, appearing elsewhere herein. Such pro forma adjustments are based upon management's assumptions described in Note 2. XYZ Company's management is responsible for the pro forma financial information.

Our review was conducted in accordance with attestation standards established by the American Institute of Certified Public Accountants. A review is substantially less in scope than an examination, the objective of which is the expression of an opinion on management's assumptions, the pro forma adjustments and the application of those adjustments to historical financial information. Accordingly, we do not express such an opinion.

The objective of this pro forma financial information is to show what the significant effects on the historical financial information might have been had the transaction (or event) occurred at an earlier date. However, the pro forma condensed financial statements are not necessarily indicative of the results of operations or related effects on financial position that would have been attained had the above-mentioned transaction (or event) actually occurred earlier.

Based on our review, nothing came to our attention that caused us to believe that management's assumptions do not provide a reasonable basis for presenting the significant effects directly attributable to the above-mentioned transaction (or event) described in Note 1, that the related pro forma adjustments do not give appropriate effect to those assumptions, or that the pro forma column does not reflect the proper application of those adjustments to the historical financial statement amounts in the pro forma condensed balance sheet as of March 31, 20X2, and the pro forma condensed statement of income for the three months then ended.

Note: Additional paragraph(s) may be added before the final paragraph to emphasize certain matters relating to the attest engagement or the subject matter.

C. The **objective of such an engagement** is to provide some degree of assurance as to (1) whether management's assumptions provide a reasonable basis for presenting the effects of the transactions (events), (2) whether the pro forma adjustments reflect those assumptions, and (3) whether the historical financial statements are appropriately adjusted.

V. **Procedures --** Obtain an understanding of the transaction, read any contracts involved and minutes of board meetings, make inquiries, discuss the assumptions with management, evaluate the computations involved, obtain "sufficient evidence" underlying the adjustments. (Note that an examination requires more evidence than a review.)

VI. **Examination Report Usually Consists of Four Paragraphs**

A. **First paragraph --** Identify the nature of the engagement, describe the pro forma information involved, and identify respective responsibilities.

B. **Second paragraph --** State that the examination was performed according to **attestation standards established by the AICPA** and express belief that the examination provides a reasonable basis for the opinion.

C. **Third paragraph --** Identify the objective of the pro forma information -- "The objective of this pro forma financial information is to show what the significant effects on the historical financial information might have been had the transaction (or event) occurred at an earlier date."

D. **Fourth paragraph --** Express positive assurance (an opinion) on three matters:

1. Whether management's assumptions provide a reasonable basis for presenting the significant effects.
2. Whether the adjustments appropriately reflect those assumptions.
3. Whether the pro forma column reflects the proper adjustments of the historical financial statements.

VII. **Basic Review Report Structure --** Usually consists of four paragraphs (essentially the same structure as the examination report, except "negative assurance" is expressed, instead of an opinion).

VIII. **Other Examination or Review Report Considerations**

A. Modify the report for any scope limitations or other known deficiencies (must convey any known deficiencies noted even if the engagement is a review).

B. The practitioner may negotiate to restrict the distribution of any pro forma report.

C. The report on pro forma information can be added to the practitioner's report on the historical financial statements, or presented separately. (If combined, and the two reports have different dates, the combined report should be "dual-dated.")

Compliance Attestation

After studying this lesson, you should be able to:

1. *Know the two types of engagements applicable to an entity's compliance issues: examination and agreed-upon procedures.*
2. *Understand the accountant's responsibilities under SSAEs when that accountant is engaged to examine or perform agreed-upon procedures regarding an entity's compliance issues.*

I. **Applicability --** When reporting on an entity's written assertion about compliance with requirements of laws, regulations, or contracts; or an assertion about the effectiveness of its internal controls related to such compliance.

  A. There are two types of engagements related to "compliance attestation:" - (1) examination; and (2) agreed-upon procedures (a "review" is not permitted!).

  B. For either an examination or agreed-upon procedures engagement - obtain management's written representations letter as evidence supporting the engagement.

II. **Examination --** Involves a positive expression of opinion relative to the established criteria. See the example of an examination report.

> **Sample Examination Report on Compliance with Specified Requirements**
>
> <u>Independent Accountant's Report</u>
>
> We have examined management's assertion about (*name of entity*)'s compliance with (*list specified compliance requirements*) during the (*period*) ended (*date*) included in the accompanying (*title of management report*). Management is responsible for (*name of entity*)'s compliance with those requirements. Our responsibility is to express an opinion on management's assertion about the Company's compliance based on our examination.
>
> Our examination was made in accordance with standards established by the American Institute of Certified Public Accountants and, accordingly, included examining, on a test basis, evidence about (*name of entity*)'s compliance with those requirements and performing such other procedures as we considered necessary in the circumstances. We believe that our examination provides a reasonable basis for our opinion. Our examination does not provide a legal determination on (*name of entity*)'s compliance with specified requirements.
>
> In our opinion, management's assertion (*identify management's assertion - for example that XYZ Company complied with the aforementioned requirements for the year ended December 31, 19x1*) is fairly stated, in all material respects.

  A. Consider **"attestation risk"** (including the component risks: inherent, control, and detection risks).

  B. **Obtain an understanding of the specific compliance requirements --** Laws, regulations, contracts, etc. (Consider recent regulatory reports and inquiries with appropriate persons inside and outside of the client organization.)

  C. **This is very similar to audit requirements --** For example, the CPA must plan the engagement appropriately; obtain sufficient evidence (including appropriate tests of controls); must perform tests of controls when assessing control risk at less than the maximum; must communicate any significant deficiencies noted; and modify the report as needed.

D. If material noncompliance is found -- Issue a qualified or adverse opinion. (In this case, report directly on the subject matter, not the written assertion.)

III. Agreed-Upon Procedures

A. Objective -- To present specific findings to assist users in evaluating the entity's compliance with specified requirements (or the effectiveness of internal control over compliance) based on agreed-upon procedures.

> **Sample Agreed-Upon Procedures Report on Compliance with Specified Requirements**
>
> Independent Accountant's Report
>
> To the Audit Committees and Managements of ABC Inc. and XYZ Fund
>
> We have performed the procedures enumerated below, which were agreed to by the audit committees and managements of ABC Inc. and XYZ Fund, solely to assist you in evaluating the accompanying Statement of Investment Performance Statistics of XYZ Fund (prepared in accordance with the criteria specified therein) for the year ended December 31, 20X1. XYZ Fund's management is responsible for the statement of investment performance statistics. This agreed-upon procedures engagement was conducted in accordance with attestation standards established by the American Institute of Certified Public Accountants. The sufficiency of these procedures is solely the responsibility of those parties specified in this report. Consequently, we make no representation regarding the sufficiency of the procedures described below either for the purpose for which this report has been requested or for any other purpose.
>
> We were not engaged to and did not conduct an examination, the objective of which would be the expression of an opinion on the accompanying Statement of Investment Performance Statistics of XYZ Fund. Accordingly, we do not express such an opinion. Had we performed additional procedures, other matters might have come to our attention that would have been reported to you.
>
> This report is intended solely for the information and use of the audit committees and managements of ABC Inc. and XYZ Fund, and is not intended to be and should not be used by anyone other than these specified parties.
>
> /signature/
>
> (Date)

B. Extents of procedures -- These procedures may be as limited or as extensive as the specified users desire, subject to the following conditions:

1. That the users participate in establishing the procedures -- need not necessarily discuss these matters directly with the users; (could base the procedures on the users' requirements or based on correspondence with them; but the CPA should then distribute a draft of the anticipated report or a proposed engagement letter with a request for the users' comments).
2. The users must take responsibility for the adequacy of these agreed-upon procedures for their purposes.

> **Note:**
> Include paragraphs to enumerate **procedures and findings** - or reference appendix (appendices) where these procedures and findings are identified.

C. Restrictions on scope -- If there are restrictions on scope due to circumstances - try to get an agreement from the users for modifying the agreed-upon procedures (otherwise must describe the restrictions in the report or else withdraw from the engagement).

D. Other report modifications involving an explanatory paragraph

1. If noncompliance is detected:
2. If a material uncertainty exists. (For example, litigation or a regulatory investigation may establish uncertainty about compliance.)
3. When compliance hinges upon interpretations of laws, etc. - consider whether "reasonable criteria" exist; may add an explanatory paragraph that describes the source of interpretations made by management.

E. Do not include "negative assurance" - **CANNOT** offer a "review" related to compliance!

Reporting on Internal Control in an Integrated Audit

After studying this lesson, you should be able to:

1. *Understand the auditor's responsibilities when reporting on internal control over financial reporting in an integrated audit of a nonissuer's financial statements in accordance with AICPA Professional Standards.*
2. *Familiarize yourself with the structure of the report on internal control over financial reporting for an engagement, whether the report is issued separately or combined with the audit report on the entity's financial statements .*

I. **Internal Control --** This section presents the AICPA's attestation standards related to reporting on internal control over financial reporting in an "integrated audit" of a non-issuer's financial statements. The AICPA issued SSAE No. 15 to supersede an earlier SSAE and, thereby, more closely align its standards with PCAOB Auditing Standard No. 5.

> **Note:**
> These AICPA standards are not applicable to reports on internal control for public companies ("issuers") which are subject to PCAOB standards!

II. **Applicability --** When engaged to perform an examination of the design and operating effectiveness of an entity's internal control over financial reporting ("examination of internal control") that is integrated with an audit of the entity's financial statements ("integrated audit").

   A. Timing of an examination of internal control - usually engaged to examine internal control over financial reporting as of the end of the entity's fiscal year. (If engaged to examine internal control for a period of time, the examination should be integrated with an audit of the financial statements covering the same period.)

   B. SSAE No. 15 does not apply to other engagements related to internal control that are addressed by other standards, such as (1) engagements to examine the suitability of design of internal control; (2) engagements to examine controls over the effectiveness and efficiency of operations; (3) engagements to examine controls over compliance with laws and regulations; (4) engagements to report on controls at a service organization; and (5) engagements to apply agreed-upon procedures on controls. (Note that an auditor should not accept an engagement to review an entity's internal control over financial reporting.)

III. **Underlying Concepts of SSAE No. 15**

   A. If one or more "material weaknesses" exist then the entity's internal control cannot be considered effective - accordingly, the auditor should plan and perform the examination to obtain sufficient appropriate evidence to obtain reasonable assurance about whether material weaknesses exist as of the date specified.

   B. The auditor is not required to search for deficiencies that are less severe than a material weakness (that is, not required to look for significant deficiencies).

   C. The auditor should use the same suitable and available control criteria to perform the examination of internal control as management uses for its evaluation of the effectiveness of the entity's internal control.

   D. Four conditions must be met for the auditor to examine internal control:

      1. Management must accept responsibility for the effectiveness of the entity's internal control;
      2. Management must evaluate the effectiveness of the entity's internal control using suitable and available criteria (for example, COSO's Internal Control-Integrated Framework);
      3. Management must support its assertion about the effectiveness of the entity's internal control with sufficient appropriate evidence;

4. Management must provide its written assertion about the effectiveness of the entity's internal control in a report that accompanies the auditor's report. (If management refuses to furnish a written assertion, the auditor should withdraw from the engagement.)

E. The auditor's basic responsibilities - the auditor should plan and perform the integrated audit to achieve the objectives of both engagements simultaneously; that is, design the tests of control to (1) obtain sufficient appropriate evidence to support the auditor's opinion on internal control as of the period end and (2) obtain sufficient appropriate evidence to support the auditor's control risk assessments for purposes of the audit of the financial statements.

IV. **Planning the Engagement --** The auditor uses the same risk assessment process to focus attention on the areas of highest risk in both engagements.

A. **Scaling the examination --** The size and complexity of the entity, its business processes, and the business units may affect the way in which the entity achieves its control objectives. (Less control testing may be needed for smaller, less complex entities.)

B. **Entities with multiple locations --** The auditor should assess the risk of material misstatement associated with the various locations/business units and correlate the amount of work with the degree of risk.

C. **Fraud risk assessment --** The auditor should incorporate the results of the fraud risk assessment performed in the financial statement audit.

D. **Using the work of others --** The auditor should assess the competence and objectivity of persons whose work the auditor plans to use. (The auditor's need to perform the work increases with the risk associated with a control.)

E. **Materiality --** The auditor should use the same materiality for both engagements.

F. **Use a "top-down approach" --** The auditor should (1) begin at the financial statement level; (2) use the auditor's understanding of the overall risks to internal control; (3) focus on "entity-level controls" (e.g., the control environment, the entity's risk assessment process, monitoring controls, etc.); (4) focus on accounts, disclosures, and assertions that have a reasonable possibility of material misstatement to the financial statements; (5) verify the auditor's understanding of the risks in the entity's processes (including "walkthroughs"); and (6) select controls for testing based on the assessed risk of material misstatement to each relevant assertion.

V. **Testing Controls and Evaluating Identified Deficiencies --** The evidence that should be obtained increases with the risk of the control being tested. (The objective is to express an opinion on the entity's overall internal control, not on the effectiveness of individual controls.)

A. **Evaluating "design effectiveness" --** Procedures include a mix of inquiry, observation of the entity's operations, and inspection of relevant documentation. (A walkthrough is usually sufficient to evaluate design effectiveness.)

B. **Evaluating "operating effectiveness" --** Procedures include a mix of inquiry, observation of the entity's operations, inspection of relevant documentation, recalculation, and reperformance of the control. (Note that these procedures are presented in order of increasing persuasiveness of the resulting evidence.)

C. **The severity of a deficiency --** Depends on the magnitude of the potential misstatement and the degree of likelihood (whether there is a "reasonable possibility") of a failure; it does not require that an actual misstatement occur.

D. **Risk factors affecting whether a misstatement may occur --** (1) the nature of the accounts, classes of transactions, disclosures, and assertions involved; (2) the susceptibility of the related asset or liability to loss or fraud; (3) the subjectivity, complexity, or judgment involved; (4) the interaction of the control with other controls; (5) the interaction among the deficiencies; and (6) the possible future consequences of the deficiency.

E. **Multiple deficiencies --** May cause a material weakness even though the deficiencies individually may be less severe.

F. **Compensating controls --** May mitigate the severity of a deficiency, although they do not eliminate the deficiency entirely.

G. **Indicators of material weaknesses --** (1) discovery of any fraud involving senior management; (2) restatement of previously issued financial statements to correct a material misstatement; (3) identification of any material misstatement during the audit that was not detected by internal control; and (4) ineffective oversight of reporting and controls by those charged with governance.

VI. Concluding Procedures

A. Review reports of other parties - the auditor should review the reports of others (such as internal auditors) during the year that address internal control issues.

B. Obtain written representations from management specific to internal control matters - management's failure to provide these representations is a scope restriction.

C. Communicate certain internal control matters identified during the integrated audit.

1. Any identified material weaknesses and significant deficiencies - should be communicated in writing by the report release date. (For governmental entities only, the written communication must occur within 60 days of the report release date.)
2. Any lesser deficiencies - should be communicated in writing to management within 60 days of the report release date (and should inform those charged with governance of that communication).
3. Communicating an absence of deficiencies - the auditor should **not** issue any report stating that "no material weaknesses" (or that "no significant deficiencies") were identified in an integrated audit.

VII. Reporting on Internal Control

A. **Separate or combined reports --** The auditor may choose separate reports on the financial statements and on internal control or a combined report on both. (If issuing separate reports, the auditor should add a paragraph to each report referencing the other report.)

Sample Combined Report on Internal Control and Financial Statements

Independent Auditor's Report

(Introductory paragraph)

We have audited the accompanying balance sheet of ABC Company as of December 31, 20XX, and the related statements of income, retained earnings, and cash flows for the year then ended. We also have audited[1] ABC Company's internal control over financial reporting as of December 31, 20XX based on (*identify criteria*). ABC Company's management is responsible for these financial statements, for maintaining effective internal control over financial reporting, and for its assertion of the effectiveness of internal control over financial reporting, included in the accompanying (*title of management's report*). Our responsibility is to express an opinion on these financial statements and an opinion on ABC Company's internal control over financial reporting based on our examination audits.

(Scope paragraph)

We conducted our audit of the financial statements in accordance with auditing standards generally accepted in the United States of America and our audit of internal control over financial reporting in accordance with attestation standards established by the American Institute of Certified Public Accountants. Those standards require that we plan and perform the audits to obtain reasonable assurance about whether the financial statements are free of material misstatement and whether effective internal control over financial reporting was maintained in all material respects. Our audit of the financial statements included examining, on a test basis, evidence supporting the amounts and disclosures in the financial statements, assessing the accounting principles used and significant estimates made by management, as well as evaluating the overall financial statement presentation. Our audit of internal control over financial reporting included obtaining an understanding of internal control over financial reporting, assessing the risk that a material weakness exists, and testing and evaluating the design and operating effectiveness of internal control based on the assessed risk. Our audits also included performing such other procedures as we considered necessary in the circumstances. We believe that our audits provide a reasonable basis for our opinions.

(Definition paragraph)

An entity's internal control over financial reporting is a process effected by those charged with governance, management, and other personnel, designed to provide reasonable assurance regarding the preparation of reliable financial statements in accordance with (*applicable financial reporting framework, such as accounting principles generally accepted in the United States of America*). An entity's internal control over financial reporting includes those policies and procedures that (1) pertain to the maintenance of records that, in reasonable detail, accurately and fairly reflect the transactions and dispositions of the assets of the entity; (2) provide reasonable assurance that transactions are recorded as necessary to permit preparation of financial statements in accordance with (*applicable financial reporting framework, such as accounting principles generally accepted in the United States of America*), and that receipts and expenditures of the entity are being made only in accordance with authorizations of management and those charged with governance; and (3) provide reasonable assurance regarding prevention, or timely detection and correction of unauthorized acquisition, use, or disposition of the entity's assets that could have a material effect on the financial statements.

(Inherent limitations paragraph)

Because of its inherent limitations, internal control over financial reporting may not prevent, or detect and correct misstatements. Also, projections of any evaluation of effectiveness to future periods are subject to the risk that controls may become inadequate because of changes in conditions, or that the degree of compliance with the policies or procedures may deteriorate.

(Opinion paragraph)

In our opinion, the financial statements referred to above present fairly, in all material respects, the financial position of ABC Company as of December 31, 20XX, and the results of its operations and its cash flows for the year then ended in conformity with accounting principles generally accepted in the United States of America. Also in our opinion, ABC Company maintained, in all material respects, effective internal control over financial reporting as of December 31, 20XX, based on (*identified criteria*).

(Signature)

(Date)

[1] SSAE No. 15 includes the following statement: "Because the examination of internal control is integrated with the audit of the financial statements and an examination provides the same level of assurance as an audit, the auditor may refer to the examination of internal control as an audit in his or her report or other communications."

B. Report date -- Should be dated when the auditor has obtained sufficient appropriate evidence to support the auditor's opinion. (If issuing separate reports, the reports should have the same date for an integrated audit.)

C. Unqualified opinion on management's assertion about internal control or on the operating effectiveness of internal control (directly) -- The structure of the auditor's report consists of six paragraphs: (1) Introductory paragraph; (2) Scope paragraph; (3) Definition paragraph; (4) Inherent limitations paragraph; (5) Opinion paragraph; and (6) Audit of financial statements paragraph.

See the following example.

Sample Examination Report on Management's Assertion

Independent Auditor's Report

(Introductory paragraph)

We have examined management's assertion, included in the accompanying (*title of management report*), that ABC Company maintained effective internal control over financial reporting as of December 31, 20XX based on (*identify criteria*). ABC Company's management is responsible for maintaining effective internal control over financial reporting, and for its assertion of the effectiveness of internal control over financial reporting, included in the accompanying (*title of management's report*). Our responsibility is to express an opinion on ABC Company's internal control over financial reporting based on our examination.

(Scope paragraph)

We conducted our examination in accordance with attestation standards established by the American Institute of Certified Public Accountants. Those standards require that we plan and perform the examination to obtain reasonable assurance about whether effective internal control over financial reporting was maintained in all material respects. Our examination included obtaining an understanding of internal control over financial reporting, assessing the risk that a material weakness exists, and testing and evaluating the design and operating effectiveness of internal control based on the assessed risk. Our examination also included performing such other procedures as we considered necessary in the circumstances. We believe that our examination provides a reasonable basis for our opinion.

(Definition paragraph)

An entity's internal control over financial reporting is a process effected by those charged with governance, management, and other personnel, designed to provide reasonable assurance regarding the preparation of reliable financial statements in accordance with [applicable financial reporting framework, such as accounting principles generally accepted in the United States of America]. An entity's internal control over financial reporting includes those policies and procedures that (1) pertain to the maintenance of records that, in reasonable detail, accurately and fairly reflect the transactions and dispositions of the assets of the entity; (2) provide reasonable assurance that transactions are recorded as necessary to permit preparation of financial statements in accordance with (*applicable financial reporting framework, such as accounting principles generally accepted in the United States of America*), and that receipts and expenditures of the entity are being made only in accordance with authorizations of management and those charged with governance; and (3) provide reasonable assurance regarding prevention, or timely detection and correction of unauthorized acquisition, use, or disposition of the entity's assets that could have a material effect on the financial statements.

(Inherent limitations paragraph)

Because of its inherent limitations, internal control over financial reporting may not prevent, or detect and correct misstatements. Also, projections of any evaluation of effectiveness to future periods are subject to the risk that controls may become inadequate because of changes in conditions, or that the degree of compliance with the policies or procedures may deteriorate.

(Opinion paragraph)

In our opinion, management's assertion that ABC Company maintained effective internal control over financial reporting as of December 31, 20XX is fairly stated, in all material respects, based on (*identified criteria*).

(Audit of financial statements paragraph)

We also have audited, in accordance with auditing standards generally accepted in the United States of America, the (*identify financial statements*) of ABC Company and our report dated (*date of report, which should be the same as the date of the report on the examination of internal control] expressed [include nature of opinion*).

(Signature)
(Date)

Sample Examination Report on the Effectiveness of Internal Control

Independent Auditor's Report

(Introductory paragraph)

We have examined ABC Company's internal control over financial reporting as of December 31, 20XX based on (*identify criteria*). ABC Company's management is responsible for maintaining effective internal control over financial reporting, and for its assertion of the effectiveness of internal control over financial reporting, included in the accompanying (*title of management's report*). Our responsibility is to express an opinion on ABC Company's internal control over financial reporting based on our examination.

(Scope paragraph)

We conducted our examination in accordance with attestation standards established by the American Institute of Certified Public Accountants. Those standards require that we plan and perform the examination to obtain reasonable assurance about whether effective internal control over financial reporting was maintained in all material respects. Our examination included obtaining an understanding of internal control over financial reporting, assessing the risk that a material weakness exists, and testing and evaluating the design and operating effectiveness of internal control based on the assessed risk. Our examination also included performing such other procedures as we considered necessary in the circumstances. We believe that our examination provides a reasonable basis for our opinion.

(Definition paragraph)

An entity's internal control over financial reporting is a process effected by those charged with governance, management, and other personnel, designed to provide reasonable assurance regarding the preparation of reliable financial statements in accordance with (*applicable financial reporting framework, such as accounting principles generally accepted in the United States of America*). An entity's internal control over financial reporting includes those policies and procedures that (1) pertain to the maintenance of records that, in reasonable detail, accurately and fairly reflect the transactions and dispositions of the assets of the entity; (2) provide reasonable assurance that transactions are recorded as necessary to permit preparation of financial statements in accordance with (*applicable financial reporting framework, such as accounting principles generally accepted in the United States of America*), and that receipts and expenditures of the entity are being made only in accordance with authorizations of management and those charged with governance; and (3) provide reasonable assurance regarding prevention, or timely detection and correction of unauthorized acquisition, use, or disposition of the entity's assets that could have a material effect on the financial statements.

(Inherent limitations paragraph)

Because of its inherent limitations, internal control over financial reporting may not prevent, or detect and correct misstatements. Also, projections of any evaluation of effectiveness to future periods are subject to the risk that controls may become inadequate because of changes in conditions, or that the degree of compliance with the policies or procedures may deteriorate.

(Opinion paragraph)

In our opinion, ABC Company maintained, in all material respects, effective internal control over financial reporting as of December 31, 20XX, based on (*identified criteria*).

(Audit of financial statements paragraph)

We also have audited, in accordance with auditing standards generally accepted in the United States of America, the (*identify financial statements*) of ABC Company and our report dated (*date of report, which should be the same as the date of the report on the examination of internal control*) expressed (*include nature of opinion*).

(Signature)

(Date)

D. Adverse opinions -- The auditor should express an adverse opinion if there is one or more material weaknesses in internal control (in this case, report directly on the effectiveness of internal control, not on management's assertion); should also consider the implications to the audit of the entity's financial statements.

Sample Report with Adverse Opinion on the Effectiveness of Internal Control

Independent Auditor's Report

(Introductory paragraph)

We have examined ABC Company's internal control over financial reporting as of December 31, 20XX based on (*identify criteria*). ABC Company's management is responsible for maintaining effective internal control over financial reporting, and for its assertion of the effectiveness of internal control over financial reporting, included in the accompanying (*title of management's report*). Our responsibility is to express an opinion on ABC Company's internal control over financial reporting based on our examination.

(Scope paragraph)

We conducted our examination in accordance with attestation standards established by the American Institute of Certified Public Accountants. Those standards require that we plan and perform the examination to obtain reasonable assurance about whether effective internal control over financial reporting was maintained in all material respects. Our examination included obtaining an understanding of internal control over financial reporting, assessing the risk that a material weakness exists, and testing and evaluating the design and operating effectiveness of internal control based on the assessed risk. Our examination also included performing such other procedures as we considered necessary in the circumstances. We believe that our examination provides a reasonable basis for our opinion.

(Definition paragraph)

An entity's internal control over financial reporting is a process effected by those charged with governance, management, and other personnel, designed to provide reasonable assurance regarding the preparation of reliable financial statements in accordance with (*applicable financial reporting framework, such as accounting principles generally accepted in the United States of America*). An entity's internal control over financial reporting includes those policies and procedures that (1) pertain to the maintenance of records that, in reasonable detail, accurately and fairly reflect the transactions and dispositions of the assets of the entity; (2) provide reasonable assurance that transactions are recorded as necessary to permit preparation of financial statements in accordance with (*applicable financial reporting framework, such as accounting principles generally accepted in the United States of America*), and that receipts and expenditures of the entity are being made only in accordance with authorizations of management and those charged with governance; and (3) provide reasonable assurance regarding prevention, or timely detection and correction of unauthorized acquisition, use, or disposition of the entity's assets that could have a material effect on the financial statements.

(Inherent limitations paragraph)

Because of its inherent limitations, internal control over financial reporting may not prevent, or detect and correct misstatements. Also, projections of any evaluation of effectiveness to future periods are subject to the risk that controls may become inadequate because of changes in conditions, or that the degree of compliance with the policies or procedures may deteriorate.

(Explanatory paragraph)

A material weakness is a deficiency, or a combination of deficiencies, in internal control over financial reporting, such that there is a reasonable possibility that a material misstatement of the entity's financial statements will not be prevented, or detected and corrected on a timely basis. The following material weakness has been identified and included in the accompanying (*title of management's report*).

(*Identify the material weakness described in management's report.*)

(Opinion paragraph)

In our opinion, because of the effect of the material weakness described above on the achievement of the objectives of the control criteria, ABC Company has not maintained effective internal control over financial reporting as of December 31, 20XX, based on (*identified criteria*).

(*Audit of financial statements paragraph*)

We also have audited, in accordance with auditing standards generally accepted in the United States of America, the (*identify financial statements*) of ABC Company. We considered the material weakness identified above in determining the nature, timing, and extent of audit tests applied in our audit of the 20XX financial statements, and this report does not affect our report dated (*date of report, which should be the same as the date of the report on the examination of internal control*), which expressed (*include nature of opinion*).

(Signature)

(Date)

E. Other report modifications -- (1) if elements of management's report are incomplete or improperly presented (add an explanatory paragraph); (2) if there is a scope limitation (either withdraw or disclaim an opinion); (3) if the opinion is based partially on the report of another auditor; or (4) management's report contains other additional information, such as commentary about corrective action taken (disclaim an opinion on the other information).

Management's Discussion and Analysis (MD&A)

After studying this lesson, you should be able to:

1. *Understand the accountant's responsibilities (and the structure of the report) when* ***examining*** *an entity's MD&A presentation in accordance with AICPA Professional Standards.*
2. *Understand the accountant's responsibilities (and the structure of the report) when* ***reviewing*** *an entity's MD&A presentation in accordance with AICPA Professional Standards.*

I. **Applicability**

A. When attesting to MD&A that has been prepared according to the requirements of the SEC and that MD&A is presented in annual reports or in other documents.

B. Can even apply to a nonpublic entity that provides a written assertion that the SEC requirements were used as criteria for the presentation of the MD&A.

1. **Precondition to accept an MD&A engagement --** Must have audited the annual financials for the latest period applicable to the MD&A presentation; any other financials involved must have been audited (or at least reviewed if interim/quarterly financials) by the practitioner or a predecessor auditor.

II. **Examination of MD&A - Results in Positive Assurance**

A. **Purpose --** To express an opinion on whether:

1. **Required elements --** The presentation includes the elements required by the SEC:
   a. Discussion of **financial condition** (liquidity and capital resources);
   b. Discussion of **changes in financial condition**;
   c. Discussion of **results of operations.**
2. **Historical amounts --** The historical financial amounts are accurately derived from the financials.
3. **Basis for conclusions --** The underlying information, assumptions, etc., provide a reasonable basis for the disclosures within the MD&A.

B. There are **four assertions** implicitly embodied in the MD&A presentation:

1. **Occurrence --** Whether reported events actually occurred during the period.
2. **Consistency with the financials --** Whether historical amounts have been accurately derived from the financials.
3. **Completeness of the explanation --** Whether the description of matters comprising the MD&A presentation is complete.
4. **Presentation and disclosure --** Whether information in the MD&A is properly classified, described, and disclosed.

C. **Primary dimensions of an examination of MD&A**

1. **Planning the examination (similar to an audit engagement) --** Develop an overall strategy that limits **"attestation risk"** to an acceptably low level.
   a. Inherent risk - varies with the assertion involved.
   b. Control risk (same as previously discussed).
   c. Detection risk (same as previously discussed).

2. **Consideration of internal control applicable to MD&A (similar to an audit) --** Pertains to assessment of control risk, documenting the understanding, and communication of significant deficiencies.
3. **Obtain sufficient evidence --** Varies with the circumstances but includes reading the MD&A for consistency with the financials, examining related documents, reading minutes, reading communications from the SEC, and obtaining written representations from management, among other things.
4. **Consideration of subsequent events --** (SEC expects MD&A to reflect events at or near the filing date) -- Read minutes and available interim financials; make inquiries of management and obtain appropriate representations in writing.

D. **Reporting on MD&A --** Financial statements with the auditor's report should accompany the document containing the MD&A (or be incorporated by reference to documents filed with the SEC).

1. **Title --** "Independent Accountant's Report."
2. **Standard examination report consists of four paragraphs**
    a. **Introductory paragraph (four sentences)**
        i. Identify MD&A presentation.
        ii. Identify management's responsibility.
        iii. Identify accountant's responsibility.
        iv. Refer to related audit report.
    b. **Scope paragraph (three sentences)**
        i. Refer to attestation standards established by AICPA.
        ii. Describe scope of examination.
        iii. Say that examination provides reasonable basis for opinion.
    c. **Explanatory paragraph (three sentences)**
        i. Comment on the need for estimates and assumptions.
        ii. Comment on the role of future expectations.
        iii. State that actual results may differ.
    d. **Opinion paragraph (one long sentence) --** Whether (1) the presentation includes elements required by SEC; (2) the historical amounts are accurately derived; and (3) the underlying information and assumptions provide a reasonable basis for the MD&A.
3. **Dating report --** As of completion of the examination procedures.
4. **Modifications of the standard report.**
    a. **Reservations as to presentation --** Results in a **qualified** or **adverse** opinion.
    b. **Reservations as to scope --** Results in a **qualified** opinion or a **disclaimer** of opinion.
    c. **Division of responsibility --** May refer to another practitioner's report on MD&A for a specific component as a partial basis for one's own report.
    d. **Emphasis of a matter --** Presented as a separate paragraph (e.g. information included beyond the SEC's requirements).

Sample Examination Report on (Annual) MD&A When Reporting Directly on the Subject Matter, Not on Management's Assertion

Independent Accountant's Report

(Introductory paragraph)

We have examined ABC Company's Management's Discussion and Analysis taken as a whole, included (incorporated by reference) in the Company's (insert description of registration statement or document). Management is responsible for the preparation of the Company's Management's Discussion and Analysis pursuant to the rules and regulations adopted by the Securities and Exchange Commission. Our responsibility is to express an opinion on the presentation based on our examination. We have audited, in accordance with auditing standards generally accepted in the United States of America, the financial statements of ABC Company as of December 31, 20X3 and 20X2, and for each of the years in the three-year period ended December 31, 20X3, and in our report dated [Month and day], 20X4, we expressed an unqualified opinion on those financial statements.

(Scope paragraph)

Our examination of Management's Discussion and Analysis was conducted in accordance with attestation standards established by the American Institute of Certified Public Accountants, and, accordingly, included examining, on a test basis, evidence supporting the historical amounts and disclosures in the presentation. An examination also includes assessing the significant determinations made by management as to the relevancy of information to be included and the estimates and assumptions that affect reported information. We believe that our examination provides a reasonable basis for our opinion.

(Explanatory paragraph)

The preparation of Management's Discussion and Analysis requires management to interpret the criteria, make determinations as to the relevancy of information to be included, and make estimates and assumptions that affect reported information. Management's Discussion and Analysis includes information regarding the estimated future impact of transactions and events that have occurred or are expected to occur, expected sources of liquidity and capital resources, operating trends, commitments, and uncertainties. Actual results in the future may differ materially from management's present assessment of this information because events and circumstances frequently do not occur as expected.

(Opinion paragraph)

In our opinion, the Company's presentation of Management's Discussion and Analysis includes, in all material respects, the required elements of the rules and regulations adopted by the Securities and Exchange Commission; the historical financial amounts included therein have been accurately derived, in all material respects, from the Company's financial statements; and the underlying information, determinations, estimates, and assumptions of the Company provide a reasonable basis for the disclosures contained therein.

(Signature)

(Date)

III. Review of MD&A - Results in Negative Assurance

A. Purpose -- To report whether the practitioner has any reason to believe that:

1. The presentation does **not** include the elements required by the SEC;
2. The historical financial amounts are **not** accurately derived from the financials;
3. The underlying information, assumptions, etc., do **not** provide a reasonable basis for the disclosures within the MD&A.

B. Primary dimensions of a review of MD&A

1. Obtain an understanding of the SEC requirements regarding MD&A.

2. Plan the engagement - develop an overall strategy.
3. Consider relevant portions of internal control affecting MD&A presentation.
4. Apply **analytical procedures** and make **inquiries** of management (usually do not have to obtain corroboration).
5. Consideration of subsequent events.
6. Obtain written representations from management.

C. **Standard review report --** Usually consists of five paragraphs (if including a "restricted use" paragraph at the end of the report); the accountant may review the entity's annual MD&A presentation or an interim MD&A presentation.

1. **Title --** "Independent Accountant's Report"
2. **Introductory paragraph (three sentences) - delete the sentence on accountant's responsibility**
    - a. Identify MD&A presentation.
    - b. Identify management's responsibility.
    - c. Refer to related audit report.
3. **Scope paragraph (four sentences) - add a disclaimer**
    - a. Refer to attestation standards established by the AICPA.
    - b. Describe a review engagement.
    - c. Say that scope is less than that of an examination.
    - d. Disclaim an opinion.
4. **Explanatory paragraph (three sentences) - same as for an examination report**
    - a. Comment on the need for estimates and assumptions.
    - b. Comment on the role of future expectations.
    - c. State that actual results may differ.
5. **Conclusions paragraph (one long sentence) --** Negative assurance as to whether presentation does not include elements required by SEC, historical amounts are not accurately derived, and underlying information and assumptions do not provide a reasonable basis for the MD&A.
6. **Restricted use paragraph (one sentence) --** Restrict the distribution when the MD&A presentation and the practitioner's report are not intended to be filed with the SEC under the 1933 and 1934 Securities Acts.
7. **Dating report --** As of completion of the review procedures.
8. **Modifications of the standard report --** Reservations as to presentation; reservations as to scope (not rendering review incomplete); division of responsibility; or emphasis of a matter.

Assurance Services

After studying this lesson, you should be able to:

1. *Know the definition of "assurance services" and understand the distinction between "auditing," "attestation," and "assurance."*
2. *Be familiar with the AICPA's established assurance services, including WebTrust, SysTrust, and PrimePlus/ElderCare.*
3. *Recognize the "Assurance Services Executive Committee" as the AICPA senior committee with responsibility for identifying evolving assurance opportunities and for developing criteria and guidance to support these AICPA initiatives.*

> **Definition:**
> *Assurance Services*: Independent professional services that improve the quality or context of information for decision makers. (Quality includes the "reliability" and "relevance" of information and "context" refers to how the decision maker uses the information.)

I. **Relationship of "Assurance" to "Auditing" and "Attestation" --** Auditing and attestation both involve enhancing the *reliability* of information (auditing specifically focuses on historical financial statement subject matter, whereas attestation is not limited to financial statements subject matter); assurance is broader than attestation, since assurance may address the relevance of information in addition to the *reliability* of information.

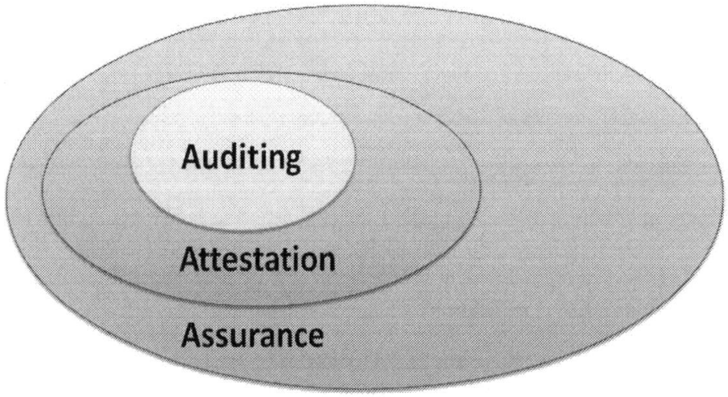

II. **AICPA Assurance Services**

A. **"Trust Services" --** The AICPA and Canadian Institute of Chartered Accountants developed "SysTrust" (to provide assurance on "systems" generating information and representations generally) and "WebTrust" (to provide assurance specifically related to e-commerce activities).

1. Five principles and criteria associated with Trust Services (these are organized in 4 broad areas: policies, communications, procedures, and monitoring):

    a. **Security --** The system is protected from unauthorized access.

    b. **Availability --** The system is available for operation and use as committed or agreed.

c. **Processing integrity --** System processing is complete, accurate, timely, and authorized.

d. **Confidentiality --** Information designated as confidential is protected as committed or agreed.

e. **Privacy --** Personal information is collected, used, retained, and disclosed in conformity with the commitments in the entity's privacy notice and with criteria set forth in generally accepted privacy principles issued by the AICPA/CICA.

2. **Web Trust --** To earn the WebTrust seal (which provides assurance to participants about transaction integrity and information security in e-commerce transactions with an entity's Web site), the entity must comply with all five of the principles above and engage a CPA licensed to provide WebTrust-related services; the seal displays a digital certificate and can be displayed until the designated expiration date (the WebTrust seal is managed by a third-party "seal manager").

3. **SysTrust --** To earn the CPA's unqualified opinion for a SysTrust engagement, an entity's system would also have to meet the above Trust Services principles; the SysTrust engagement would evaluate management's written assertions about the effectiveness of controls over the entity's system relative to applicable attestation standards.

B. **PrimePlus** (formerly known as "ElderCare") **Services --** PrimePlus has a connotation primarily involving financial/lifestyle planning issues, whereas ElderCare has a connotation primarily involving healthcare (the AICPA says it will continue to support both brands).

Definition:
PrimePlus/ElderCare services: "A unique and customizable package of professional services - both financial and nonfinancial - intended to help older adults maintain, for as long as possible, their desired lifestyle and financial independence."

1. **Financial services** include the following: receiving, disposing, and accounting for client receipts; making bill payments and handling banking services; submitting claims to insurance companies; estate planning; providing tax planning and tax return preparation; evaluating investments and trust activity; managing portfolios; protecting elderly from predators; etc.

2. **Nonfinancial services** include the following: coordinating support and healthcare services; communicating family expectations to care providers; managing real estate and other assets; establishing performance monitoring systems; managing real estate and other assets; coordinating services involving healthcare, legal, and other professionals; etc.

3. Markets for PrimePlus/ElderCare services - there are three primary markets: (a) older clients themselves; (b) children of older adults; and (c) other professionals who deal with those older adults (such as lawyers and healthcare professionals).

C. The AICPA has established a senior committee known as the **"Assurance Services Executive Committee"** (ASEC) to oversee the ongoing development of assurance services.

1. ASEC's role - to identify trends and assurance opportunities; to develop assurance guidance (including applicable criteria); to communicate those opportunities and guidance to AICPA members; and to create alliance with industry, government, or others to facilitate those assurance opportunities.

2. ASEC has appointed several task forces to focus on developing assurance opportunities: (a) XBRL Assurance Task Force (regarding the development of guidance on the assurance of XBRL-related documents); (b) Trust/Data Integrity Task Force (regarding the development of principles/criteria for assurance on the security, availability, process integrity of systems and the confidentiality and privacy of information); and (c) Risk Assurance Task Force (regarding enterprise risk management issues).

Sample Reports

Examination of Forecast

Independent Accountant's Report

To the Board of Directors and Stockholders

ABC Company

We have examined the accompanying forecasted balance sheet, statements of income, retained earnings, and cash flows of ABC Company as of December 31, 20X1, and for the year then ending. ABC Company's management is responsible for the forecast. Our responsibility is to express an opinion on the forecast based on our examination.

Our examination was conducted in accordance with attestation standards established by the American Institute of Certified Public Accountants and, accordingly, included such procedures as we considered necessary to evaluate both the assumptions used by management and the preparation and presentation of the forecast. We believe that our examination provides a reasonable basis for our opinion.

In our opinion, the accompanying forecast is presented in conformity with guidelines for presentation of a forecast established by the American Institute of Certified Public Accountants, and the underlying assumptions provide a reasonable basis for management's forecast. However, there will usually be differences between the forecasted and actual results, because events and circumstances frequently do not occur as expected, and those differences may be material. We have no responsibility to update this report for events and circumstances occurring after the date of this report.

/s/ CPA firm (signed by engagement partner)

Date (usually the last day of field work)

AUP of Forecast

Sample Agreed-Upon Procedures Report on Forecast Financial Information

Independent Accountant's Report on Applying Agreed-Upon Procedures

Board of Directors - XYZ Corporation

Board of Directors - ABC Company

At your request, we have performed certain agreed-upon procedures, as enumerated below, with respect to the forecasted balance sheet and the related forecasted statements of income, retained earnings, and cash flows of DEF Company, a subsidiary of ABC Company, as of December 31, 20XX, and for the year then ending. These procedures, which were agreed to by the Boards of Directors of XYZ Corporation and ABC Company, were performed solely to assist you in evaluating the forecast in connection with the proposed sale of DEF Company to XYZ Corporation. DEF Company's management is responsible for the forecast.

This agreed-upon procedures engagement was conducted in accordance with attestation standards established by the American Institute of Certified Public Accountants. The sufficiency of these procedures is solely the responsibility of the specified parties. Consequently, we make no representation regarding the sufficiency of the procedures described below either for the purpose for which this report has been requested or for any other purpose.

[Include paragraphs to enumerate (or reference) procedures and findings]

We were not engaged to and did not conduct an examination, the objective of which would be the expression of an opinion on the accompanying prospective financial statements. Accordingly, we do not express an opinion on whether the prospective financial statements are presented in conformity with AICPA presentation guidelines or on whether the underlying assumptions provide a reasonable basis for the presentation. Had we performed additional procedures, other matters might have come to our attention that would have been reported to you. Furthermore, there will usually be differences between the forecasted and actual results, because events and circumstances frequently do not occur as expected, and those differences may be material. We have no responsibility to update this report for events and circumstances occurring after the date of this report.

This report is intended solely for the information and use of the Boards of Directors of ABC Company and XYZ Corporation and is not intended to be and should not be used by anyone other than these specified parties.

Compilation of Forecast

<u>Accountant's Compilation Report</u>

We have compiled the accompanying forecasted balance sheet, statements of income, retained earnings, and cash flows of ABC Company as of December 31, 20X1, and for the year then ending, in accordance with attestation standards established by the American Institute of Certified Public Accountants.

A compilation is limited to presenting in the form of a forecast information that is the representation of management and does not include evaluation of the support for the assumptions underlying the forecast. We have not examined the forecast and, accordingly, do not express an opinion or any other form of assurance on the accompanying statements or assumptions. Furthermore, there will usually be differences between the forecasted and actual results, because events and circumstances frequently do not occur as expected, and those differences may be material. We have no responsibility to update this report for events and circumstances occurring after the date of this report.

Examination of Pro Forma

Independent Accountant's Report

We have examined the pro forma adjustments reflecting the transactions [or event] described in Note 1 and the application of those adjustments to the historical amounts in the accompanying pro forma financial condensed balance sheet of ABC Company as of December 31, 20X1, and the pro forma condensed statement of income for the year then ended. The historical condensed financial statements are derived from the historical financial statements of ABC Company, which were audited by us, and of XYZ Company, which were audited by other accountants, appearing elsewhere herein. Such pro forma adjustments are based upon management's assumptions described in Note 2. ABC Company's management is responsible for the pro forma financial information. Our responsibility is to express an opinion on the pro forma financial information based on our examination.

Our examination was conducted in accordance with attestation standards established by the American Institute of Certified Public Accountants and, accordingly, included such procedures as we considered necessary in the circumstances. We believe that our examination provides a reasonable basis for our opinion.

The objective of this pro forma financial information is to show what the significant effects on the historical financial information might have been had the transaction [or event] occurred at an earlier date. However, the pro forma condensed financial statements are not necessarily indicative of the results of operations or related effects on financial position that would have been attained had the above-mentioned transaction [or event] actually occurred earlier.

In our opinion, management's assumptions provide a reasonable basis for presenting the significant effects directly attributable to the above-mentioned transaction [or event] described in Note 1, the related pro forma adjustments give appropriate effect to those assumptions, and the pro forma column reflects the proper application of those adjustments to the historical financial statement amounts in the pro forma condensed balance sheet as of December 31, 20X1, and the pro forma condensed statement of income for the year then ended.

Note:
Additional paragraph(s) may be added to emphasize certain matters relating to the attest engagement or the subject matter.

Review of Pro Forma

Independent Accountant's Report

We have reviewed the pro forma adjustments reflecting the transactions [or event] described in Note 1 and the application of those adjustments to the historical amounts in the accompanying pro forma financial condensed balance sheet of XYZ Company as of March 31, 20X2, and the pro forma condensed statement of income for the three months then ended. The historical condensed financial statements are derived from the historical unaudited financial statements of XYZ Company, which were reviewed by us, and of ABC Company, which were reviewed by other accountants, appearing elsewhere herein. Such pro forma adjustments are based upon management's assumptions described in Note 2. XYZ Company's management is responsible for the pro forma financial information.

Our review was conducted in accordance with attestation standards established by the American Institute of Certified Public Accountants. A review is substantially less in scope than an examination, the objective of which is the expression of an opinion on management's assumptions, the pro forma adjustments and the application of those adjustments to historical financial information. Accordingly, we do not express such an opinion.

The objective of this pro forma financial information is to show what the significant effects on the historical financial information might have been had the transaction [or event] occurred at an earlier date. However, the pro forma condensed financial statements are not necessarily indicative of the results of operations or related effects on financial position that would have been attained had the above-mentioned transaction [or event] actually occurred earlier.

Based on our review, nothing came to our attention that caused us to believe that management's assumptions do not provide a reasonable basis for presenting the significant effects directly attributable to the above-mentioned transaction [or event] described in Note 1, that the related pro forma adjustments do not give appropriate effect to those assumptions, or that the pro forma column does not reflect the proper application of those adjustments to the historical financial statement amounts in the pro forma condensed balance sheet as of March 31, 20X2, and the pro forma condensed statement of income for the three months then ended.

Note:
Additional paragraph(s) may be added to emphasize certain matters relating to the attest engagement or the subject matter.

Examination for Compliance

Independent Accountant's Report

We have examined management's assertion about (*name of entity*)'s compliance with (*list specified compliance requirements*) during the (*period*) ended (*date*) included in the accompanying (*title of management report*). Management is responsible for (*name of entity*)'s compliance with those requirements. Our responsibility is to express an opinion on management's assertion about the Company's compliance based on our examination.

Our examination was made in accordance with standards established by the American Institute of Certified Public Accountants and, accordingly, included examining, on a test basis, evidence about (*name of entity*)'s compliance with those requirements and performing such other procedures as we considered necessary in the circumstances. We believe that our examination provides a reasonable basis for our opinion. Our examination does not provide a legal determination on (*name of entity*)'s compliance with specified requirements.

In our opinion, management's assertion (*identify management's assertion - for example that XYZ Company complied with the aforementioned requirements for the year ended December 31, 19x1*) is fairly stated, in all material respects.

AUP for Compliance

Independent Accountant's Report

To the Audit Committees and Managements of ABC Inc. and XYZ Fund

We have performed the procedures enumerated below, which were agreed to by the audit committees and managements of ABC Inc. and XYZ Fund, solely to assist you in evaluating the accompanying Statement of Investment Performance Statistics of XYZ Fund (prepared in accordance with the criteria specified therein) for the year ended December 31, 20X1. XYZ Fund's management is responsible for the statement of investment performance statistics. This agreed-upon procedures engagement was conducted in accordance with attestation standards established by the American Institute of Certified Public Accountants. The sufficiency of these procedures is solely the responsibility of those parties specified in this report. Consequently, we make no representation regarding the sufficiency of the procedures described below either for the purpose for which this report has been requested or for any other purpose.

We were not engaged to and did not conduct an examination, the objective of which would be the expression of an opinion on the accompanying Statement of Investment Performance Statistics of XYZ Fund. Accordingly, we do not express such an opinion. Had we performed additional procedures, other matters might have come to our attention that would have been reported to you.

This report is intended solely for the information and use of the audit committees and managements of ABC Inc. and XYZ Fund, and is not intended to be and should not be used by anyone other than these specified parties.

/signature/

[Date]

Note:
Include paragraphs to enumerate **procedures and findings** - or reference appendix (appendices) where these procedures and findings are identified.

Sample Combined Report on I/C and F/S

Independent Auditor's Report

(Appropriate Addressee)

(Introductory paragraph)

We have audited the accompanying balance sheet of ABC Company as of December 31, 20XX, and the related statements of income, retained earnings, and cash flows for the year then ended. We also have audited[1] ABC Company's internal control over financial reporting as of December 31, 20XX based on (identify criteria). ABC Company's management is responsible for these financial statements, for maintaining effective internal control over financial reporting, and for its assertion of the effectiveness of internal control over financial reporting, included in the accompanying (title of management's report). Our responsibility is to express an opinion on these financial statements and an opinion on ABC Company's internal control over financial reporting based on our examination audits.

(Scope paragraph)

We conducted our audit of the financial statements in accordance with auditing standards generally accepted in the United States of America and our audit of internal control over financial reporting in accordance with attestation standards established by the American Institute of Certified Public Accountants. Those standards require that we plan and perform the audits to obtain reasonable assurance about whether the financial statements are free of material misstatement and whether effective internal control over financial reporting was maintained in all material respects. Our audit of the financial statements included examining, on a test basis, evidence supporting the amounts and disclosures in the financial statements, assessing the accounting principles used and significant estimates made by management, as well as evaluating the overall financial statement presentation. Our audit of internal control over financial reporting included obtaining an understanding of internal control over financial reporting, assessing the risk that a material weakness exists, and testing and evaluating the design and operating effectiveness of internal control based on the assessed risk. Our audits also included performing such other procedures as we considered necessary in the circumstances. We believe that our audits provide a reasonable basis for our opinions.

(Definition paragraph)

An entity's internal control over financial reporting is a process effected by those charged with governance, management, and other personnel, designed to provide reasonable assurance regarding the preparation of reliable financial statements in accordance with (applicable financial reporting framework, such as accounting principles generally accepted in the United States of America). An entity's internal control over financial reporting includes those policies and procedures that (1) pertain to the maintenance of records that, in reasonable detail, accurately and fairly reflect the transactions and dispositions of the assets of the entity; (2) provide reasonable assurance that transactions are recorded as necessary to permit preparation of financial statements in accordance with (applicable financial reporting framework, such as accounting principles generally accepted in the United States of America), and that receipts and expenditures of the entity are being made only in accordance with authorizations of management and those charged with governance; and (3) provide reasonable assurance regarding prevention, or timely detection and correction of unauthorized acquisition, use, or disposition of the entity's assets that could have a material effect on the financial statements.

(Inherent limitations paragraph)

Because of its inherent limitations, internal control over financial reporting may not prevent, or detect and correct misstatements. Also, projections of any evaluation of effectiveness to future periods are subject to the risk that controls may become inadequate because of changes in conditions, or that the degree of compliance with the policies or procedures may deteriorate.

(Opinion paragraph)

In our opinion, the financial statements referred to above present fairly, in all material respects, the financial position of ABC Company as of December 31, 20XX, and the results of its operations and its cash flows for the year then ended in conformity with accounting principles generally accepted in the United States of America. Also in our opinion, ABC Company maintained, in all material respects, effective internal control over financial reporting as of December 31, 20XX, based on (identified criteria).

(Auditor's signature)

(Date of the auditor's report)

[1]SSAE No. 15 includes the following statement: "Because the examination of internal control is integrated with the audit of the financial statements and an examination provides the same level of assurance as an audit, the auditor may refer to the examination of internal control as an audit in his or her report or other communications."

Sample Separate Report on I/C (Mgt's Assertion)

Independent Auditor's Report

(Appropriate Addressee)

(Introductory paragraph)

We have examined management's assertion, included in the accompanying (*title of management report*), that ABC Company maintained effective internal control over financial reporting as of December 31, 20XX based on (*identify criteria*). ABC Company's management is responsible for maintaining effective internal control over financial reporting, and for its assertion of the effectiveness of internal control over financial reporting, included in the accompanying (*title of management's report*). Our responsibility is to express an opinion on ABC Company's internal control over financial reporting based on our examination.

(Scope paragraph)

We conducted our examination in accordance with attestation standards established by the American Institute of Certified Public Accountants. Those standards require that we plan and perform the examination to obtain reasonable assurance about whether effective internal control over financial reporting was maintained in all material respects. Our examination included obtaining an understanding of internal control over financial reporting, assessing the risk that a material weakness exists, and testing and evaluating the design and operating effectiveness of internal control based on the assessed risk. Our examination also included performing such other procedures as we considered necessary in the circumstances. We believe that our examination provides a reasonable basis for our opinion.

(Definition paragraph)

An entity's internal control over financial reporting is a process effected by those charged with governance, management, and other personnel, designed to provide reasonable assurance regarding the preparation of reliable financial statements in accordance with (applicable financial reporting framework, such as accounting principles generally accepted in the United States of America). An entity's internal control over financial reporting includes those policies and procedures that (1) pertain to the maintenance of records that, in reasonable detail, accurately and fairly reflect the transactions and dispositions of the assets of the entity; (2) provide reasonable assurance that transactions are recorded as necessary to permit preparation of financial statements in accordance with (*applicable financial reporting framework, such as accounting principles generally accepted in the United States of America*), and that receipts and expenditures of the entity are being made only in accordance with authorizations of management and those charged with governance; and (3) provide reasonable assurance regarding prevention, or timely detection and correction of unauthorized acquisition, use, or disposition of the entity's assets that could have a material effect on the financial statements.

(Inherent limitations paragraph)

Because of its inherent limitations, internal control over financial reporting may not prevent, or detect and correct misstatements. Also, projections of any evaluation of effectiveness to future periods are subject to the risk that controls may become inadequate because of changes in conditions, or that the degree of compliance with the policies or procedures may deteriorate.

(Opinion paragraph)

In our opinion, management's assertion that ABC Company maintained effective internal control over financial reporting as of December 31, 20XX is fairly stated, in all material respects, based on (identified criteria).

(Audit of financial statements paragraph)

We also have audited, in accordance with auditing standards generally accepted in the United States of America, the (*identify financial statements*) of ABC Company and our report dated (*date of report, which should be the same as the date of the report on the examination of internal control expressed include nature of opinion*).

(Auditor's signature)

(Date of the auditor's report)

Examination of MD&A

Sample Examination Report on (Annual) MD&A When Reporting Directly on the Subject Matter, Not an Assertion

Independent Accountant's Report

We have examined ABC Company's Management's Discussion and Analysis taken as a whole, included (incorporated by reference) in the Company's (insert description of registration statement or document). Management is responsible for the preparation of the Company's Management's Discussion and Analysis pursuant to the rules and regulations adopted by the Securities and Exchange Commission. Our responsibility is to express an opinion on the presentation based on our examination. We have audited, in accordance with auditing standards generally accepted in the United States of America, the financial statements of ABC Company as of December 31, 20X3 and 20X2, and for each of the years in the three-year period ended December 31, 20X3, and in our report dated (Month and day), 20X4, we expressed an unqualified opinion on those financial statements.

Our examination of Management's Discussion and Analysis was conducted in accordance with attestation standards established by the American Institute of Certified Public Accountants, and, accordingly, included examining, on a test basis, evidence supporting the historical amounts and disclosures in the presentation. An examination also includes assessing the significant determinations made by management as to the relevancy of information to be included and the estimates and assumptions that affect reported information. We believe that our examination provides a reasonable basis for our opinion.

The preparation of Management's Discussion and Analysis requires management to interpret the criteria, make determinations as to the relevancy of information to be included, and make estimates and assumptions that affect reported information. Management's Discussion and Analysis includes information regarding the estimated future impact of transactions and events that have occurred or are expected to occur, expected sources of liquidity and capital resources, operating trends, commitments, and uncertainties. Actual results in the future may differ materially from management's present assessment of this information because events and circumstances frequently do not occur as expected.

In our opinion, the Company's presentation of Management's Discussion and Analysis includes, in all material respects, the required elements of the rules and regulations adopted by the Securities and Exchange Commission; the historical financial amounts included therein have been accurately derived, in all material respects, from the Company's financial statements; and the underlying information, determinations, estimates, and assumptions of the Company provide a reasonable basis for the disclosures contained therein.

Review of MD&A

Sample Review Report on (Interim) MD&A When Reporting Directly on the Subject Matter, Not an Assertion

Independent Accountant's Report

We have reviewed ABC Company's Management's Discussion and Analysis taken as a whole, included in the Company's [insert description of registration statement or document]. Management is responsible for the preparation of the Company's Management's Discussion and Analysis pursuant to the rules and regulations adopted by the Securities and Exchange Commission. We have reviewed, in accordance with standards established by the American Institute of Certified Public Accountants, the interim financial information of ABC Company as of June 30, 20X2 and 20X1, and for the three-month and six-month periods then ended, and have issued our report thereon dated July XX, 20X6.

We conducted our review of Management's Discussion and Analysis in accordance with attestation standards established by the American Institute of Certified Public Accountants. A review of Management's Discussion and Analysis consists principally of applying analytical procedures and making inquiries of persons responsible for financial, accounting, and operational matters. It is substantially less in scope than an examination, the objective of which is the expression of an opinion on the presentation. Accordingly, we do not express such an opinion.

The preparation of Management's Discussion and Analysis requires management to interpret the criteria, make determinations as to the relevancy of information to be included, and make estimates and assumptions that affect reported information. Management's Discussion and Analysis includes information regarding the estimated future impact of transactions and events that have occurred or are expected to occur, expected sources of liquidity and capital resources, operating trends, commitments, and uncertainties. Actual results in the future may differ materially from management's present assessment of this information because events and circumstances frequently do not occur as expected.

Based on our review, nothing came to our attention that caused us to believe that the Company's presentation of Management's Discussion and Analysis does not include, in all material respects, the required elements of the rules and regulations adopted by the Securities and Exchange Commission, that the historical financial amounts included therein have not been accurately derived, in all material respects, from the Company's financial statements, or that the underlying information, determinations, estimates, and assumptions of the Company do not provide a reasonable basis for the disclosures contained therein.

This report is intended solely for the information and use of (list or refer to specified parties) and is not intended to be and should not be used by anyone other than the specified parties.

Sarbanes-Oxley Act of 2002 and the PCAOB

PCAOB Responsibilities

The Sarbanes-Oxley Act of 2002 (SOA) was enacted by Congress in response to a series of highly visible financial reporting frauds and audit failures that undermined investor confidence in the U.S. capital markets. Said to be the most significant revision of securities laws since the 1930s, SOA ended self-regulation of the accounting profession and created the Public Company Accounting Oversight Board (PCAOB), a private-sector not-for-profit corporation, to provide a new regulatory mechanism over auditors of public companies, among other things.

After studying this lesson, you should be able to:

1. *Know the five primary responsibilities of the Public Company Accounting Oversight Board established by the Sarbanes-Oxley Act of 2002.*
2. *Understand the primary sections ("Titles") of the Sarbanes-Oxley Act of 2002 that directly affect auditors of public companies ("issuers").*

I. The Sarbanes-Oxley Act of 2002 and the PCAOB

A. Public Company Accounting Oversight Board (PCAOB) - five primary responsibilities

1. **Registration of public accounting firms --** U.S. and non-U.S. accounting firms that prepare audit reports of any U.S. public company ("issuer" of securities) must register with the PCAOB. (This includes non-U.S. accounting firms that play a substantial role in the preparation of such audit reports.)
2. **Inspections of registered public accounting firms --** PCAOB is directed to conduct a continuous program of inspections that assess compliance with SOA, PCAOB rules, SEC rules, and applicable professional standards. (A written report is required for each such inspection.)
   - **a.** Firms that provide audit reports for at least 100 issuers - PCAOB must inspect annually.
   - **b.** Firms that provide audit reports for fewer than 100 issuers - PCAOB must inspect every three years ("triennially").
3. **Standard setting --** PCAOB is directed to establish auditing and related attestation, quality control, ethics and independence standards and rules to be used by registered public accounting firms in the preparation of audit reports for issuers. (The Office of the Chief Auditor and the Standing Advisory Group (SAG) assist PCAOB in establishing such auditing and professional practice standards.)
4. **Enforcement --** PCAOB has broad authority to investigate registered public accounting firms and persons associated with such firms.
   - **a.** PCAOB rules require cooperation by registered public accounting firms and associated persons - must produce documents and provide testimony as directed. (PCAOB may also seek information from others, including clients of registered firms.)
   - **b.** PCAOB sanctions may range from revocation of a firm's registration or barring a person from participating in audits of public companies to lesser sanctions such as monetary penalties or imposition of remedial measures, including additional training or new quality control procedures.
5. **Funding --** PCAOB's budget is funded by (1) registration and annual fees from public accounting firms and (2) an annual "accounting support fee" assessed on issuers (based on their relative monthly market capitalization).

II. Overview of the Sarbanes-Oxley Act of 2002

A. **Purpose of the legislation --** To address a series of perceived corporate misconduct and alleged audit failures (including Enron, Tyco, and WorldCom, among others) and to strengthen investor confidence in the integrity of the U.S. capital markets.

B. The Sarbanes-Oxley Act of 2002 consists of 11 "Titles" (the first four of which are directly applicable to auditors).

C. **Title I --** Established the PCAOB, gave standard-setting authority to the PCAOB (regarding auditing, quality control, and independence standards), and created its role in overseeing the accounting firms required to register with the PCAOB.

D. **Title II --** Established independence requirements for external auditors, which addressed perceived conflicts of interest (limiting non-audit services, establishing a five-year rotation for the audit partner and review partner, and restricting members of the audit firm from taking key management positions (including CEO, CFO, controller, or chief accounting officer) during the one-year period preceding the audit engagement).

   1. Services that the auditor is prohibited from providing: (1) bookkeeping or other services related to the accounting records; (2) financial information systems design and implementation; (3) appraisal or valuation services; (4) actuarial services; (5) internal audit outsourcing services; (6) management functions or human resources; (7) broker or dealer, investment advisor, or investment banking services; (8) legal services and expert services unrelated to the audit; and (9) any other service that the PCAOB determines is impermissible.

   2. The issuer's audit committee is required to approve any non-audit services (including tax services) that are not specifically prohibited.

E. **Title III --** Established requirements related to "corporate responsibility" to make executives take responsibility for the accuracy of financial reporting (including a requirement for certification by the entity's "principal officers") and to make it illegal for management to improperly influence the conduct of an audit.

F. **Title IV --** Addressed a variety of "enhanced financial disclosures," the most well known of which deals with required internal control reporting (Section 404), among other matters.

Auditing Standard No. 1

After studying this lesson, you should be able to:

1. *Know the audit report (and review report) requirements applicable to issuers under PCAOB Auditing Standard No. 1.*

I. **"References in Auditors' Reports to the Standards of the (PCAOB)" --** Approved by the SEC on May 14, 2004.

II. **Standards Adopted --** PCAOB adopted the AICPA's auditing standards in existence on April 16, 2003, as "interim standards, on an initial, transitional basis."

III. **Required Changes --** Made the following required changes to the auditor's report, relative to AICPA guidelines.

   A. **Title of the report --** Replaced "Independent Auditor's Report" with "**Report of Independent Registered Public Accounting Firm**."

   B. **Scope paragraph --** Replaced reference to "auditing standards generally accepted in the United States of America" with "**the standards of the Public Company Accounting Oversight Board (United States)**."

   C. **Opinion paragraph --** Replaced reference to "accounting principles generally accepted in the United States of America" with "**U.S. generally accepted accounting principles**."

   D. **Signature --** Required firms to **add their city and state** (or country, as applicable) along with their signature and date of their audit report.

IV. **Examples of Reporting Language Specified by PCAOB**

> **Sample Audit Report Using the PCAOB's Template: Report No. 1**
>
> <u>Report of Independent Registered Public Accounting Firm</u>
>
> We have audited the accompanying balance sheets of ABC Company at December 31, 20X3 and 20X2, and the related statements of operations, stockholders' equity, and cash flows for each of the three years in the period ended December 31, 20X3. These financial statements are the responsibility of the Company's management. Our responsibility is to express an opinion on these financial statements based on our audits.
>
> We conducted our audits in accordance with the standards of the Public Company Accounting Oversight Board (United States). Those standards require that we plan and perform the audit to obtain reasonable assurance about whether the financial statements are free of material misstatement. An audit includes examining, on a test basis, evidence supporting the amounts and disclosures in the financial statements. An audit also includes assessing the accounting principles used and significant estimates made by management, as well as evaluating the overall financial statement presentation. We believe that our audits provide a reasonable basis for our opinion.
>
> In our opinion, the financial statements referred to above present fairly, in all material respects, the financial position of ABC Company at December 31, 20X3 and 20X2, and the results of its operations and its cash flows for each of the three years in the period ended December 31, 20X3, in conformity with U.S. generally accepted accounting principles.
>
> (Signature)
>
> (City and State or Country)
> (Date)

Sample Review Report Using the PCAOB's Template: Report No. 2

Report of Independent Registered Public Accounting Firm

We have reviewed the accompanying (*describe the interim financial information or statements reviewed*) of ABC Company as of September 30, 20X3 and 20X2, and for the three-month and nine-month periods then ended. This interim financial information (statements) is (are) the responsibility of the company's management.

We conducted our review in accordance with the standards of the Public Company Accounting Oversight Board (United States). A review of interim financial information consists principally of applying analytical procedures and making inquiries of persons responsible for financial and accounting matters. It is substantially less in scope than an audit conducted in accordance with the standards of the Public Company Accounting Oversight Board, the objective of which is the expression of an opinion regarding the financial statements taken as a whole. Accordingly, we do not express such an opinion.

Based on our review, we are not aware of any material modifications that should be made to the accompanying interim financial information (statements) for it (them) to be in conformity with U.S. generally accepted accounting principles.

(Signature)

(City and State or Country)

(Date)

Auditing Standard No. 3

After studying this lesson, you should be able to:

1. *Know the PCAOB documentation requirements under Auditing Standard No. 3.*
2. *Know the primary differences between PCAOB documentation requirements for issuers relative to AICPA documentation requirements for nonissuers (regarding documentation retention and the documentation completion date).*

I. **"Audit Documentation" --** Approved by the SEC on August 25, 2004.

> **Definition:**
> *Audit Documentation*: The written record of the basis for the auditor's conclusions that provides the support for the auditor's representations. Also serves as a **basis for the review** of the quality of the audit work - the documentation should be prepared in sufficient detail to permit an experienced auditor without prior connection to the engagement to understand the procedures performed and the conclusions reached (and to determine who performed the work and on what date).

II. **Basic Documentation Requirement --** (1) Demonstrate that the engagement complied with PCAOB standards; (2) support the basis for the auditor's conclusions regarding every relevant financial statement assertion; and (3) demonstrate that the underlying accounting records agree to or reconcile with the financial statement elements.

III. **Documentation of Specific Matters**

A. Document audit procedures involving inspection of documents (including walkthroughs, tests of controls, and substantive tests of details) - identify the specific items tested (or the source and specific selection criteria); include abstracts or copies of significant contracts or agreements examined.

B. For matters documented in a **"central repository"** or in a particular office of the public accounting firm (including issues such as auditor independence, staff training, client acceptance/retention, etc.) - the audit documentation should appropriately reference the central repository.

C. Must document all **"significant findings or issues"** (also document the actions taken to address them and the basis for the conclusions reached) - including the application of accounting principles, circumstances causing modification of planned audit procedures, matters that could result in modification of the auditor's report, material misstatements, significant deficiencies or material weaknesses in internal control over financial reporting, difficulties in applying audit procedures, and disagreements among members of the engagement team about final conclusions on significant matters, among other things.

D. All significant findings or issues must be identified in an **"engagement completion document"** in sufficient detail so that a reviewer can obtain a thorough understanding of the matters.

IV. **Retention of and Subsequent Changes to Audit Documentation**

A. Must retain audit documentation for **seven years** from the **"report release date"** - the report release date is when the auditor grants permission to use the auditor's report in connection with the issuance of the company's financial statements. (Recall that the AICPA requires a retention period of five years for audits of "nonissuers.")

B. A complete and final set of audit documentation should be assembled no later than **45 days** after the report release date - that is called the "**documentation completion date**." (Recall that the AICPA allows auditors of "nonissuers" to have a maximum of 60 days for this purpose.)

C. After the documentation completion date - no documentation can be deleted, but documentation can be added (must indicate the date the information was added, the name of the person preparing the additional documentation, and the reason for adding it).

D. The office of the firm issuing the auditor's report is responsible for ensuring that all documentation complies with PCAOB requirements - documentation of other auditors associated with the engagement (in other offices of the firm or in different firms) must be retained or accessible to the office issuing the report.

Auditing Standard No. 4

After studying this lesson, you should be able to:

1. *Know the PCAOB requirements, in general, when engaged to report on whether a previously reported material weakness in internal control over financial reporting continues to exist under Auditing Standard No. 4.*
2. *Know management's specific responsibilities before an auditor can report on whether a previously reported material weakness in internal control over financial reporting continues to exist.*
3. *Understand the auditor's specific responsibilities when reporting on whether a previously reported material weakness in internal control over financial reporting continues to exist.*

I. **"Reporting on Whether a Previously Reported Material Weakness Continues to Exist" --** Approved by the SEC on February 6, 2006.

II. **Applicability --** When engaged to report on whether a previously reported material weakness in internal control over financial reporting continues to exist as of a date specified by management. (The date specified by management must be a date after that of management's most recent annual assessment.) PCAOB standards do not require reporting on whether a previously reported material weakness continues to exist, so such an engagement is voluntary.

III. **The Auditor's Objective --** In an engagement to report on whether a previously reported material weakness continues to exist to express an opinion about the existence of a specifically identified material weakness as of a specified date (does not relate to the overall effectiveness of internal control over financial reporting); may report on more than one material weakness as part of the same engagement.

IV. **Conditions for Engagement Performance --** Cannot report on whether a previously reported material weakness continues to exist unless all of the following are met:

   A. Management accepts responsibility for the effectiveness of internal control over financial reporting;

   B. Management evaluates the effectiveness of the specific control(s) that it believes addresses the material weakness using the same control criteria that management used for its most recent annual assessment of internal control over financial reporting and management's stated control objective(s);

   C. Management asserts that the specific control(s) identified is (are) effective in achieving the stated control objective;

   D. Management supports its assertion with sufficient evidence, including documentation;

   E. Management presents a written report that will accompany the auditor's report that contains all the elements required by the PCAOB.

      1. Statement of management's responsibility for establishing and maintaining effective internal control over financial reporting;
      2. Statement identifying the control criteria used by management to conduct the required annual assessment of internal control;
      3. Identification of the material weakness that was identified as part of management's annual assessment (or by the auditor's report on it);
      4. Identification of the control objective(s) addressed by the specified controls and a statement that the specified controls achieve the stated control objective(s) as of a specified date;

5. Statement that the identified material weakness no longer exists as of the specified date because the specified controls address the material weakness.

V. Performing the Engagement

A. An individual material weakness may be associated with a single stated control objective (or more than one) - a "stated control objective" is the specific control objective identified by management that, if achieved, would result in the material weakness no longer existing.

B. Auditor uses materiality at the financial-statement level, rather than at the individual account-balance level, in evaluating whether a material weakness exists.

C. Obtaining an understanding of internal control over financial reporting:

   1. The extensiveness of the required understanding of internal control increases with the pervasiveness of the effects of the material weakness.

   2. Must perform a walkthrough for all major classes of transactions that are directly affected by controls specifically identified by management as addressing the material weakness - an auditor who has reported on internal control in accordance with Auditing Standard No. 5 for the most recent annual assessment is not required to perform a walkthrough for this engagement.

   3. Successor auditors may determine that they are unable to obtain a sufficient basis for reporting on whether a previously reported material weakness continues to exist without performing a complete audit of internal control over financial reporting in accordance with Auditing Standard No. 5 .

D. Testing and evaluating whether a material weakness continues to exist:

   1. If management has not supported its assertion with sufficient evidence (a required condition) - the auditor cannot complete this engagement.

   2. Auditor should evaluate the appropriateness of management's chosen date - for example, controls that operate daily and continuously can be as of almost any date of management's choosing; controls that operate over the company's period-end reporting process can usually only be tested in connection with a period-end.

   3. Auditor should obtain evidence about the effectiveness of all controls specifically identified in management's assertion (all controls that are necessary to achieve the stated control objective should be specifically identified and evaluated) - determine whether the specified control operated as designed and whether the person performing the control possesses the authority and qualifications to perform the control effectively.

E. Using the work of others - the auditor may consider the work of others in deciding the nature, timing, or extent of the work that should be performed. (The auditor should perform any walkthroughs, however, because of the judgment involved.)

F. Obtain written representations from management about various matters (ranging from management's responsibility for establishing and maintaining internal control, management's evaluation of the effectiveness of the specified controls, describing any fraud issues, and stating whether there were material subsequent events, among other matters).

VI. Auditor's Report -- On whether a previously reported material weakness continues to exist may only issue an **unqualified opinion** or a **disclaimer of opinion** (cannot issue a qualified opinion - any limitation on the scope precludes an expression of opinion).

A. See the sample below for a "continuing auditor" who has previously reported on the company's internal control over financial reporting in accordance with Auditing Standard No. 5 as of the company's most recent year-end.

B. Report modifications - for any of the following conditions:

   1. Other material weaknesses that were reported previously by the company as part of the company's annual assessment of internal control are not addressed by the auditor's opinion.

2. A significant subsequent event has occurred since the date reported on.
3. Management's report contains additional information - express a disclaimer of opinion on the additional information.

Sample Auditor's Report for a Continuing Auditor Expressing an Opinion That a Previously Reported Material Weakness No Longer Exists

Report of Independent Registered Public Accounting Firm

We have previously audited and reported on management's annual assessment of XYZ Company's internal control over financial reporting as of December 31, 200X based on (*identify control criteria, for example, "criteria established in Internal Control - Integrated Framework issued by the Committee of Sponsoring Organizations of the Treadway Commission (COSO)."*) Our report, dated (*date of report*), identified the following material weakness in the Company's internal control over financial reporting:

(*Describe material weakness*)

We have audited management's assertion, included in the accompanying (*title of management's report*), that the material weakness in internal control over financial reporting identified above no longer exists as of (*date of management's assertion*) because the following control(s) addresses the material weakness:

(*Describe control(s)*)

Management has asserted that the control(s) identified above achieves the following stated control objective, which is consistent with the criteria established in (*identify control criteria used for management's annual assessment of internal control over financial reporting*): (*state control objective addressed*). Management also has asserted that it has tested the control(s) identified above and concluded that the control(s) was designed and operated effectively as of (*date of management's assertion*). XYZ Company's management is responsible for its assertion. Our responsibility is to express an opinion on whether the identified material weakness continues to exist as of (*date of management's assertion*) based on our auditing procedures.

Our engagement was conducted in accordance with the standards of the Public Company Accounting Oversight Board (United States). Those standards require that we plan and perform the engagement to obtain reasonable assurance about whether a previously reported material weakness continues to exist at the company. Our engagement included examining evidence supporting management's assertion and performing such other procedures as we considered necessary in the circumstances. We obtained an understanding of the company's internal control over financial reporting as part of our previous audit of management's annual assessment of XYZ Company's internal control over financial reporting as of December 31, 200X and updated that understanding as it specifically relates to changes in internal control over financial reporting associated with the material weakness described above. We believe that our auditing procedures provide a reasonable basis for our opinion.

In our opinion, the material weakness described above no longer exists as of (*date of management's assertion*).

We were not engaged to and did not conduct an audit of internal control over financial reporting as of (*date of management's assertion*), the objective of which would be the expression of an opinion on the effectiveness of internal control over financial reporting. Accordingly, we do not express such an opinion. This means that we have not applied auditing procedures sufficient to reach conclusions about the effectiveness of any controls of the company as of any date after December 31, 200X, other than the control(s) specifically identified in this report. Accordingly, we do not express an opinion that any other controls operated effectively after December 31, 200X.

Because of its inherent limitations, internal control over financial reporting may not prevent or detect misstatements. Also, projections of any evaluation of the effectiveness of specific controls or internal control over financial reporting overall to future periods are subject to the risk that controls may become inadequate because of changes in conditions or that the degree of compliance with the policies or procedures may deteriorate.

(Signature)

(City and State/or Country)

(Date)

Auditing Standard No. 5

After studying this lesson, you should be able to:

1. *Understand the auditor's responsibilities when reporting on internal control over financial reporting in an integrated audit of an issuer's financial statements in accordance with PCAOB Auditing Standard No. 5.*
2. *Be familiar with the structure of the report on internal control over financial reporting for such an engagement, whether the report is issued separately or combined with the audit report on the entity's financial statements.*

I. **"An Audit of Internal Control Over Financial Reporting That Is Integrated with An Audit of Financial Statements" --** Approved by the SEC on July 25, 2007.

II. **Applicability of Standard --** When engaged to "perform an audit of management's assessment of the effectiveness of internal control over financial reporting" (ICFR); the objective of such an engagement is to express an opinion on the effectiveness of ICFR.

III. **Some Important Definitions**

A. **"Control deficiency" --** When the design or operation of a control does not allow management or employees, in the normal course of performing their assigned functions, to prevent or detect misstatements on a timely basis.

1. **Deficiency in design --** When a control necessary to meet the control objective is missing or when an existing control is not properly designed so that, even if the control operates as designed, the control objective is not always met.
2. **Deficiency in operation --** When a properly designed control does not operate as designed or when the person performing the control does not possess the necessary authority or qualifications to perform the control effectively.

B. **"Material weakness" --** A deficiency, or a combination of deficiencies, in ICFR such that there is a reasonable possibility that a material misstatement of the company's annual or interim financial statements will not be prevented or detected on a timely basis. (If one or more material weaknesses exist, the company's ICFR is not considered to be effective.)

C. **"Significant deficiency" --** A deficiency, or a combination of deficiencies, in ICFR that is less severe than a material weakness, yet important enough to merit attention by those responsible for oversight of the company's financial reporting.

IV. **Planning the Audit --** The audit of ICFR should be integrated with the audit of the financial statements (that is, the tests of controls should be designed to address both the objectives of the audit of ICFR and the audit of the financial statements).

A. **Role of risk assessment --** "Risk assessment underlies the entire audit process described by this standard, including the determination of significant accounts and disclosures and relevant assertions, the selection of controls to test, and the determination of the evidence necessary for a given control."

1. There is a direct relationship between the risk of material weakness and the amount of audit attention that is needed.
2. Materiality - should use the same materiality considerations in planning the audit of ICFR as for the audit of the company's annual financial statements.

B. **Using the work of others --** The auditor may use the work of others to reduce the work the auditor might otherwise have to perform.

1. Includes internal auditors, other company personnel, service auditors (when a service organization is involved), and third parties working under the direction of management or the audit committee; the auditor should assess the competence and objectivity of those whose work the auditor plans to use.

2. As the risk associated with a control increases, the auditor should take increasing responsibility for performing the work instead of using the work of others.

V. **Using a "Top-down" Approach --** Begins at the financial statement level and with the auditor's understanding of the overall risks to ICFR; the auditor then focuses on "entity-level" controls and works down to significant accounts and disclosures and their relevant assertions.

A. Identifying entity-level controls - the auditor must test those entity-level controls that are important to the conclusion about the effectiveness of ICFR.

1. **Entity-level controls --** Include controls related to the control environment, controls over management override, the company's risk assessment process, controls to monitor results of operations or other controls, controls over the period-end financial reporting process; and policies that address significant business control and risk management practices.

2. **Control environment --** Because of its importance to ICFR, the auditor must evaluate the control environment at the company.

3. **Period-end financial reporting process --** Because of its importance to ICFR, the auditor must evaluate the period-end financial reporting process.

B. Identifying significant accounts and disclosures and their relevant assertions.

1. **Relevant assertions --** Those financial statement assertions that have a reasonable possibility of containing a material misstatement. (Auditing Standard No. 5 specifically refers to (1) existence or occurrence; (2) completeness; (3) valuation or allocation; (4) rights and obligations; and (5) presentation and disclosure.)

2. **Risk factors --** The auditor should consider risk factors relevant to the identification of significant accounts and disclosures and their relevant assertions, including the nature of the account or disclosure; size and composition of the account, susceptibility to misstatement, volume of activity and complexity of transactions; and changes from the prior period, among others.

C. Understanding likely sources of misstatement:

1. **The auditor should achieve these control objectives --** (a) Understand the flow of transactions related to the relevant assertions; (b) verify that the auditor has identified the points within the company's processes at which a material misstatement could arise; (c) identify the controls that management has implemented to address these potential misstatements; and (d) identify the controls that management has implemented over the company's assets that could materially misstate the financial statements.

2. **Performing walkthroughs --** Following a transaction from origination through the company's processes until reflected in the financial records is frequently the most effective way to achieve the objectives above. (Procedures usually include inquiry, observation, inspection of relevant documentation, and re-performance of controls.)

D. Selecting controls to test - the auditor should test those controls that are important to the conclusion about whether the company's controls sufficiently address the assessed risk of misstatement to each relevant assertion.

VI. **Testing Controls**

A. **Nature of tests of controls --** (From least to most evidence) Inquiry, observation, inspection of relevant documentation, and re-performance of a control:

1. **Testing design effectiveness --** Procedures include inquiry of appropriate personnel, observation of the company's operations, and inspection of relevant documentation (may be addressed by appropriate walkthroughs).

2. **Testing operating effectiveness --** Procedures include inquiry of appropriate personnel, observation of the company's operations, inspection of relevant documentation, and re-performance of the control.

B. **Timing of tests of controls --** Testing controls over a greater period of time provides more evidence than testing over a shorter period of time; testing closer to the date of management's assessment provides more evidence than testing performed earlier in the year.

C. **Extent of tests of controls --** The more extensively a control is tested, the greater the evidence to evaluate the effectiveness of the control.

D. **Roll-forward procedures --** When operating effectiveness has been tested at an interim date, the auditor should consider what additional testing for the remaining period may be necessary.

VII. Evaluating Identified Deficiencies

A. **Basic responsibility --** The auditor must evaluate identified control deficiencies to determine whether, individually or in combination, they constitute material weaknesses as of the date of management's assessment (based on whether there is a "reasonable possibility" that the controls will fail to prevent or detect a material misstatement, not whether a misstatement has actually occurred).

B. **Indicators of material weaknesses --** Examples include (1) identification of fraud involving senior management (whether or not material); (2) restatement of previously issued financial statements; (3) identification by the auditor of a material misstatement of the financial statements in the current period; and (4) ineffective oversight of the company's external financial reporting and internal control by the company's audit committee.

C. **Communicating identified deficiencies**

1. The auditor must communicate (in writing) all **material weaknesses** identified to **management and the audit committee.**

2. The auditor must also communicate (in writing) other **significant deficiencies** identified to the **audit committee.**

3. The auditor should communicate (in writing) all other deficiencies in ICFR to **management** and inform the audit committee that such a communication has been made.

4. If the auditor concludes that the audit committee's oversight of financial reporting and ICFR is ineffective - must communicate that conclusion in writing to the board of directors.

VIII. Reporting on Internal Control over Financial Reporting

A. Separate or combined reports - the auditor may choose to issue a combined report on the financial statements and on ICFR or separate reports.

B. Title of report should include the word "independent" (e.g., "Report of Independent Registered Public Accounting Firm").

C. Combined report - an unqualified report on the financial statements and on ICFR consists of five paragraphs: (1) introduction; (2) scope; (3) definition; (4) inherent limitations; and (5) opinion.

D. Separate reports - the auditor should add an additional paragraph to the audit report on the financial statements that references the report on ICFR; and the auditor should add an additional paragraph to the report on ICFR that references the audit report on the financial statements.

E. Report date - if separate reports are issued, they should be dated the same (the date as of which the auditor has obtained sufficient competent evidence).

F. If one or more material weakness exists - the auditor must express an adverse opinion (unless there is a scope limitation).

1. When expressing an adverse opinion - the auditor's report must include the definition of a material weakness and refer to management's assessment of the material weakness. (If not included in management's assessment, the auditor's report should state that fact.)
2. Should determine the effect the adverse opinion on ICFR has on the opinion on the entity's financial statements.

G. If there is a scope limitation - the auditor should disclaim an opinion or withdraw from the engagement.

Sample Report on the Effectiveness of Internal Control Over Financial Reporting

(Separate From Audit Report on Financial Statements)

<u>Report of Independent Registered Public Accounting Firm</u>

<u>Separate Audit Report on ICFR</u>

(*Introductory paragraph*)

We have audited ABC Company's internal control over financial reporting as of December 31, 20X2, based on (*Identify control criteria, for example, "criteria established in Internal Control - Integrated Framework issued by the Committee of Sponsoring Organizations of the Treadway Commission (COSO)"*). ABC Company's management is responsible for maintaining effective internal control over financial reporting and for its assessment of the effectiveness of internal control over financial reporting, included in the accompanying (*title of management's report*). Our responsibility is to express an opinion on the company's internal control over financial reporting based on our audit.

(*Scope paragraph*)

We conducted our audit in accordance with the standards of the Public Company Accounting Oversight Board (United States). Those standards require that we plan and perform the audit to obtain reasonable assurance about whether effective internal control over financial reporting was maintained in all material respects. Our audit of internal control over financial reporting included obtaining an understanding of internal control over financial reporting, assessing the risk that a material weakness exists, and testing and evaluating the design and operating effectiveness of internal control based on the assessed risk. Our audit also included performing such other procedures as we considered necessary in the circumstances. We believe that our audit provides a reasonable basis for our opinion.

(*Definition paragraph*)

A company's internal control over financial reporting is a process designed to provide reasonable assurance regarding the reliability of financial reporting and the preparation of financial statements for external purposes in accordance with generally accepted accounting principles. A company's internal control over financial reporting includes those policies and procedures that (1) pertain to the maintenance of records that, in reasonable detail, accurately and fairly reflect the transactions and dispositions of the assets of the company; (2) provide reasonable assurance that transactions are recorded as necessary to permit preparation of financial statements in accordance with generally accepted accounting principles, and that receipts and expenditures of the company are being made only in accordance with authorizations of management and directors of the company; and (3) provide reasonable assurance regarding prevention or timely detection of unauthorized acquisition, use, or disposition of the company's assets that could have a material effect on the financial statements.

(*Inherent limitations paragraph*)

Because of its inherent limitations, internal control over financial reporting may not prevent or detect misstatements. Also, projections of any evaluation of effectiveness to future periods are subject to the risk that controls may become inadequate because of changes in conditions, or that the degree of compliance with the policies or procedures may deteriorate.

(*Opinion paragraph*)

In our opinion, ABC Company maintained, in all material respects, effective internal control over financial reporting as of December 31, 20X2, based on (*identify control criteria, for example, "criteria established in Internal Control - Integrated Framework issued by the Committee of Sponsoring Organizations of the Treadway Commission (COSO)"*).

(*Explanatory paragraph*)

We have also audited, in accordance with the standards of the Public Company Accounting Oversight Board (United States), the (*identify financial statements*) of ABC Company and our report dated (*date of report, which should be the same as the date of the report on the effectiveness of internal control over financial reporting*) expressed (*include nature of opinion*).

(Signature)

(City and State or Country)

(Date)

Sample Combined Audit Report on Financial Statements and on the Effectiveness of Internal Control Over Financial Reporting

Report of Independent Registered Public Accounting Firm

Combined Audit Reports on Financial Statements and ICFR

(*Introductory paragraph*)

We have audited the accompanying balance sheets of ABC Company as of December 31, 20X2 and 20X1, and the related statements of income, stockholders' equity and comprehensive income, and cash flows for each of the years in the three-year period ended December 31, 20X2. We have also audited ABC Company's internal control over financial reporting as of December 31, 20X2, based on (*Identify control criteria, for example, "criteria established in Internal Control - Integrated Framework issued by the Committee of Sponsoring Organizations of the Treadway Commission (COSO)"*). ABC Company's management is responsible for these financial statements, for maintaining effective internal control over financial reporting, and for its assessment of the effectiveness of internal control over financial reporting, included in the accompanying (*title of management's report*). Our responsibility is to express an opinion on these financial statements and an opinion on the company's internal control over financial reporting based on our audits.

(*Scope paragraph*)

We conducted our audits in accordance with the standards of the Public Company Accounting Oversight Board (United States). Those standards require that we plan and perform the audits to obtain reasonable assurance about whether the financial statements are free of material misstatement and whether effective internal control over financial reporting was maintained in all material respects. Our audits of the financial statements included examining, on a test basis, evidence supporting the amounts and disclosures in the financial statements, assessing the accounting principles used and significant estimates made by management, and evaluating the overall financial statement presentation. Our audit of internal control over financial reporting included obtaining an understanding of internal control over financial reporting, assessing the risk that a material weakness exists, and testing and evaluating the design and operating effectiveness of internal control based on the assessed risk. Our audits also included performing such other procedures as we considered necessary in the circumstances. We believe that our audits provide a reasonable basis for our opinions.

(*Definition paragraph*)

A company's internal control over financial reporting is a process designed to provide reasonable assurance regarding the reliability of financial reporting and the preparation of financial statements for external purposes in accordance with generally accepted accounting principles. A company's internal control over financial reporting includes those policies and procedures that (1) pertain to the maintenance of records that, in reasonable detail, accurately and fairly reflect the transactions and dispositions of the assets of the company; (2) provide reasonable assurance that transactions are recorded as necessary to permit preparation of financial statements in accordance with generally accepted accounting principles, and that receipts and expenditures of the company are being made only in accordance with authorizations of management and directors of the company; and (3) provide reasonable assurance regarding prevention or timely detection of unauthorized acquisition, use, or disposition of the company's assets that could have a material effect on the financial statements.

(*Inherent limitations paragraph*)

Because of its inherent limitations, internal control over financial reporting may not prevent or detect misstatements. Also, projections of any evaluation of effectiveness to future periods are subject to the risk that controls may become inadequate because of changes in conditions, or that the degree of compliance with the policies or procedures may deteriorate.

(*Opinion paragraph*)

In our opinion, the financial statements referred to above present fairly, in all material respects, the financial position of ABC Company as of December 31, 20X2 and 20X1, and the results of its operations and its cash flows for each of the years in the three-year period ended December 31, 20X2 in conformity with accounting principles generally accepted in the United States of America. Also in our opinion, ABC Company maintained, in all material respects, effective internal control over financial reporting as of December 31, 20X2, based on (*identify control criteria, for example, "criteria established in Internal Control - Integrated Framework issued by the Committee of Sponsoring Organizations of the Treadway Commission (COSO)"*).

(Signature)

(City and State or Country)

(Date)

Auditing Standard No. 6

After studying this lesson, you should be able to:

1. *Understand the auditor's responsibilities under PCAOB Auditing Standard No. 6 to identify issues related to "consistency" involving either a change in accounting principle or a restatement to correct previously issued financial statements.*

I. **"Evaluating Consistency of Financial Statements" --** Approved by the SEC on September 16, 2008.

II. **PCAOB Auditing Standard No. 6 --** Establishes requirements and provides direction for the auditor's evaluation of the consistency of financial statements and the effect of that evaluation on the auditor's report (regarding the second reporting standard of Generally Accepted Auditing Standards).

   A. Identifies two types of issues related to consistency that might affect the auditor's report: (1) a change in accounting principle; and (2) an adjustment to correct a misstatement in previously issued financial statements (i.e., "restatements").

   B. When reporting on two or more periods - evaluate the consistency between those periods and with the prior period, if that prior period is presented along with the financial statements reported on.

III. **Changes in Accounting Principle --** Involving a change from one generally accepted accounting principle to another, including the situation where the accounting principle formerly used is no longer generally accepted.

   A. GAAP is specified by FASB Statement No. 154, "Accounting Changes and Error Corrections." Auditing Standard No. 6 points out that, when a company uses retrospective application to account for a change in accounting principle, the financial statements generally will be viewed as consistent. (However, the previous years' financial statements will appear different from those that the auditor previously reported on.)

   B. When there is a change in accounting principle - the auditor should evaluate whether **(1) the newly adopted principle is GAAP; (2) the method of accounting for the effect of the change conforms to GAAP; (3) the disclosures related to the change are adequate; and (4) the company has justified that the alternative accounting principle is preferable.**

      1. When the four criteria have been met - the auditor should add an explanatory paragraph to the auditor's report to identify the inconsistency.

      2. When the four criteria have not been met - the auditor should treat the matter as a GAAP departure and modify the audit report appropriately.

      3. When an investor uses the "equity method" and the investee has a change in accounting principle that is material to the investor's financial statements - the auditor should add an explanatory paragraph to emphasize the matter.

   C. When there is a change in accounting estimate effected by a change in accounting principle - the auditor should evaluate and report on the matter like other changes in accounting principle.

   D. When there is a change in the reporting entity resulting from a transaction or event, such as the purchase or disposition of a subsidiary - it does not require recognition in the auditor's report. (However, if there is a change in the reporting entity that does not result from such a transaction or event, then an explanatory paragraph would be required.)

IV. **Correction of a Material Misstatement in Previously Issued Financial Statements**

A. The correction of a material misstatement in previously issued financial statements should be recognized in the auditor's report by the addition of an explanatory paragraph.

B. Restatements of previously issued financial statements require related disclosures to be made - the auditor should evaluate the adequacy of the company's disclosures.

V. Change in Classification

A. Changes in classification in previously issued financial statements normally do not require recognition in the auditor's report (unless the change represents a change in accounting principle or the correction of a material misstatement).

B. Accordingly, the auditor should evaluate a material change in financial statement classification (and the related disclosure) to determine whether such a change is also a change in accounting principle or a correction of a material misstatement.

> The auditing requirements under PCAOB Auditing Standard No. 6 are substantially the same as those of the AICPA's clarified auditing standards (specifically, AU 708, "Consistency of Financial Statements." The now-superseded SAS No. 1 (specifically, AU 420, "Consistency of Application of [GAAP]," previously stated that "error correction not involving principle" (e.g., mathematical mistakes, oversight, or misuse of facts) did not have to be identified in the auditor's report. However, the guidance in the clarified auditing standard now treats restatements as an inconsistency that warrants mention in the auditor's report, similar to PCAOB requirements.

Auditing Standard No. 7

After studying this lesson, you should be able to:

1. *Understand the auditor's responsibilities for an "engagement quality review" (and for concurring approval of issuance) under PCAOB Auditing Standard No. 7.*
2. *Know the primary differences between the requirements of PCAOB Auditing Standard No. 7 and the AICPA's Statements on Quality Control Standards (SQCS).*

I. "Engagement Quality Review" Approved by the SEC, January 2010

II. Introduction and Overview

A. Applicability of standard - requires an engagement quality review (and concurring approval of issuance) for engagements conducted under PCAOB standards (1) for an audit and (2) for a review of interim financial information.

B. Objective of the engagement quality reviewer - to perform an evaluation of the significant judgments made by the engagement team and the related conclusions reached and in preparing any engagement report(s).

C. Qualifications of an engagement quality reviewer - (1) must be an "associated person" of a registered public accounting firm; and (2) must have competence, independence, integrity, and objectivity:

1. **"Associated person" of a registered public accounting firm** -- should be able to withstand any pressure from the engagement partner or others and may be someone from outside the firm; if the reviewer is from within the firm, he/she should be a partner or have an equivalent position. (There is no such requirement for a reviewer from outside the firm.)
2. **Competence** -- must be qualified to serve as the engagement partner on the engagement under review.
3. **Objectivity** -- the engagement quality reviewer (and any assisting personnel) should not make engagement team decisions or assume any responsibilities of the engagement team.
4. **"Cooling off" restriction --** the person serving as engagement partner during either of the two audits preceding the audit subject to engagement quality review is not permitted to serve as engagement quality reviewer (unless the registered firm qualifies for a specific exemption to this requirement).

> **Note:**
> "An outside reviewer who is not already associated with a registered public accounting firm would become associated with the firm issuing the report if he or she ... (1) receives compensation from the firm issuing the report for performing the review or (2) performs the review as agent for the firm issuing the report."

III. Engagement Quality Review for an Audit or a Review under PCAOB Standards

A. Engagement quality review process -- to evaluate the significant judgments and conclusions of the engagement team, the engagement quality reviewer should (1) hold discussions with the engagement partner and other members of the engagement team; and (2) review documentation.

B. Evaluation of engagement documentation -- the engagement quality reviewer should evaluate whether the documentation that was reviewed (1) indicates that the engagement team responded appropriately to significant risks; and (2) supports the conclusions reached by the engagement team.

C. Concurring approval of issuance

1. The engagement quality reviewer cannot express such approval if there is any "significant engagement deficiency" (when (a) the engagement team failed to obtain sufficient appropriate evidence; (b) the engagement team reached an inappropriate overall conclusion; (c) the engagement report is not appropriate; or (d) the firm is not independent of its client).
2. The firm cannot give permission to the client to use the engagement report until the engagement quality reviewer provides concurring approval of issuance.

IV. Documentation of an Engagement Quality Review

- **A.** Documentation should contain sufficient information to permit an experienced auditor, having no prior association with the engagement, to understand the procedures performed and conclusions reached by the engagement quality reviewer.
- **B.** Documentation of an engagement quality review should be included in the engagement documentation (and be subject to other PCAOB requirements regarding retention of and changes to audit documentation).

V. Auditing Standard No. 7 Identified Several Differences Relative to AICPA's Statements on Quality Control Standards (SQCS)

- **A.** **Engagement quality review --** SQCS do not require an engagement quality review for any type of engagement, whereas Auditing Standard No. 7 establishes such a requirement.
- **B.** SQCS do not impose a "cooling off" restriction or a requirement that the reviewer must be an associated person of a registered public accounting firm.
- **C.** **Concurring approval of issuance --** SQCS require any engagement quality review performed be completed before the engagement report is released without requiring a concurring approval of issuance.
- **D.** **Documentation retention and changes --** SQCS do not specifically require that engagement quality review documentation must be retained with other engagement documentation and be subject to specific policies regarding retention and changes.

Auditing Standard 8-15

After studying this lesson you should be able to:

1. *Recognize the set of pronouncements that comprise the PCAOB's "risk assessment" project.*
2. *Understand the auditor's fundamental responsibilities associated with the various risk assessment Auditing Standards issued by the PCAOB.*
3. *Know the primary differences between the risk-assessment-related standards of the PCAOB and those of the AICPA.*

I. PCAOB "Risk Assessment Standards" -- The PCAOB issued a suite of eight Auditing Standards comprising their "risk assessment" project in 2010 (approved by the Securities and Exchange Commission in December, 2010). In general, these PCAOB risk assessment standards are remarkably similar to the risk assessment standards previously issued (and now clarified) by the AICPA (Statements on Auditing Standards) and by the International Federation of Accountants (International Standards on Auditing), although a few (mostly minor) differences are identified below.

- **A.** PCAOB Auditing Standard No. 8, "Audit Risk"
- **B.** PCAOB Auditing Standard No. 9, "Audit Planning"
- **C.** PCAOB Auditing Standard No. 10, "Supervision of the Audit Engagement"
- **D.** PCAOB Auditing Standard, No. 11, "Consideration of Materiality in Planning and Performing an Audit"
- **E.** PCAOB Auditing Standard, No. 12, "Identifying and Assessing Risks of Material Misstatement"
- **F.** PCAOB Auditing Standard, No. 13, "The Auditor's Responses to the Risks of Material Misstatement"
- **G.** PCAOB Auditing Standard, No. 14, "Evaluating Audit Results"
- **H.** PCAOB Auditing Standard, No. 15, "Audit Evidence"

II. PCAOB vs. AICPA -- The table below compares those PCAOB risk assessment standards with the corresponding clarified auditing standards issued by the AICPA's Auditing Standards Board.

PCAOB's Risk-Related Standards:	AICPA's (Clarified) Risk-Related Standards:
AS #8, "Audit Risk"	Audit risk is addressed in AU§200, "Overall Objectives of the Independent Auditor and the Conduct of an Audit in Accordance with [GAAS]"
AS #9, "Audit Planning"	AU§300, "Planning an Audit"
AS #10, "Supervision of the Audit Engagement"	(These topics are addressed in AU§300 above)
AS #11, "Consideration of Materiality in Planning and Performing an Audit"	AU§320, "Materiality in Planning and Performing an Audit"
AS #12, "Identifying and Assessing the Risks of Material Misstatement"	AU§315, "Understanding the Entity and Its Environment and Assessing the Risks of Material Misstatement"
AS #13, "The Auditor's Responses to the Risks of Material Misstatement"	AU§330, "Performing Audit Procedures in Response to Assessed Risks and Evaluating the Audit Evidence Obtained"
AS #14, "Evaluating Audit Results"	(These topics are addressed in AU§330 above)
AS #15, "Audit Evidence"	AU§500, "Audit Evidence"

III. **Structural Differences --** These PCAOB Auditing Standards are applicable to integrated audits of an issuer's financial statements and the internal controls over financial reporting - in contrast these AICPA's Statements on Auditing Standards focus solely on audits of non-issuers' financial statements.

IV. **Summaries --** Summaries of the essence of these PCAOB risk assessment standards.

A. **PCAOB Auditing Standard No. 8, "Audit Risk"**

1. Auditor's objective - to conduct the audit of financial statements in a manner that reduces audit risk to an appropriately low level.
2. "Reasonable assurance" means reducing audit risk to an appropriately low level - the auditor must plan and perform the audit to obtain reasonable assurance about whether the financial statements are free of material misstatements due to error or fraud.
3. The auditor should assess the risks of material misstatement at two levels: (1) at the financial statement level (where the risk of material misstatement is pervasive and potentially involves many assertions); and (2) at the assertion level (where the risk of material misstatement involves inherent risk and control risk).

B. **PCAOB Auditing Standard No. 9, "Audit Planning"**

1. Auditor's objective - to plan the audit so that the audit is conducted effectively.
2. "Planning the audit includes establishing the overall audit strategy for the engagement and developing an audit plan, which includes, in particular, planned risk assessment procedures and planned responses to the risks of material misstatement. Planning is not a discrete phase of an audit but, rather, a continual and iterative process that might begin shortly after (or in connection with) the completion of the previous audit and continues until the completion of the current audit."
    a. Overall strategy - involves rather high level audit resource allocation issues involving the scope, timing, and direction of the audit (guides the development of the more specific audit plan).
    b. Audit plan - deals with the planned nature, timing, and extent of the risk assessment procedures, the tests of controls, the substantive procedures, and any other procedures required to comply with PCAOB standards.

3. Engagement partner responsibilities - "The engagement partner is responsible for the engagement and its performance. Accordingly, the engagement partner is responsible for planning the audit and may seek assistance from appropriate engagement team members in fulfilling this responsibility."

C. **PCAOB Auditing Standard No. 10, "Supervision of the Audit Engagement"**

1. Auditor's objective - to supervise the audit engagement so that the work is performed as directed and supports the conclusions reached.
2. The extent of supervision required varies with the engagement's circumstances, including the size and complexity of the company, the nature of the work assigned to engagement personnel, the capabilities of each engagement team member, and the risks of material misstatement. (The extent of supervision should be commensurate with those risks.)
3. Engagement partner responsibilities - "The engagement partner is responsible for the engagement and its performance. Accordingly, the engagement partner is responsible for proper supervision of the work of engagement team members and for compliance with PCAOB standards, including standards regarding using the work of specialists, other auditors, internal auditors, and others who are involved in testing controls."

D. **PCAOB Auditing Standard, No. 11, "Consideration of Materiality in Planning and Performing an Audit"**

1. Auditor's objective - to apply the concept of materiality appropriately in planning and performing audit procedures.
2. The auditor should plan and perform the audit to detect misstatement that, individually or in the aggregate, would result in material misstatement of the financial statements.
3. The auditor should use the same materiality considerations for planning the audit of internal control over financial reporting as for the audit of the financial statements.
4. The materiality level for the financial statements should be expressed as a specified amount to determine the nature, timing, and extent of audit procedures.
5. The auditor should determine tolerable misstatement for purposes of assessing risks of material misstatement at the account or disclosure levels.

E. **PCAOB Auditing Standard, No. 12, "Identifying and Assessing Risks of Material Misstatement"**

1. Auditor's objective - to identify and appropriately assess the risks of material misstatement, thereby providing a basis for designing and implementing responses to the risks of material misstatement.
2. The auditor should perform risk assessment procedures sufficient to provide a reasonable basis for identifying and assessing the risks of material misstatement and designing further audit procedures.
3. These risk assessment procedures should include (a) obtaining an understanding of the company and its environment; (b) obtaining an understanding of internal control over financial reporting; (c) considering information from the client acceptance/retention evaluation, planning activities, prior audits, and other engagements for the company; (d) performing analytical procedures; and (e) inquiring of the audit committee, management, and others within the company about the risks of material misstatement.
4. The auditor should begin by identifying and assessing the risks of material misstatement at the financial statement level and then work down to the significant accounts and disclosures and their relevant assertions.

F. **PCAOB Auditing Standard, No. 13, "The Auditor's Responses to the Risks of Material Misstatement"**

1. Auditor's objective - to address the risks of material misstatement through appropriate overall audit responses and audit procedures.

2. Overall responses - the auditor should consider (a) making appropriate assignments of responsibilities based on capabilities of team members; (b) providing appropriate supervision; (c) incorporating a degree of unpredictability in planned procedures; (d) evaluating the company's selection and application of significant accounting principles (especially in subjective areas); and (e) determining whether it is necessary to make pervasive changes to the nature, timing, and extent of audit procedures.
3. Responses involving the nature, timing, and extent of audit procedures - the auditor should address the assessed risks of material misstatement for each relevant assertion of each significant account and disclosure.
    a. There are two categories of audit procedures performed in response to the assessed risks of material misstatement: (1) tests of controls; and (2) substantive procedures.
    b. The auditor should perform substantive procedures that are responsive to any identified "significant risks" (including fraud risks).
    c. In responding to fraud risks, the auditor should address the risk of management override of controls by examining journal entries, reviewing accounting estimates for biases, and evaluating the business rationale for significant unusual transactions.

G. **PCAOB Auditing Standard, No. 14, "Evaluating Audit Results"**

1. Auditor's objective - to evaluate the results of the audit to determine whether the audit evidence obtained is sufficient and appropriate to support the opinion.
2. The auditor must reach a conclusion as to whether sufficient appropriate audit evidence has been obtained to support the opinion.
3. The auditor should consider all relevant audit evidence (whether it corroborates or contradicts the financial statements) and evaluate the following:
    a. The results of analytical procedures performed as the overall review.
    b. Misstatements (other than "trivial" ones) accumulated during the audit (with emphasis on uncorrected misstatements).
    c. The qualitative aspects of the company's accounting practices, including potential for management bias.
    d. Conditions identified related to fraud risk.
    e. The presentation of the financial statements (including disclosures) relative to the applicable financial reporting framework.
    f. The sufficiency and appropriateness of the evidence obtained.

H. **PCAOB Auditing Standard, No. 15, "Audit Evidence"**

1. Auditor's objective - to plan and perform the audit to obtain appropriate audit evidence that is sufficient to support the opinion.
2. Sufficient appropriate audit evidence.
    a. Sufficiency relates to the QUANTITY of evidence required - the amount of evidence needed increases as the risk of material misstatement increases; the amount of evidence needed decreases as the quality of the underlying evidence increases.
    b. Appropriateness relates to the QUALITY of evidence, which involves (1) relevance and (2) reliability.
3. Financial statement assertions are factual representations that are implicitly or explicitly made by management - the PCAOB identified the five traditional financial statement assertions previously presented in a now-superseded Statement on Auditing Standards.
    a. Existence - that the assets or liabilities exist at a given date or that the recorded transactions have occurred during a given period.

b. Completeness - that there are no omissions of transaction or accounts that should have been recorded.

c. Rights and obligations - that the company has the rights to the assets and the obligations for the liabilities at a given date.

d. Valuation or allocation - that the financial statement elements are presented at appropriate amounts relative to the applicable accounting framework.

e. Presentation and disclosure - that the elements of the financial statements are properly classified, described, and disclosed relative to the applicable accounting framework.

> **Note:** The PCAOB's discussion about these five traditional financial statement assertions is a relatively major difference compared to the AICPA's Statement on Auditing Standards dealing with audit evidence. The SAS presents the discussion of assertions in three categories: (1) account balances at the period end (four assertions); (2) transactions and events during the period (five assertions); and presentation and disclosure (four assertions).
> The Auditing Standards Board replaced an earlier SAS that had focused on the five traditional financial statement assertions in order to make U.S. auditing standards more consistent with International Standards on Auditing.
> The PCAOB AS addressed the alternative treatments of assertions: "The auditor may base his or her work on financial statement assertions that differ from those in this standard if the assertions are sufficient for the auditor to identify the potential misstatements... "

V. Summary of Differences -- Summary of fundamental differences between the PCAOB risk assessment standards and the AICPA Auditing Standards Board risk assessment standards.

A. The PCAOB risk assessment standards apply to integrated audits of issuers (encompassing both the company's financial statements and internal control over financial reporting), whereas the AICPA risk assessment standard apply solely to audits of non-issuers' financial statements.

B. The PCAOB standards tended to provide a bit more specific guidance in certain areas (such as the engagement partner's responsibilities) that were originally addressed in somewhat more general terms in the AICPA standards; however, the AICPA's clarified auditing standards are now very similar to PCAOB auditing standards in these areas.

C. A more significant difference involves the treatment of "assertions" in their respective standards dealing with the topic of audit evidence - the PCAOB focuses on the five traditional financial statement assertions (as presented in an earlier SAS that has since been superseded in an attempt to align U.S. auditing standards more closely with international standards); the resulting current AICPA standard classifies 13 assertions into three categories: (1) account balances at the period end (for which there are four assertions); (2) transactions and events for the period (for which there are five assertions); and (3) presentation and disclosure (for which there are four assertions).

Auditing Standard No. 16

I. **"Communications With Audit Committees"** -- Released by the PCAOB on August 15, 2012 Approved by the SEC on December 20, 2012.

II. **Introduction** -- AS #16 encourages effective *two-way communication* between the auditor and the audit committee. Specifically, it requires the auditor to communicate with a company's audit committee regarding the conduct of an audit and to obtain information from the audit committee relevant to the audit. It also requires the auditor to establish an understanding of the terms of the engagement with the audit committee and to obtain an engagement letter. Communications are required only to the extent that the matters are relevant to the integrated audit, so there may be fewer matters to communicate when auditing a smaller, less complex company.

> **Definitions:**
> *Audit committee*: A committee (or equivalent body) established by and among the board of directors of a company for the purpose of overseeing the accounting and financial reporting processes of the company and audits of the financial statements of the company; if no such committee exists with respect to the company, the entire board of directors of the company.
>
> *Critical accounting estimate*: An accounting estimate where (a) the nature of the estimate is material due to the levels of subjectivity and judgment necessary to account for highly uncertain matters or the susceptibility of such matters to change and (b) the impact of the estimate on financial condition or operating performance is material.
>
> *Critical accounting policies and practices*: A company's accounting policies and practices that are both most important to the portrayal of the company's financial condition and results, and require management's most difficult, subjective, or complex judgments, often as a result of the need to make estimates about the effects of matters that are inherently uncertain.

III. **Objectives** -- The auditor's objectives are to: (1) communicate to the audit committee the auditor's responsibilities regarding the audit and establish an understanding of the terms of the audit engagement with the audit committee; (2) obtain information from the audit committee relevant to the audit; (3) communicate to the audit committee information about the strategy and timing of the audit; and (4) provide the audit committee with timely observations about the audit that are significant.

IV. **Appointment and Retention**

- **A.** Significant issues discussed with management in connection with the auditor's appointment or retention -- The auditor should discuss with the audit committee any significant issues that the auditor discussed with management in connection with the auditor's appointment/retention.
- **B.** Establish an understanding of the terms of the audit.
    1. The auditor should establish an understanding of the terms of the engagement with the audit committee, including the following matters: (a) the objective of the audit; (b) the auditor's responsibilities; and (c) management's responsibilities.
    2. The auditor should provide an engagement letter to the audit committee annually.

V. **Obtaining Information and Communicating the Audit Strategy**

- **A. Obtaining information relevant to the audit** -- The auditor should inquire of the audit committee about matters relevant to the audit, including their knowledge of (possible) violations of laws or regulations.

B. Overall audit strategy, timing of the audit, and significant risks -- The auditor should communicate an overview of the audit strategy (including timing of the audit) and discuss any significant risks identified during the auditor's risk assessment. The auditor should communicate the need for specialized skills or knowledge and plans to use the work of the entity's internal auditors or others (including other CPA firms) in the integrated audit.

VI. Results of the Audit

A. Accounting policies and practices, estimates, and significant unusual transactions -- The auditor should communicate the following matters: (1) *significant* accounting policies and practices; (2) *critical accounting policies and practices* (and the reasons they are considered critical); (3) *critical accounting estimates* (including a description of management's processes, significant assumptions, and significant changes to those processes or assumptions); and (4) significant unusual transactions (matters that are outside the normal course of business). If management communicates any of those matters, the auditor is not required to communicate them again at the same level of detail.

B. Auditor's evaluation of the quality of financial reporting -- The auditor should communicate the following matters:

1. Qualitative aspects of significant accounting policies and practices (including any indications of management bias);
2. Assessment of critical accounting policies and practices;
3. Conclusions regarding critical accounting estimates;
4. Significant unusual transactions (and their business rationale);
5. The conformity of the financial statement presentation with applicable financial reporting framework;
6. Any new accounting pronouncements affecting financial reporting; and
7. Alternative accounting treatments discussed with management.

C. Other information in documents containing audited financial statements -- The auditor should communicate the auditor's responsibilities for *other information* presented in documents containing the audited financial statements.

D. Difficult or contentious matters -- The auditor should communicate any difficult or contentious matters for which the auditor consulted outside the engagement team.

E. Management consultation with other accountants -- The auditor should communicate views about any known instances where management consulted with other accountants about significant accounting or auditing matters.

F. Going concern issues -- The auditor should communicate about the following going concern matters: (1) The conditions or events causing the auditor to have *substantial doubt about the company's ability to continue for a going concern for a reasonable period of time*; (2) the basis for the auditor's conclusion, if the auditor concludes that such substantial doubt is alleviated by management's plans; and (3) if the auditor concludes that substantial doubt remains after considering management's plans, the effect on the financial statements and the auditor's report.

G. Uncorrected and corrected misstatements

1. **Uncorrected misstatements --** The auditor should provide the audit committee with a schedule of uncorrected misstatements that the auditor presented to management, and discuss with the audit committee the basis for the determination that the uncorrected misstatements were immaterial.
2. **Corrected misstatements --** The auditor should communicate those corrected misstatements (other than those that are clearly *trivial*) that were detected by the auditor, and discuss the implications of those matters relative to internal control over financial reporting.

H. **Material written communications --** The auditor should communicate *other material written communications* between the auditor and management.

I. **Departure from the auditor's standard report --** When the auditor expects to modify the opinion or include explanatory language to the audit report (or an explanatory paragraph), the auditor should communicate the reasons for that.

J. **Disagreements with management --** The auditor should communicate any disagreements with management over significant matters, whether or not satisfactorily resolved.

K. **Difficulties encountered in performing the audit --** The auditor should communicate any significant difficulties encountered, such as: (1) significant delays or the unavailability of personnel; (2) unreasonable time pressures to complete the audit; (3) unreasonable management restrictions; and (4) unexpected difficulties in obtaining sufficient appropriate audit evidence.

L. **Other matters --** The auditor should communicate any other matters arising out of the audit that are significant to overseeing the company's financial reporting.

VII. **Form and documentation of communications --** The auditor's communications may be oral or in writing, unless otherwise specified.

VIII. **Timing --** The auditor should communicate all of these required matters to the audit committee on a timely basis and prior to the issuance of the auditor's report.

Auditing Standard No. 17

After studying this lesson you should be able to :

1. *Know the auditor's responsibilities for reporting on supplemental information under PCAOB auditing standards.*
2. *Know the auditor's responsibility for performing audit procedures on supplemental information under PCAOB auditing standards.*
3. *Know the meaning of the term "supplemental information" as used by the PCAOB.*

I. **"Auditing Supplemental Information Accompanying Audited Financial Statements" --** Approved by the SEC: February, 2014

II. **Introduction and Overview**

A. AS #17 was issued primarily because of recent changes in the regulatory environment. For example, the 2010 Dodd-Frank Act gave the PCAOB oversight responsibility for audits of brokers and dealers registered with the SEC. These brokers and dealers are required to file certain schedules of information with the SEC. The previous PCAOB standards on supplemental information (adopted from the AICPA standards in 2003) addressed supplemental information only in "auditor-submitted documents" and did not specify audit procedures to be applied to supplemental information that is filed with a regulatory authority, such as the SEC. AS #17 is applicable to supplemental information, whether it is required by regulatory authorities or provided voluntarily, when audited in connection with financial statements under PCAOB auditing standards.

B. Objective—The auditor's objective is "to obtain sufficient appropriate audit evidence to express an opinion on whether the supplemental information is fairly stated, in all material respects, in relation to the financial statements as a whole."

> **Definition: Supplemental Information:** "Refers to the following information when it accompanies audited financial statements:
>
> a. Supporting schedules that brokers and dealers are required to file pursuant to Rule 17a-5 under the Securities Exchange Act of 1934;
>
> b. Supplemental information (i) required to be presented pursuant to the rules and regulations of a regulatory authority and (ii) covered by an independent public accountant's report on that information in relation to financial statements that are audited in accordance with PCAOB standards; or
>
> c. Information that is (i) ancillary to the audited financial statements, (ii) derived from the company's accounting books and records, and (iii) covered by an independent public accountant's report on that information in relation to the financial statements that are audited in accordance with PCAOB standards."

C. Overview of the performance and reporting requirements associated with AS #17

1. The auditor is required to perform audit procedures specifically to test the supplemental information.
2. The auditor is required to evaluate (a) whether the supplemental information is fairly presented in relation to the audited financial statements; and (b) whether the supplemental information complies with the relevant regulatory requirements (or other criteria, if applicable).

3. The auditor is required to coordinate audit work on the supplemental information with audit work on the related financial statements.

4. The auditor is required to clearly report the auditor's responsibilities and conclusions when reporting on supplemental information.

III. Performing Audit Procedures on the Supplemental Information

A. The nature, timing, and extent of the procedures to be applied to the supplemental information may vary with the circumstances, including the following: (1) the risk of material misstatement; (2) the applicable materiality levels relevant to the information; (3) the audit evidence obtained with respect to the financial statements; and (4) the type of opinion expressed on the financial statements.

B. In performing procedures on the supplemental information, the auditor should:

1. Obtain an understanding of the purpose of the information and the criteria used by management for its presentation;

2. Obtain an understanding of the methods used to prepare the information, evaluate the appropriateness of those methods, and determine whether those methods are consistent with those used in the prior period;

3. Inquire of management about any significant assumptions underlying the presentation of the information;

4. Determine that the information reconciles to the financial statements or other applicable records;

5. Perform procedures to test the completeness and accuracy of the information (if not already tested in connection with the audit of the financial statements);

6. Evaluate whether the information complies with relevant regulatory requirements (or other applicable criteria); and

7. Obtain appropriate management representations: (a) that management acknowledges responsibility for the fair presentation of the information; (b) that management believes the information is fairly stated; (c) that the methods used have not changed from the prior period (if changed, state that the reasons for the changes are appropriate); (d) that the information complies with regulatory requirements or other applicable criteria; and (e) that management believes any underlying assumptions are appropriate.

IV. Evaluation of Audit Results

A. **Overall evaluation** -- The auditor should evaluate whether the information is fairly stated in relation to the financial statements, including whether the information is presented in conformity with regulatory requirements or other applicable criteria.

B. **Accumulated misstatements** -- The auditor should communicate accumulated misstatements to management to give management a chance to make corrections.

C. **Uncorrected misstatements** -- The auditor should evaluate whether uncorrected misstatements are material (based on relevant quantitative and qualitative factors).

V. Reporting on Supplemental Information

A. **Combined or separate reports permitted** -- Unless prohibited by regulatory requirements, the auditor may either issue a separate report on the supplemental information and the financial statements or issue a combined report on both.

B. **Effects of modifications to the report on financial statements** -- The auditor should evaluate whether any modification of the report on the financial statements is relevant to the opinion to be expressed on the supplemental information.

1. **Qualified opinion on the financial statements** -- The auditor should express a qualified opinion on the supplemental information if the basis for the qualification also applies to the supplemental information.

2. **Adverse opinion (or disclaimer) on the financial statements --** The auditor should likewise express an adverse opinion (or disclaimer) on the supplemental information.

PCAOB's Sample (Separate) Report on Supplemental Information:

The (identify supplemental information) has been subjected to audit procedures performed in conjunction with the audit of (Company's) financial statements. The (supplemental information) is the responsibility of the Company's management. Our audit procedures included determining whether the (supplemental information) reconciles to the financial statements or the underlying accounting and other records, as applicable, and performing procedures to test the completeness and accuracy of the information presented in the (supplemental information). In forming our opinion on the (supplemental information), we evaluated whether the (supplemental information), including its form and content, is presented in conformity with (specify the relevant regulatory requirement or other criteria, if any). In our opinion, the (identify supplemental information) is fairly stated, in all material respects, in relation to the financial statements as a whole.

International Auditing Issues

IFAC and International Standards on Auditing

After studying this lesson, you should be able to:

1. *Understand the nature of the International Federation of Accountants (IFAC) and its role as a global standard-setting body in auditing, ethics, public sector accounting, and education.*
2. *Understand the role of IFAC's "International Auditing and Assurance Standards Board" (IAASB) as a global auditing standard-setting body, in general, and the structure of the IAASB's International Standards on Auditing (ISAs), in particular.*
3. *Understand the role of IFAC's "International Ethics Standards Board for Accountants" (IESBA) as a global ethics standard-setting body, which is responsible for IFAC's Code of Ethics for Professional Accountants.*
4. *Understand the primary differences between clarified ISAs and existing PCAOB Auditing (and Interim) Standards and, thereby, the primary differences between ISAs and AICPA Professional Standards.*

I. The International Federation of Accountants (IFAC)

A. Membership

1. IFAC is comprised of more than 150 member and associate organizations, which collectively represent more than 2.5 million accounting professionals globally.
2. U.S. CPAs are represented through the AICPA's membership in IFAC -- individual CPAs cannot be members of IFAC.

B. Brief history

1. IFAC was established in 1977 with the following purposes: (a) to develop and support high quality international standards; (b) to facilitate cooperation among member bodies; (c) to collaborate with other international organizations; and (d) to serve as the primary international spokesperson for the accountancy profession.
2. Over time, IFAC has expanded its focus to become increasingly involved in regulation of the international profession and coordinating interactions among the largest public accounting firms (through the "Forum of Firms" representing more than twenty large firms/affiliations of firms that perform transnational audits), among other activities.

II. IFAC's Role as a Standard-Setting Body -- IFAC has four specific standard-setting boards.

A. The International Auditing and Assurance Standards Board (IAASB)

> **Note:**
> **IFRSs** are issued by the **International Accounting Standards Board** (IASB), which is an independent accounting-standard setter and is not part of IFAC! IFAC is not the global "accounting" standard-setting body.

1. **Purposes --** To set high quality standards related to auditing, review, other assurance services, and quality control; and to facilitate convergence of national and international standards.
2. **Composition of IAASB --** The Board is comprised of eighteen members: ten are nominated by member bodies; three are so-called "public" members; and five are nominated by the "Transnational Auditors Committee" (TAC is the acting executive committee of the "Forum of Firms"); there are also four "observers" (non-voting), including one from the U.S. PCAOB.
3. **Standards issued by the IAASB**

a. **International Standards on Auditing (ISAs) -- Applicable to the audit of historical financial information**; ISAs distinguish professional requirements from explanatory material in each standard (similar to recently issued AICPA Statements on Auditing Standards that are modeled on the structure of ISAs).

b. **Other standards issued by the IAASB --** International Standards on Review Engagements (ISREs) applicable to the review of historical financial information; International Standards on Assurance Engagements (ISAEs) applicable to assurance engagements not involving historical financial information; International Standards on Related Services (ISRSs) applicable to agreed-upon procedures and compilation engagements; and International Standards on Quality Control (ISQCs) applicable to a firm's services under those ISAs, ISAEs, and ISRSs.

4. **Due process --** The IAASB adheres to due process in the issuance of ISAs, which includes issuance of exposure drafts and a period for public comments; a separate "basis for conclusions" is issued for every final pronouncement that addresses comments received.

5. "International Auditing Practice Statements" provide guidance and assistance to practitioners in implementing ISAs (similar Practice Statements are issued with respect to ISAEs and ISRSs).

6. **IAASB's "Clarity Project" --** In line with its commitment to facilitate convergence between national and international standards (and similar to a comparable initiative of the AICPA's Auditing Standards Board), the IAASB initiated a "Clarity Project."

   a. **Purpose of the Clarity Project --** To enhance the quality of practice by making standards as clear/understandable and capable of consistent application as possible.

   b. **Impact on ISAs --** Each ISA specifies an objective and establishes the auditor's responsibilities in relationship to that objective.

7. **Public Interest Oversight Board (PIOB) --** Provides oversight of the IAASB to ensure that IFAC's auditing standards are responsive to the public interest and to enhance investor confidence in these standards.

B. **The International Ethics Standards Board for Accountants (IESBA)**

1. **Purposes --** To set ethical standards and provide related guidance to accounting professionals and to promote good ethical practices globally.

2. Ethical standards issued by the IESBA comprise the Code of Ethics for Professional Accountants; the IESBA also issues Interpretations of the Code of Ethics.

3. **Due process --** The IESBA follows the same due process as the IAASB.

4. **Public Interest Oversight Board (PIOB) --** Provides oversight of the IESBA to ensure that IFAC's ethics standards are responsive to the public interest.

C. The International Public Sector Accounting Standards Board (IPSASB) issues international standards dealing with accounting issues affecting local, regional, and national governmental entities and their constituents. (The Board's pronouncements are called "International Public Sector Accounting Standards.")

D. The International Accounting Education Standards Board (IAESB) issues international standards dealing with accounting education around the world with particular emphasis on (1) the elements of accreditation (including tests of professional competence) and (2) continuing professional education. (The Board's pronouncements are called "International Education Standards.")

III. **Comparison of International Standards on Auditing (ISAs) and the PCAOB's Auditing Standards --** Based on a 2009 study (conducted by the Maastricht Accounting, Auditing and Information Management Research Center on behalf of the European Union).

A. **Objective of the Study --** Identify the primary differences between IFAC's clarified ISAs and the PCAOB Auditing (and Interim) Standards and the effect of those differences on audit practice and the perceptions of financial statement users.

B. The 2009 Maastricht study identified five primary areas where ISAs and PCAOB standards differ in ways that might be significant to auditing:

   1. **Evaluating and reporting on internal control over financial reporting --** PCAOB auditing standards require the auditor to report on internal control over financial reporting in an "integrated audit" (as mandated by the Sarbanes-Oxley Act, specifically Sections 302 and 404); whereas, there is no similar requirement under ISAs for an integrated audit or an expression of opinion on internal control over financial reporting.

   2. **Documentation requirements --** The PCAOB is viewed as somewhat more specific ("prescriptive") in their documentation requirements (for example, an engagement completion memorandum is necessary); whereas, ISA documentation requirements are viewed more generally as a matter of professional judgment.

   3. **Reference to "other auditors" --** PCAOB auditing standards permit the primary auditor to signal a division of responsibility by referring to other auditors; whereas, no such reference is permitted under ISAs.

   4. **Going concern issues --** PCAOB standards focus on the foreseeable future defined as a period not to exceed twelve months; whereas, ISAs are not limited to twelve months in addressing such going concern issues.

C. The 2009 Maastricht study identified minor differences regarding **auditing related party transactions** (ISA requirements are more extensive than PCAOB standards) and **inquiry of a client's attorney** about litigation, etc. (PCAOB requirements are more extensive than ISAs).

D. Other than the differences identified above - the 2009 Maastricht study indicated that there were practically no differences between PCAOB standards and ISAs for other audit-related topics (including materiality, quality control, analytical procedures, confirmations, written representations, sampling, responsibilities for fraud and illegal acts, fair values, subsequent events, the role of an entity's internal audit function, using specialists, audit communications, etc.).

E. The PCAOB "risk assessment" standards issued in 2010 result in additional differences relative to International Standards on Auditing - the most significant difference is that the PCAOB Auditing Standards focus on five traditional financial statement assertions, whereas the ISAs focus on 13 assertions across three categories of assertions (which is consistent with the treatment of the Auditing Standards Board's corresponding Statement on Auditing Standards).

> An article entitled "Auditing Standards Don't Have Far to Converge" (dated August 21, 2009) on WebCPA commented about the 2009 Maastricht study as follows:
>
> "A new study indicates that differences between the international and U.S. auditing standards are fairly negligible and won't present the challenge now facing the convergence of U.S. GAAP with International Financial Reporting Standards.... However, there will remain significant differences because of Sarbanes-Oxley requirements for separate reporting by auditors on internal control over financial reporting."

Code of Professional Conduct

Introduction and Preface

After studying this lesson you should be able to :

1. *Understand the basic organizational structure of the new electronic version of the Code of Professional Conduct.*
2. *Explain the six key principles on which the code is based.*

I. Introduction

A. The AICPA dramatically reorganized the Code of Professional Conduct so that its new electronic format would be easily searchable by members who needed answers regarding their professional responsibilities. The code is available at: http://pub.aicpa.org/codeofconduct. While there were minor substantive changes, most of the changes were organizational. The following materials reflect the new electronic version of the code (which can now be easily updated). Most of the provisions are effective December 15, 2014. Some, mostly those dealing with the Conceptual Framework, are effective December 15, 2015.

B. Two major changes deserve mention in this introduction. First, the code now divides professional responsibilities in terms of the role that members play. Part 1 of the code sets out rules for members in public practice, such as independent auditors. This includes, of course, independence rules but also rules regarding integrity, objectivity, and discreditable acts. Part 2 of the code sets out rules for members in business, such as internal auditors at a corporation. They need not worry about independence rules, and many of the other rules for members in business are identical (or nearly so) to the nonindependence rules that apply to members in public practice. Part 3 sets out rules for other members, such as those who are unemployed or retired, who are expected to avoid discreditable acts.

C. Second, following the lead of the International Federation of Accountants, the AICPA has put into place (effective December 15, 2015), a Conceptual Framework for answering questions that arise that are not answered even by the many detailed code provisions and interpretations. In virtually every subject matter area of the entire code, if there is no clear answer, the Conceptual Framework should be applied.

II. Preface (Part 0)

A. Overview

1. The code is divided into three main parts:

- **a.** Part 1 applies to members in public practice .
- **b.** Part 2 applies to members in business.
- **c.** Part 3 applies to other members.

2. Members serving in multiple roles should choose the most restrictive applicable provisions.

B. Principles and rules of conduct contained in the code are supplemented by:

1. Interpretations

2. Definitions

3. Applications

4. Where applicable, standards promulgated by other bodies such as

- **a.** State certified public accounting (CPA) societies

b. Securities and Exchange Commission

c. Public Company Accounting Oversight Board

d. Government Accountability Office

e. Department of Labor

f. Various taxing authorities

C. Principles of Professional Conduct

1. By voluntarily joining the AICPA, members assume an obligation of self-discipline above and beyond legal requirements.

2. The six major principles "call for "an unswerving commitment to honorable behavior, even at the sacrifice of personal advantage":

   a. "Responsibilities principle. In carrying out their responsibilities as professionals, members should exercise sensitive professional and moral judgments in all their activities."

      i. This principle imposes a continuing responsibility on members to "cooperate with each other to:

         1. "improve the art of accounting,

         2. "maintain the public's confidence, and

         3. "carry out the profession's special responsibilities for self-governance."

   b. "Public Interest principle. Members should accept the obligation to act in a way that will serve the public interest, honor the public trust, and demonstrate a commitment to professionalism."

> **Note:**
> "A distinguishing mark of a profession is acceptance of its responsibility to the public."

   c. "Integrity principle. To maintain and broaden public confidence, members should perform all professional responsibilities with the highest sense of integrity."

      i. "Integrity is measured in terms of what is right and just"; members should always ask "Am I doing what a person of integrity would do?"

   d. "Objectivity and Independence principle. A member should maintain objectivity and be free of conflicts of interest in discharging professional responsibilities. A member in public practice should be independent in fact and appearance when providing auditing and other attestation services."

      i. "Objectivity is a state of mind" that requires:

         1. impartiality,

         2. intellectual honesty, and

         3. freedom from conflicts of interest.

      ii. Only members in public practice must act with independence, but all members performing all services must act with objectivity and integrity.

   e. "Due care principle. A member should observe the profession's technical and ethical standards, strive continually to improve competence and the quality of services, and discharge professional responsibility to the best of the member's ability."

      i. Perfection is not required.

      ii. Competence requires a commitment to continued learning—hence, continuing professional education.

      iii. Members may derive competence from research or consultation with experts.

iv. Due care entails

1. Adequate planning of engagements and

2. Supervision of professional activities for which members are responsible.

f. "Scope and nature of services principle. A member in public practice should observe the Principles of the Code of Professional Conduct in determining the scope and nature of services to be provided."

g. At a minimum, members should:

i. Practice in firms that have good internal quality control procedures,

ii. Use their individual judgments to determine whether the scope and nature of services provided to an audit client would create a conflict of interest, and

iii. Individually assess whether a contemplated activity is consistent with their role as professionals.

	Audit	**Compilation**	**Tax**	**Consulting**
Integrity	Yes	Yes	Yes	Yes
Objectivity	Yes	Yes	Yes	Yes
Independence in Fact	Yes	No	No	No
Independence in Appearance	Yes	No	No	No

D. Definitions

1. Part 0 contains approximately 50 definitions, ranging from "Acceptable Level" to "Threats." This study guide sets out various definitions as they become relevant to the substantive provisions being discussed, but it couldn't hurt to read through the definitions.

Example:
Partner equivalent. A professional employee who is not a partner of the firm but who either (a) has the ultimate responsibility for the conduct of an attest engagement, including the authority to sign or affix the firm's name to an attest report or issue, or authorize others to issue, an attest report on behalf of the firm without partner approval; or (b) has the authority to bind the firm to conduct an attest engagement without partner approval. For example, the professional employee has the authority to sign or affix the firm's name to an attest engagement letter or contract to conduct an attest engagement without partner approval.

Members in Public Practice

MIPPs Introduction and Conceptual Framework

After studying this lesson you should be able to :

1. *Apply the Conceptual Framework to answer questions of professional responsibility that are not clearly answered in the code itself.*

I. Introduction

A. Part 1of the Code of Professional Conduct applies to members in public practice (MIPPs), which includes not only members in firms doing attest work, but also government auditors within a government audit organization.

II. Conceptual Framework -- Where the code's rules and interpretations do not provide a clear answer to a particular situation, members should always apply the threats-and-safeguards Conceptual Framework in order to determine whether **threats** to a member's compliance with the rules (independence and otherwise) can be reduced to an **acceptable level** (defined as "a level at which a reasonable and informed third party who is aware of the relevant information would be expected to conclude that a member's compliance with the rules is not compromised") by application of **safeguards**.

A. There are three main steps to applying the Conceptual Framework:

1. Identify threats
2. Evaluate the significance of the threats
3. Identify and apply safeguards

B. There are seven broad categories of threats:

1. Adverse interest threats. Examples:
   - **a.** Client sues or threatens to sue firm
   - **b.** Subrogee makes claim against firm to recover payments it made to client
2. Advocacy threats. Examples:
   - **a.** Member provides forensic accounting services to client in lawsuit with third party
   - **b.** Firm acts as investment advisor, underwriter, promoter, or registered agent for a client
3. Familiarity threats. Examples:
   - **a.** Member's spouse, parent, sibling, or close friend is employed by the client
   - **b.** Former firm partner joins client in a key position
4. Management participation threats. Example:
   - **a.** Member takes on role of client management
5. Self-interest threats. Examples:
   - **a.** Member has a financial interest in a client that may be affected by outcome of professional services the firm is providing
   - **b.** Firm relies excessively on revenue from a single client
6. Self-review threats. Examples:
   - **a.** Member relies on work product of own firm
   - **b.** Member does client's bookkeeping

    c. Partner in firm was an officer or director of client

  7. Undue influence threats. Examples:

    a. Client threatens to fire firm or to withhold future business unless firm accedes to client's wishes

    b. Client's major shareholder threatens to withdraw or terminate a professional service unless the member reaches desired conclusion

C. Three kinds of safeguards exist.

  1. Safeguards created by the profession, legislation, or regulation. Examples:

    a. Ethics education and training requirements, including continuing professional education (CPE)

    b. Professional standards and threat of discipline

    c. External reviews of a firm's quality controls

    d. Legislation regulating firm's professionals

    e. Licensure requirements

    f. Professional resources, such as ethics hotlines

  2. Safeguards implemented by the client. The client has, for example:

    a. Knowledgeable and experienced managers

    b. Appropriate tone at the top regarding ethics and compliance

    c. Appropriate policies and procedures for compliance and fair reporting

    d. Appropriate ethics policies and procedures

    e. Appropriate governance structure, including an active audit committee

    f. Policies to prevent client from hiring a firm to provide services that would impair independence or objectivity

  3. Safeguards implemented by the firm. Examples:

    a. Strong leadership emphasizing compliance and acting in the public interest

    b. Policies and procedures to implement and monitor engagement quality control

    c. Designation of qualified senior manager to oversee firm's quality control system

    d. An effective internal disciplinary system

    e. Rotation of engagement team senior personnel

    f. Policies precluding partners from being compensated for selling nonattest services to attest client

    g. And so on.

MIPPs Nonindependence Rules

Conflicts of Interest, Directorships, and Gifts

After studying this lesson you should be able to :

1. *Understand and be able to apply the Code of Professional Conduct's rules regarding: a0 General conflicts of interest; b) Members serving on corporate boards; c) Gifts and entertainment (which can pose a threat to member integrity and objectivity).*

I. Conflicts of Interest

A. In evaluating possible conflicts of interest, members should ask: Would a "reasonable and informed third party" conclude that a conflict exists?

B. There are two main types of conflicts:

1. Between interests of two clients

2. Between interests of client on one hand and firm and/or its members on the other.

Example:

1. Simultaneously advising two clients trying to acquire the same company

2. Preparing valuation of assets to two clients who are simultaneously the potential seller and the potential buyer of the same assets

3. Representing both a husband and a wife in a divorce proceeding

4. Advising a client to invest in a business owned by a member or member's relatives

5. Advising a client on acquisition of assets that the firm also seeks to acquire

6. Providing forensic accounting services to one client to assist it in deciding whether to sue another client

7. Providing personal financial planning services to several members of a family or group known to have conflicting interests

8. Referring a client to a service provider that, in turn, refers clients to member under an exclusive arrangement.

C. **Identification --** Before accepting an engagement, members should identify potential conflicts that threaten independence and objectivity, and should continue to monitor as engagement progresses.

1. When **network firms** are involved, members are **not** required to take specific steps to identify conflicts of interest of other network firms but should apply the conceptual framework if they **know or have reason to know** that a conflict exists or might arise.

D. **Evaluation --** When an actual conflict is identified by any member, the Conceptual Framework should be applied and engagements should be refused or terminated if risk of violation is unacceptably high. Safeguards that might reduce threats to an acceptable level include:

1. Implementing mechanisms to prevent unauthorized disclosure of confidential information when providing services to multiple clients with conflicting interests, including use of:

a. Separate engagement teams

b. Policies and procedures to limit access to client files, confidentiality agreements and physical and electronic separation of confidential information

2. Regular review by a senior manager not involved in the engagement

3. Consulting with third parties, such as a professional body or legal counsel.

E. **Disclosure --** Conflicts should be disclosed to clients and affected third parties, even if threats to compliance are at an acceptable level.

1. General disclosure (e.g., "We audit several firms in your industry sector") may suffice.

2. Specific disclosure (e.g., "We advise your closest competitor who would love to have access to your confidential information that we possess") may be needed, however.

F. Documenting the threat-reducing process is wise.

G. Members should always comply with federal (including Internal Revenue Service Circular 230), state, or local provisions that are more restrictive than the code.

II. Director Positions

A. Objectivity is threatened when a member serves as a client entity's director.

B. It is preferable to serve as a mere consultant to a client's board.

C. The Conceptual Framework should be applied to determine whether the threat to objectivity is unacceptably high.

III. Gifts and Entertainment

A. Objectivity and integrity are threatened if the client (including its officers, directors, and 10% shareholders) give gifts or entertainment to the firm or its members (or vice versa).

B. A violation is presumed if:

1. The member receives gifts or entertainment from a client that violate the member's or client's policies or applicable laws and regulations

2. The member knows or is reckless in not knowing of the violation.

C. If no rules are violated, then there is no problem if the gifts or entertainment are "reasonable in the circumstances."

D. Factors in determining reasonableness include:

1. The nature of the gift or entertainment

2. The occasion giving rise to the gift

3. The cost or value of the gift or entertainment.

4. The nature, frequency, and value of other gifts

5. Whether the entertainment was associated with active conduct of the business.

Reporting Income and Subordination of Judgment

After studying this lesson you should be able to :

1. *Understand and be able to apply the new electronic Code of Professional Conduct's provisions regarding how to report income without violating the code.*
2. *Understand how to apply the rules and process governing how to avoid a subordination of judgment.*

I. Preparing and Reporting Income

A. Obviously there would be a violation of the Code if a member has:

1. Made, permitted, or directed another to make materially false and misleading entries in an entity's financial statements or records,

2. Failed to correct misstatements when having the authority to do so, or

3. Signed, permitted, or directed another to sign misleading documents.

II. Subordination of Judgment

A. Assume that members have a disagreement with a superior over how to record potential earnings (or some other issue). The members are not supposed to simply do what the superior wants and subordinate their judgment.

B. The proper procedure is to:

1. Evaluate whether the threat is at an **unacceptable level**, which occurs if the position taken would result in a material misrepresentation or legal violation. If the threat is **not significant**, then nothing further need be done.

2. But if there is such a significant threat, the member should discuss the matter with the supervisor.

3. If discussion with the supervisor does not resolve the difference of opinion, the member should go over the supervisor's head.

4. If, after discussion with people up the chain, the member is still worried that the right thing is not going to be done, the member should, in no particular order, invoke the following safeguards:

a. Determine whether the organization's policies and procedures have any additional requirements for reporting differences of opinion.

b. Determine whether there is a duty to report to external authorities.

c. Consult legal counsel.

d. Fully document the situation.

5. If the member ultimately concludes that the threat of misrepresentation or legal violation cannot be reduced to an acceptable level, he or she should consider quitting the firm and taking appropriate steps to eliminate his or her exposure to subordination of judgment.

6. Although the code does not **require** the member to quit, only to consider it, it goes on to say that "nothing in this interpretation precludes a member from resigning from the organization at any time."

7. Resigning from the firm would not necessarily discharge all obligations, such as to report to regulatory authorities or an external auditor.

Advocacy, Third-Party Service Providers (TSPs), General Standards, and Accounting Principles

After studying this lesson you should be able to :

1. *Understand members' responsibilities regarding basic accounting principles.*
2. *Master the general standards that apply to members.*
3. *Explain and apply the Code of Professional Conducts rules regarding advocacy on behalf of clients and the outsourcing of work to third-party service providers.*

I. Client Advocacy

A. Members doing attest work may not advocate for their attest clients.

B. Members providing nonattest services may advocate for their clients, but should be careful and conservative so as to preserve credibility and avoid the "zealous" advocacy that lawyers often provide.

II. Use of a Third-Party Service Provider (TSP)

A. Outsourcing work to third-party service providers can threaten objectivity or integrity.

B. There is no problem if the third-party service provider provides only **administrative support** (e.g., record storage, software application hosting, authorized e-file transmittal services).

C. If substantive services are outsourced, clients should be notified, preferably in writing, before any confidential information is provided to the third-party service provider.

D. If the client objects, the member should:

1. Not outsource, or
2. Decline the engagement

III. General Standards

A. Members must follow rules set by appropriate bodies, meaning in part:

1. Take on jobs only if you can reasonably expect to complete them with **professional competence**.
2. You need not be perfect but should always exercise **due professional care** when providing all professional services
3. Always **adequately plan and supervise** your provision of professional services.
4. Never render conclusions or recommendations without **sufficient relevant data** to support them.

B. **Competence** means that the member or his/or her staff has appropriate technical qualifications and the member can supervise and evaluate quality of work performed.

1. Decline an engagement unless you have necessary knowledge or can acquire it through research or consultation with others.
2. If you employ a specialist to provide consulting services, you should have the ability to define the tasks and evaluation the results.

C. **Using third-party service providers**

1. Ensure any third-party service providers you use have the required professional qualifications, technical skills, and needed resources.

2. Adequately plan and supervise the third-party service providers' services and obtain the data needed to evaluate the job.

IV. Accounting Principles

A. Follow generally accepted accounting principles (GAAP) and other relevant accounting principles.

B. **Exceptions --** Departure from GAAP is appropriate if the member:

   1. Demonstrates that due to unusual circumstances, following GAAP would mislead

   2. Describes:

      a. The departure,

      b. Its approximate effects,

      c. The reasons why compliance with GAAP would mislead.

C. Circumstances justifying departure include:

   1. New legislation

   2. Evolution of a new form of business.

D. Circumstances **not** justifying departure include:

   1. An unusual degree of materiality

   2. Conflicting industry practice.

E. Departure from GAAP is permitted when other accounting principles apply, such as:

   1. Financial reporting frameworks generally accepted in foreign country

   2. Frameworks prescribed by contract

   3. Other special- purpose frameworks required by a law or by a domestic or foreign regulatory agency.

Discreditable Acts

This part mostly surveys the discreditable acts, some of which are covered in more detail elsewhere (such as the confidentiality duty). But it dives into detail regarding the fairly complicated rules regarding a member's obligation to produce accounting records pursuant to a client's request.

After studying this lesson you should be able to :

1. *Understand the (nonexclusive) list of acts that the Code of Professional Conduct deems to be discreditable acts by members in public practice.*

I. **Discreditable Acts --** Members shall not commit discreditable acts, including:

   A. Discrimination and harassment in employment practices.

   B. Solicitation or disclosure of CPA Exam questions and answers.

   C. Failure to file a tax return (including one's one personal return or his or her firm's) or failure to pay a tax liability.

   D. Negligence in the preparation of financial statements or records.

   E. Material departure from the audit standards of government bodies, commissions, or other regulatory agencies.

   F. Failure to follow additional government standards over and above generally accepted accounting standards where applicable.

   G. Improper use of indemnification and limitation of liability provisions in violation of regulatory requirements.

   H. Confidential information obtained from employment or volunteer activities. (More detail in the Advertising and Confidentiality lesson).

   I. False, misleading, or deceptive acts in promoting or marketing professional services.

   J. Use of the CPA credential in violation of rules and regulations.

   K. Records requests. (more detail below).

   L. Removing client files or proprietary information from a firm after termination.

   M. Use of confidential information obtained from a prospective client or nonclient without consent.

   N. **Records Requests**

      1. **Four categories of records**

         a. **Client-provided records** are records given by the client to the member.

         b. **Member-prepared records** are those the member was not specifically engaged to prepare and are not in the client's books and records, rendering the client's financial information incomplete. Example: adjusting, closing, combining or consolidating journal entries and supporting schedules and documents that the member proposed or prepared as part of an engagement.

         c. **Member's work products** are deliverables set forth in the engagement letter, such as a tax return.

         d. **Working papers** are all other items prepared solely for purposes of the engagement, including items prepared by both the member (e.g., audit programs, analytical review schedules, and statistical sampling and analysis) and the client (e.g., papers prepared at the member's request and reflecting testing or other work done by the member).

2. **Proper treatment of requests from client**
    a. **Client-provided records** should be delivered to the client at the client's request, even if the client has not paid its bill to the member.
    b. **Member-prepared records** related to a completed and issued work product should be delivered to the client at the client's request, **except** that they may be withheld if fees are due for that specific work product.
    c. **Work products** should be delivered to the client at the client's request, except that they may be withheld under four circumstances:
        i. Fees are due for the specific work product
        ii. The work product is incomplete
        iii. To comply with professional standards (e.g., withholding an audit report because of unresolved audit issues)
        iv. If threatened or outstanding litigation exists concerning the engagement or the member's work.
    d. **Working papers** are the member's property and need not be provided to the client (unless some regulation or contractual provision requires production).
3. Members may charge a reasonable fee for the time and expense incurred in producing records.
4. Members need not convert records that are not in electronic format to electronic format.
5. Sometimes state laws are more demanding of accountants, and those laws must be followed.
6. Generally, client requests should be honored within **45 days**.

Fees

After studying this lesson you should be able to :

1. *Understand how members in public practice are supposed to handle contingent fees (mostly by avoiding them).*
2. *Understand how members in public practice are supposed to handle commissions and referral fees (mostly by avoiding them).*

I. Contingent Fees

A. Members shall not receive contingent fees **for any service** performed for a client for whom he or she performs any of the following attest services:

   1. A financial statement audit or review,

   2. A financial statement compilation reasonably expected to be used by a third party that does not disclose a lack of independence, or

   3. An examination of prospective financial information.

B. Nor may a member prepare an original or amended tax return or claim for a tax refund for a contingent fee for **any client**, even nonattest clients.

C. The definition of a **contingent fee** ["a fee established for the performance of any service pursuant to an arrangement in which no fee will be charged unless a specified finding or result is attained, or in which the amount of the fee is otherwise dependent upon the finding or result of such service"] excludes fees "fixed by courts or other public authorities, or, in tax matters, if determined based on the results of judicial proceedings or the finding of government agencies."

D. A member may do tax work for nonattest clients in exchange for contingent fees if Internal Revenue Service rules are not to the contrary (which they sometimes are).

E. Examples of some permitted contingent fees in the tax area include:

   1. Representing a client before a revenue agent examining the client's income tax return.

   2. Filing an amended federal or state income tax return claiming a refund based on a tax issue that is the subject of a test case involving a different taxpayer.

   3. Filing an amended federal or state income tax return (or refund claim) claiming a tax refund in an amount that will be examined by a tax authority, such as the Joint Committee on Taxation.

   4. Helping a client obtain a private letter ruling or influencing the drafting of a regulation or statute.

F. Contingent fees are not permitted if a member prepared an amended return claiming a refund because of an error in the original return.

G. The code contains additional rules regarding services performed by a member's spouse for a contingent fee and contingent fees in connection with investment advisory services that are not covered here.

II. Commissions and Referral Fees

A. Referral fees and commissions are prohibited for attest clients.

B. For nonattest clients, they are permitted, but must be disclosed.

C. A member's spouse may receive a commission from the member's attest client, so long as the spouse's activities are separate from the member's practice and the member is not significantly involved in the spouse's activities.

D. Members taking title to a product and assuming risks of ownership may resell the product to a client at a profit without disclosure.

E. Similarly, members may subcontract services to third parties and mark up the cost of the services to the client without this being considered a commission.

Advertising and Confidentiality

After studying this lesson you should be able to :

1. *Explain and apply the relatively straightforward code restrictions on advertising.*
2. *Explain and apply the relatively more complicated rules on the confidentiality obligation that members in public practice owe to clients.*

I. Advertising

A. Members are responsible not only for their own promotional efforts, but also for those of third parties if they are asked to perform professional services for the client or customer of a third party.

B. Promotional efforts are a discreditable act if they are false, misleading, or deceptive (i.e., if they contain any claim that would likely cause a reasonable person to be misled), which would be the case if they:

1. Create false or unjustified expectations of favorable results
2. Imply the ability to influence any court, tribunal, regulatory agency or similar body
3. Contain a representation that the member will perform services for stated fees when it is likely at the time that the fees will be substantially increased.

II. Confidential Information

A. General rule -- A member in public practice shall not disclose confidential client information (defined as "any proprietary information pertaining to the employer or any organization for whom the member may work in a volunteer capacity that is not known to be available to the public and is obtained as a result of such relationships") without the specific consent of the client.

1. It is a discreditable act to inappropriately disclose confidential client information.
2. Members should take reasonable steps to ensure that staff members do not improperly disclose confidential information.
3. The confidentiality duty survives the employment relationship.

B. Exceptions -- Disclosures allowed where:

1. The client consents.
2. Disclosure is permitted by law **and authorized by the employer**.
3. Disclosure is **required by law**, for example, to:
   a. Comply with a validly issued and enforceable subpoena or summons
   b. Inform appropriate public authorities of violations of the law
4. Members may have responsibility or right to disclose the information, when not prohibited by law, to:
   a. Initiate an ethics complaint with the American Institute of Certified Public Accountants (AICPA), a state board of accountancy, and so on,
   b. Comply with professional standards and other ethics requirements
   c. Report potential concerns regarding questionable accounting, auditing, or other matters to the employer's confidential complaint hotline or those charged with governance

5. Disclosure is permitted on behalf of the employer to:
    a. Obtain financing from lenders
    b. Communicate with vendors, clients, and customers
    c. Communicate with the external accountant, attorneys, regulators, and others

C. Members should be sensitive to disclosing a client's confidential information when providing services to its competitors.

D. If taking on a new client would likely lead to disclosure of confidential information from an existing, identifiable client, the member should not take on new client without informed consent from the existing client.

E. When a member withdraws from an engagement due to, say, irregularities in a client's tax return, the member should, if contacted by a potential successor firm, suggest that the potential successor firm contact the client to ask permission to discuss all matters freely with the successor .

F. If a member prepares a tax return for a married couple, both are clients, so if during a divorce one spouse directs the member to withhold joint tax information from the other, the member may provide information to both spouses. When receiving conflicting directions from the spouses, the member should seek an attorney's advice.

G. When outsourcing work to a third-party service provider (TSP), a member should do one of the following **before** disclosing confidential information:
    1. Bind the third-party service provider contractually to maintain confidentiality and ensure that the third-party service provider has effective procedures in place.
    2. Obtain specific consent from the client.

H. Members involved in a peer review must keep information they receive confidential and not use it for their advantage.

I. If a third party, such as a trade association or member of academia, asks a member to disclose confidential information for purposes of publication or the like, the member should obtain the client's specific consent, preferably in writing, before disclosing.

J. Members who are directors of organizations must be cautious, because their fiduciary duty to the organization might conflict with their duty to clients who might, for example, be customers of the organization. The threats-and-safeguards conceptual framework should be utilized.

K. Disclosing clients' names is permissible, unless to do so discloses confidential information. Example: where the member does primarily bankruptcy work and disclosing clients' identities signals that clients are in financial difficulty.

Form of Organization and Names

After studying this lesson you should be able to :

1. *Explain what names they may use for denominating their firms.*
2. *Explain and apply the code's rules regarding what form of organization members in public practice may practice in.*

I. Form of Organization

A. Basic rules

1. Members in public practice may practice only in a form of organization permitted by law.
2. Members in public practice may not practice under misleading firm name.
3. Names of past owners may be included in the name of a successor firm.
4. A firm may not designate itself as "Members of the AICPA" unless *all* its CPA owners are members of the AICPA.

B. Ownership of a separate business

1. A member may own an interest in a separate business that performs accounting, tax, or consulting services, but if the member *controls* the separate business, then its owners and professional employees must comply with the code for issues such as commissions and referral fees. And regarding an attest client, independence rules would have to be complied with as well.
2. But if the member's interest is not a controlling one, then the code's provisions apply to him but not to the separate firm or its employees.

C. Partner designation

1. Only members of a firm who are legally partners should use the designation "partner."

D. Responsibility for nonmember practitioners

1. If a member becomes an employee of a firm made up of one or more nonmembers, he or she still must comply with the code. And if the member is a partner in the firm, he or she is responsible or the firm's professional employees.

E. *Attest engagement performed with a former partner*

1. Two former partners may continue to jointly perform an attest engagement, but to make it clear that a partnership no longer exists, they should present their report on plain paper (with no letterhead).

F. Alternative practice structures

1. If a firm does attest work,
   a. CPAs must own a majority of its financial interests.
   b. CPAs must remain responsible, financially and otherwise, for a firm's attest work.
2. CPAs are responsible for compliance with laws and regulations, for enrollment in an AICPA-approved practice monitoring program, for compliance with independence rules, and for compliance with all other applicable standards within their firms.

II. Firm Name

A. If two firms merge, they may use in the newly formed firm's name the name of retired or other partners in either or both of the former firms.

B. A CPA member who is in partnership with non-CPAs may sign reports in the firm's name and also affix the designation "CPA" to his or her own signature if it is clear that the firm is not holding itself out as entirely comprised of CPAs.

C. No misleading name that causes confusion about the legal form of the firm or its owners' identities should be used.

D. Firms within a network may share a common brand or common initials as part of their firm name without misleading. To be part of a network, the firms should share one or more of the following with other network firms:

1. Common control among the firms.
2. Profits or costs.
3. Common business strategy.
4. Significant portions of professional resources.
5. Common quality control policies and procedures.

MIPPs Independence Rules

Introduction to MIPPs Independence Rules

After studying this lesson you should be able to :

1. *Understand the big picture regarding the independence obligations of members in public practice and be able to answer: a) what are the threats to independence; b) who must comply with the rules; c) what time period is relevant?*

I. Introduction

A. Members in public practice (MIPPs) shall be independent when performing attest services.

B. If the code and its interpretations do not resolve independence issues, the **Conceptual Framework should be applied**.

C. **Threats and safeguards**

1. The "threats" to independence detailed in the code are very much the same as the threats to integrity and objectivity discussed elsewhere in these materials: adverse interest threats, advocacy threats, familiarity threats, management participation threats, self-interest threats, self-review threats, and undue influence threats.

2. The "safeguards" that may be applied to reduce the threats to independence come from the same three sources as those relevant to integrity and objectivity:

a. The profession, legislation, or regulation

b. The attest client

c. The firm

D. The threats to independence (adverse interest, advocacy, etc.) are concentrated in four areas:

1. **Financial relationships --** Example: An attest partner should not own stock in an audit client

2. **Employment relationships --** Example: Attest partners should not be on an audit client's board of directors

3. **Family relationships --** Example: An attest partner should not audit a client whose chief executive officer is the partner's spouse.

4. **Consulting relationships --** Example: An attest firm should not provide internal audit services to an attest client.

E. **Time period --** Independence rules must be followed when relationships exist during:

1. The period covered by the financial statements

2. The period of the professional engagement

F. "Covered members" must comply with the independence rules for financial interests (and many others):

1. An individual on the attest engagement team ("team member")

2. An individual in a position to influence the attest engagement

3. A partner, partner equivalent (defined as "a person who is not a partner of the firm but either has the ultimate responsibility for the conduct of an attest engagement, or has the authority to bind the firm to conduct an attest engagement without partner approval"), or manager who provides more than 10 hours of nonattest services to the attest client within any fiscal year ("10-hour person")

4. A partner or partner equivalent in the office in which the lead attest engagement partner or partner equivalent practices in connection with the attest engagement ("other partner in office")
5. The firm, including the firm's employee benefit plans
6. An entity whose operating, financial, or accounting policies can be controlled by any of the individuals or entities described in items (1) through (5) or two or more such individuals or entities if they act together.

Network Firms and Affiliates

After studying this lesson you should be able to :

1. *Understand and be able to apply the independence rules regarding network firms that band together to increase their competitiveness vis-à-vis the Big Four and other competitors.*
2. *Understand the rules regarding affiliates of clients. Obviously, if auditors cannot own a direct and material financial interest in an attest client, they also probably should not own a direct and material financial interest in a firm that controls the client or a firm controlled by the client.*

I. Affiliates

A. Independence problems can arise if covered members, while not having a financial, consulting, employment, and so on, relationship with the attest client, have such a relationship with an "affiliate" of the client.

B. The code sets out numerous examples of such "affiliates," including:

1. An entity that a client can control.
2. An entity in which a client has a direct and material financial interest.
3. An entity that controls a client when the client is material to such entity.
4. An entity with a direct and material financial interest in the client when that entity has significant influence over the client.
5. A sister entity of a client if the client and sister entity are each material to the entity that controls both.
6. A trustee that is deemed to control a trust financial statement attest client that is not an investment company.
7. The sponsor of a single employer employee benefit plan financial statement attest client.

C. Although there are significant exceptions (not covered here), in general, covered members must abide by independence rules for both their attest clients and their clients' affiliates. There are similar rules (and exceptions) when a firm audits some units, but not all, of related governmental agencies.

Reissues, Engagement Letters, ADR, and Unpaid Fees

After studying this lesson you should be able to :

1. *Explain and apply rules regarding when no longer independent firms can put their names on a report that was signed when they were independent.*
2. *Explain and apply rules regarding what an engagement letter may contain without impairing independence.*
3. *Explain and apply rules regarding when an engagement letter properly mandates alternative dispute resolution.*
4. *Explain and apply rules regarding under what circumstances unpaid fees endanger independence.*

I. Reissued Reports

A. Covered members or their firms that were independent when they first issued an audit report may reissue that report or consent to its incorporation by reference, even if they are no longer independent, so long as they do not perform new procedures that would require updating the date (or "dual dating") of the original report.

B. In this connection, it is acceptable if necessary to assess the effect of recent facts on the original report to:

1. Make inquiries of successor auditors
2. Read subsequent financial statements
3. Undertake similar procedures

II. Engagement Contractual Terms

A. Although the Securities and Exchange Commission (SEC) and other regulators disapprove of engagement contracts that indemnify auditors for the effects of their own mistakes, it is okay for an engagement letter to require an attest client to indemnify or hold harmless a member firm for liability and costs **resulting from knowing misrepresentations by the client's management**.

B. It would impair independence for a covered member to agree to indemnify an attest client for losses resulting from the client's own acts.

III. Alternative Dispute Resolution

A. Engagement letters may require use of alternative dispute resolution (ADR) to resolve disagreements with clients.

B. However, if alternative dispute resolution is initiated, binding arbitration is sufficiently similar to litigation that it could place the member in public practice and the client in positions of material adverse interests and thereby impair independence, so the Conceptual Framework should be applied.

IV. Unpaid Fees

A. A member in public practice (MIPP) may not sign a current-year audit report if it has unpaid fees from the client for services provided more than one year prior.

B. Fees are "unpaid" even if:

1. They are unbilled

2. The client has issued to the firm a note receivable.

C. If the client is in bankruptcy, this rule does not apply.

Financial Interests

Overview and Unsolicited Financial Interests

After studying this lesson you should be able to :

1. *Explain and apply the rules that govern a situation where a financial interest unexpectedly comes the way of a member in public practice.*
2. *Know that members in public practice may not own direct or material indirect interests in an attest client.*
3. *Recognize the terms that are important in understanding the financial interests that can cause independence problems for an attest firm.*

I. **Overview --** If a covered member has or is committed to acquire any direct (whether material or not) or any material indirect financial interest in an attest client, independence is impaired. Only if interests are both indirect and immaterial is independence not impaired.

II. **Definitions**

   A. **Financial interest --** Includes ownership (or an obligation to obtain ownership) in equity, debt, or derivatives issued by an entity.

   B. **Direct financial interest --** An interest:

      1. Owed directly (even if managed by others)
      2. Under one's control (even if managed by others)
      3. Beneficially owned through an investment vehicle, estate, trust, or other intermediary when the beneficiary either:

         a. Controls the intermediary or
         b. Has the authority to supervise or participate in the intermediary's investment decisions.

   C. **Indirect financial interest --** An interest beneficially owned through an investment vehicle, estate, trust, or other intermediary when the beneficiary neither:

      1. Controls the intermediary nor
      2. Has the authority to supervise or participate in its investment decisions.

   D. **Beneficial ownership --** Occurs when an individual or entity is not the record owner but has a right to some or all of the underlying benefits of ownership, such as to:

      1. Direct the voting
      2. Dispose of the interest
      3. Receive its economic benefits

III. **Financial Interests --** These rules about financial interests normally apply only to "covered members"; however, even if a partner or professional employee of a firm is not a covered member, that person (and his or her immediate family, or any group of such persons acting together) cannot own more than 5% of a client's ownership interests without impairing independence.

IV. **Unsolicited Financial Interests**

   A. If covered members receive or learn they will receive an unsolicited financial interest in an attest client (perhaps through gift or inheritance), independence will not be impaired if they dispose of the interest as soon as practicable but no later than **30 days**.

B. If the covered member does not yet have the right to dispose of the interest (perhaps a relative who wrote a will is still alive), independence will not be impaired if:

1. The member does not participate on the attest engagement team
2. The interest is not material to the covered member.

Mutual Funds and Retirement Plans

After studying this lesson you should be able to :

1. *Apply those rules in order to avoid independence problems arising from personal investments in mutual funds retirement plans.*
2. *Understand the rules to avoid independence problems arising from personal investments in mutual funds retirement plans.*

I. Mutual Funds

A. A covered member who owns shares in a mutual fund has a direct financial interest in the fund itself.

B. If the member owns 5% or less of the outstanding shares of a **diversified** mutual fund, the interest in the underlying investments of the fund is **indirect**. Immaterial and indirect interests do not impair independence.

C. However, if the covered member owns more than 5% of a diversified fund's shares **or** owns a financial interest in an **undiversified** fund, then the member must evaluate the fund's underlying investments to determine whether he or she holds a material indirect financial interest in any of the underlying investments.

D. The code gives this illustration:

> "If:
> Chapter 1 :a nondiversified mutual fund owns shares in attest client Company A,
> Chapter 2 :the mutual fund's net assets are $10,000,000,
> Chapter 3 :the covered member owns 1% of the outstanding shares of the mutual fund, having a value of $100,000, and
> Chapter 4 :the mutual fund has 10% of its assets invested in Company A,
>
> then the indirect financial interest of the covered member in Company A is $10,000 and this amount should be measured against the covered member's net worth (including the net worth of his or her immediate family) to determine if it is material."

II. Retirement, Savings, Compensation, or Similar Plans

A. If covered members or their immediate family members (IFMs) self-direct their investments into such a plan or have the ability to supervise **or** participate in the plan's investment decisions, then the financial interests held by the plan are direct financial interests that impair independence even if they are immaterial.

B. Two examples:

1. A covered member is trustee of a retirement plan and supervises its investments, which include shares of an attest client.
2. A covered member participates in a retirement plan and has discretion to direct its investments, which include shares of an attest client.

C. If covered members (or their immediate family members) do not self-direct or supervise or participate in a plan's investment decisions, the underlying investments are **indirect** and therefore do not create independence issues unless they are material.

D. When a **defined benefit plan** is involved, interests held by the plan are not interests held by the covered members unless the covered members (or their immediate family members) are trustees of the plan or otherwise have the ability to supervise or participate in the plan's investment decisions.

E. Allocated shares held in an employee stock option plan are beneficially owned by the covered members but are indirect interests **until** the members have the right to dispose of them. At that point, they become direct financial interests.

Partnerships, 529s, Trust and Estates, Employee Benefit Plans

After studying this lesson you should be able to :

1. *Understand how to minimize problems through trusts and estates.*
2. *Understand how to minimize problems in employee benefit plans.*
3. *Understand how to minimize problems in 529 plans.*
4. *Understand how to minimize problems in relation to investments in partnerships and limited liability corporations.*

I. Partnerships and Limited Liability Corporations (LLCs)

A. **General partnership --** A general partner (GP) has authority to influence investments, so a general partner's financial interests in both the partnership itself and its underlying investments are **direct**.

B. **Limited partnership**

C. A general partner has authority to influence investments, so a general partner's financial interests in both the limited partnership itself and its underlying investments are **direct**.

D. A limited partner's interest in the limited partnership is direct, but usually he or she will not have influence over its investments so this partner's financial interest in its underlying investments will be **indirect**.

   1. If the limited partner has authority to supervise or participate in investment decisions or the ability to replace the general partner(s), then his or her interest in the underlying investments will be direct .

E. **Limited liability companies (LLCs)**

   1. If a limited liability company is member-managed, then it is sufficiently like a general partnership that members' interests in both the firm and its underlying investments are direct.
   2. If a limited liability company is agent-managed, then members are more like limited partners and their interests in the underlying investments are viewed as indirect unless the members have the authority to control the limited liability company or to supervise or participate in its investments.

II. Section 529 Plans

A. **Prepaid tuition plans --** Owners of a 529 account used to prepay tuition have a direct interest in the plan but only an indirect interest in its underlying investments. Owners of such plans are essentially buying tuition credits. The state has an obligation to provide the education regardless of the investments' performance.

B. **B. Savings plans --** Owners of these accounts have a direct financial interest in both the plan and its investments because they may decide in which sponsor's 529 savings plan to invest and can determine before investing which firms the plan will investe in.

III. Trusts and Estates

A. The fact that a covered member is asked to serve as trustee of a trust or executor of an estate does not by itself create an independence problem if an attest client's shares are owned by the trust or estate. However, there is a problem if:

   1. The covered member has the ability to make investment decisions for the trust or estate

2. The trust or estate owns or is committed to acquiring more than 10% of the attest client's ownership interests
3. The value of the trust's or estate's ownership interest in the client exceeds 10% of its total assets

B. **Grantor --** If a covered member acts as a grantor to set up a trust, its investments are **direct** financial interests if:

1. The covered member has the ability to amend or revoke the trust
2. The covered member has authority to control the trust
3. The covered member has the ability to supervise or participate in the trust's investment decisions
4. The underlying trust investments ultimately will revert to the covered member as the grantor

C. **Beneficiary --** If a covered member is a beneficiary of a trust, then the covered member's interest in it is direct and his or her interest in the trust's underlying investments is indirect, unless the covered member controls the trust or supervises or participates in its investment decisions, in which case the interest becomes direct.

D. **Blind trust --** Because the investments ultimately will revert to the grantor who typically retains the right to amend or revoke, both a blind trust **and** its underlying investments are considered to be direct financial interests of the grantor.

IV. Participation in Employee Benefit Plans (EBP)

A. Independence is impaired if a covered member participates in an employee benefit plan that is an attest client or sponsored by one. Two exceptions apply:

1. When a covered member is an employee of a government organization that sponsors an employee benefit plan and the covered member is required by law to audit the plan, then it is acceptable to do so if all of the following safeguards are in place:
    a. The covered member is required to participate in the plan as a condition of employment
    b. The plan is offered to all employees in comparable positions
    c. The covered member is not a director, officer, employee, promoter, or the like of the plan
    d. The covered member has no influence or control over the investment strategy, benefits, or other management activities of the plan.
2. When the covered member formerly was associated with an attest client but is no longer, then independence is not impaired.

Depository Accounts, Brokerage Accounts, and Insurance Policies

After studying this lesson you should be able to :

1. *Avoid independence problems that might arise from investing in the stock market using a stockbroker.*
2. *Avoid independence problems that might arise from auditors using bank accounts and insurance policies.*

I. Depository Accounts

A. Firm -- Firms may maintain depository accounts at a bank that is an attest client if they conclude that the likelihood is remote that the bank will experience financial difficulties.

B. Individual -- Individual covered members may maintain such accounts if any of three conditions is met:

1. The balance in the depository account is fully insured, OR
2. Any uninsured amounts were not material to the covered member's worth, OR
3. If uninsured accounts are considered material, they are reduced to an immaterial amount within 30 days of becoming material.

II. Brokerage Accounts

A. A covered member's brokerage account at an attest client broker-dealer would **not** impair independence only if **both** of the following apply:

1. The attest client's services were rendered under the attest client's normal terms, procedures, and requirements
2. Any covered member's assets subject to the risk of loss are immaterial to the covered member's net worth.
   - **a.** In determining risk of loss, the question is not whether the assets' market value might decline but whether the client might become insolvent or commit fraud. Protection by regulators and insurance are relevant factors in determining risk of loss.

III. Insurance Policies

A. An insurance policy is not a financial interest unless it offers an investment option.

B. If there is an investment option, there would still not be an independence problem if the covered member bought the policy under normal terms and conditions, unless the covered member had either:

1. The ability to select the policy's underlying investments
2. The authority to supervise or participate in the investment decision and the covered member invested in an attest client.

Loans, Leases, and Business Relationships

After studying this lesson you should be able to :

1. *Understand how to minimize the independence complications that might arise for members in public practice from: a) borrowing money; b) leasing (and leasing out) real estate; c)entering into various business relationships, such as co-ownership.*

I. Loans

A. If a covered member borrows from (or loans to) an attest client or any of its officers, directors, or 10% owners, there is likely an independence problem, especially if the client is not a lending institution.

B. If the attest client is a lending institution making a loan to covered members or their immediate family members, independence would not be impaired if it is (a) an immaterial unsecured loan, (b) a home mortgage, or (c) a secured loan, so long as **all** of these safeguards are met:

1. Normal lending procedures, terms, and requirements applied
2. The loan occurred before the lending institution become an attest client, or came from a lending institution for which independence was not required and later sold to an attest client
3. Loans are kept current, and terms are not altered by extending maturity date, lowering interest rate, and so on
4. The estimated fair value of the collateral equals or exceeds the outstanding balance; any deficit is not material to the covered member's net worth

C. If a covered member keeps payments current and otherwise complies with loan or lease terms, these also do **not** impair independence:

1. Auto loans and leases collateralized by the car
2. Loans fully collateralized by cash surrender value of an insurance policy
3. Loans fully collateralized by cash deposits at the same lending institutions (e.g., passbook loans)
4. Aggregate outstanding balances from credit card and overdraft reserve accounts of $10,000 or less

II. Leases

A. Capital leases (leases to own) impair independence.

B. Operating lease arrangements do not impair independence if all of these safeguards are met:

1. The lease meets the generally accepted accounting principles criteria for an operating lease
2. The terms and conditions are comparable with similar leases
3. All amounts are paid in accordance with the terms of the lease

III. Business Relationships

A. **Cooperative ventures --** Cooperating with an attest client to provide services to a third party or to develop a product is problematic. A cooperative venture does not exist where all these safeguards are present:

1. Participation of the firm and client is governed by separate agreements that do not create obligations between them
2. Neither assumes responsibilities for the other's activities or results
3. Neither has authority to act as the other's agent

B. Joint closely held investments -- Joint financial investments may create an independence problem also.

1. Permissible: The firm and an attest client could both own the stock of a widely held public company, like Microsoft.
2. Impermissible:
    a. The firm and a client both own material stakes in a small company
    b. A covered member and an officer of an attest client jointly buy a sailboat

Family Relationships

After studying this lesson you should be able to :

1. *Understand which restrictions apply to each category.*
2. *Understand to what the label "close relatives" applies.*
3. *Understand to what the label "immediate family members" applies.*

I. Introduction

A. Two categories of family relationships create potential independence problems:

1. **Immediate family members**: spouses, spousal equivalents, and dependents
2. **Close relatives**: parents, siblings, and nondependent children.

II. Immediate Family Members

A. With substantial exceptions that are about to be spelled out, immediate family members of covered members must comply with the same independence rules as covered members themselves. They may not work for attest clients or own financial interests in them (unless the interests are both indirect and immaterial).

B. Irrespective of the exceptions below, immediate family members cumulatively may not own more than 5% of an attest client.

C. Immediate family members employed by attest client -- A covered member's immediate family members may work for an attest client, just not in a "key position" such as one in which an employee has:

1. Primary responsibility for significant accounting functions that support material components of the financial statement;
2. Primary responsibility for the preparation of the financial statement; or
3. The ability to exercise influence over the contents of the financial statement, including when the individual is a member of the board of directors or similar governing body, chief executive officer, president, chief financial officer, chief operating officer, general counsel, chief accountancy officer, controller, director of internal audit, director of financial reporting, treasurer, or any equivalent position.

D. Immediate family member participation in an employee benefit plan -- Immediate family members may not only work for an attest client in a nonkey position, they may also participate in an employee benefit plan that is an attest client or is sponsored by an attest client, so long as all of the following safeguards are followed:

1. The plan is offered to all employees in comparable employment positions;
2. The immediate family member does not serve in a position of governance for the plan; and
3. The immediate family member does not have the ability to supervise or participate in the plan's investment decisions or in the selection of the investment options made available to plan participants

E. Immediate family member participation in an employee benefit plan with financial interests in an attest client -- An immediate family member might work for a company that is not an attest client but participate in its employee benefit plan and learn that the plan holds stock of an attest client. The general rule is that in this setting an immediate family member may hold a direct financial interest or material indirect financial interest in an attest client if all of the following safeguards are met:

1. The covered member is neither on the attest team nor in a position to influence. (So, the immediate family member could be a 10-hour person or other partner in the office but not a team member or in a position to influence in relationship to the attest client);
2. Such investment is an unavoidable consequence of such participation; the immediate family member had no other investment options available for selection.
3. If the plan creates an option that would allow the immediate family members to invest in a nonattest client, the immediate family members should select that option and dispose of the attest client shares as soon as practicable but within 30 days.

III. Close Relatives

- **A.** Generally, close relatives of covered members must follow the same independence rules as the covered members themselves, but the restrictions are looser than for immediate family members and they are looser for close relatives of covered members who are not on the engagement team.
- **B.** Independence is impaired if the close relative of an audit team member has **either** of the following:
  1. A key position with the attest client, or
  2. A financial interest in the attest client that:
     - **a.** The team member knows or has reason to know was material to the close relative, or
     - **b.** Enabled the close relative to exercise significant influence over the attest client.
- **C.** Independence is impaired if the close relative of a person in a position to influence or other partner in the office has **either** of the following:
  1. A key position with an attest client, or
  2. A financial interest that:
     - **a.** The person in a position to influence or other partner in office has reason to believe was material to the close relative, *and*
     - **b.** Enabled the close relative to exercise significant influence over the attest client.
- **D.** There are no specific restrictions on close relatives of 10-hour people (though the Conceptual Framework should always be kept in mind).

Employment Relationships

Current Employment

After studying this lesson you should be able to :

1. *Apply the rules that, to preserve independence, prevent various members of an accounting firm from working for an audit client in a wide range of positions.*
2. *Understand the rules that govern a situation where an attest client's employee wishes to come to work for the audit firm.*

I. Current Employment

A. The employment rules focus on partners and professional employees of attest firms. They may not, without impairing independence, serve in these roles for an attest client: director, officer, employee, promoter, underwriter, voting trustee, or trustee for any pension or profit-sharing trust of the client's, or in any equivalent management position.

B. Professors -- Partners and professional employees may serve as adjunct faculty members at a college that is an attest client so long as the following safeguards are all accurate regarding the faculty member. He or she:

1. Does not hold a key position with the client
2. Is not on the attest engagement team
3. Is not in a position to influence
4. Is on a part-time and non-tenure basis
5. Does not participate in any employee benefit plan sponsored by the school, unless participation is required
6. Does not assume any management responsibilities or set policies.

C. Honorary director or trustee of a not-for-profit organization -- Partners and professional employees may lend the prestige of their names to a not-for-profit that is an attest client so long as all of the following safeguards are in place:

1. The position is clearly honorary
2. The partner or professional employee cannot vote and takes no management role in the organization
3. All externally circulated materials identify the position as honorary.

D. Member of an advisory board -- If criteria similar to those mentioned in the previous section are met, partners and professional employees may serve on an attest client's advisory board without impairing independence.

E. Member of governmental advisory committee -- Independence considerations do not prevent partners or professional employees from serving on a citizen's advisory committee studying possible changes in the form of a county government that is an attest client, or on an advisory committee appointed to study the financial status of the state in which the county is located.

F. Campaign treasurer -- Independence considerations preclude a firm from auditing a campaign organization whose campaign manager is a partner or professional employee of the firm. However, the firm can still audit the political party of the candidate or the governmental unit that the candidate will head if he or she wins the election.

G. Member of federated fund-raising organization -- If a firm's partner or professional employee serves as director or officer of a federated fund-raising organization such as United Way, which not only gives funds to a particular local charity but also exercises control over that charity, then the firm may not audit that local charity. Even if United Way does not exercise control, there are sufficient independence concerns that the Conceptual Framework should be invoked.

H. **Member of organization that receives funds from fund-raising organization --** When a partners or professional employee is a director of an organization that receives funding from a foundation that exists solely to raise funds for that organization, the firm may not audit the foundation, **unless** the directorship is clearly honorary.

II. Former Employment or Association with an Attest Client

A. Independence concerns arise when people who are employed by attest clients or who were associated with them as officers, directors, promoters, underwriters, voting trustees, or trustees for a pension fund or profit-sharing fund of the clients, join the firm as **covered members.**

B. Independence is impaired if one of these people participates as a **team member** or someone in a **position to influence** when the attest engagement covers any of period of time when the person was employed by or associated with the audit client.

C. However, if the people become merely other partners in the office or 10-hour people, then independence is not impaired so long as they **dissociate** themselves from the client **prior** to becoming a covered member. Dissociation includes **all** of the following five steps:

1. Ceasing to participate in all the client's health and welfare benefit plans, unless the client is legally required to allow the covered member to participate in the plan (e.g., COBRA), and the covered member pays 100% of his or her portion of the cost.
2. Ceasing to participate in all other employee benefit plans by liquidating or transferring all vested benefits in the client's defined benefit plans, defined contribution plans, and similar arrangements at the earliest permissible.
3. Disposing of any direct or material indirect financial interest in the client.
4. Collecting or repaying any loans to or from the client other than those specifically permitted or grandfathered by the code.
5. Assessing other relationships with the client to determine if they create threats to independence that would require the application of safeguards to reduce threats to an acceptable level.

Subsequent Employment

After studying this lesson you should be able to :

1. *Know the rules that must be followed to preserve independence when certain covered members are considering going to work for an attest client.*
2. *Know the rules that must be followed to preserve independence when covered members do go to work for an attest client.*

I. Considering Subsequent Employment with an Attest Client

A. When an attest team member or person in a position to influence is considering employment with the attest client, independence is impaired unless the team member:

1. Promptly reports such consideration or offer to an appropriate person in the firm, and
2. Removes him- or herself from the engagement until the offer is rejected or the position is no longer sought.

B. When a "covered member" learns that a team member or a person in a position to influence is considering employment with a client and has not taken the steps listed above, that member should alert the firm.

1. The firm must consider what additional procedures may be necessary to provide "reasonable assurance" that the person acted properly.
2. The policy does not explicitly cover other partners in office or 10-hour people.

II. Subsequent Employment with an Attest Client

A. A firm's independence will be considered impaired when a partner or professional employee goes to work for an attest client in a "key position," unless all of the following conditions are met:

1. Amounts due the former employee for ownership interest in the firm an unfunded, vested retirement interests are not material to the firm, and the underlying formula used to calculate payments remains fixed.
2. The former employee is not in a position to influence the accounting firm's operations or financial policies.
3. The former employee does not participate or **appear** to participate in the firm's business and is not associated with the firm (even if unpaid). An "appearance of participation" results from such actions as:
   - **a.** The former employee consults with the firm.
   - **b.** The firm provides the former employee with an office and related amenities.
   - **c.** The individual's name is included in the firm's office directory.
   - **d.** The individual's name is included as a member of the firm in other membership lists of business, professional, or civic organizations, unless designated as retired.
4. The ongoing attest considers modifying audit procedures to adjust for the risk created by the former employee's knowledge of the audit plan that he or she has now taken to the client. Also, it should consider whether remaining team members can appropriately stand up to a former employee if they have to deal with him or/ her.
5. If the former employee joins the client in a **key position within one year of dissociating from the firm**, and has significant interaction with the attest engagement team, an appropriate professional in the firm should review the subsequent engagement to determine whether appropriate skepticism was maintained.

B. Sarbanes-Oxley (SOX) imposes stricter rules where public companies are involved. SOX imposes a one-year cooling-off period that requires the lead partner, the concurring partner, or any other member of the audit engagement team who provides more than 10 hours of audit, review, or attest services to observe a one-year cooling-off period before going to work for a client in financial oversight positions. The positions that cannot be assumed within the one-year period include (a) chief executive officer, chief financial officer, controller, chief accountancy officer, or any equivalent officers; (b) any financial oversight role; and (c) any position preparing financial statements. If a former audit firm employee violates these rules, independence is impaired. The one-year cooling-off period is that year preceding the beginning of the audit, so the cooling-off period actually can extend to nearly two years if the member has begun an audit cycle before going to work for the client.

Other Associations and Relationships

After studying this lesson you should be able to :

1. *Appreciate the intricacies of avoiding independence problems while in various relationships with attest clients, such as social clubs, trade associations, condominium associations, and credit unions.*
2. *Know the rules that govern the giving of gifts and entertainment in an attest setting.*

I. **Member of Social Club --** If a covered member belongs to a social club, such as a country club, that is an attest client, there should be no independence problem if the membership is primarily a social matter.

II. **Member of a Trade Association --** Independence is impaired if a covered member belongs to a trade association that is an attest client. If a partner or professional employee is employed by or associated with a trade association in an important role (director, trustee, etc.), independence is again impaired.

III. **Member of a Common Interest Realty Association (CIRA) --** If a covered member buys an interest in a condominium, cooperative, or other common interest realty association, his or her firm may nonetheless audit the common interest realty association, but only if **all** of the following safeguards are met:

   A. The common interest realty association performs functions similar to local governments, such as public safety, road maintenance, and utilities

   B. The covered member's annual assessment is not material to either the common interest realty association or the member

   C. Liquidation of the common interest realty association or sale of common assets would not result in a distribution to the covered member; and

   D. The common interest realty association's creditors would not be permitted to recover out of the member's assets if the common interest realty association became insolvent

IV. **Member of a Credit Union --** When a covered member is a member of a credit union and became eligible to join only because of the professional services he or she provided to the credit union, independence is impaired. However, if the member individually qualifies to join the credit union irrespective of professional services provided, then independence is not impaired.

V. **Gifts and Entertainment**

   A. **Gifts --** Independence is impaired if the firm, a team member, or someone in a position to influence accepts a gift from an attest client, unless the value is clearly insignificant to the recipient.

   B. **Entertainment --** Entertainment may be accepted without impairing independence so long as it is reasonable in the circumstances. The circumstances to be considered include:

      1. Nature of the gift or entertainment
      2. Occasion giving rise to the gift or entertainment
      3. Cost or value of the gift or entertainment
      4. Nature, frequency, and value of other gifts and entertainment
      5. Whether the entertainment was associated with the active conduct of business
      6. Whether other attest clients also participated in the entertainment; and
      7. Client and firm employees who participated in the entertainment

VI. Actual or Threatened Litigation

A. **Litigation between client and member --** If the client (or its management) sues the audit firm (or vice versa), the key question is whether the firm and client are in threatened or actual positions of material adverse interests. A minor dispute or one not related to the engagement (such as a billing dispute) would not impair independence. However, the code gives these examples of impaired independence:

   1. An **attest client's current** management sues or seriously threatens to sue firm alleging deficiencies in the audit work.

   2. A **covered member** sues the client's current management alleging fraud or deceit.

B. **Litigation by client security holders --** Client shareholders filing a suit claiming securities fraud or some other wrong by both the client and the audit firm presumptively does **not** automatically impair independence. But if there are cross-claims between the client and its managers on one hand and the attest firm of the other (or a serious risk of them), independence is impaired if there is a "significant risk" that a material settlement or judgment will result.

C. **Other third- party litigation --** Litigation by non-shareholder third parties, such as lenders, who might also sue the auditor and/or the client is treated similarly.

D. Final resolution of litigation or other dispute eliminates the independence threat and reduces it to an acceptable level.

Nonaudit Services

Code Provisions

After studying this lesson you should be able to :

1. *Understand the differences between the code's approach and Sarbanes-Oxley's approach to the provision of nonaudit services to public company attest clients.*
2. *Understand and be able to apply the "big picture" code rules, such as the general requirements that always must be met for those who provide nonaudit services to attest clients.*

I. Introduction

A. The code governs provision of nonaudit services to private company audit clients and indicates that communications about the following matters that would **not** normally be considered nonaudit services:

1. The client's selection and application of accounting standards or policies and financial statement disclosure requirements;
2. The appropriateness of the client's methods used in determining accounting and financial reporting;
3. Adjusting journal entries that the member has prepared or proposed for client management consideration; and
4. The form or content of the financial statement.

B. Covered members should monitor the total amount of their nonaudit services to ensure that their total involvement with the client does not become so extensive that it would constitute performing a separate service.

C. **Management responsibilities --** Members must not assume any management responsibilities of attest clients. "Management responsibilities involve leading and directing an entity, including making significant decisions regarding the acquisition, deployment, and control of human, financial, physical, and intangible resources." Examples of such impermissible activities include:

1. Setting policy or strategic direction for the attest client
2. Directing or accepting responsibility for actions of the attest client's employees except to the extent permitted when using internal auditors to provide assistance for services performed under auditing or attestation standards
3. Authorizing, executing, or consummating transactions or otherwise exercising authority on behalf of an attest client or having the authority to do so
4. Preparing source documents, in electronic or other form, that evidence the occurrence of a transaction
5. Having custody of an attest client's assets
6. Deciding which recommendations of the member or other third parties to implement or prioritize
7. Reporting to those charged with governance on behalf of management
8. Serving as an attest client's stock transfer or escrow agent, registrar, general counsel or equivalent
9. Accepting responsibility for the management of an attest client's project

10. Accepting responsibility for the preparation and fair presentation of the attest client's financial statements in accordance with the applicable financial reporting framework

11. Accepting responsibility for designing, implementing, or maintaining internal control.

II. General Requirements for Performing Nonaudit Services -- When covered members do provide nonaudit services for an attest client, **if other rules do not state otherwise**, independence would not be impaired if **all** of the following three safeguards are met.

A. In order to ensure that the ultimate management of the attest client stays with the client's management, the members must determine that the client and its management agree to:

1. Assume all management responsibilities;

2. Oversee the service, by designating an individual, preferably within senior management, who possesses the skill, knowledge, and/or experience to do the job. The member should assess the situation to ensure that the individual is up to the task;

3. Evaluate the adequacy and results of the services performed

4. Accept responsibility for the results of the services.

B. The members must **not** assume management responsibilities (as outlined above) and additionally must satisfy themselves that the audit client and its management will:

1. Be able to meet the criteria listed in the previous paragraph

2. Make an informed judgment on the results of the member's nonaudit services

3. Accept responsibility for making the significant judgments and decisions that are the proper responsibility of management.

C. Before performing nonaudit services, members must establish (and document in writing) their understanding with the attest client regarding:

1. Objectives of the engagement

2. Services to be performed

3. The attest client's acceptance of its responsibilities

4. The member's responsibilities

5. Any limitations on the engagement.

D. If all of these general requirements are met, then independence is not impaired, unless other rules (that we are about to explore) so provide.

E. If the general requirements are met, then a member may:

1. Provide advice, research materials, and recommendations to assist management in performing its functions and making decisions;

2. Attend board meetings as a nonvoting advisor

3. Interpret financial statements, forecasts, or other analyses

4. Provide management with advice regarding its potential plans strategies, or relationships.

III. Sarbanes-Oxley (SOX)

A. SOX limits the nonattest (also known as consulting or advisory services) that attest firms may provide to attest clients that are **public companies**. SOX does not apply if the firms are not public companies, so the code governs if an accounting firm audits a private company.

B. SOX limitations on nonaudit services are based on three fundamental notions: (a) accounting firms should not audit their own work, (b) auditors should not advocate for their clients, and (c) accounting firms should not serve as their clients' managers.

C. SOX provides that an independent auditor cannot perform the following nonaudit services for a public company audit client:

1. Bookkeeping or other services related to the accounting records of financial statements
2. Financial information systems design and implementations
3. Appraisal or valuation services, fairness opinions, or contributions-in-kind reports
4. Actuarial services
5. Internal audit outsourcing services
6. Management functions or human resources
7. Broker or dealer, investment advisor, or investment banking services
8. Legal services and expert services unrelated to the audit
9. Any other service that the Public Company Accounting Oversight Board (PCAOB) determines is impermissible.

D. SOX does not prohibit attest firms from providing tax services to their attest clients, but PCAOB rules do provide that a public company's auditor's independence is impaired regarding a tax client if the firm:

1. Enters into a contingent fee arrangement with an audit client
2. Provides marketing, planning, or opinion services in favor of the tax treatment of a "confidential transaction," or if the transaction is based on an "aggressive" interpretation of tax law
3. Provides tax services to members of management who serve in a financial reporting oversight role for a client (or to their immediate family).

E. SOX requires that rather than the audit client's management selecting the auditor, client **audit committees** should select, evaluate, and compensate the auditors. In addition, these audit committees, which are to be composed entirely of outside directors and therefore presumably independent of overt management influence, must **preapprove** any permitted nonaudit services (such as tax services) purchased by a company from its auditor.

F. Also, when a firm seeks the permission of an audit client's audit committee to provide tax services, it must: (a) describe the proposed services in writing to the committee, (b) discuss with the committee the potential effects on independence, and (c) document that discussion.

Specific Services

After studying this lesson you should be able to :

1. *Understand the types of nonaudit services that can be provided to a private company attest client.*
2. *Understand the types of nonaudit services that cannot be provided to a private company attest client .*

Overview

Appraisal, Valuation, or Actuarial	Impaired	Not Impaired
Results would be material to the financial statement and services involve high degree of subjectivity*	x	
Services not requiring high degree of subjectivity†		x
Services performed for nonfinancial statement purposes‡		x
*Ex: valuing employee stock option plan, business combination, or appraisals of assets and liabilities.		
†Ex: valuing a client's pension or postemployment benefit liabilities.		
‡Ex: appraising or actuarial services for tax planning, estate and gift taxation, and divorce proceedings.		

Benefit Plan Administration	Impaired	Not Impaired
Communicate summary plan data to plan trustee		x
Advise client management regarding impact of plan provisions		x
Process transactions initiated by plan participants		x
Prepare account valuations		x
Prepare and transmit participant statement to plan participants		x
Make policy decisions on client's behalf	x	
Interpret plan for participants without management's concurrence	x	
Make disbursements on plan's behalf	x	
Take custody of plan assets	x	
Serve as a plan fiduciary	x	

See the following illustration.

Bookkeeping, Payroll, and Other Disbursements	Impaired	Not Impaired
Record management-approved transactions in client's general ledger		x
Post client-coded transactions to client's general ledger		x
Prepare financial statements based on client's trial balance information		x
Post client-approved journal entry to client's trial balance		x
Propose standard, adjusting, or correcting journal entries		x
Generate unsigned checks using client's source documents		x
Process a client's payroll using client-provided records		x
Transmit client approved payroll or other disbursement information to a financial institution chosen by client		x
Prepare reconciliation for client's evaluation		x
Determine or make changes in accounting records without client approval	x	
Approve or authorize client transactions	x	
Prepare source documents	x	
Make changes to source documents without client approval	x	
Accept responsibility to authorize payment of client funds	x	
Accept responsibility to sign or cosign checks	x	
Maintain client's bank account, take custody of client funds, or make credit or banking decisions for client	x	
Approve vendor invoices for payments	x	

Business Risk Consulting	Impaired	Not Impaired
Assist management in its assessment of client's business risk control processes		x
Recommend a plan for improving control processes and assisting in implementation		x
Make or approve business risk decisions	x	
Present business risk consideration to board on management's behalf	x	

See the following illustration.

Corporate Finance Consulting	Impaired	Not Impaired
Assist in developing corporate strategies		x
Assist in identifying sources of capital meeting client's criteria		x
Introduce management to sources of capital meeting client's criteria		x
Assist management in analyzing effects of proposed transactions		x
Advise client in transaction negotiations		x
Assist in drafting offering documents		x
Participant in transaction negotiations in advisory capacity		x
Be named as financial advisory in client's offering documents		x
Commit the client to a transaction	x	
Consummate transaction on client's behalf	x	
Act as a promoter, underwriter, broker-dealer, or guarantor of client's securities	x	
Act as a distributor of client's offering documents	x	
Maintain custody of client's securities	x	

Executive or Employee Search	Impaired	Not Impaired
Recommend position description or candidate specifications		x
Solicit, screen, and recommend candidates based on client-approved criteria		x
Recommend qualified candidates based on client-approved criteria		x
Advise employer on employee hiring or benefits		x
Hire or terminate client employees	x	
Commit client to employee compensation or benefits	x	

See the following illustration.

Forensic Accounting Services	Impaired	Not Impaired
Expert witness for a client	x	
Expert for a large group where attest clients (a) < 20% of members, voting interest, and claims (b) are not "lead" plaintiffs, and (c) do not have sole decision-making power to select expert witness		x
Fact witness		x
Litigation consulting: providing advice to attest client (without serving as expert witness)		x
Litigation consulting: serving as trier of fact, special master, court-appointed expert, or arbitrator	x	
Litigation consulting: mediator		x

Information Systems	Impaired	Not Impaired
Install or integrate a client's financial information system if it is off-the-shelf (not designed by member)		x
Assist in setting up client's chart of accounts and financial statement format		x
Design, develop, install, or integrate client's information system that is unrelated to client's financial statements or accounting records		x
Provide training and instruction to client's employees on information and control system		x
Perform network maintenance		x
Design or develop a client's financial information system	x	
Make other than insignificant modifications to source code underlying a client's existing financial information system	x	
Supervise client personnel in the daily operation of financial information system	x	
Operate client's network	x	

See the following illustration.

Internal Audit	Impaired	Not Impaired
Assess whether performance complies with management policies		x
Identify opportunities for improvement		x
Recommend improvement for management consideration		x
Performing ongoing monitoring activities or control activities (e.g., reviewing customer credit info as part of sales process) that affects execution of transactions	x	
Performing separate evaluations of a significant control such that member is, in effect, performing routine operations built into client's business process	x	
Having management rely on member's work as primary basis for client's assertions on design of operating effectiveness of internal controls	x	
Determining which, if any, recommendations for improving internal control system should be implemented	x	
Reporting to board or audit committee on behalf of management regarding internal audit affairs	x	
Approving or being responsible for overall internal audit work including determining internal audit risk and scope, project priorities, and frequency of performance of audit procedures	x	
Being connected with client as employee or in any management position (e.g., being listed as an employee in client's directory)	x	

Investment—Advisory or Management	Impaired	Not Impaired
Recommend allocation of funds that client should invest in various asset classes		x
Perform bookkeeping and reporting of client's portfolio balance		x
Review management of client's portfolio by others to determine if managers are meeting client's investment objectives		x
Transmit client's investment selection to broker		x
Make investment decisions on client's behalf	x	
Execute transactions to buy or sell for client	x	
Take custody of client assets, such as a security purchased by client	x	

See the following illustration.

Tax Services	Impaired	Not Impaired
Assuming that CPA does not have custody or control over client's funds and that client employee reviews and approves tax return prior to transmission to taxing authority, and, if required for filing, signs tax return, then:		
- Preparing tax return		x
- Transmitting tax return to taxing authority		x
- Transmitting payment		x
Signing and filing tax return on behalf of client management if authorized by management and requirements are met	x	
Representing client in administrative proceedings before taxing authority		x
Representing client in court resolve a tax dispute	x	

Members in Business

After studying this lesson you should be able to :

1. *Have a good appreciation for how the rules that govern members in business differ from those that govern members in public practice.*
2. *Understand the specifics of professional obligations for members in business.*

I. Introduction

A. **Members in business** are members who are "employed or engaged on a contractual or volunteer basis in an executive, staff, governance, advisory, or administrative capacity in such areas as industry, the public sector, education, the not-for-profit sector and regulatory or professional bodies." This would include staff accountants, internal auditors, and other accountants not engaged in public practice.

B. Members in business do not have to worry about independence rules. They have other responsibilities that generally mirror those of members in public practice, so it should not take long to master their part of the Code of Professional Conduct.

II. Conceptual Framework

A. The Conceptual Framework for members in business generally tracks that of members in public practice. Six of the seven threats identified for members in public practice also apply to members in business:—(a) adverse interest threats, (b) advocacy threats, (c) familiarity threats, (d) self-interest threats, (e) self-review threats, and (f) undue influence threats. The examples given differ, naturally, because of the difference in work setting.

B. Examples of adverse interest threats include:

1. A member in business's close relative is an investor in her employer's closest competitor.
2. A member in business has sued her employer.

C. Examples of advocacy threats include:

1. Obtaining favorable financing is dependent on the information that the member in business includes in a prospectus.
2. The member in business gives or fails to give information that he knows will unduly influence the conclusions reached by a third party.

D. Examples of familiarity threats include:

1. A member in business has a long relationship with a third party and therefore stops reviewing the quality of the third-party's work.
2. A member in business hires a relative as a subordinate.
3. A member in business regularly accepts gifts or entertainment from a firm that sells goods or services to the member's employer.

E. Self-interest threats include:

1. A member in business's close relative owns stock in the employer.
2. A member in business is eligible for a performance-related bonus, and its value will be directly affected by the member in business's decisions.

F. Self-review threats include:

1. An internal auditor accepts work that she previously performed before she was promoted to her current position.

2. A member in business accepts work that she previously performed that will be the basis for providing another professional—for example, Sally gives tax advice to her client and later, while doing attest work for the client, automatically accepts the validity of the tax advice.

G. Undue influence threats include members in business being pressured to

1. Become associated with misleading information
2. Deviate from company policy, or
3. Change a conclusion regarding a tax or accounting position :

H. When attempting to eliminate these threats or reduce them to an acceptable level, members in business cannot turn to safeguards generated by their accounting firm, of course, but can turn to those created by:

1. The profession, legislation, or regulation, or
2. Their employer.

III. **Integrity and Objectivity**

A. **Offering or accepting gifts or entertainment --** Members in business should not accept any gifts or entertainment that would violate the law or the policies of other firms of their own employer. Gifts or entertainment **not reasonable in the circumstances** would create a violation of the integrity and objectivity rule.

B. **Preparing and reporting information --** Members in business must never:

1. Make or direct another to make a false entry
2. Fail to correct inaccurate financial statements or entries; or
3. Sign or permit another to sign a document containing materially false information.

C. **Subordination of judgment --** The rules against subordination of judgment for members in business are essentially identical for those of members in public practice that are contained in Part 1of the Code of Professional Conduct.

D. **Obligation of a member to his or her employer's external accountant --** Members in business are to "be candid and not knowingly misrepresent facts or knowingly fail to disclose material facts to their employers" external auditor.

E. **Educational services --** When teaching at a university or performing other educational services, a member in business is viewed as performing professional services and therefore must act with integrity and objectivity.

IV. **General Standards**

A. Like members in public practice, members in business must:

1. Act with professional competence
2. Act with due competence
3. Act with due professional care
4. Adequately plan and supervise performance of professional services, and
5. Have sufficient relevant data to back up any conclusions or recommendations they make.

B. Members in business are expected to:

1. Comply with applicable standards promulgated by bodies like the Securities and Exchange Commission and Internal Revenue Service, and

2. Not imply that financial statements they are preparing and submitting to third parties were prepared in accordance with independence rules when they were not.

V. Accounting Principles

A. Like members in public practice, members in business may not claim that financial statements are presented in accordance with generally accepted accounting principles when they are not.

VI. Acts Discreditable -- Members in business are held to essentially the same standards as members in public practice when it comes to defining discreditable acts, which include:

A. Discrimination and harassment in employment

B. Solicitation or disclosure of CPA exam questions and answers

C. Failure to file a tax return or pay a tax liability

D. Negligence in preparing financial statement or other records

E. Failure to follow the rules for preparation of financial statements required by agencies like the Securities and Exchange Commission, Federal Communications Commission, and state commissioners

F. Entering into prohibited indemnification agreements and limited liability provisions

G. Disclosing confidential information without the employer's permission or the application of another recognized exception (such as validly issued subpoena, etc.)

H. Promoting or marketing their firm by use of false, misleading, or deceptive ads, and

I. Improper (misleading) use of the CPA credential.

Other Members

After studying this lesson you should be able to :

1. *Understand that they should not engage in discreditable acts.*
2. *Recognize the two basic types of "other members"; retired and unemployed.*

I. Definition -- "Other members" are, by definition, unemployed, retired, or otherwise not working in the profession, so most of the code that applies to members in public practice and members in business does not apply to them.

II. Discreditable Acts -- Other members are, at a minimum, not to engage in discreditable acts, including:

A. Discrimination and harassment in employment practices.

B. Solicitation or disclosure of CPA Examination questions and answers.

C. Failure to file a tax return or pay a tax liability.

D. Improper disclosure of confidential information obtained from former employment or previous volunteer work.

E. False, misleading, or deceptive acts in promoting or marketing services.

F. Improper (misleading) use of the CPA credential.

Other Ethics Codes

Securities and Exchange Commission (SEC)

After studying this lesson you should be able to :

1. *Understand that the SEC's basic independence rules are quite similar to the AICPAs.*
2. *Know how to describe in detail those extra SOX requirements.*
3. *Realize that Sarbanes-Oxley (SOX) created many additional independence rules regarding the audit of public companies that go beyond or conflict with the AICPA Code's Rule 101.*

I. Basic Independence Rules

A. The SEC has its own set of independence rules for auditors, but they were developed with an eye toward the AICPA rules at a time around the turn of the century when both sets of standards migrated simultaneously from a firm-oriented approach to an audit team-oriented approach.

B. Although there are some differences in terminology, the ultimate results in independence situations are almost always the same under the SEC rules and the AICPA's Rule 101.

C. Therefore, this section will not address the basic SEC rules, but will instead address important changes that the Sarbanes-Oxley Act of 2002 (SOX) mandated for the audit of public companies. Where these rules clash with the AICPA Code, they overrule the AICPA for any audit of public companies.

II. Sarbanes-Oxley Audit Provisions

A. The AICPA Code allows audit firms to provide nonaudit services (NAS) to audit clients, with certain restrictions (e.g., don't make management decisions, don't audit your own work, don't take custody of client assets). However, after the debacles of the Enron era, Congress enacted SOX to simply prohibit the performance of many NAS where the purchaser of those services is a public company audit client of the provider. So if PriceCoopersHouse (PCH) is auditing ABC Co. (a public company), PCH may not provide it with these NAS:

1. Bookkeeping or other services related to the accounting records of financial statements;
2. Financial information systems design and implementation;
3. Appraisal or valuation services, fairness opinions, or contributions-in-kind reports;
4. Actuarial services;
5. Internal audit outsourcing services;
6. Management functions or human resources;
7. Broker or dealer, investment adviser, or investment banking services;
8. Legal services and expert services unrelated to the audit;
9. Any other service that the PCAOB determines is impermissible.

B. Keep in mind that:

1. Audit firms may provide these services to nonaudit clients and to private companies (even if they are audit clients) so long as AICPA restrictions are followed.
2. Other NAS may be performed for public company audit clients, such as tax services, but only if:
   a. pre-approved by the client's audit committee; and

b. disclosed in the client's periodic reports filed with the SEC.

3. Although the SEC and PCAOB decided not to bar provision of tax services to public company audit clients, the PCAOB did issue rules that bar provision of two types of tax services:

   a. those involving confidential or aggressive tax transactions (tax shelters); and

   b. personal tax services provided to a person in a Financial Reporting Oversight Role (FROR) at the audit client, such as the CFO.

C. Audit partner rotation. Sarbanes-Oxley did not require that public companies rotate audit *firms*.

1. However, audit firms of public companies must rotate both the lead audit partner and the reviewing audit partner at least every five years. They must then serve at least a five-year "time out" before returning to the client. So, it's five-on, five-off, five-on, etc. for the lead audit partner and the reviewing partner.

2. Other partners playing a significant role in the audit are subject to a seven-year rotation requirement with a two-year time out period. For them it is seven-on, two-off, seven-on, etc.

D. **Auditor compensation**

1. Under SOX, a public company audit firm is not independent if any partner earns or receives compensation based on that partner selling NAS to an audit client.

E. **Audit report to audit committee**

1. All audit firms for public companies are now selected and compensated by the audit committee rather than by management;

2. Each audit firm must timely report to the client's audit committee

   a. all critical accounting policies and practices to be used;

   b. all alternative treatments of financial information within GAAP that have been discussed with management officials, ramifications of the use of such alternative disclosures, and the treatment preferred by the accounting firm; and

   c. other material written communications between the accounting firm and the issuer's management, such as any management letter or schedule of unadjusted differences.

F. **Cooling-off periods**

1. Sarbanes-Oxley provides that an audit firm may not perform an audit for a client if its CEO, controller, CFO, CAO, or any person serving in an equivalent FROR was employed by the audit firm and participated in the audit during a one-year period preceding the date of the initiation of the audit.

2. If the individual worked for the audit firm but did not participate in the client's audit, it is not considered a problem.

3. Because a complete audit cycle must pass between the time that an auditor leaves the accounting firm until he or she starts to work for the client in one of these FRORs, the total cooling-off period could end up being nearly two years.

Example:
ABC Co.'s audit cycle runs May 15 to May 15. Sandy is on PriceCooperHouse (PCH)'s audit team. She resigns on June 15, just one month into an audit cycle. She must wait until the end of that cycle, and then allow a complete cycle to pass before she can go to work for ABC in an FROR capacity. Had she quit on May 14, 2011, she could have started at ABC on May 15, 2012. But if she resigned on June 15, 2011, she would have had to wait until May 15, 2013.

III. Public Company Accounting Oversight Board (PCAOB)

A. **Creation --** Sarbanes-Oxley created the PCAOB to oversee auditors of public companies.

B. The SEC role in overseeing the PCAOB and PCAOB's powers are discussed in the next section.

Sarbanes-Oxley and the PCAOB

The audit profession has traditionally been self-regulating through self-promulgated professional standards, peer reviews, etc. The 2002 Sarbanes-Oxley Act (SOX) changed this situation and directly affects the accounting profession in several ways. In this section, we focus upon the PCAOB. Impact on audit independence rules were mentioned in the preceding section on the SEC.

After studying this lesson you should be able to :

1. *Be conversant with some key Sarbanes-Oxley criminal provisions.*

I. Public Company Accounting Oversight Board (PCAOB)

A. Sarbanes-Oxley created the PCAOB to have power over auditors similar to that exercised by FINRA over broker-dealers.

1. The SEC oversees the PCAOB.

2. The PCAOB's members (five, three of whom may not be accountants) are selected by the SEC.

B. The PCAOB does not regulate firms that service only private companies.

C. Principal functions of the PCAOB

1. Register public accounting firms.

2. Establish auditing, quality control, ethics, independence, and other standards relating to the preparation of audit reports, or adopt such standards as proposed by existing professional groups or new advisory committees.

3. Conduct inspections of registered public accounting firms.

4. Conduct investigations and disciplinary proceedings concerning registered public accounting firms and associated persons.

5. Enforce compliance with SOX, the PCAOB's rules, professional standards, and the securities laws relating to the preparation of audit reports by registered public accounting firms and associated persons.

6. Perform such other services as the PCAOB or the SEC determines are necessary or appropriate to promote high professional standards, protect investors or further the public interest.

D. Registration with the PCAOB

1. In order to prepare, issue, or participate in the preparation or issuance of any audit report with respect to any public company, a public accounting firm must register with the PCAOB.

2. Information to be disclosed will include:

a. the names of all audit clients in the past year;

b. annual fees for audit and nonaudit services received from each client;

c. a statement of firm quality control policies;

d. a list of all accountants associated with the firm who participated in the audits;

e. information relating to criminal, civil, or administrative proceedings pending against the firm or any associated person in connection with any audit report;

f. copies of any disclosure filed by a client with the SEC in the last calendar year disclosing a disagreement between the auditor and the firm; and

g. any other information that the PCAOB or the SEC believe should be disclosed.

3. Each firm must also submit an annual report and pay a registration fee each year.

E. **New standards**

1. The PCAOB has broad power to consult experts to establish auditing, quality control, ethics, and independence standards.

2. The auditing standards must include at least these three rules:

a. For at least seven years, auditors must retain audit work papers and other information in sufficient detail to support the conclusions reached in the audit report.

b. An accounting firm must provide a concurring or second partner to review and approve each audit report.

c. In each audit report, the firm must describe the scope of the auditor's testing of the internal control structure and procedures of the issuer and present the findings of such testing, an evaluation of the internal control structure, a description of material weaknesses in such internal controls, and any material noncompliance found.

3. The PCAOB has initially adopted the AICPA's independence rules, as limited and affected by SOX requirements, but is slowly issuing its own rules, such as:

a. Rule 3526, which requires public company auditors to communicate in writing to the client's audit committee *prior to accepting an initial engagement*, relationships that might reasonably be thought to bear on the auditor's independence and to affirm annually their compliance with PCAOB independence rules; and

b. Rule 3523, which prohibits a registered audit firm from providing tax services to executives in financial reporting oversight roles for public company audit clients.

F. **Inspections of registered public accounting firms**

1. PCAOB must conduct a "program of inspections" to assess registrant's compliance with the 1934 Securities Exchange Act, SEC and PCAOB rules, and professional standards.

a. Annual inspections are conducted for firms doing more than 100 audits per year.

b. Inspections are conducted every three years for firms doing fewer than 100 audits.

2. Firms can seek SEC review of PCAOB inspection reports if they disagree.

3. Inspection reports are posted on the PCAOB website.

G. **Investigations and disciplinary proceedings**

1. The PCAOB is authorized to investigate any act, practice, or omission by a registrant to any associated person that may violate any provision of the Act, the PCAOB's rules, securities rules, or professional standards.

2. The PCAOB can require testimony and production of audit work papers or other documents.

3. The PCAOB must notify the SEC and coordinate with its enforcement division.

4. The PCAOB may refer any investigation to the SEC, other federal regulators, or, at the SEC's direction, federal prosecutors.

5. In any disciplinary proceeding, the PCAOB must bring specific charges, give notification, allow for an opportunity to defend, and keep a record of the proceedings (which will generally be nonpublic).

6. **Board sanctions may include**

a. temporary suspension or permanent revocation of registration of a firm (only for intentional or knowing conduct, or repeated negligent conduct);

b. temporary or permanent suspension or bar of a person from working with a registered public accounting firm (only for intentional or knowing conduct, or repeated negligent conduct);

c. temporary or permanent limitation on the activities, functions or operations of a firm or person (only for intentional or knowing conduct, or repeated negligent conduct);

d. a civil penalty for each violation, up to $100,000 for an individual and $2 million for an entity, or, in the case of intentional or knowing conduct repeated negligent conduct, up to $750,000 for an individual and $15 million for an entity;

e. censure;

f. required professional education or training; and/or

g. any other appropriate action.

7. The PCAOB may sanction a firm or its supervisors if they failed to reasonably supervise an "associated person" who violated rules or standards.

H. Foreign accounting firms are presumptively subject to the Act, but the SEC may create exemptions.

I. **SEC oversight**

1. The SEC must approve all PCAOB rules.
2. The SEC has broad power to oversee the board, limit its activities, and remove its members.
3. Creation of the PCAOB does not limit in any way the SEC's authority to enforce the securities laws, set standards for auditors, or take legal action.
4. A violation of the Act, any SEC rule based on the Act, or any PCAOB rule is deemed equivalent to a violation of the 1934 Securities Exchange Act.

J. **Standard setting body**

1. The SEC is authorized to adopt generally accepted accounting principles (GAAP) promulgated by any body that meets certain criteria.
2. Those criteria just happen to describe FASB.

II. **Auditor Independence**

A. An independent auditor cannot perform the following services for an audit client:

1. Bookkeeping or other services related to the accounting records of financial statements.
2. Financial information systems design and implementations.
3. Appraisal or valuation services, fairness opinions, or contributions-in-kind reports.
4. Actuarial services.
5. Internal audit outsourcing services.
6. Management functions or human resources.
7. Broker or dealer, investment adviser, or investment banking services.
8. Legal services and expert services unrelated to the audit.
9. Any other service that the PCAOB determines is impermissible.

B. Firms may provide these services to nonaudit clients and to private companies.

C. Other nonaudit services may be performed for public audit clients *if* pre-approved by the audit committee and disclosed in the client's periodic reports.

D. **Audit partner rotation**

1. There are no requirements for issuers to rotate audit *firms*.
2. Audit firms must rotate both the lead audit partner and the reviewing audit partner at least every 5 years.

E. **Auditor report to audit committee**

1. Audit firms are now selected and compensated by the audit committee rather than management.
2. Each firm must timely report to the client's audit committee:
   a. all critical accounting policies and practices to be used;
   b. all alternative treatments of financial information within GAAP that have been discussed with management officials, ramifications of the use of such alternative disclosures, and the treatment preferred by the accounting firm; and
   c. other material written communications between the accounting firm and the issuer's management, such as any management letter or schedule of unadjusted differences.

F. **Cooling-off periods**

1. An audit firm may not perform an audit for a client if its CEO, controller, CFO, CAO, or any person serving in an equivalent capacity was employed by the firm and participated in the audit during a one-year period preceding the date of the initiation of the audit.
2. If the individual worked for the audit firm but did not participate in the client's audit, there is no problem.

III. **Other Provisions**

A. **Financial statement requirements**

1. Financial statements for public companies must reflect "all material correcting adjustments."
2. Financial statements must contain all material off-balance sheet transactions.
3. Pro forma figures must be reconciled to GAAP.

B. It is now unlawful for officers, directors, or others to coerce, manipulate, or mislead company auditors.

C. The SEC received additional authority to discipline professionals, including auditors, under Rule 102(e).

D. **Ethical standards**

1. **Interim ethical standards --** As interim ethics standards, the PCAOB adopted Rule 3500T, which applies AICPA Rule of Professional Conduct 102, along with its interpretations and rulings.
2. **Definitions --** Rule 3501 adopts several clarifying definitions (e.g., "audit client," "confidential transaction," "contingent fee"), but the terms are generally consistent with AICPA practice and do not deserve separate treatment.
3. **Reckless contribution to violations --** Most recently, the PCAOB adopted Rule 3502, which imposes a responsibility to not knowingly *or recklessly* contribute to violations of SOX, PCAOB rules, or federal securities laws. The contribution could occur by an action or by an omission. So if someone associated with a registered accounting firm takes or omits to take an action knowing, or recklessly not knowing, that the act would directly and substantially contribute to such a violation, the person has violated Rule 3502.

Government Accountability Office (GAO)

After studying this lesson you should be able to :

1. *Understand the General Accountability Office's independence rules for firms that audit government agencies and entities that receive government funds.*

I. General Accountability Office's Government Auditing Standards - Ethical Principles

A. The GAO's guidelines apply to those who conduct audits of government entities (e.g., federal, state, and local) and entities that receive government awards (e.g., colleges, trade schools, charities, local governments) in compliance with generally accepted government auditing standards (GAGAS).

B. Independence and Ethical Principles. Those who audit pursuant to GAGAS are expected to audit:

1. Independently; and

2. In accordance with these key Ethical Principles:

a. The public interest;

b. Integrity;

c. Objectivity;

d. Proper use of government information, resources, and position; and

i. Government information, resources, or positions are to be used for official purposes and not for an auditor's personal gain.

e. Professional behavior.

i. Professional behavior includes compliance with laws and regulations, avoidance of conflicts of interest, sensitivity to appearances of impropriety and putting forth an honest effort to meet technical and professional standards.

C. Independence standards

1. Audit organizations (AOs) and individual auditors, whether government or public, must be free from three types of independence impairments (and must avoid the appearance of such impairments):

a. Personal impairments;

b. External impairments; and

c. Organizational impairments.

2. ***Personal impairments* include, for example**

a. Family relationships (e.g., a close family member is an officer of the audited entity);

b. Financial interests (e.g., the auditor has an indirect material interest in the audited entity or program);

c. Employment relationships (e.g., the auditor serves in a decision making function for the audited entity);

d. Prospective employment (e.g., the auditor seeks employment with the audited organization during the audit);

e. Self-review (e.g., auditing source documents that the same auditor prepared);

f. Bias (e.g., preconceived ideas toward individuals, groups or organizations that could bias the audit and political, ideological, or social convictions that could bias the audit).

3. To identify personal impairments and ensure compliance with independence requirements, AOs should:

    a. establish policies and procedures to identify, report, and resolve personal impairments;

    b. communicate the AO's policies and procedures to all auditors;

    c. establish internal policies and procedures to monitor compliance;

    d. establish a disciplinary mechanism;

    e. stress the importance of independence and the expectation that auditors will always act in the public interest; and

    f. maintain documentation of steps taken to identify potential personal independence impairments.

4. If a personal impairment is identified, the AO should promptly eliminate the problem by, for example, removing the auditor from the audit or requiring the auditor to eliminate the cause of the impairment.

5. ***External impairments*** include, among others:

    a. External interference or influence that could improperly limit or modify the scope of the audit (e.g., the audited entity exerting pressure to inappropriately reduce the extent of the work performed in order to reduce costs or fees).

    b. External interference with the selection or application of audit procedures or in the selection of transactions to be examined;

    c. Unreasonable restrictions on the time allowed to complete the audit;

    d. Externally-imposed restrictions on access to records, government officials, or other individuals needed to conduct the audit.

    e. External interference over the assignment, appointment, compensation, and promotion of audit personnel;

    f. Threat of replacing auditors over a disagreement with the contents of an audit report.

6. ***Organizational impairments*** result when:

    a. the audit function is organizationally located within the reporting line of the areas under the audit; or

    b. the auditor is assigned or takes on responsibilities that affect operations of the area under audit.

7. Audit organizations are presumed to be free from organizational impairments if the AO is:

    a. at a level of government other than the one to which the audited entity is assigned (e.g., federal auditors auditing a state government program); or

    b. in a different branch of government (e.g., an executive branch program is audited by legislative auditors).

8. Audit organizations are also resumed to be free from organizational impairment if their head is elected by voters, selected by a legislative body, or appointed by a statutorily-created governing body.

9. In addition, AOs may avoid organizational impairment of independence by a number of other means, including statutory protections that do such things as prevent the audited entity from abolishing the AO, prevent the audited entity from interfering with the audit report, and grant the AO sole authority over selection, retention, and dismissal of its staff.

10. **Internal audit**

    a. The GAO guidelines urge internal auditors to use the Institute of Internal Auditors (IIA) International Standards for the Professional Practice of Internal Auditing in conjunction with GAGAS.

    b. Under GAGAS, a government internal audit function is presumed free from organizational impairments to independence for reporting internally if the AO's head:

        i. is accountable to the head or deputy head of the government entity or to those charged with governance;

        ii. reports the audit results both to the head or deputy head of the government entity and to those charged with governance;

        iii. is located organizationally outside the staff or line-management function of the unit under audit;

        iv. has access to those charged with governance; and

        v. is sufficiently removed from political pressures to conduct audits and report findings, opinions, and conclusions objectively without fear of political reprisal.

D. **Nonaudit services**

1. Nonaudit services (NAS) receive substantial attention in the GAO guidelines.

2. Auditing organizations must use professional judgment in determining whether provision of certain types of NAS to audited government entities will impair or appear to impair independence.

3. Overarching Independence Principles for NAS. When assessing the impact of NAS performance on independence, AOs must keep in mind two overarching principles (that are consistent with AICPA principles in the area of NAS):

    a. AOs must not provide NAS that involve performing management functions or making management decisions; and

    b. AOs must not audit their own work or provide NAS in situations in which the NAS are significant or material to the subject matter of the audits.

4. NAS fall into three categories:

    a. Those that do not impair independence and therefore do not require compliance with *supplemental safeguards*.

    b. Those that do not impair independence so long as the AO complies with *supplemental safeguards*.

    c. Those that impair independence in such a way that compliance with *supplemental safeguards* will not overcome the impairment.

5. **NAS that do not impair independence --** These are often performed in response to a statutory requirement, at the discretion of the authority of the AO, or for a legislative oversight body. They usually involve auditors providing technical advice based on their technical knowledge, such as:

    a. Participating in activities such as commissions and task forces to advise entity management on issues based on the auditor's knowledge;

    b. Providing tools and methodologies, such as guidance and good business practices, that can be used by management; and

    c. Providing targeted and limited technical advice to assist management in such activities as answering technical questions and providing training.

6. *NAS that do not impair independence so long as the AO complies with supplemental safeguards.* Examples in this category include:

a. Providing basic accounting assistance;

b. Providing payroll services when payroll is not material to the audit objectives;

c. Providing appraisal or valuation services that are limited to services, such as reviewing the work of the entity or valuing an entity's pension, provided management has taken responsibility for all significant assumptions and data;

d. Providing advisory services on information technology;

e. Providing basic human resources services, such as reviewing the applications of at least three individuals in order to provide input to management for its decision regarding whom to hire;

f. Preparing routine tax filings based on information prepared by the audited entity.

7. The *supplemental safeguards* that can prevent independence from being impaired when the AO provides the NAS mentioned in the previous section require the AO to do all of the following:

   a. Document its consideration of the NAS, including its conclusions about the impact on independence;

   b. Establish in writing an understanding with the audited entity regarding the objectives, scope of work, deliverables, and management's responsibility for the substantive outcome of the work;

   c. Exclude personnel who provided NAS from planning, conducting, or reviewing the audit work; and

   d. Do not reduce the scope or extent of the audit work below the level that would be appropriate if the NAS were being provided by a third party.

8. **NAS that impair independence so that *supplemental safeguards* cannot eliminate the impairment**. These activities are generally consistent with AICPA prohibitions on performing management functions, auditing your own work, and taking control of client assets. The GAO theory is that, by their nature, certain types of NAS directly support the audited entities' operations and would impair the AO's ability to comply with the two overarching independence principles. Examples include:

   a. Maintaining or preparing the audited entity's basic accounting or financial records that the AO will audit;

   b. Posting transactions to the audited entity's financial records;

   c. Determining account balances or capitalization criteria;

   d. Designing, developing, installing, or operating the audited entity's accounting system or other information systems that are significant to the audit;

   e. Providing payroll services that are material to the subject matter of the audit or involve making management decisions;

   f. Providing appraisal or valuation services that go beyond the limited appraisal and evaluation services described above that do not generally impair independence;

   g. (In the HR realm) Recommending a single individual for a specific position that is key to the entity or program being audited;

   h. Developing an entity's performance measurement system when it is significant to the subject matter of the audit;

   i. Developing an entity's policies, procedures, and internal controls;

   j. Performing management's assessment of internal controls when they are significant to the audit;

- **k.** Providing services that are intended to be used as management's primary basis for making decisions that are significant to the subject matter under audit;
- **l.** Carrying out internal audit functions; and
- **m.** Serving as voting members of an entity's management committee or board of directors, making policy decisions that affect future direction and operation of an entity's program, supervising entity employees, developing programmatic policy, authorizing an entity's transactions, or maintaining custody of an entity's assets.

E. Professional judgment

1. The GAO standards repeatedly emphasize the importance of auditors using professional judgment in planning and performing audits.
2. Professional judgment includes:
   - **a.** exercising reasonable care;
   - **b.** exercising professional skepticism;
   - **c.** applying professional knowledge in good faith and with integrity;
   - **d.** complying with independence standards;
   - **e.** achieving technical competence;
   - **f.** considering the risk level of each assignment; and
   - **g.** documenting significant decisions.

F. Competence

1. The staff assigned to perform an audit must collectively possess adequate professional competence for the task required.
2. An AO's management is responsible for hiring, training, and supervising a competent workforce.
3. Competence is derived from a blending of education and expertise.

G. Continuing professional education (CPE).

1. Auditors performing under GAGAS should complete, every two years, at least 24 hours of CPE that directly relates to government auditing and an additional 56 hours (for a total of 80 hours) of CPE that enhances the auditor's professional proficiency to perform audit or attest engagements.

Department of Labor (DOL)

After studying this lesson you should be able to :

1. *Understand the Department of Labor's independence rules for the auditing of employee benefit plans regulated by ERISA.*

I. **Department of Labor --** Interpretive Bulletin Relating to Guidelines on Independence of Accountant Retained by Employee Benefit Plan.

   A. Employee Benefit Plans (plans) are broadly regulated by the Department of Labor's (DOL's) Employee Benefits Security Administration (EBSA) pursuant to the Employee Retirement Income Security Act (ERISA).

   B. Statutory law provides that an accountant retained by a plan to examine plan financial information and render an opinion on the financial statements and schedules required to be contained in a plan's annual report must be "independent."

   C. Unfortunately, despite having been strongly urged to simply adopt AICPA guidelines for independence, DOL's guidelines, contained in 29 C.F.R. 2509-75-9, date to the 1970s and are inconsistent with modern independence rules.

   D. The rules provide that an accountant will **not** be considered independent with respect to a plan, due to the following:

      1. **Financial ties --** Independence will be considered to be impaired if during the period of the engagement, at the date of the opinion, or during the period covered by the Financial Statements, "the accountant or his or her firm or a member thereof had, or was committed to acquire, any direct financial interest or any material indirect financial interest in such plan, or the plan sponsor ..."

         a. Because this provision covers any member of an accountant's firm, its coverage is much broader than that of current AICPA guidelines.

         b. The term "member" means all partners or shareholder employees in the firm and all professional employees participating in the audit or located in an office of the firm participating in a significant portion of the audit.

      2. **Employment ties --** During the same period, the same entities may not be connected to a plan or plan sponsor as a:

         a. Promoter;

         b. Underwriter;

         c. Investment advisor;

         d. Voting trustee;

         e. Director;

         f. Officer; or

         g. Employee of the plan or plan sponsor.

      3. However, employees of a plan or plan sponsor who have left to join the accounting firm may nonetheless be deemed independent if:

         a. They have completely disassociated themselves from the plan or plan sponsor; and

         b. Do not participate in auditing Financial Statements of the plan covering any period of his or her employment by the plan or plan sponsor.

4. However, independence may be considered impaired if an accountant or a member of an accounting firm maintains financial records for the plan. An accounting firm should not audit its own work.

E. According to the rule, an engagement to provide professional services, including actuarial services, to the plan sponsor does not ruin an accountant's independence so long as the accountant does not violate the rules on financial ties and employment mentioned above.

F. However, the firm should take care not to engage in a prohibited transaction pursuant to 29 U.S.C. 1106(a)(1)(C), which prohibits certain transactions between a plan and a "party in interest" to minimize conflicts of interest and thereby prevent fiduciaries from lining their own pockets with the plan's funds.

International Federation of Accountants (IFAC)

After studying this lesson you should be able to :

1. *Understand the basic operation of the International Federation of Accountants (IFAC).*
2. *Understand the background of the IFAC Ethics Code.*
3. *Comprehend the difference between a rules-based approach and IFAC's principles-based approach to constructing a code of ethics.*
4. *Comprehend the basic provisions of the IFAC Ethics Code.*
5. *Identify similarities and differences between the IFAC Code and the AICPA's Code of Professional Conduct.*

I. Introduction

A. **The International Ethics Standards Board for Accountants --** The International Ethics Standards Board for Accountants (IESBA), one of the International Federation of Accountants (IFAC)'s standard-setting agencies, promulgated the Code of Ethics for Professional Accountants (the IFAC Code).

B. **The IFAC Code --** This code has been adopted in more than 100 countries and accountants and accounting firms operating abroad or with clients operating abroad will increasingly need to be familiar with the IFAC Code's provisions. As cross-border tax and audit work increase, the importance of the IFAC Code will grow.

C. **Standards application --** As a member of IFAC, the AICPA has pledged that it will use its best efforts to apply standards that are not lower than those of the IFAC Code. Just as there is conscious convergence in international auditing standards (e.g., the IFRS and U.S. GAAP), IFAC and the AICPA have begun to merge ethical frameworks. Therefore, the IFAC Code is broadly consistent with the AICPA Code and would generally produce similar results in similar cases. Importantly, the AICPA's Professional Ethics Executive Committee (PEEC) participates in IESBA's activities to ensure that the AICPA's views are adequately considered. If a particular country has a statute or regulation that prevents an accountant there from complying with a portion of the IFAC Code, he or she should nonetheless comply with the other applicable portions.

D. **The IFAC Code vs. the AICPA's Code of Professional Conduct --** Two major differences between the IFAC Code and the AICPA's Code of Professional Conduct stand out.

   1. First, whereas the AICPA Code has many specific rules that are supplemented by a *conceptual framework* that encourages accountants to resolve gray areas by identifying *threats to compliance* with professional duties, evaluating those threats, and applying *safeguards* in order to reduce the threats so that compliance with fundamental principles is not compromised, the IFAC Code begins with that framework in its Part A. It then gives specific guidance for applying the conceptual framework in Parts B and C. The AICPA Code might be termed a rules-based approach while the IFAC Code is a principles-based approach. This is somewhat a mere difference in emphasis, especially after a recent revision to the IFAC Code changed a large number of "shoulds" to "shalls."

   2. Second, IFAC's Code covers not only accountants in public practice (termed *Professional Accountants in Public Practice* [PAPPs]) but also accountants who work for businesses, governments, and other employing agencies (termed *Professional Accountants in Business* [PABs]). Thus, Part B of the IFAC Code applies Part A's guidelines to PAPPs in ways that strongly resemble much of the AICPA Code. Part C of the IFAC Code applies Part A's principles to PABs, whereas the AICPA has generally left it to the Institute of Internal Auditors (IAA) and Institute of Management Accountants (IMA) to issue codes of conduct for that type of activity.

E. Two less significant differences are also worth mentioning at the beginning.

1. First, consistent with the international nature of its application, the IFAC Code specifically mentions *network firms* to indicate that accounting firms under common control or management that cross borders will presumptively have to be broadly considered in applying these rules. This concept was adopted in 2010 by PEEC (ET section 101.19).

2. Second, IFAC has two sections on what it terms "assurance" engagements. One section focuses on independence and other rules for financial statement audit clients. The second focuses on other sorts of assurance engagements. For example, consider a situation where an accounting firm is asked to provide assurance services regarding a consulting firm's report on the sustainability practices of a company. This is an assurance engagement even though a financial statement would not be involved (although such a company could, of course, also be a financial statement assurance engagement client). Independence standards are generally more demanding if audits of financial statements are involved.

F. The IFAC Code is also more demanding when the financial statement audit client is a *listed firm* (a public company) than when it is not.

II. Part A

A. **Fundamental principles --** The IFAC Code is based on certain *fundamental principles* that accountants should not compromise. These are:

1. Integrity;
2. Objectivity;
3. Professional competence and due care;
4. Confidentiality; and
5. Professional behavior.

B. The first four of these should be familiar, as they are heavily emphasized in the AICPA's Code of Professional Conduct. *Professional behavior* means following laws and regulations and avoiding acts that would discredit the profession.

C. **Types of threats --** The IFAC Code's conceptual framework involves identifying threats to these five fundamental principles. If a threat is not *clearly insignificant* (meaning both trivial and inconsequential), then various *safeguards* must be considered. There are five primary types of threats:

1. **Self-interest threats --** The threat that a financial or other interest will inappropriately influence the professional accountant's judgment or behavior. An auditor should obviously not own stock in an audit client.

2. **Self-review threats --** The threat that a professional accountant will not appropriately evaluate the results of a previous judgment made or service performed by the professional accountant, or by another individual within the professional accountant's firm or employing organization, on which the accountant will rely when forming a judgment as part of providing a current service. An auditor should not audit its own work.

3. **Advocacy threats --** The threat that a professional accountant will promote a client's or employer's position to the point that the professional accountant's objectivity is compromised.

4. **Familiarity threats --** The threat that due to a long or close relationship with a client or employer, a professional accountant will be too sympathetic to their interests or too accepting of their work.

5. **Intimidation threats --** The threat that a professional accountant will be deterred from acting objectively because of actual or perceived pressures, including attempts to exercise undue influence over the professional accountant.

D. If such threats are identified and evaluated as sufficiently significant that they might threaten compliance with fundamental principles, the professional accountant shall consider whether they may be reduced to an acceptable level by application of two types of safeguards:

1. Safeguards created by the profession, legislation or regulation; and
2. Safeguards in the work environment.

E. *Safeguards created by the profession, legislation or regulation* include, but are not restricted to:

1. education, training, and experience requirements for entry into the profession;
2. continuing professional development requirements;
3. corporate governance regulations;
4. professional standards;
5. professional or regulatory monitoring and disciplinary procedures;
6. external review by a legally empowered third part of the reports, returns, communications, or information produced by a professional accountant.

F. **Types of safeguards --** There are two general types of *safeguards in the work environment*: firm-wide safeguards and engagement-specific safeguards.

1. Examples of **firm-wide work environment safeguards** include:
   a. Leadership of the firm that stresses the importance of compliance with the fundamental principles.
   b. Leadership of the firm that establishes the expectation that members of an assurance team will act in the public interest.
   c. Policies and procedures to implement and monitor quality control of engagements.
   d. Using different partners and engagement teams with separate reporting lines for the provision of non-assurance services to an assurance client.
   e. A disciplinary mechanism to promote compliance with policies and procedures.
2. Examples of **engagement-specific work environment safeguards** include:
   a. Having a professional accountant who was not involved with the non-assurance service review the non-assurance work performed or otherwise advise as necessary.
   b. Having a professional who was not a member of the assurance team review the assurance work performed or advise as otherwise necessary.
   c. Consulting an independent third party, such as a committee of independent directors, a professional regulatory body, or another professional accountant.
   d. Discussing ethical issues with those charged with governance of the client.
   e. Involving another firm to perform or re-perform part of the engagement.

III. Part B

A. Part B applies the basic IFAC Code concepts to Professional Accountants in Public Practice (PAPPs), that is, accountants working for accounting firms. It begins by addressing basic concepts such as conflicts of interest, contingency fees, advertising, gifts, custody of client assets, and the like. Then it addresses independence rules, addressing largely the same financial, employment, family, and consulting issues as the AICPA Code.

B. In all these settings, the results tend to be pretty similar to results from the AICPA Code, in part because both have the "threat and safeguard" conceptual framework as background. As with the AICPA Code, for example, assurance team members should not own a material financial interest in an audit client, should not borrow money from an assurance client under unusually favorable terms, should not provide assurance services to a firm whose CEO is an immediate family member of a team member, etc.

C. **The IFCA Code vs. the AICPA Code - Similarities --** To illustrate the similarities, consider several examples.

1. Under the AICPA Code, five primary categories of actors must be independent (a) audit team members; (b) those in a position to influence audit team members, (c) other partners in the office of the attest engagement team partner and other partners and managers providing at least 10 hours of non-audit services, and (e) the firm itself. Additionally, any entity composed of or controlled by the first five actors must be independent.
2. The IFAC Code is similar, but different. It presumptively covers all the firms in a *network*, which is defined as a larger structure that is (a) aimed at co-operation and (b) aimed at profit or cost sharing or shares common ownership, control or management, common quality control policies and procedures, common business strategy, the use of a common brand name, *or* a significant part of professional resources. In other words, if PwC's Chicago office has an assurance engagement with ABC Co., its Rome and Hong Kong offices may have to meet independence standards.
   a. The "audit team" is broadly defined to include all members of the engagement team (including experts contracted with) and "(a)ll others within the firm who can directly influence the outcome of the assurance engagement." This includes those who recommend compensation for or supervise the assurance engagement partner (including all successive senior levels to the top of the firm), those who provide consultation regarding technical or industry specific issues, and those who provide quality control for the assurance engagement. The assurance team also includes all those within a network firm who can directly influence the outcome of the engagement.
   b. Although the IFAC Code does not include other partners or managers who provide 10 hours of non-assurance services (NAS) to an audit client in the definition of the "audit team," it does elsewhere prohibit partners and managerial employees who provide NAS to the audit client, except those whose involvement is "minimal," and their immediate family members (IFMs), from holding a direct or material indirect financial interest in the audit client.
3. The IFAC Code independence provisions are concerned with the same general areas as the AICPA Code and SOX - financial ties, employment relationships, family connections, and consulting (NAS). Many of the IFAC rules are quite similar to the AICPA Code. The IFAC Code focuses on direct and material indirect financial relationships, as does the AICPA Code. It is concerned both with employees from the accounting firm who go to the client and those who go the other direction. It has guidelines for complications caused by immediate family members (IFMs) and close family members (CFMs - comparable to the AICPA's "close relatives"). It provides guidance regarding provision of NAS such as tax services (no problem), internal audit, IT systems services, litigation support, human resources, etc. that are provided to assurance clients.

D. Although the IFAC Code is largely principles-based, it is not without definitive rules. For example, the self-interest threat to objectivity would be so great that no safeguards could be taken that would allow a member of an assurance team to own a material financial interest in an assurance client or to accept a significant gift from such a client.

1. To illustrate similarities and differences, note that the AICPA Code provides that an IFM of an audit team member cannot hold a direct or material indirect interest in an audit client. The IFAC Code agrees. The AICPA further provides that a CR of an audit team member cannot hold a financial interest in an audit client that the team member knows or has reason to know is material to the CR. The IFAC Code has a slightly different approach. It defines a CFM the same as a CR, but does not have a black-and-white rule. It calls for application of the contextual framework. First, the self-interest threat must be evaluated. Its significance will depend upon such factors as (a) the nature of the relationship between the team member and the CFM and (b) the materiality of the

financial interest to the CFM. Then, safeguards shall be applied to reduce the threat to an acceptable level, such as (a) the CFM disposing as soon as practicable of all or most of the interest, (b) having a professional accountant review the work of the team member, or (c) removing the individual from the team.

2. The provisions regarding NAS services are neither as stringent as SOX provisions where public company audit clients are concerned, nor as objective as AICPA provisions. Nonetheless, they have many of the same key features as the AICPA Code - largely forbidding the PAPP from making management decisions, ensuring that the client takes ownership of the process, discouraging the PAPP from taking custody of client assets, ensuring that NAS services are provided by employees who are not on the assurance team, encouraging full disclosure, etc.

3. As an illustration of the IFAC approach to NAS, consider provision of IT systems services to a financial statement audit client. The Code notes that design and implementation of financial information technology systems that will be used to generate information forming part of the financial statements that the assurance firm will audit creates a self-review threat, which is likely to be too significant to allow unless appropriate safeguards ensure that:

   a. The audit client acknowledges its responsibility for establishing and monitoring a system of internal controls;

   b. The audit client designates a competent employee, preferably within senior management, with the responsibility to make all management decisions with respect to the design and implementation of the hardware and software system;

   c. The audit client makes all management decisions with respect to the design and implementation process;

   d. The audit client evaluates the adequacy and results of the design and implementation of the system; and

   e. The audit client is responsible for the operation of the system (hardware or software) and the data used or generated by the system.

4. The Code also suggests that the firm *consider* as a safeguard ensuring that the IT work be performed only by employees not involved in the audit engagement. If the IT engagement is design *or* implementation of financial information technology systems, the self-review threat is not as great as with a design *and* implementation engagement. Still, the firm must evaluate the threat and consider safeguards that might be appropriate.

5. Finally, the IFAC Code indicates that provisions of services in connection with the assessment, design, and implementation of *internal accounting controls* and *risk management controls* are not considered threats to independence so long as the firm or network firm personnel do not perform management functions.

IV. Part C

A. Part C's provisions for Professional Accountants in Business (PABs) are common sense provisions. They recognize that PABs have a responsibility to further the legitimate aims of their employing organizations (EOs), but emphasize a counterbalancing responsibility to comply with the fundamental principles (integrity, objectivity, etc.). These provisions address topics such as potential conflicts of interest, the duty to accurately prepare and report information, acting with sufficient expertise, coping with conflicts created by financial interests, and pressures to accept or offer improper inducements.

B. Without going through all these provisions, consider an example that will illustrate the IFAC Code's suggested approach. Assume that a PAB is being pressured to manage earnings by a CFO interested in hitting the EO's projected numbers no matter what.

   1. The IFAC Code instructs the PAB to evaluate the significance of the threats arising from pressure to violate the law. Clearly, the PAB may face an intimidation threat as the CFO may expressly or impliedly threaten to demote or even to fire the PAB should he or she not comply with the improper request. Yet the PAB has an obligation to maintain

information in a manner that clearly describes the true nature of the business transaction, assets or liabilities; classifies and records information in a timely and proper manner; and represents the facts accurately and completely in all material respects.

2. The IFAC Code requires the PAB to consider safeguards to reduce the threat such as:
   a. Obtaining advice where appropriate from within the EO, an independent professional advisor, or a relevant professional body;
   b. Utilizing a formal dispute resolution process within the EO; and
   c. Seeking legal advice.
3. If these and other steps do not sufficiently reduce the threat of noncompliance to fundamental principles, the PAB may consider resigning from the EO.

Alphabetical Index

21317187R00277

Made in the USA
San Bernardino, CA
16 May 2015